THE CAMBRIDGE CULTURAL HISTORY

VOLUME 6   THE ROMANTIC AGE IN BRITAIN

The Cambridge Cultural History

The Cambridge Cultural History of Britain

edited by
BORIS FORD

VOLUME 6

THE ROMANTIC AGE IN BRITAIN

CAMBRIDGE
UNIVERSITY PRESS

Published by the Press Syndicate of the University of Cambridge
The Pitt Building, Trumpington Street, Cambridge CB2 1RP
40 West 20th Street, New York, NY 10011–4211, USA
10 Stamford Road, Oakleigh, Victoria 3166, Australia

First published 1989 as *The Cambridge Guide to the Arts in Britain:
Romantics to Early Victorians*
First paperback edition 1992

Printed and bound in Great Britain by
BPCC Hazells Ltd
Member of BPCC Ltd

A catalogue record for this book is available from the British Library

Library of Congress cataloguing in publication data

Cambridge guide to the arts in Britain.
The Cambridge cultural history/edited by Boris Ford.
    p. cm.
Previously published as: The Cambridge guide to the arts in Britain. 1988–1991.
Includes bibliographical references and indexes.
Contents: v.1. Early Britain – v.2. Medieval Britain – v.3. Sixteenth-century
Britain – v.4. Seventeenth-century Britain – v.5. Eighteenth-century Britain –
v. 6. The Romantic Age in Britain – v. 7. Victorian Britain – v.8. Early
twentieth-century Britain – v.9. Modern Britain.
ISBN 0-521-42881-5 (pbk.: v.1). – ISBN 0-521-42882-3 (pbk.: v.2). – ISBN
0-521-42883-1 (pbk.: v.3). – ISBN 0-521-42884-X (pbk.: v.4). – ISBN 0-521-42885-8
(pbk.: v.5). – ISBN 0-521-42886-6 (pbk.: v.6). – ISBN 0-521-42887-4 (pbk.: v.7). –
ISBN 0-521-42888-2 (pbk.: v.8). – ISBN 0-521-42889-0 (pbk.: v.9)
1. Arts, British.   I. Ford, Boris.   II. Title.
[NX543.C36   1992]
700′.941–dc20   91–43024
                                                                                                            CIP

ISBN 0 521 30979 4 hardback
ISBN 0 521 42886 6 paperback

Contents

Notes on Contributors

John Beer is Professor of English Literature at Cambridge University and Fellow of Peterhouse. As well as having published several volumes on Blake and Coleridge, his most recent contributions to Romantic studies are *Wordsworth and the Human Heart* and *Wordsworth in Time*.

Christopher Gillie is a retired lecturer in English. His books include the *Longman Companion to English Literature* (reissued and updated as *Bloomsbury Guide to English Literature*, ed. M. Wynne-Davies, 1989), and *A Preface to Jane Austen*.

John Harvey is a Lecturer in English at Cambridge University and Fellow of Emmanuel College. He is the author of *Victorian Novelists and their Illustrators*; and of three novels, *The Plate Shop*, winner of the David Higham Prize in 1979, *Coup d'Etat*, and, most recently, *The Legend of Captain Space*.

Pat Kirkham is Principal Lecturer in the History of Architecture and Design at Leicester Polytechnic. Her books include *William and John Linnell, Harry Peach, Dryad and the DIA, The London Furniture Trade 1830–1980* and *A View from the Interior: Feminism, Women and Design*.

David Punter is Professor of English at Stirling University. His books include *The Literature of Terror, Romanticism and Ideology, The Hidden Script, Introduction to Contemporary Cultural Studies and The Romantic Unconscious.*

H.C. Robbins Landon, who is honorary Professorial Fellow of University College, Cardiff, founded the Haydn Society in 1949 to issue the Collected Works of Haydn. His books include *Haydn: Chronicle and Works, Handel and his World, 1791: Mozart's Last Year* and *Mozart: the Golden Years*.

Michael Rosenthal is a Senior Lecturer in the History of Art at Warwick University. His books include *British Landscape Painting* and the prize-winning *Constable: The Painter and his Landscape*.

Alexandra Wedgwood is a freelance writer and lecturer on architecture, and set up and maintains the Architectural Archive at the Houses of Parliament. She worked with Sir Nikolaus Pevsner on *The Buildings of England*, contributing the entry on Birmingham; and she catalogued the Pugin Collection at the Victoria & Albert Museum.

Tom Williamson is a Lecturer in Landscape History and Material Culture at the Centre of East Anglian Studies at the University of East Anglia. With his wife, Liz Bellamy, he is co-author of *Ley Lines in Question* and *Property and Landscape*, and co-editor of the periodical *Rural History: Economy, Society, Culture*.

Alexander Youngson was formerly Director of the Research School of Social Sciences at the Australian National University, Canberra, Professor of Economics at the University of Hong Kong and Chairman of the Royal Fine Art Commission for Scotland. His publications include *The Making of Classical Edinburgh, After the '45, The Prince and the Pretender* and *Urban Development and the Royal Fine Art Commissions.*

General Introduction

BORIS FORD

If all people seem to agree that English literature is pre-eminent in the world, the same would not often be claimed for Britain's arts as a whole. And yet, viewed historically, Britain's achievements in the visual and decorative arts and in architecture and music, as well as in drama and literature, must be the equal, as a whole, of any other country.

The Cambridge Cultural History of Britain is not devoted, volume by volume, to the separate arts, but to all the arts in each successive age. It can then be seen how often they reinforce each other, treating similar themes and speaking in a similar tone of voice. Also it is striking how one age may find its richest cultural expression in music or drama, and the next in architecture or the applied arts; while in a later age there may be an almost total dearth of important composers compared with a proliferation of major novelists. Or an age may provide scope for a great range of anonymous craftsmen and women.

The nine volumes of this *Cambridge Cultural History* have been planned to reveal these changes, and to help readers find their bearings in relation to the arts and culture of an age: identifying major landmarks and lines of strength, analysing changes of taste and fashion and critical assumptions. And these are related to the demands of patrons and the tastes of the public.

These volumes are addressed to readers of all kinds: to general readers as well as to specialists. However, since virtually every reader is bound to be a non-specialist in relation to some of the arts under discussion, the chapters do not presuppose specialist knowledge.

This sixth volume of the series covers the period 1785 to 1851 – from shortly after the death of Dr Johnson, which can be taken as signalling the end of the Augustan age, to the Great Exhibition. It is thus concerned with the arts of the Romantics and the early Victorians, in a period of profound social and industrial changes. Turner's wonderfully evocative painting of the Great Western Railway offers a glimpse of the energy and bustle of the new age and of the misty grandeur of the neo-classical world it was superseding.

In the arts, the period was unusually rich in individual talent. For sheer profusion, this was perhaps the greatest of all ages of British literature, with

Blake and the great Romantic poets, and with such major, yet very contrasting novelists as Jane Austen, Scott, Dickens, and the Brontës. One of the paradoxes of the age, which also saw the work of two of England's greatest artists, Constable and Turner, and some of its major architects, like Soane, Nash and Barry, is that it lacked a single composer of importance at a time when the rest of Europe was experiencing an outpouring of musical creation. And there was a strange dearth in the theatre. If the chapters that follow are hardly able to account for this paradox, at least they reveal it very clearly and copiously.

This volume, with a considerably more detailed bibliography, was originally published in a hardcover edition as *Romantics to Early Victorians*, under the series title *The Cambridge Guide to the Arts in Britain*.

Part I
The Cultural and Social Setting

The Fighting Temeraire tugged to her last Berth to be broken up. *This picture and*
Rain, Steam and Speed *(1844), both by J.M.W. Turner, provide a nostalgic and yet*
bustling and even optimistic view of the old world giving way to a new one (detail; 1839).

Romantics to Early Victorians

DAVID PUNTER

The period between 1785 and 1851, from shortly after the death of Dr Johnson to the Great Exhibition, was one of intense activity in the arts in Britain. We think of great names – of poets like Blake, Wordsworth and Coleridge, Keats, Byron and Shelley, and later Tennyson and the two Brownings, Robert and Elizabeth Barrett; novelists like Scott, the 'magician of the North', the 'incomparable' Jane Austen, Dickens, Thackeray, the Brontë sisters; painters and visual artists (never prolific in Britain) like Blake, Constable and Turner; even of musicians, although many of them were visitors to these shores; and, of course, of architects and figures in the more 'public' applied arts, men like Soane, Nash, Barry and Pugin who forever changed the face of Britain as we know it.

We think also of great movements, most obviously of Romanticism, which swept through many of the arts, altering perceptions and attitudes among practitioners and audiences alike; but also of the beginning of that amorphous but powerful bundle of social and aesthetic codes which we now call 'Victorianism'; and also of a host of more shadowy schools and currents, Gothicism, exoticism, historicism, Regency, Pre-Raphaelitism, the survival and development, in architecture especially, of a particularly British form of neo-classicism.

What lay behind this efflorescence of activity? It has to be said – even though it is repeated, ad nauseam, of every historical period – that this time was one of profound change in the ways people lived. To begin with, it was these years that saw the full arrival in Britain of that force which for long after was going to condition British attitudes to the rest of the world and to consolidate for a further century the central position which it had already achieved through colonialism and trade: the force of industry, whose arrival can virtually be dated to the two decades after 1765. As an example: at the beginning of the eighteenth century, the second city in Britain, after of course London, the centre of all things economic and cultural and Johnson's touchstone for the life worth living, was Norwich, primarily an agricultural centre thriving on its connection with the European wool trade. By the end of our period, Norwich is insignificant: overtaken in terms of population and cultural centrality by the great industrial cities of the North, cities founded on coal, iron and cotton; by Birmingham, for example, which had outgrown Norwich by the time of the census of 1801. Also growing were Bristol and Liverpool, the great ports without which British manufacture could not reach the four corners of the globe and assure the burgeoning capitalists of these great conurbations of the profits they required to maintain the acceleration of output.

The massive increase in industry changed the whole pattern of labour and working life in Britain. The older cottage industries gradually disappeared, as huge factories opened; more flexible habits of work were replaced by rigid working days based on the necessity of keeping the machines rolling. Along with these changing habits went the prospects of increased wages for working people; and not only that, but also an increasing range of reasonably cheap consumer goods on which to spend the new money – manufactured goods, but also artistic 'goods': new books and new ways of borrowing them, if they could not be afforded; new opportunities for listening to music or for attending various kinds of theatrical and near-theatrical entertainment.

All over Britain there was a steady flow of population towards the new cities, not reversed even when, on occasion, it turned out that there were no golden pavements but instead a life of drudgery made even worse by the removal of those seasonal and diurnal imperatives which had conditioned life on the land. And thus too there came an emptying of the countryside, frequently noticed and regretted, as by George Crabbe in *The Village* (1783), by Wordsworth and William Cobbett; sometimes turned to ephemeral new use as when areas which had previously been economically thriving saw themselves turned instead into tourist sites for the throngs with new access to money for travel and, because of the steady succession of European wars, with nowhere to go except into the heart of Britain. So they went to Tintern Abbey in the Wye Valley, for example, where we are informed by a seasoned traveller of the time that no enjoyment there can be complete without plenty of wine with the picnic and preferably the hiring of a Welsh harper from Chepstow.

Yet these changes were ambiguous. Historians are not agreed on whether there was even any general economic betterment of life between 1780 and 1850. Some of the early Victorian social commentators, Thomas Carlyle foremost among them, became painfully aware that the cities were not merely filling up with people, as Thomas Malthus and David Ricardo were also to note; they were in effect spawning a new class, a class without obvious political affiliations and sometimes with little love for the alliance of party politicians and big industrialists who could too easily be seen as constituting an unrepresentative parliament. Every now and then, this new class would erupt, at Peterloo in 1819 and during the various Chartist agitations; noises would be made in the centres of power, and a new breed of social explorer would head off with trepidation into the gloomy courts of London and elsewhere to attempt to interpret this curious new class on which, regrettably, the whole edifice of industry depended, a breed eventuating in Friedrich Engels and his *Condition of the Working Class in England in 1844*.

As a mirror image of this new class, there emerged a new bourgeoisie, a new middle class no longer based merely in the traditional professions but now also coming from the employers and magnates of the great new towns. On neither side could it be pretended that all was harmony in this new Britain; and if anybody had been disposed to such a rosy view, there was always the sporadic stream of revolutions and other disturbances uncomfortably close to the other side of the Channel to remind people of the vast array of different interests flung up by the new society. Edmund Burke in the 1790s could argue that the traditional way of doing things had divine right on its side; Tom Paine could argue back – and become Britain's best-selling author of the time by doing so – that society had to be reconstituted from the ground up.

In terms of party politics, the period was dominated by the Tory party of William Pitt, Lord Liverpool, George Canning and Robert Peel, with the Whigs only able to achieve power through the Tories' internal divisions. A major theme was the demand for broadening of the parliamentary franchise, which bore some fruit in the Whig Reform Act of 1832. The principal effects were to ratify changes already occurring in the country at large by giving the vote to a new block of the manufacturing and commercial middle class and by redistributing representation to reflect the development of the new towns. Towards the end of the period, in 1846, Peel undertook his famous repeal of the Corn Laws, virtually splitting the Tory party in the process.

People had to contend not only with the price of food and new ways of earning a living, but also with a wealth of developments of other kinds: scientific developments which made the unthinkable possible, and technological developments which produced machines which were, certainly, convenient but which also threatened already to supersede the people who were supposed to operate them. A very brief list would include the remarkable development of steam power and its use industrially and in ships and railways; the discovery of electricity and electro-magnetism; the virtual founding of many of the organic sciences; a long series of astronomical discoveries, including the planets Uranus and Neptune; the development of precision tools; the beginnings of photography, gas street lighting, telegraphy, and so on to matches, Portland cement, chloroform and Macintosh's waterproof fabric. And alongside these there were also, of course, developments in ideas, culminating in the revelations of Charles Darwin (1809–82) which appeared to challenge the whole basis on which human life and its meanings and purposes had been evaluated for centuries.

Alfred Lord Tennyson (1809–92) wrestled with the problem manfully, insisting on humanity as 'the heir of all the ages, in the foremost files of time'; but if we are indeed descended from the apes, then how are we to think about God's purposes for us?

> They say,
> The solid earth whereon we tread
>
> In tracts of fluent heat began,
>   And grew to seeming-random forms,
>   The seeming prey of cyclic storms,
> Till at the last arose the man;   (*In Memoriam* 118)

But, Tennyson asked,

> Are God and Nature then at strife,
>   That Nature lends such evil dreams?
>   So careful of the type she seems,
> So careless of the single life;

(*In Memoriam* 55)

Are we then not a hand-picked species with a morality whose object is to render us capable of individual and universal salvation? If not, then what are we, and by whose laws are we to be judged? Is there no law above man's, and what recourse can we have against manifest injustice?

Many of these considerations may have been beyond the ken of the average citizen, who proved able to continue, albeit sometimes uneasily, with a mixed bag of epistemological and religious assumptions. Yet more and more people were in fact able to consider these issues in an informed way, principally because of the spread of education, the upsurge of literacy after 1780. Although a long way from the ideas of free education for all which became the hallmark of the mid-twentieth century, nevertheless education did spread, evidenced in the growth of elementary schools, the consequent creation of a teaching profession, the beneficial effects of the 1833 Factory Act; and with it a whole set of new habits of reading.

William Wordsworth (1770–1850) was to complain that much of this new education was a waste of time, and worse, because it exposed people to all manner of trivia, 'frantic novels, sickly and stupid German Tragedies, and deluges of idle and extravagant stories in verse', food for exaggerated tastes which had lost contact with the eternal rural verities. Perhaps; but other percipient observers made the leap into realising that, whatever the faults in this cultural expansion, it was here to stay. The dominant Victorian ideals thus became those of enlightened paternalism, prefigured at its extreme in the schemes of Robert Owen at New Lanark, with his clean factories and insistence on workers' education; and of a version of self-help derived eventually from the theories of utilitarianism. As Matthew Arnold was later to say with vehemence, it behoved the classes with power at their command to think carefully about the cultural diet they provided for their underlings, because it might well be on that that the future stability of the State would depend.

Communications and transport within Britain were going through their own series of revolutions. In effect, the country was getting smaller. Journeys which might have seemed unthinkable in the mid-eighteenth century could be achieved even by the end of the century with a comparative minimum of effort; better stage-coaches were available, roads were vastly improved, the new Post Office meant that communication with long-distant relatives was no longer impossible and the coaches provided for it by John Palmer provided a new model of freedom from delay and danger. To the government's frequent irritation, news now travelled fast; this was good for business, but it also tended towards the foundation of large groups of people with perceivably common interests.

Yet this revolution was itself a brief one; in 1825 the Stockton to

Darlington Railway was opened, and the world was never to be the same again. The railways, as Carlyle put it, 'have set all the Towns of Britain a-dancing' in a turmoil of change. The first great London terminus was opened at Euston Square in 1838; Thomas Cook was in business by 1841. A new age of speedy and reliable travel had arrived. People came to refer to many of the attendant issues under the heading of the 'condition-of-England question'. In what state was this new country? How healthy were its inhabitants and its prospects? Cobbett rode hundreds of miles a year looking over the countryside and assessing its condition, and we can see some of his reports in *Rural Rides* (1830); Henry Mayhew and others were later to inspect the cities from all angles and were variously grim about what they saw. And with all this it also became possible for literary and artistic fame to travel faster; concert halls would be packed at the news of a new virtuoso performer from Europe (the émigré conductor Louis Jullien was a cardinal example, conducting regular full-scale orchestral tours of the provinces), London exhibitions, which had only begun in 1760, would suddenly become profitable exercises, crowds would be clamouring at the new circulating libraries for the latest novels or for the most recent instalments of magazine fiction.

And all of this was based on an overall population explosion. The population of England and Wales had perhaps trebled between 1400 and 1780; it trebled again during the period under discussion with, of course, important and direct consequences for architecture and building in particular.

Global and imperial influences

Ever since Elizabethan days the British had been renowned seafarers and travellers. From many parts of the globe were coming the raw materials of new industry and new tastes, the cotton for the mills of Lancashire, for instance; but much of this had been unknown to the common people, whose daily ambit might never have brought them within sight of a coastline, let alone within thinking distance of Persia or Araby. One of the great events which began to change all that was the loss of the American colonies in 1783. Here, indeed, was something new and frightening: a subject land standing up for its own rights and rejecting the British yoke.

The consequences were considerable. It was in 1787 that the first ships sailed for Botany Bay, a new place to which to transport convicted criminals; and thus began a new expansion of the British Empire, which was to embrace the vast tracts of Australia, New Zealand, the south of Africa, and Canada, itself founded on the conflicts of the American states. India was already closely linked with Britain, but its role in the Empire was being transformed from very early on in the eighteenth century, culminating in the revision of the East India Company Charter in 1833, which produced from a vast trading station a governed state.

Paine had been to America, as he was to be wherever trouble threatened for a quarter of a century, and it was his belief that the Americans were well within their natural rights in throwing off the burden of 'taxation without representation'. This view helped to release a considerable debate around the question of empire. The portrayal which became most dear to the Victorians was of honourable, patient Britain devoting itself to the improvement of living standards in various far-flung parts of the world, and to the improvement of the mental and spiritual health of benighted natives by the distribution of Bibles and moral homilies.

But, as Asa Briggs points out, frequently the outcome was a battle in far-flung parts of the world between Bibles and gin, both imported, for there were various groups in England interested in the Empire, 'investors, foreign trading concerns, missionary societies, and a small section of the radicals'. That was true; but there was also a larger sector of interest, the public imagination itself with its burgeoning taste for things exotic, tales of returned travellers, and the products of the 'mystic' orient.

And this is not surprising. Egypt; the West Indies; the Nile; the Niger: all these were on the routes of explorers and travellers, even in the 1790s. Farther afield, William Bligh and George Vancouver were making their voyages through the perilous straits of the South Seas and the North Pacific, and sending home new Odysseys resounding with accounts of curious customs and extraordinary opportunities for gain. It was, after all, not that long since Daniel Defoe had been able to claim with perfect seriousness that God had placed Africa on the surface of the globe in order to provide decent Europeans with extra riches, and had constructed the oceans in order to facilitate free trade.

The dominions were at this time of considerable size: the loss of the American states seemed only to have multiplied the spreading areas which were coloured red on the map. And there seemed to be a corresponding British skill when it came to 'seeding' new territories where nothing had existed before; the cardinal example would be Singapore, which was founded virtually from scratch, and against the policy of the British government, by Sir Stamford Raffles in 1819.

The certainties which had been Defoe's, however, were not universally shared. William Blake (1757–1827), coming from a dissenting religious background quite similar to Defoe's, was nonetheless certain that the benefit of the subject peoples was less at the root of the motivation of empire than was the maintenance of slavery itself, that detestable trade based on Bristol and the other ports, which was now to come under the scrutiny of William Wilberforce and to be eventually abolished in 1833. The slave trade made Samuel Taylor Coleridge (1772–1834) uneasy in Bristol too; and there crept into people's minds an uneasy sense that Britain might not be the centre of the world. In a poem like Coleridge's *Ancient Mariner* (1798), it is clear that 'crossing the line' is not a simple matter; exploration in seas that might not be one's own encourages a closer dealing with retribution and wrath than might be the lot of the ordinary man, although the Mariner himself seems to have no compunction about revisiting this wrath on the unsuspecting stay-at-home, the unfortunate wedding guest whose time for listening has come. There is a marvellous and fearsome visual echo of this problematic of slavery, empire and the sea in *Slave Ship*, painted by Joseph Mallord William Turner (1775–1851) in 1840.

Especially for the wealthy and for those with aesthetic pretensions, there was a great deal to be said for the Empire, and for this new sense that the world itself was shrinking. For the 'subject' peoples, the matter was somewhat different. For the Chinese the consequences of this British zest were nothing less than catastrophic. True, the regulated Anglo-Chinese trade of the early years of the century seemed not to engender disasters; but the momentary freedom accorded by the renegotiation of the East India Company's treaty in 1839 began the long chain of unequal dealings which resulted in the cession of the treaty ports and the long opium stain on Britain's reputation in the East, which no Victorian missionary society could totally remove.

But for all this, cargoes of tea and domestic and commercial exotica – sugar, molasses, tobacco, wines – were arriving on Britain's coasts faster and in more profusion than ever before. And in the late eighteenth century, there was a whole cultural movement dedicated to interest in the 'exotic'; in the third quarter of the century solid country gentlemen had begun to feel out of place if at least one room of their home was not done up in 'chinoiserie'. *Vathek* (1786) by William Beckford began a strong taste for novels with oriental settings, as the Grand Tour was extended to the Near East and even on occasions to India.

Perhaps the most famous visible manifestation of this fascination was the Brighton Pavilion, designed by John Nash (1752–1835), built by the Prince Regent in 1815 and the object of extended debate for years afterwards. Was it evidence of strong artistic taste, the kind of taste we should expect from a potential monarch who laid claim to patronage of the arts? Or was it a vulgar monstrosity, a testimony to a new willingness to waste time and very large amounts of money on all sorts of frippery, provided they were 'foreign-made' on the price tag?

Canning in 1826 could claim, on the announcement of the new republics of Mexico, Buenos Aires and Colombia, that he had 'called the New World into existence to redress the balance of the Old'; that was true in more than one sense, since the emigration figures from the British Isles climbed from 2000 in 1815 to a quarter of a million per year in the 1840s. Charles Kingsley was to speak enthusiastically of

brave young England longing to wing its way out of its island prison, to discover and to traffic, to colonise and to civilise, until no wind can sweep the earth which does not bear the echoes of an English voice.

(*Westward Ho*, 1855)

And he was probably right; but the question remains as to how these processes affected the people back home, and to find the keys to that, we have to look at relationships closer to home and to the situation in continental Europe.

European influences

If the loss of the American colonies forever destroyed some of the old British certainties, the eruption of the French Revolution in the late 1780s completed the traumatic rending of the curtain. It is difficult for us now to think ourselves back into the extreme improbability of the Revolution, and perhaps more particularly of the execution of the French monarch. As far as many Englishmen at the end of the century were concerned, the world had indeed been turned upside down, and Leviathan and Behemoth paraded in all their panoply of destruction and licentiousness a few short miles across the English Channel.

Not of course, that relations between the French and the English had ever been easy. Amid the confusion of sentiments called up by the events in France there was a goodly crop of old-fashioned xenophobia. Some of this was certainly endemic, and the lesson thus derived was simply that the beastly French had once more proved themselves capable of unutterable extremes; some again was probably engineered by agents of the Tory government as a long-stop against the threat that revolutionary ambitions might spread into the purity of the British soul, or soil. One effect was the emergence of 'Church and King' mobs who made it their business to seek out anybody who betrayed the least trace of radical sympathies.

This spectre of Jacobinism in due course modified itself into the more practically frightening figure of Napoleon, and Britain found itself embroiled in twenty years of war with the would-be dictator of Europe. Again, with hindsight it is difficult to keep in mind that the outcomes of wars are not predetermined, or predictable in advance; it never seemed very likely that Napoleon could successfully invade Britain, but on the other hand it was also far from clear how the monster who had brought the rest of Europe to its knees could be defeated. There were years of waiting and doubt, climaxing in the 'false victory' of Napoleon's first imprisonment; and there emerged a culture, too, of heroism dedicated to celebrating the exploits of Nelson, Wellington and Britain's heroic fighting men, fighting always against colossal odds and, in the popular mind at least, against the new barbarians. In 1815 the British Institution offered a £1000 prize for a 16 × 21-foot painting on the triumph of Wellington; Nelson's Column was put up in 1843.

The peace which came to Europe in 1815 was an uneasy one, in two ways. First, the promised fruits of peace were not readily available; the British economy and British social life had been vastly disrupted by the war effort, and victory produced a massive economic slump, fuelled by the demobilisation of 400,000 troops and reflected in the prices of wheat. Second, the radical ideas engendered by the revolution, however far they may have fallen short of their original objects, did not simply vanish, but continued to inflame popular European feeling and to erupt sporadically, especially in the crucial years of 1830 and 1848.

But now there was a difference; from being ideas of democracy and of the overthrow of authority, whether God-given or not, they now came more to be seen in terms of small nations, notably Greece and Italy, fighting for independence and national self-determination. It was these ideas with which Wordsworth (*Poems dedicated to National Independence and Liberty*, 1802–16), Percy Bysshe Shelley (*Hellas*, 1821) and Byron associated themselves in various ways. And it was also in relation to these European ideas, and to their practical outcomes, that a whole wave of British politicians acquired their fame, men like Viscount Castlereagh, Canning, Lord Palmerston whose public base at home depended also on the commanding figure they cut variously on the European stage.

Towards the middle of the nineteenth century, another factor in Europe was the shifting of political attention away to its eastern frontiers, where the famously tottering Turkish Empire continued to totter under the impact of Greek independence. It was because of the vacuum created in this area that Russia reappeared on the European scene, with consequences which were in due course to lead to the outbreak of the Crimean War.

What was perhaps most important culturally about all these events was the flow of proud patriotism to which they gave birth. From the early days of the Napoleonic wars, through the triumphalism of Trafalgar and Waterloo, and then on into the great but ambivalent Victorian certainties about Britain's role as arbiter of the world's fortunes, there is a continuity. Interestingly, it was in 1850 when this spirit of national self-congratulation was at its height that Britain finally became a net food importer, relying on manufactured exports for foreign exchange. Again, it was to be the increasingly mournful tones of Tennyson which marked the new problems, religious, national and ethical, and which came to haunt the later years of Victorianism. His masterpiece *In Memoriam* (1850) is among other things a lament for the passing away of a social order and of a certain definition of Britishness, a plangent meditation on the frailty of certainty. Thus also implicitly it marks an awareness of the vast range of new things in the world which were coming to pass outside the national consensus, and which were already eating away at Victorian confidence.

Indeed, this can be seen from the wars themselves. The attempt to convert the revolutionary and Napoleonic wars into the stuff of myth was largely successful, in painting as well as in literature, one of the cardinal heroic images being Benjamin West's *Apotheosis of Nelson* (1807). West, perhaps not surprisingly, had succeeded Sir Joshua Reynolds, who died in 1792, as President of the Royal Academy, a post he was to hold for almost 30 years. We may, however, have some sympathy with Wellington's well-known and unromantic moment of doubt when confronting his men: 'I don't know what effect these men will have upon the enemy, but, by God, they frighten me.' By the time it came to the Crimea the toll of life, the uncertainty of the goals, the sheer mud and misery, were to prove more resistant to the need for glory.

It was also in connection with these European events that the 'condition-of-England' question, which was principally a domestic one, came to acquire a more international counterpart, in the search for a 'national purpose'. In part, this was a device for unification; what better way to pacify the new masses than to convince them that Britain had a collective national destiny? But in part it was also a genuine reflection of the uncertainties which lay at the heart of Victorian self-confidence. What was it that made this small island special – or indeed, was it not so special at all, was it also destined to be overtaken by the vast fluxes of history which seemed to be sweeping so much of the old order aside? 'As an anarchic multitude on mere Supply-and-demand', as Carlyle put it, it is 'inevitable that we dwindle in horrid suicidal convulsion, and self-abrasion, frightful to the imagination, into Chactaw Workers' (*Past and Present*, 1843).

One thing that *was* certain was that the British knew more, and more accurately, about the rest of the world than they had ever previously done. In part this was because, under the pressure of the wars, newspaper reportage improved immensely; in part it was due to general developments in communications; in part to changes in the methods of book production. For over twenty years, direct travel through Europe had been very difficult, and when the barriers finally came down there was a desire for foreign experience to be satisfied, so avid that it was referred to as the 'British mania', well traced by Donald Low in *That Sunny Dome* (1977). The Grand Tour became more socially widespread as the economic base of society shifted, and at the same time travellers became more adventurous, venturing out beyond Europe, partly under the influence of Byron, to the Eastern Mediterranean; and thus to Africa and the East. This new Grand Tour served to remind the British that the island's barriers were becoming more permeable all the time.

In cultural terms, a crucial example is in music, where British openness to foreign influences became more widespread; European composers and performers from Franz Joseph Haydn to Felix Mendelssohn were welcomed and popular, English music itself benefited from exposure to European styles and techniques; Ludwig van Beethoven's 9th Symphony, commissioned by the Royal Philharmonic Society (founded 1813), was first performed here in 1825. In ideas too, European philosophies came to add dimensions to British thinking – evidenced particularly in the work of Carlyle and, perhaps, Coleridge – which had been notably absent from the down-to-earth political philosophies of Thomas Hobbes and John Locke, a dimension of speculation unfettered by parochial considerations.

Context for the arts: patronage and the market

When approaching the arts themselves, one starting-point is the new wealth which was generated by this rapidly industrialising society, which created new patrons and new markets. The most outstanding of these was certainly the market for fiction. The novel as we know it had its origins in the work of Defoe, Samuel Richardson and Henry Fielding only in the early to mid-eighteenth century; yet by the end of the century, the market was solidly established, and it was even possible for novel-writers to make respectable livings from their work without the previous necessity for literary hackwork.

Popular Gothic and historical novelists, Ann Radcliffe for instance, were being paid handsome advances for their forthcoming work. In the new circulating libraries, people were queueing up for the latest books. Sir Walter Scott (1771–1832) is emblematic of a worthy Victorian attitude. Already a successful writer, but very much less successful when it came to the management of his financial affairs, he went spectacularly bankrupt, and vowed that he would write to pay off his debts. He never did, quite, but the shining example which he thus held up of a combination of literary popularity and scrupulous probity went down very well with the public.

Later on in the period, the market went through a further stage of revolution with the intensification of serial publication. Charles Dickens

(1812–70) is the outstanding example; but there were many others, for example G.W.M. Reynolds, whose serialised works sold in their millions and were read out loud in the markets of London every morning. Reynolds padded his material out with inserted pieces of a more factual, informative nature: the audience to whom he was speaking wanted a good melodramatic plot but they also wanted information, and they were willing to wade through prodigious numbers of pages to get it.

Thus, between the beginning of the eighteenth century and the middle of the nineteenth, the whole economic base of literature changed. No longer was it a matter of aristocratic patronage and gentlemanly libraries; the rise of the novel brought a literature of incident, character and, occasionally, high moral concern within the purview of a broad public. The outstanding cause of change was the enormous increase in literacy. Initially confined to those whose occupations, while menial in themselves, brought them into contact with chances for self-improvement – domestic servants are the obvious example. Later this urge for self-improvement spread like wildfire, probably faster than the institutional means of satisfying it. One reason was that, with the societal changes that were going on, all sorts of areas of public questioning were opened up; for it was becoming no longer possible to presume that life next year would proceed in much the same way as life last year. There was consequently a spreading desire for knowledge about society and the world; and the reading public by no means restricted itself to novels – biographies, travellers' tales, ethical and political pamphlets were all part of the 'literary' explosion.

And the cities spawned a lust for new forms of entertainment. It has been argued that with the demise of the old village festivals, people were virtually forced to discover new sources of enjoyment and reassurance. Much of this new fiction has been seen as escapist, to do more with people's dissatisfaction with their new lives than with any desire for 'improvement'. But 'escapist' is a difficult word, and even some of the cheapest and most sensational chapbooks of popular tales and ballads served either to open the imagination or, prefiguring the Victorian fascination with crime, to probe into some of the more mysterious and bizarre ways in which people behaved. At all events, 'improvement', in all its varied senses, economic and cultural, was a controlling motif of the age.

What was also emerging as a concomitant of this expansion was a class-divided audience: Scott's audience and Jane Austen's (1775–1817) would not have comprised the readers of the 'penny dreadfuls'. Fiction was used to discover how other sectors of society lived, in both directions: the middle classes reading about the doings of the criminal sub-proletariat in the prolific works of writers like William Harrison Ainsworth, or about the aristocracy in, for example, the 'silver-fork' fiction of the 1820s. Perhaps the single most important factor in the composition of the reading public was the predominance of women, through a combination of greater leisure and increased opportunities for education. Although the institutional manifestation of this move towards equality can only be dated, at the earliest, from events like the establishment of the North London Collegiate School in 1850, writers had been aware of the female audience for the previous century.

In the painting of the period we can again trace the erosion of the patronage system and the emerging possibility of living by one's own brush, along with an improvement in the painter's social status, prefigured by Reynolds and the founding of the Academy in 1768. Whereas in the eighteenth century we encounter a dismal host of painters accompanying their patrons' sons on the Grand Tour, providing topographies on demand, by the middle of the nineteenth a painter of genius like Turner can be fully independent. Of course, this had its problems: in order to survive, the painter had to become involved, at least to an extent, in the evaluation of public taste, a difficult thing at the best of times and especially complex in such times of change. Turner was tremendously and instinctively good at this; but for a painter like John Crome, no metropolitan academy could suffice, and thus he sets up his own 'academy on the banks of the Yare'.

Certainly it became more possible to survive on the basis of exhibitions, which became more systematic during the first half of the nineteenth century. In terms of public taste in painting, however, history tells us a confusing story. When we think of the great artists of the period, Turner and John Constable (1776–1837) emblematic among them, we see an enormous divergence, although one which is parallel in many ways to divergences within literary romanticism. Constable we could see as aligned with Wordsworth in his love of locality, of the countryside, and his concentration on the changeless aspects of experience; Turner represents all the more passionate side of romanticism, the fire and wreck and battle, that sense of a new world which made Byron and Shelley so restless in sheltered Britain. Yet a distinctively British school of painting can be seen to continue throughout, in for example the portraiture of Henry Raeburn, Thomas Lawrence and John Hoppner, and more importantly in the unique development of watercolour in the period, even though there was here a variousness which clearly shows the broadening of the markets.

In music a somewhat similar picture obtained. Composers became more dependent on the sales of published works, and correspondingly freer from the needs to compose to order or for great occasions. The breaking of the old ties of patronage meant a greater responsiveness to public taste, and there was again a corresponding rise in social status. However, the requirement of public performance placed considerable strain on the musician and the obverse side of this new freedom, which was a Europe-wide phenomenon, was the fate of so many nineteenth-century composers whose work failed to find the right audience, Beethoven and Franz Schubert among others.

The history of British music in the period is not so much centred around composition, which was in a state of considerable decline, but around performances and trends in public taste, initially particularly around the eventual supersession of the long-lived and intense cult of George Frederic Handel after, for example, the great Handel Festivals of 1784–91. What was noticeable was a considerable spread of musical access, evidenced in the growth of concert series (the Ancient Concerts, 1776–1848; the Vocal Concerts, 1792–1822; the endeavours of Johann Peter Salomon to establish his philharmonic concerts, 1791–4); the founding of the Philharmonic Society in 1813 and the Royal Academy of Music in 1823, tours by the great

composers which found ready audiences in many parts of the country
(Mendelssohn's *Elijah* was a sensation when first performed in Birmingham
in 1846 and, like Handel's *Messiah* (1741) before it, drew enormous
audiences). Again, we can trace in this the importance of the evolution of new
forms of entertainment, and behind it the new importance of middle-class
money. Opera remained significant, but for the most part securely in the
hands of the Italians, despite the contributions of Stephen Storace and
William Shield.

In the fields of architecture, urban and rural, and town planning the major
effect of patronage was the restructuring of London which took place during
the Regency; and the most important figure on the scene after Sir John
Soane's long work on the Bank of England was Nash. He was a man of
tremendous and sometimes rather suspect versatility who, while living
through that reliance on commissions which had become inevitable in the
field, was nevertheless able to use those commissions in an individual way,
starting from the construction of Regent Street (1811), and proceeding regally
via the Brighton Pavilion to Buckingham Palace (1825). Behind Nash still lies
the model of the enlightened patron, surviving of course into the nineteenth
century and embodied neatly in the portly but enlightened person of the
Prince Regent himself. In the rush of urbanisation and in the importance
attached to economic practicality, many opportunities for the beautification of
the environment were lost; yet it is a wonder that they were not all lost, and
that the aesthetic impulse continued to exert an influence even over urban
development.

Print and the development of literacy

Many of these matters, then, had to do with the development of literacy and
artistic access; many also had to do with what we might usefully call a
diffusion of public concern. Affairs both domestic and foreign which in earlier
times had been exclusively the fief of nobility and politicians were now
everybody's, whether beneficially or not. In no area was this change
registered more keenly than in the Press. Despite a series of attempts at
restriction from the early days of Pitt through to the stamp duty controls of
the post-war years, there was a massive burgeoning of the newspaper
industry. One of the vital landmarks was the introduction in 1814 by *The
Times* (founded 1788) of steam-driven machinery, which revolutionised print
runs.

A great deal of this expansion was, on the whole, at the expense of the
credibility of governments; an exemplary case here is Cobbett's successive
publishing enterprises, particularly *The Political Register*, which became
Britain's first cheap periodical in 1816. In it he claimed to be giving voice to
that sector of the population which would otherwise be speechless. Many
newspapers during the period trod a thin political line. Certainly there were
plenty of time-serving editors who saw it as their bounden duty to rehearse
party politics, on all available sides; but there were others who found,
whether honourably or not, that there was a thirst for news which

transcended these squabbles and who saw furthermore that technological development had placed in their hands the means of satisfying it. The now traditional distinction between daily and Sunday papers was already in place, with the popular Sundays evolving the sensationalist mix which was to coalesce into the *News of the World* (first published 1843, ironically the year *The Economist* first saw the light of day), while the dailies on the whole prided themselves more on their ability to capture and transmit up-to-the-minute news stories, a habit at which they had already become exceptionally and sometimes illegally agile during the years of the European blockades. *The Observer* was founded in 1791, the *Manchester Guardian* in 1821, the *Sunday Times* in 1822, the *Evening Standard* in 1827.

We can also trace a vast increase, in production and in scope, on the part of the reviews; the early nineteenth century was the great age in which the *Edinburgh Magazine* (founded 1802), the *Quarterly Review* (founded by Scott and other Tories in 1809) and *Blackwood's Magazine* (1817, with John Wilson as editor) thundered their different versions of literary taste and the classical canon across Britain. What they had to say, even about erudite matters of poetic style, was frequently regarded as publicly important, for we are looking here at a time when many of the separations we now regard as conventional had not occurred, and when a healthy literature and art were regarded as essential to the general health of the body politic. Conversely, the breath of scandal or decadence in the arts would set reviewers and belletrists huffing and puffing about decline in moral standards; Byron and John Keats felt the chill breath of these moralising pronouncements, and so did Blake's followers and friends, Henry Fuseli among them, as they tried to probe rather more deeply into the psychological underworld than was socially permissible.

The immediate post-war period of the Regency has been seen as characterised by an almost frenzied impulse towards freedom; yet looking back we can now see it equally as a prelude to the more restricted atmosphere of the great Victorian years. This duality cannot be denied. Perhaps the best way of envisioning that pivotal time is in terms of a patrolling of the boundaries: when the newspapers and magazines set themselves up as arbiters of political opinion and artistic taste, they found themselves acting both as the channel through which new opinions and attitudes could come, and also as the protector of standards which this flood of new ideas and activity might otherwise sweep away. The seeds of uncertainty and instability, the birth of a thoroughly dissenting academy, are there from the very beginning; the question becomes one of how much tolerance the evolving State was going to have for these voices of dissent.

The middle ground was struck very significantly in the age's satire. *Headlong Hall* (1816) and *Nightmare Abbey* (1818) by Thomas Love Peacock come particularly to mind, but more importantly the line of satirical painting and engraving which flowed down from William Hogarth into the brilliant caricatures of Thomas Rowlandson, whose detailed and comic appreciations of life in both city and country, from *Vauxhall Gardens* (1784) to the *Dance of Life* (1816), make him one of the most important recorders of manners and customs of the time. Increasing sales of prints made such mirrors of life ever more available, as British people were encouraged to laugh not only at their faintly ridiculous 'confrères' across the Channel, which was by now a tradition, but also at themselves. Rowlandson's *Tour of Doctor Syntax*, originally published in the *Poetical Magazine* between 1809 and 1811, became a firm favourite with the public.

Rowlandson and his collaborator William Combe on the one hand, and Blake on the other, demonstrate for us how much the art of the period was responding to technical changes, and to developments in the available modes of production. The art of illustration, the fitting together of literary and painterly subject-matter, was a keynote and not only an aesthetic development; it was also an evolution of new forms to suit the different modes of dissemination which were now available. We may note Blake's illustrations to the Book of Job (*c.*1820–2); Thomas Bewick's and John James Audubon's bird illustrations; illustrations in magazines like *Good Words* and *Cornhill*; the works of James Gillray and George Cruikshank; the numerous illustrations to Dickens, Ainsworth and others.

It was perhaps in the illustrated works of Dickens that these new mixed forms, part pictorial, part discursive, produced their greatest fruit. Of all the great British novelists – and these years produced more than their share – it was Dickens who proved most able, in novels like *Pickwick Papers* (1836–7) and the later *Great Expectations* (1860–1), to combine an awareness of popular taste with the brilliant handling of moral and political materials. He was to prove uniquely attuned to the new ways in which his countrymen saw their own lives, and uniquely able to blend a remarkable accuracy when it comes to social and cultural detail with the more exaggerated and caricatured modes which, through forms like pantomime and Punch-and-Judy shows, had for long been a staple of working-class taste. In fact when one thinks in terms of popular taste it becomes apparent, even looking through the design of Christmas cards today, that alongside Dickens the novelist there is also a Dickensian mode, a whole apparatus of ways of portraying Britain – and especially London – which relied not only on the written word but also on illustration.

This kind of popularity cannot be achieved by a writer alone, however accomplished; it can happen only in terms of a remarkable conjunction between his own perceptions and the popular imagination. In many ways, it is only Dickens among the British writers who provides us with a parallel with Shakespeare. In both cases, the achievement rests upon the discovery of a form which can straddle the class divisions of the available audience, offer something to the groundlings as well as something to the élite, and encourage an interplay between these audience factions which, if not fully harmonious, is at least tolerant and large-minded – in Dickens's case, 'comic' in the widest and wisest sense of that word. In the fiction and theatre of the early Victorian period we find a great deal of this 'comic' interaction between classes (the tone is set by Pierce Egan's *Life in London*, 1821) in the attempt, perhaps, to resist the brutal facts of economic separatism.

In terms of music, we can find similar motifs operating; not perhaps at the soaring heights of the art, but in the early evolution of music hall as an art form (the Mogul Saloon opened in 1847, the Canterbury Hall in 1849) and in the consequent coining of popular songs which marks the period. Music in its higher reaches may be the art form which attains the purest states of the abstract; but there is also an area of music which echoes the national pulse, whether it be the war songs of the early years of the century or the Cockney rhymes of the middle years; and in this kind of music the age was proficient and even on occasion innovative. People were flocking to hear entertainment with a musical content, at for example the great pleasure gardens of Vauxhall and Ranelagh, and were enjoying the benefits of a popular theatre which even now can be seen to have contributed much to the development of the national self-image.

The Romantic experience

This may, perhaps, sound rather cosy: worlds first of Regency beaux and dandies, later of gas-lamps and London lanes in snow. And this was all part of the period; but there was of course another part, more concerned with the country than the city, more with the wilder reaches of imagination than with social mores, more with the difficult integrity of the lone artist than with the vagaries of popular taste. There was that whole area of sensibility and response for which we now use that difficult term 'Romanticism'. What strands can we pick out as typical, if not definitive, of British Romanticism during the years 1785–1851?

It is useful to begin from a negative: much Romantic art stood, in one way or another, in opposition to the classicism of the earlier eighteenth century. This classicism revered tradition; took formal order as an assumption of the arts; saw the artist's public duty as paramount; worried ceaselessly, if somewhat aristocratically, about whether the petty present was capable of matching up to the awe-inspiring achievements of the past. By contrast Romanticism extolled the virtues of innovation; explored the realms of chaos in human experience; gave great emphasis to the artist's overriding responsibility to the maintenance of his own integrity; looked forward, albeit with frequent trepidation, into new ages, while at the same time essaying a quite different version of the past canon in which the 'ill-formed' brilliances of Shakespeare and the sublimity of Milton are at least as important as the regularities and symphonies of Greek and Roman architecture. Two emblematic European figures were Beethoven and Berlioz whose distinct influences became commanding in the mid-nineteenth century.

Yet the works of Wordsworth, Coleridge and many others also bespeak an intense concern with the social role of the poet, and Constable for one was almost desperate at times to demonstrate to the public that painting was a 'mechanical' craft like any other. And Romanticism did not exclude the survival of some previous habits; but, as Frederick Hart has insisted, 'except in architecture, neo-classicism was relatively weak in England'; and even in architecture neo-classicism takes its due place only among the host of revivalisms of the early Victorian years. The crucial questions here are about priority. The Romantic artist did not see himself as correctly acquitting his responsibility by fitting the awkwardnesses and nightmares of his personal vision into the framework of the established State. Rather, he saw himself as providing a better model for the health and intelligence of the individual by laying out his own individual dilemmas and uncertainties, his peculiar perception, which may in the end appear to part company with the ostensible object entirely; and by helping to ensure that the whole soul of man, rather than merely the rational faculties, are engaged with the great problems of integrity and development in that all-embracing way which Coleridge, in *Biographia Literaria* (1817), classified under the great heading of 'imagination'.

Blake, the poet, painter, engraver and visionary, is a cardinal example here. His aesthetic was distinctive and widely misunderstood: for him 'vision' is precisely that which is 'Determinate & Perfect', the opposite of cloudiness or vapouring; and it is in the exact and vivid world of the imagination and not in the smudged and jarring world of 'vegetable' reality that we can make precise distinctions and learn about the nature of life. The entire realm of oil painting he saw as a realm of imprecision and false grandiosity; better by far to concentrate on the exactitudes of the imagination, and to this end he evolved a range of new painting and engraving techniques designed to force our attention onto the exact shapes of the gods, or 'principles' of human life, as he saw them. Blake was also emblematic in his attitude towards the interplay between art and commerce; he saw perhaps more clearly than anybody in the period the way in which, alongside all this burgeoning and growth in the arts, the danger existed of a levelling out, a flattening of differences until all art would become insipid. 'The Foundation of Empire', he wrote, 'is Art & Science. Remove them or Degrade them, & the Empire is No More' ('Annotations to Reynolds', *c.*1808).

In poetry we also find this visionary impulse very strongly in Shelley, who in so much of his work – *Ode to the West Wind* (1819) is the best-known example – seems to be 'overflying' the world and seeking in it the 'eternal lineaments' in terms of which it makes so much more sense than when we look at it amid the clutter of quotidian experience. We can see some reflection of this concern in Constable (who also uses the word 'visionary' of himself, although with a rather different meaning), with his insistence on the clouds as the true centre of landscape, the form below which everything else lives and moves and has its being; the sky as 'the keynote' of depiction. We can see it in an exemplary if exaggerated form in the massive paintings of John Martin (1789–1854), with their dwarfed human figures lost in mighty supernatural landscapes, *The Bard* (1817), for instance, or *The Fall of Nineveh* (1833). It was already there in a particularly interesting condition in Joseph Wright of Derby, the first artist who was able to conjoin this Romantic sensibility with industrial scenes in paintings like *Experiment on a Bird in the Air Pump* (1768) and *Iron Forge* (1772).

And we can find it at its most superb in the works of Turner. Turner, the greatest of British artists, epitomises many things about the first half of the nineteenth century. He practised precisely those modes of painting which Reynolds, the great arbiter of eighteenth-century painting, had not long before dismissed as trivial, and thus asserts the multifariousness of artistic endeavour so beloved of the Romantics. From an early realism, he comes increasingly to concentrate on pure problems of colour and form, putting together great masses of light and shade in his paintings of sea and sky. He too, much more impressively than Wright, has a real sense of how the new world connects onto the old: *Rain, Steam and Speed* (1844) is both a recognisably real train and at the same time, with its gold and blue veils, a symbol of an ambivalent divine wrath, a 'holy terror' which is in some ways too great, too new, for us to judge, but must be perceived, apprehended in all its magnificence.

Turner spent his life probing more and more deeply into these intensely personal visions, yet the Professor of Perspective, who had been elected to full membership of the Royal Academy when only 27 years old, remained a public man for all that. Where for so many other Romantics the strain of personal vision proved too much and culminated either in compromise or in lapses into madness or alienation, in Turner we see a man who was resolutely Janus-like, one face looking into the swelling world of the individual imagination, while with the other he registered the enormous changes through which his society was going. Turner asserted implicitly that all could yet be saved provided we preserve that essential moment of individual confrontation between the massive forces of nature and the human world of endeavour. *Hannibal Crossing the Alps* (1812) is a splendid example of this match between human achievement and natural splendour.

But Romantic experience can also be more simply characterised. For example, we can see in it a constant search for settings adequate as models of and correlatives for the human mind. For the Romantics, mind – or better, psyche – was a vastly wider organism than it had been for their predecessors. It is here that we first begin to glimpse – in Coleridge's *Kubla Khan* (1797), say, or in the visionary landscapes of Samuel Palmer (1805–81) – those inarticulable depths which we have now grown accustomed to calling the 'unconscious'. But this grander view of mind, wherein the conscious, rational faculty is but the tip of the invisible and dangerous iceberg, requires a corresponding broadening of man's view of nature: hence the *mise-en-scène* of the early eighteenth century, the architecture of regularity and architectonic syntax, was replaced by a quite different series of scenes. Typically, the Romantics looked north or south: to the Lake District (as Byron so ironically points out in *Don Juan*, 1819–24) where a more spreading scenery can even be found on British soil, or even farther to Scott's Highlands; or to Southern Europe, to the rocks and crags of the Alps or Pyrenees, to the mountainous, precipitous landscapes so beloved of the Gothic writers and of a succession of travelling artists from Francis Towne onwards.

In all this we see a counterbalance to urbanisation, but again to call it escape is too simple: Blake and Turner certainly were not much bothered about being 'mid the din/Of towns and cities' (Wordsworth, *Tintern Abbey*, 1798), since to one variant of Romantic the imagination can work regardless of immediate stimulus. The point is that the process of social change reminded the Romantics of the limitless potential of the human psyche: change in the industrialising sense might be right or wrong, but change in general is of the essence of humankind, and essentially these great poetic and painterly landscapes, with their flashing waterfalls and sudden avalanches of words, sound, colour, are reminders of the constant possibility of change.

Among the things they therefore remind us of is the impermanence of human life, the double message of mortality.

In this period we find these questions of change and mortality underlined in a parallel way in the sustained interest in childhood, from Blake's carefully described state of innocence, through Wordsworth's interest in the world before the 'Shades of the prison-house begin to close/Upon the growing Boy' (*Intimations of Immortality*, 1802–4), to Dickens's masterpieces of child portraiture in *Oliver Twist* (1837–8), *Dombey and Son* (1848) and *David Copperfield* (1849–50). There is clearly in these writers – and perhaps we can see it in Constable, in for example the pristine yet poised landscape of *The White Horse* (1825), and the lesser landscape painters as well – a fear of contamination. Alongside that fear there is also a belief in the possibility that within everybody there survives the visionary faculty, the gift of imagination, the creative impulse, essentially the ability to *play*; not to be drowned by the encroaching world of work, but to retain the possibility of what Blake calls 'infant joy', some faculty to recreate that pure scenery of childhood in all its rich tones.

Maybe there is and was little room for this kind of pleasure in the harsh world of capitalism and the profit motive. Certainly many of the Romantics and early Victorians could wax bitter about this at times. Maybe, indeed, the fate of this type of 'innocent experience' is precisely to be condemned as madness. For we find a strong theme of madness running through Romanticism: the accusations of it levelled at Blake; the depictions of it by Byron and Shelley; the worship, frequently, of the 'fine frenzy', as in Carlyle, who believed that the whole structure of the English language, so painfully worked up since Johnson's time, was being destroyed under the pressure of social change; the emblematic breakdown of John Stuart Mill (1806–73), caught like so many of his contemporaries between speculation and utility, the expansion of the mind and the concentration of efficiency. The crucial opposition was between madness and civilisation: what was it, the Romantics asked themselves, nostalgically, bitterly or angrily according to their taste, which had been lost in the long process of civilising? What was missing?

The dream; the unconscious spasm of memory; the moment of desire; the slippage of visual focus: all of these were among the losses which the Romantics recorded and set about portraying. For they were trying to do nothing less than describe the indescribable: this was exactly their task and their contradiction. The wonder of it is that, given the internal strain of their programme, they proved able to supply us, across the European spectrum, in literature, painting and music with some of the most brilliant, memorable and glowing images that the arts have produced. Britain participated amply in these achievements.

Heroes and hero-worship

Although they made much of privacy, the individual and incommunicable experience, it was not all the major Romantics who chose to hide their light under a bushel. Blake's light, it is true, ended up under a bushel for a number of years but we can find no blushing spirits among Byron, Shelley, Keats, Carlyle and so forth. Still less can we find shrinking violets among the important political thinkers of the age, people like Paine, Mary Wollstonecraft, Cobbett, Jeremy Bentham, who had much in common with the Romantics in their convictions about liberty and equality, even if their taste for argument would situate them rather differently from the apostles of the imagination.

For the period we are discussing was a period of heroes and hero-worship, as Carlyle above all people perceived, and as we can see from the grandiose art of Benjamin West and Benjamin Robert Haydon. Byron was rapidly to seize this available coronet and clap it upon the head of the heroic man of letters; or, in other words, his own – in this case in the flimsy guise of Childe Harold:

> But I have lived, and have not lived in vain:
> My mind may lose its force, my blood its fire,
> And my frame perish even in conquering pain;
> But there is that within me which shall tire
> Torture and Time, and breathe when I expire . . .
>
> (*Childe Harold's Pilgrimage* canto 4, 1818)

Modesty was not Byron's greatest virtue.

Indeed, Byron was very important during these years: not by any means only, or even most importantly, as a poet, but as a living legend, as, in Hyppolite Taine's description, the age's 'ruling personage; that is, the model that contemporaries invest with their admiration and sympathy'. What was the substance of the legend which surrounded this fat, limping, rather unhealthy minor aristocrat? Was it mostly to do with his undoubted poetic gifts? Probably not. It had a lot to do with the search for excitement which erupted at the cessation of hostilities and with the idea that here was somebody who could cock a snook at authority. But the public infatuation with Byron was short-lived and two-faced, and rapidly turned to ridicule. Byron's own position as the democrat and supporter of the great cause of national liberation who also happened to be the epitome of aristocratic manners and even *droit de seigneur* was striated with contradiction.

What Byron was *not* was bourgeois. The infatuation with the heroic in this period was the flip side of the social descent, as it could be perceived, into bourgeoisification; even an aristocracy which, in other ways, could be seen as hopelessly decadent and archaic could take on a mythic value when it came to finding a symbolic opponent to this drift towards standardisation. Prometheus; Lucifer; Milton's Satan; the figures blazing in the darkness of Martin's illustrations (1824–8) to *Paradise Lost*: all these heroes of the struggle against the unjust gods are part of the imaginative substance of the period. Even Frankenstein, although apparently a scientist, was really an alchemist in the Humphry Davy mould, an original of brilliant inspiration. A major manifestation of this tendency was the whole phenomenon of Gothic, whose importance in these years cannot be overestimated. In fiction, in poetry, in painting, in the theatre, in architecture, the distinctive tones of the Gothic were felt; everywhere there were innocent maidens clad in white gauze standing back aghast and uttering strangely articulate speeches of defiance as they were approached by sinister noblemen clad in black and silver muttering designs variously upon their honour, their persons and/or their fortunes. In architectural terms, the equivalent of these grandiosely dramatic tones is to be found not so much in Horace Walpole's jokey Strawberry Hill as in, for example, the Parliament Buildings in London, designed by Charles Barry and Augustus Welby Northmore Pugin in the 1830s, where medieval formalities, pretensions and hierarchies are taken altogether more seriously.

Interestingly, what is least memorable about all this is the so-called heroes themselves. Emblematically in the work of Charlotte and Emily Brontë it is the hero/villains, Rochester and Heathcliff, who attract and distract us. Who remembers the name of the ostensible hero of Radcliffe's *Mysteries of Udolpho* (1794)? This 'Byronic/Satanic' personage is dangerous, unpredictable, the very personification of the Romantic unconscious; although the Regency dandies and beaux in the Beau Brummell mould were for the most part ephemeral sparks which burnt for a few brief moments and then went out leaving debts scattered all over London. Yet they too had their place in the society of the time: perhaps indeed as models of conspicuous consumption, as aids to forgetting about the austerities of the war years. This too was the real message of the Brighton Pavilion: it was now possible again to play, to invent, to indulge; better to think new than to drift back into the staid paths of our ancestors. Hence one of the peculiarities of Romanticism, this relentless surge forward, as it thought of itself, which nevertheless kept on recoining images of the past, and eventually modulated, through Wordsworth's epitaphs, into the elegiac tones of the mid-century.

These various insistences on the role of the hero found their popular apotheosis in the emergence of melodrama, which was to dominate the English stage for the rest of the century. In a sense, melodrama could never go out of fashion – and never has – because it was never precisely *in* fashion. It was always deliberately archaic; it dealt partly in folk memories of the great villains of Jacobean tragedy, partly in more recent but still very secondhand memories of the eighteenth-century aristocracy. From near and far came villains with supercharged moustaches intent on disarming all resistance. In its early inceptions, as for example with the work of Thomas Holcroft (1745–1809), and his translations from August von Kotzebue and R.-C. de Pixérécourt, melodrama had a definite and tantalising connection with the exposure of social injustice; after the late 1820s, as in the enormously popular *Maria Marten; or, The Murder in the Red Barn*, crime became the vital keynote.

The other side of this heroism is victimisation; it could be said that a great deal of art of this period deals to a point of oppression with victims and their state of mind. Matthew Gregory Lewis and Radcliffe among the Gothics come to mind; a certain quality of gloating in Keats's *Isabella* (1820); a gallery of Victorian heroines, including not only Jane Eyre, and Catherine in *Wuthering Heights* (both these novels appeared in 1847), but a host of Dickens heroines and also, in a way, Jane Austen's chastened and 'improved' women, even the women of Fuseli's nightmares; everywhere in this period there are victims, and they are usually women.

In the musical field, who is the counterpart of the dashing, twirling Victorian villain? Why, the performer on the pianoforte, that new hero of the concert-halls, dominating an instrument first heard in England only in the 1760s. For the pianoforte was new, superseding the harpsichord around 1800, and its single bound onto the musical stage in these years constituted a revolution from which music was never to recover. Now, suddenly, there arrived the great age of composer/performers: writers of music who were also, in various ways, great showmen, and who built up a personal following not only on their technical skills but also on their 'virtuosity' – such a different word from 'virtue' – that is, their charisma. For the first time, people were going to concerts not merely to be entertained, but to be thrilled, to be moved to the depths of their being by the great pianist 'storming the keys', as Auden was aptly to put it.

As the period drew on, this taste for heroes was to receive an apocalyptic and a gloomy inflection from Carlyle and Tennyson, respectively. Carlyle, in books like *Heroes and Hero-Worship* (1841) and *Past and Present*, would have none of this business of unsung heroes dying in garrets: his version of the hero was of a martial figure – whether soldier, politician or artist – who strode above the ranks of common humanity, possessed of vision and the promise of a better life. Carlyle, a High Victorian castigator of bourgeois values, embodied a crucial nineteenth-century contradiction: nothing, for him, flowed from this new world of money but the need to evolve yet another category of hero, the great man of affairs, the great profiteer.

Tennyson, as was his wont, was not so sure. Certainly he saw the loss of quality of life among the people; but he was not certain that heroes knew how to countermand this social de-evolution. For him there was only the wistful conjuring of the past, the second coming of Arthur; the imaginary rather than practical politics. The dilemma Tennyson expresses in poems like *The Palace of Art* (1832–42) and *The Lotos-Eaters* (1833) prefigures a melancholy withdrawal of the artist from a public life overweighted with materialist pressures.

As time went on, the heroine suffered even more, so many Marianas chanting their plaint for ever in the moated grange which they must inhabit in the knowledge of their lost hero. There is a certain displaced social truth in this; in fact, for middle-class and upper-class women, there were some improvements in social status, education and prestige. However, for many more women brought under the yoke of factory labour there was indeed a fearful separation from previous certainties of family and work, and the 'wailing for her demon lover' (Coleridge, *Kubla Khan*) took a more practical form of yearning for equality, while the development of capitalism seemed set to intensify the old injustices. These suffering women became artistically beautified in a tradition which gave rise, in 1848, to the founding by Holman Hunt, Sir John Everett Millais and Dante Gabriel Rossetti of the Pre-Raphaelite Brotherhood, which was to seek to replace what it saw as a brutalisation of life and social relations by a return to an idealised medieval past. But this was hardly to constitute a direct address to these problems of inequality and servitude.

Countryside: escape and preservation

Where, in the end, could the impulse towards bourgeoisification best be resisted? Not, indeed, in London, where the tumult of life and of change all too readily reminded the artist of social disorder; and not in the growing industrial towns of the North, with their practical businessmen and factory smoke. Only in the countryside, then, could there remain some solid ground on which to stand. In painting, it is this urge towards the steady depiction of landscape which becomes the mainstream in the years between 1800 and about 1840, when Crome, Turner, Constable break decisively with the artificiality of eighteenth-century landscape.

In the earlier years of the period, however, a myth was born, which was that, somehow, through these social changes the countryside could endure. Like all myths it grew around a nugget of truth; we cannot suggest that the mills and winding deep lanes which Constable depicts in *Dedham Lock and Mill* (1820), *The Hay Wain* (1821) and elsewhere are things merely of the imagination. On the contrary, they are the products of a meticulous habit of observation, and also of an extraordinary power of self-identification with natural forces and with atmosphere, paralleled only perhaps by Shelley in, for example, parts of *Alastor* (1816). As Constable himself said, his art can be found in Suffolk 'under every hedge, and in every lane'. But the dimension of the mythic creeps in with a writer like Wordsworth, with his implicit claim that the countryside is the repository of eternal verities, truths of the imagination which will survive in unchanged form when the urbanisation of Britain has receded like a muddy tide. 'How oft', as he puts it,

> In darkness and amid the many shapes
> Of joyless daylight; when the fretful stir
> Unprofitable, and the fever of the world,
> Have hung upon the beatings of my heart –
> How oft, in spirit, have I turned to thee,
> O sylvan Wye! thou wanderer through the woods,
> How often has my spirit turned to thee!
>
> (*Tintern Abbey*, 1798)

The countryside was not, of course, an invention of the late eighteenth century; we have only to think back to the strictures of many of the mid-eighteenth-century poets, novelists and critics – Johnson in some moods, Tobias Smollett and many others – upon the contaminations of city life to see that there was a much older, indeed a classical habit of holding the countryside up as a corrective mirror. It is when Tom Jones reaches the city that all his troubles begin; it is only when he is reunited with his Sophia, that rurally-based wisdom which he had foolishly come near to losing, that his soul can be healed. But Fielding himself wrote at least in part as a city sophisticate; and we may justly detect an underlying tone of irony in his work.

What Wordsworth brings to this ironic tradition in *Lyrical Ballads* (1798), *The Prelude* (1805) and elsewhere is an undeviating seriousness. The writer or artist who remains in the city is not merely foolish but immoral; he is cutting himself off from all that is best in humanity, and thus the quality of his work is bound to suffer. Poor Coleridge was taken in by this time and time again, and resolved to live the good life in Nether Stowey or in the Lake District; yet he came slinking back to the sanctuary of the city because he detected, rightly, that while for one kind of artist the countryside may indeed be necessary, it is not so for all.

Romantic views of the countryside are by no means escapist; on the contrary, there is a strenuousness about this set of beliefs. One goes to the country to receive a proper education, away from the distractions of town life; one goes to concentrate, to put in hard work on the healing of the fragmentation of the psyche reckoned to be endemic to the city. We can find this single-minded attachment to the countryside as a source of healing at its strongest in a determinedly local painter like Crome; in the vibrant calm of, for example, *The Edge of a Common* (c.1815) or *A Road near Bury St Edmunds* (c.1816).

The Romantic belief in the countryside attains the status of an articulated moral and educational recommendation in Wordsworth's treatment of the old Cumberland beggar (1798). Here we are required to observe the beggar, not as an object of aesthetic perception, but because from him we can learn the real truths about human life, the nature of social and communal bonding. In all this there is a problem, about what happens to the beggar himself; clearly his consent is not sought before he comes to be held up as a moral object-lesson, and indeed it is Wordsworth's argument that it need not be. The purpose of the beggar's life is not to be found in or for himself; instead it is to be found in the way in which his 'weary journey' reminds the village folk of the seasons and the weathers, in the way in which his indigence provides a constant call on their charity and thus their better natures. The 'mild necessity of use compels/To acts of love'.

Arguments about charity were important in the period. We can find them in poets like Blake and Wordsworth, in artists like Rowlandson, in novelists like Dickens. There were two sides. One said that charity is a human duty, the other that charity in itself is but a cold thing. 'Pity would be no more', as Blake ironically put it in *The Human Abstract*, 'If we did not make somebody Poor'. Perhaps the poor are always with us; but as the nineteenth century wore on they became increasingly visible, in the arts as in life, partly as a result of the decay of rural family systems which had the flexibility and capacity to take care of the sick and the aged, and the inability of the new urban environments to evolve alternative systems of welfare; Kingsley's *Alton Locke* (1850) was one of the most influential accounts.

Thus instead of the well-ordered village, in which the plight of each member is at least noticed by his or her neighbours, we have that newly anonymous monster, the crowd. The most extraordinary symbolic description comes from America, and is that of Edgar Allan Poe, in *The Man of the Crowd* (1840), where the narrator observes an old man walking through the city streets and resolves to follow him. Twenty-four hours later he is still wandering, and the narrator comes to the conclusion that there is no end to this journey; he gives up in terror and doubt before this manifestation of the soullessness and anonymity of city life.

In the formation of an enduring myth of the countryside there was also a continuing hunt for peasant poets. Why, after all, if country air and village habits promoted the most intense communions with all that was best and purest in the world, should we not find the greatest and truest poets in the humblest surroundings and company, for indeed had not artists like the painter Paul Sandby, the theorist William Gilpin and others claimed to have found the truest embodiments of the 'picturesque' in such settings?

And so arose some dubious exploitation, some success, some political difficulties. These are best expressed in the life of John Clare (1793–1864), the Northamptonshire poet: a writer of great skill and vision, he found himself being courted by various factions beyond his ken, and was eventually committed to an asylum. For behind the apparently innocent myth of the countryside there lurked, in the early nineteenth century, darker considerations. For the Church and King rednecks, belief in village life necessarily implied a reactionary adherence to ancient values and feudal social forms; for the libertarians, it implied the country as a scenario for freedom, for setting free forces of the imagination which would in the end conduce to social change.

The rural poets were taken from the beginning to exhibit one or the other of these ideals, most violently in the form of Hannah More's *Shepherd of Salisbury Plain*, that paragon of rustic virtue and sensibility whose main message to the world is that it is just fine the way it is. We see that there was not just one morality of nature in the period but competing ideologies, and as time went on the debate grew more heated. There was, after all, nature 'red in tooth and claw', a symbol for a very different, and far more pessimistic, assessment of human society, an assessment in which to remind ourselves of 'nature' was simply to confirm the inevitability of competition and aggression.

We are thus a long way now from Blake's lamb and the world of innocence. We are closer, perhaps, to the stark wilderness of *Wuthering Heights*, where 'nature' forms an objective correlative not for peace and tranquillity but for the storms of overmastering passion. Whereas in earlier years the city was experienced as a place of panic and confusion, and therefore what was needed was a refuge, later the city came to be apprehended, by Dickens above all, as a site of tedium and drudgery and the needed alternative was a place where men and women could recall and re-enact the wild feelings which had been exiled by this new world of organisation. Thus as the perceptions of social life changed, so the images of the countryside changed, and Romantic viewpoints swung from the world of innocence to that of passion, from lost childhood to lost emotional freedom.

Rediscovery and remaking of history

One of the things which people derived from the experience of the French Revolution was a sense of history in the making, of history being changed; at the same time, more people came to have the sense that they themselves were part of history, that history was not solely to do with the activities of the great, or with huge impersonal forces clashing beyond the purview of the ordinary person.

In this process of constant revision of the history of the recent and not so recent past, a crucial figure is Scott (1771–1832). Sometimes Scott's knowledge of history seems more focused on details of setting and costume than on accuracy of a grander kind; but the most important thing about his fiction was that it provided a view of historical action and event while at the same time situating the 'ordinary person' within those events. The central figures in *Heart of Midlothian* (1818) and *Ivanhoe* (1819) are not aristocrats or political manipulators; they are humble people who are blown hither and thither by change, revolution, intrigue, and yet during the course of these manifold accidents they come to their own views of the events around them.

These were figures with whom a wide audience could identify, representatives of common humanity. The vein of writing which Scott originated stayed highly popular throughout the period, with the prolific novels of George Payne Rainsford James and Ainsworth eventually becoming best-sellers in the new market of 'railway reading'. In some ways James and Ainsworth developed from Scott; in other ways they provided an interestingly 'Victorian' revision of Scott's view of history. Scott was a conservative, but a benevolent one, a paternalist, whereas the later writers were always liable to veer towards a more purely reactionary position, to move back from the common people towards kings, queens and nobles.

To these revisions of history, there were radical responses, from Paine on; Frances Trollope, Benjamin Disraeli and particularly Elizabeth Gaskell in *Mary Barton* (1848) are important contributors to the debate. But on the whole it is fair to say that popular historical fiction retreated from a serious engagement with history and, as the nineteenth century became more conformist, so it tended increasingly to side with the 'haves' of history rather than the 'have-nots'. Similarly, the massive biblical and historical canvases of Haydon, for example, which were not well regarded either by his contemporaries or by later critics, nevertheless represent something significant within the period. It has to do with past grandeur; perhaps as a compensation for the trivialities of the present, perhaps more simply as a mode of memory in times of change. It is as though the grandiosity of Haydon and the other history painters was born out of a strange combination of pride and fear: pride in Britishness and civilisation, fear about what might be swept away in the new world of cities and urban crowds.

A similar tendency can be discerned in the extreme popularity in the 1820s of 'silver-fork' fiction, which is set exclusively in the parlours and country parks of a vanishing aristocracy. A major writer who sews these threads together in a revealing way is Bulwer Lytton, immensely popular in his time, who sets many of his novels, *The Last Days of Pompeii* (1834) being the outstanding example, in recherché folds of history without ever really convincing us that the past world was really much different from the present. The eventual message of Lytton's massive 'oeuvre' is that we can all take comfort in a certainty that, really, times do not change that much. Thus did Victorianism try to heal the yawning gap in historical certitude reflected in the incidents happening around them.

This complex set of attitudes to history – as the place of a past barbarity and yet also as the place whence we can derive such confidence as we have in a continuous future – was also reflected in the theatre. Although there had been historical drama before, the historical melodrama of the early nineteenth century concentrated intensely on accuracy of costume and setting. In all of this, perhaps there is a tinge of social regret; clearly this sense was shared right down the social spectrum, because the audiences for melodrama themselves were generally living in social worlds many millions of miles removed from the swirling dresses and elaborate coiffures of the fiction and theatre which was entertaining them.

So here we have a combination, even a contradiction, of two societal myths. On the one hand, there is the solacing reversion to 'the world we have lost'; on the other there is 'the barbarity we have put behind us', the half-ironic sense that the march of human reason is to continue behind the frock-coats and watch-chains of a new class of merchant rulers. And behind all that, what we can sense is a new puzzlement, amply evidenced in the many attempts, not merely to recount history, but to find a *theory* of history, a way of conceptualising change and stability. Perhaps the greatest exponent of this intellectually imperialist urge came from Europe, in the august and impenetrable figure of George Wilhelm Friedrich Hegel; but the British historians, Henry Hallam, Lord Macaulay, Henry Hart Milman, Thomas Arnold, however much they might pride themselves on their pragmatic cast of mind, were not immune to this pressing need to make sense of the welter of incident with which they were surrounded.

Nikolaus Pevsner provides us with an interesting addition to these arguments about historicity when he points out that

England was the first country to break the unity of interior and exterior and wrap buildings up in clothes not made for them but for buildings of other ages and purposes. Your country-house might be Grecian or Gothic, a summer-house in a garden even Chinese or Moorish. After 1830 a club would be like the palace of a princely merchant in Italy, a grammar school would be Gothic, a gaol Romanesque . . .

(*The Englishness of English Art*, 1956)

Clearly history as authenticity and history as clothing might cut two ways.

Impact of scientific and technological development

The sheer pace of scientific and technological development during the period was enormous. New research institutes were finding money; new schools of thought were emerging, it seemed, constantly; new inventions, as we have mentioned, were promoting practical changes right across social life, from transportation and agriculture to the arts. Perhaps most importantly, new theories of the very origin of life were being propounded from Charles Lyell's *Principles of Geology* (1830) to Darwin.

A crucial myth of this age of improvement is Mary Shelley's *Frankenstein* (1818), which bears a very close relation to the fears which were occupying the minds of British people during the early years of the nineteenth century. Interestingly, Mary Shelley catches up both the thread of absorption in the remote past and the fascination with scientific development. Frankenstein's discovery of the principle of life is held up to us as a more or less natural development from discoveries then current in the sciences – galvanism, the precursor of electricity, is the chief example – yet at the same time the actual apparatus of equipment and ideas with which the great inventor works is more reminiscent of the archaic world of the alchemists.

What lies behind it is the fear that science may get out of control. Essentially it is the symbolic beginning of a still absorbing argument about how human beings can retain control over objects they have made when those objects prove too complex or revolutionary for us to continue to understand. Behind the monster is also the shadow of the political monster of the Revolution, as before him lies the great unnameable monster of the city mob. The monster represents the beginning of humanity, in his childlikeness and his ready openness to learning; he represents the end of humankind in his uniqueness, although it is of course Frankenstein himself, already scared and tested beyond endurance by the existence of this surrogate child, who denies his monster a mate.

What, indeed, would the consequences have been if Frankenstein's monster had reproduced? Among other things, it would, of course, have been a blasphemy, because Frankenstein had arrogated to himself the role of creator. Mary Shelley is obviously aware of the theological ramifications of this issue; and yet, she is implicitly asking, who is this God whom we worship yet who does not protect us from wars and terrors and who might perhaps not even have made us uniquely in his own image? For as we question Frankenstein's usurpation of divine prerogative, as that of Milton's Satan before him, and as Prometheus's before *him*, we are forced to begin also to question the motives and record of this God whom we seek to defend and yet who appears to send us little of his sacred peace.

Where, in particular, is God amid this new Northern wasteland of furnaces and mills, the 'unhealthy, smoky, sunless place', as Mrs Gaskell put it? Were people to feel despair as the railway came thundering through, or an admixture of hope, as Dickens muses in relation to the destruction of Staggs's Gardens in *Dombey and Son* (1846–8), where

the old by-streets now swarmed with passengers and vehicles of every kind; the new streets that had stopped disheartened in the mud and waggon-ruts, formed towns within themselves, originating wholesome comforts and conveniences belonging to themselves, and never tried nor thought of until they sprung into existence. Bridges that had led to nothing, led to villas, gardens, churches, healthy public walks.

Who was in control of all this? The increase in political and economic understanding cut two ways. Some questions, in the good old days, would never have been asked; it was obvious and incontrovertible that the squire exercised his prerogative over a man's body and his labour as the parson did over his spirit. But, as Cobbett tells us, now the solid old oak table which symbolises these certitudes has been broken up, sold off to the new developers, and the old ample habits of entertainment and responsibility have been replaced by tawdry, paper-thin substitutes; and what spirit of English resistance shall people conjure?

What needs to be seen is a connection between all these monsters. Fuseli's nightmare sitting grinning on the breast of innocence, tempting with a knowledge which dare not be admitted; Frankenstein's monster rampaging around the countryside searching for human comfort but finding only an intensification of misunderstanding; the railway engine which mows down the appalling Carker in *Dombey* with an utterly impersonal justice just when he thought he was home and dry; Blake's Urizen stooped over his compasses and measuring rods, not noticing the other monsters which are growing from the ground behind him as he works. Here there is a gallery of images which cannot be paralleled from the eighteenth century. To some extent they have a bearing on uncertainties about the mind itself; but more, they have to do with doubts about social control. It is as though the early years of the century were seen as both too controlled (in the political sense) and too full of libido; thus we can see the Victorian reaction as a natural successor to a state of affairs which in some ways seemed to be on the brink of a great liberation, but in others promised only fright and continuing uncertainty.

And so we come upon a curious contradiction which crops up in a peculiarly intensified form in this period. For the whole point of technology is to give people more control over their environment and more understanding of it, and indeed the great inventions of the agricultural and industrial revolutions, seen from one angle, did exactly this. This aspect of scientific and technological change is well exemplified in the extraordinary achievements of Humphry Davy (1778–1829), of whom Coleridge once said that had he not been the greatest chemist of his age, he would have been its greatest poet; here we have a symbol for the integration of mind and imagination which was so important at the time. But for whose actual benefit were the new machines going to be used? This was the question asked in violent form by the Luddites (1812–18). Also such developments, while apparently harmless or even helpful in themselves, nonetheless carried with them the odour of the pit. They moved people closer to the brink of their own lack of understanding, and thus to that tabooed dividing line between men and gods, that brink of insanity over which Clare and others tumbled, along with the first Mrs Rochester in *Jane Eyre* (1847), all under the pressures of social conformism.

Victorianism consolidating

The early Victorians found ways of dealing with the monster; it might prowl outside, but it could not invade the civilised drawing-room, the well-stocked parlour. The Victorian interior, though only in its infancy by 1850, is one of the great 'locales' of British history: cluttered, cosy, warm to the point of suffocation, it formed a pointed antithesis to the spacious and soaring architecture of previous ages. It is truly in the early Victorian age that an Englishman's home becomes his castle, with an imaginary Landseer in every room (*Chevy Chase* was painted in 1826, *Monarch of the Glen* 1851), albeit a castle of brick rather than stone and one which, in its most important lower-middle-class manifestation, cannot even afford to support one live-in servant.

In many of these homes, economy is all, provided the necessary social status is kept up; thus the sovereign importance of curtains, to conceal economic realities from prying eyes.

After the wilder excesses of the Romantics and the Prince Regent, we now have the consolidating virtues of the realist novelists and the great Queen herself, an exemplar of home life who also happens to occupy a throne; not to mention the earnest model of Prince Albert (1819–61), with his keen interest in matters social and industrial. The Victorian age is the great age of English fiction, and we may enumerate some of its composite merits. An intense eye to details of behaviour (Dickens, to the point of parody); an equally intense focus on ethical norms and the ways in which people try to live up to them and are variously affected by their inevitable, although usually partial, failure (Peacock and William Thackeray in comic mode, the Brontës in tragedy); more problematically, a reliance on *deus ex machina* endings – the sudden bequest, the equally sudden removal to distant corners of the globe; a sense of certainty, nevertheless, about geography, history, correctness both in one's metaphysical and theological dealings with the greater world and also in one's codes of dress and comportment. The greatest of these writers, Jane Austen pre-eminent among them, produce this material slightly and penetratingly seamed with irony. Even for the most central figures like George Eliot (although her writing career did not really begin until 1858), there is often something significantly unstable about these figures of moral and social rectitude – Bulstrode the banker with his hidden past, Casaubon with his apparent scholasticism concealing a pathology of competition and failure.

But the achievement of the Victorian novelists can hardly be overstated. Here we have as complete a picture of social life, across all, or almost all, classes and types, as has been produced since Chaucer and Shakespeare. A primary concern was with the processes of maturation; where the Romantics tended to generalise about these matters, the realist novelists were well aware that they can be best observed through detailed depiction of the complex processes of family life; there were important questions for the Victorian about what formed the criminal, the delinquent, the model of socially correct behaviour, and it is as though they knew instinctually, before depth psychology had come along to validate their findings, that these are matters of the family.

In Victorian fiction, the family is all (and correspondingly, the condition of being an orphan is frequently and tellingly explored); as the century evolved, the novel increasingly turned into a family chronicle, sometimes lasting over several generations. Omnipresent though the vast forces of history are in the works of Scott, Lytton, Dickens and Disraeli, it is also the way you were treated by your mother, the way you absorbed or reacted to the role models set by father, sisters, cousins, that determine the moral texture of society.

In many of the arts in the age of Victoria, we can detect a drive towards comfort, even consolation; it is as though, as the world outside gets larger and larger, so there emerges a need for security, reflected in an apparent retreat into the interior of the Victorian drawing-room. The furniture and decor we find so brilliantly represented by Jane Austen's interiors, which had striven for a cosmopolitan feel and for a sense of spaciousness and light, are replaced

by the heavy woods and deep textures of classic Victorianism; the apparently
careless, graceful lines of the Regency and Georgian periods are replaced by
an intensity of detail, a filling in of the interior landscape, much as
Middlemarch is to become a civic space almost totally filled by webs of
relationship and gossip.

In the midst of this clutter the notion of 'accomplishments' which had
flourished in the eighteenth century throve and took new turns: the roles
available for women were deliberately bounded by the domestic space, both
in the sense of housework and in the sense of the skills – playing the
pianoforte, sketching, knitting, sewing – which were regarded as essential to
marriageable girls. Thus the piano, in particular, comes to carry a double
significance during the period: on the one hand it has its wild side, its
contribution to heroism and melodrama, while on the other its presence in
the drawing-room comes to confirm the centrality of the domestic space.

What are we to make of the consolidation of Victorianism, of this
revaluation of domestic and civic virtue? Partly a reaction, as we have said, to
the freedoms of the Regency; partly also a new seriousness, a new emphasis
on respectability which, in socio-psychological terms, probably arose from the
very conditions of city life itself. In the older world of the village and the
country town, demarcations of role and class were strongly and inexorably
marked and did not need reinforcement; a certain libertarianism on the part
of the aristocracy was only to be expected. But in the city all kinds of people
were thrown together without prior knowledge of each other; small wonder
that a new, confused and confusing society needed to set up a new range of
social markers and to adhere to them at all costs.

We may also, perhaps, choose to see it in religious terms. The earlier part
of our period had seen the cultural importance of the Evangelicals, those
Anglicans who did not go with the Methodist secession of the 1780s but who
continued to advance fundamentalist ideas and the authority of scripture.
Among them was Wilberforce, and later the Earl of Shaftesbury who was
active in industrial reform in the 1830s and 1840s. But the most significant
element in these later years was the Oxford Movement, a High Church
conservatism associated with John Keble, John Henry Newman and Henry
Manning, which has been described as a 'corrective and a complement' to the
evangelical revival, but which certainly shared with it nothing of its social
liberalism. The Oxford Movement spoke instead of the absolute authority of
tradition and morality, and thus very much addressed Victorianism in its own
tones.

Women and the arts

In all of this the role of women was crucial. The importance of Mary
Wollstonecraft's *Vindication of the Rights of Women* (1792) can hardly be
overestimated. Although Wollstonecraft's claims now hardly seem extreme,
the fact that women could be perceived as having 'rights' at all outraged
many of the male intellectuals of the late eighteenth century. There rapidly
followed during the early nineteenth century a series of practical *exempla*, of

which the most notorious became the case of Lady Caroline Norton, which
centred on the right of a woman to keep something of the matrimonial
property after divorce and on the custody of children.

Hidden within this are the seeds of a whole new order of things, in which
the contribution of women – through housework, the rearing of children, and
similar labours which are financially unrewarded – is to become recognised as
a contribution to the household and family equal in real value to the wage-
earning capacity of the man of the house; but the history of the early
Victorian period is the history of resistance to this development. In this
context, we can see that the crucial figure of the Victorian patriarch was an
unstable one, as indeed the female Gothic novelists had already perceived. It
takes but a small step to portray the patriarch at the head of the dining table
as the domestic tyrant against whom all the forces of women's liberation need
to be directed; and this was a step which women novelists were not loth to
take. Increasingly, as the century progressed, it is to them that we have to
look in order to see the aspirations and demands of women in the early
nineteenth century; at least partly because, as readers, women's participation
in the literary and intellectual world was increasing with a rapidity which
surprised and indeed terrified many of their male counterparts.

Under these pressures, one of the major developments was in the range of
available portrayals of women as literary characters. If we look back to
eighteenth-century fiction, what we largely find is a gallery of caricatures and
stereotypes: the dutiful and inexperienced girl (Sophia in *Tom Jones*, 1749);
the embittered spinster (Tabitha in Tobias George Smollett's *Humphry
Clinker*, 1771); the victim (Samuel Richardson's *Clarissa* and *Pamela*); the
wise mother, and so forth. It is in the works of Fanny Burney (1752–1840),
Jane Austen and their descendants that this mould is broken, and the
complexity of women's emotions and behaviour becomes a central topic of
literary investigation. Austen's *Emma* is strong both in her own conviction of
her powers and in her intended and actual effects on others, and Austen was
fully aware of what a cardboard 'knight' Knightley seems when confronted
with Emma's determination and her certainty about her own societal
centrality.

With the Brontës, we see women writers moving into and authoritatively
claiming a different area, the area of passion and desire. Here the achievement
is twofold: on the one hand there is the detailed exploration of the female
psyche itself, on the other there is the provision of a set of male characters
who are clearly conjured not from outdated male myths of heroism but rather
from female fantasy, and who are therefore enduringly fraught with the
ambivalence which is latent within the whole notion of the hero from the
Gothic writers on.

So the period sees two contradictory developments in the participation of
women in cultural life. On the one hand, there is the excessive formalisation
and reduction of women's roles which is endemic to conservative
Victorianism: the insistence that a woman's place is in the home, the
codification, so brilliantly explored by Steven Marcus, of the classic double-
bind whereby women cannot be seen as persons in their own right, but only
as goddesses or whores. But on the other hand, there is the steady and

unstoppable evolution of a whole range of depictions of women – strong women, justifiably bitter women, passionate women, angry women – tilting at the complacency of Victorian men. No wonder, indeed, that daughters needed to be seen as protected; if they were not, they might emerge from their prolonged chrysalis as Catherines, howling their desires across the moors, to the infinite shock of one's suburban neighbours.

To all this, the education of women brought enormous added impetus. No longer was it sufficient to suppose that a woman's imagination or vision could be circumscribed by the needs and wants of her husband and children. One of the interesting moot points here is what the contribution of Victoria herself was: obviously she was hardly the kind of monarch to give direct encouragement or sympathy to women's rights, but the fact remained that she was at once an enormously powerful political figure, and also a wife and a mother, and a competent painter, whose family life dominated the press and the popular imagination. In the face of this, it became increasingly difficult to maintain that women were debarred by nature from holding high office or from social and intellectual success.

Of course there were many vicissitudes to be endured before legal obstacles to women's equality were to be modified; but there is no doubt that some of the seeds of this change were sown during the period, evidenced, for the working classes, by the Factory Acts of 1844 and 1847 and, for the middle classes, by, for example, the founding of Bedford College in 1849. The great question which came to beset Victorian England in this area was indeed one of class. Even if one could dream of admitting middle-class, clever women to some variety of intellectual equality, what about the working classes, the mass of women workers who had been spawned by the industrial revolution and who were not for long willing to keep quiet about their fears and hopes, even with the new provision of a ten-hour working day?

Forms of popular art

The whole period is remarkable for the interflow which we can detect between the popular arts and those arts restricted to an élite audience. There is the avidity with which poets followed folk models of the kind collected by Thomas Percy in his *Reliques of Ancient English Poetry* (1765), although these were perhaps 'technically' popular rather than being potentially accessible to a contemporary popular audience. The real or supposed use of the ballad form runs through the early work of all the great poets of the period – Robert Burns (1759–96), Blake, Wordsworth, Coleridge, Keats, Scott, Tennyson – and forms part of the longing for simplicity and stability which, as we have seen, was one side of the Romantic experience. And it is worth remembering that the genuine sung ballad with news content did not die out until after the Crimean War; also that this whole period was incomparably rich, in England and in Scotland, in folk-song.

The Gothic in all its forms – not only literary but architectural and decorative – reinforced this interest in what was significantly taken to be 'British art' as writers and builders and designers attempted to find a strength in British tradition which could be properly measured against the dominance of the classics and against the more recent French, German and Italian dominance of crucial arts. Often these popular forms were but imperfectly understood; occasionally, as in the case of the 'Ossian' poems, they were partly invented. However, the impetus remained to find a mode of expression which would, from one point of view, justify Britain's international dominance as a centre of empire and trade, even when, by an important contemporary paradox, the content and meaning of these forms was seen as at least partly anti-imperial and anti-commercial.

The continuing success of the sensationalist novel was shadowed and encouraged by a lower but larger market of chapbooks and pamphlets: retellings of famous gory and criminal episodes from the past, narratives of present murders and trials told in the utmost detail – among these the influence of translations from the German from J.C.F. Schiller on was particularly important. While the middle-class audience was developing that taste for realism which had already been set up in the eighteenth century, the lower classes were evolving their own popular tastes which were based far more on sensationalism, melodrama, violent humour; were requiring, as Peacock's Mr Flosky put it in *Nightmare Abbey*, a 'perpetual adhibition of *sauce piquante* to the palate of its depraved imagination . . .'.

The greatest legacy of these tastes was melodrama; but the classic Victorian melodrama was only one among a number of popular forms, others of which have since disappeared. The circus; the pantomime; the equestrian, aquatic and military spectacle; all of these were forms of entertainment which relied on grandiosity and caricature in varying proportions. They were also forms which were to come to have a great deal of commercial success.

Pantomime, a form whose peculiarity has been said to be that it is shaped less by authors than by audiences, is perhaps particularly interesting since, like many of the popular forms of the Victorian years, it represents a formalisation of a tradition which was genuinely old but which now received a new codification and became bound into a rigid set of assumptions and conventions. It is in these years that the stock repertoire of pantomime was beginning to be formed, loosely based on the childhood genres of fairy tale and nursery rhyme.

These years also saw an enormous growth in hymn-writing; some, like Samuel Wesley's, were of a noble musical quality, but many of them shared with melodrama and the Gothic the bloodier side of the arts of the time, tending less to present idealised pictures of heavenly benison and peace than to continue in an older tradition which threatened congregations with the tortures of hell and awesome pictures of the consequences of sin. In part these hymns reflect the newly necessary methods of social order, the need to frighten people into submission when older links in the chain of authority had been broken by geographical mobility and sentiments for change. In part they reflect a genuine folk consciousness, in which it has always been easier to draw pictures of Satan than to convince by direct portrayals of a white-bearded God sitting enthroned on the clouds. In painting, this is the world of John Martin, where man is dwarfed by enormous supernatural figures and conflicts. We can now see his pictures as just reflections of an age where the divine status of man was newly under question and where the individual was threatened with a chronic loss of identity in the midst of a burgeoning population. Even though it is the empty spaces of the universe which Martin depicts with his dark and glowing palette, we also see the facelessness of the crowd in these renditions of man at the brink of a precipice and disappearance.

In terms of the urban environment, perhaps the best cultural fable of this deep split in the arts and the social atomisation which it represented comes rather later in the century. Robert Louis Stevenson was born in 1850; in his *Dr Jekyll and Mr Hyde* (1886) we can readily see that the change which overtakes Jekyll in the midst of the Victorian city is deeply affected by the very situation of his house and laboratory. When he leaves this house through the front door, he emerges into a world of regulation and respectability; thus he is himself respectable, a man of social status and measured judgement. But when he emerges from his back door, he passes into a teeming underworld of half-seen figures, the criminal night in which the grossest pleasures – albeit unnamed, and thus unnameable – are readily available; and in this alternative world, Mr Hyde moves easily, deformed and a caricature of evil. Here we have the lasting echo of the divisions of the period: the arts of life and the arts of death, as Blake put it, the arts of day and the arts of night, that which belongs to respectability, reason and conscience and that which cannot be dissociated from passion, violence, criminality and the beast.

Arts and public life

During these years and through to 1851 and the triumphant culmination of British commercial and cultural power celebrated in the Great Exhibition, the arts in Britain had an enormous impact on public life at every level. In the early years, the building of Regent Street was only the most obvious among many successfully completed projects which transformed London into a more modern capital. If these developments represent triumphs of planning by an enlightened monarch and an architectural genius, it is also true that only a strong centralised government which did not object to displacing great numbers of people in the name of what was perceived to be the greater good could have brought such schemes to a successful completion.

In the country, something of the same pattern obtained. The new roads and canals made possible by the technical advances of men like Thomas Telford and John McAdam brought undoubted benefits in terms of communication and transport; but these advantages were probably more significantly prized by the industrialists and the substantial farmers, whose overheads were consequently reduced, than by the rural inhabitants. For these latter the new roads and canals did indeed mean added possibilities for travel, provided they could afford the fares; but they also meant a further stage in the disintegration of homogeneous village life, and placed many more lives at the direct mercy of market forces and of moral 'evil' from the conurbations.

Above all, as the nineteenth century wears on, we find ourselves in the age of iron: the ironmaster becomes the ruler of industry, and iron itself becomes – apart from red brick – the material most memorable about Victorian public architecture, as a host of railway stations will bear witness. In one sense, iron is symbolic of permanence; here is the material which will resist changes caused either by weather or by social turmoil; if Ozymandias had been made of iron he would not now have been rotting in the desert surrounded by the ruins of empire. There can be great beauty in iron and glass, as the Palm House at Kew (1844–8) and Robert Stephenson's Britannia Bridge over the Menai Strait (1845–50) demonstrate. But there is also something inhuman about iron, about the architectural leaps and shapes and voids which it permits, about its separateness from the previous material bases of architecture domestic and public.

Iron became, as it were, a public architecture. No longer would the country house, for example, be seen simply as the largest and most opulent version of a general architecture; now the great public places began to belong to a world different in kind from the residential house, just as the accumulation of capital increasingly separated off a new class of the rich from their workers. And thus the ambiguity of the Crystal Palace; it was constructed in a remarkable nine months in 1850–51 (the British Museum, finished in 1847, had been twenty-five years in the building), and yet it served later to demonstrate an unsuspected vulnerability to fire. In itself it was perhaps only a precursor of the greater age of steel which was so soon to be made possible by Henry Bessemer's process of 1855.

In painting and in poetry, we can see also this growth of an official establishment set over against artistic spontaneity. True, the development of the Royal Academy from its eighteenth-century roots meant the possibility of further recognition for the artist; but it also set up a system of connections which in some respects was little more flexible than the older systems of aristocratic patronage. In poetry, it was Robert Southey and Wordsworth as poets laureate who spearheaded this revived version of conservatism, to the fury of their more radical colleagues; and the production of 'occasional' celebration, again an old practice, received a new impetus from the many triumphs which the British were called upon to celebrate in this era of apparent confidence. A good example of this important art of celebration is Turner's small masterpiece, *Richmond Hill, on the Prince Regent's Birthday* (1819).

Music too became very much more part of a visible public life. The arrival of visiting European musicians like Haydn, 'the god of Science', in 1791 and of Mendelssohn in 1829 were public events; tickets for concerts became the basis of a growing and lucrative entertainment industry. Orchestras, choirs, festivals, the Philharmonic Societies stood on this double edge: in bringing music to the people, they simultaneously helped the formation of a new subclass of appreciators who had the wherewithal to keep themselves abreast of the very latest developments in taste and performance. Much of this was in any case facilitated by improvements in instrument-making techniques as a result of developments in precision tools. There was also a more genuinely populist aspect of these changes; as W.C. Smith put it:

The Industrial Revolution largely created conditions which compelled the ordinary people . . . to find their own recreations cheaply amongst themselves – and they therefore endeavoured to make their own music. Many tried to play the pianoforte and other musical instruments, and to sing as soloists or in part-songs, choruses, etc.

(*Music Publishing in the British Isles*, 1970)

In music, the greatest symbol of these changes was the emergence of that colossal new form of composition which we now take so much for granted, the symphony, developed by Beethoven from roots in Haydn and Mozart, although puzzlingly without a single leading British exponent. Here we have larger orchestras, more complex and organised works than ever before; a greater canvas on which the composer could paint his work and a greater repertoire of tone and shade than ever previously available, a development of music which parallels architectural development. It is one of the most remarkable features of burgeoning Victorianism in general that the tendency towards grandiosity, which was one of its hallmarks, by no means totally overwhelmed the real grandeur which we now see as marking many of its most characteristic artistic productions.

This grandeur found its most remarkable apotheosis in the Exhibition of 1851, held in the Crystal Palace. In part we may see this as the display of a whole way of life. The assertion which lay behind the Exhibition was about the benefits of progress. There was much emphasis on how the growth of technology and the wealth of new inventions in fact made the lot of the common man and woman easier; on how all the hard work and systematisation of industrial life would in the end conduce to a more leisured, a more humane way of life for the majority.

This previsioned coming of the age of leisure was thinkable only for the future; the Exhibition was a matter of hopes and promises, of deferred gratification, and behind it lay a myth of social harmony, the idea that if all English men and women worked together regardless of class, status and wealth, all would be well. Coming as it did so soon after the various events of 1848 had rocked Europe and reminded it of the political and social insecurities of 1789, it attempted to serve the purpose of promoting social cohesion.

In this the arts were also to play their part; the dournesses of the new cities were also to be informed by artistic growth, such that each of these locales of labour was also to be a base for cultural renewal, replete with orchestras and exhibition halls. But it was also the year 1851 which saw the beginnings of important artistic transitions away from this 'public' art; in painting, in particular, where Millais's *The Return of the Dove to the Ark* (1851) and Hunt's *The Hireling Shepherd* (1852) emerged as the vanguard of Pre-Raphaelite reaction. It was also in 1851 that Turner died.

Conclusions: themes and trends

Much of this panorama consists of contradictions, paradoxes, uncertainties. How are we to come at a description of continuing themes and trends during this period, at, in William Hazlitt's term, the 'spirit of the age'?

Despite Romanticism, the habits and styles of neo-classicism did not suddenly die in 1780. Neo-classicism continued, and indeed we can see its lineaments in some of the ethical pronouncements of Wordsworth, in some of the early works of Turner, most especially in the survival of neo-classical architecture, albeit as part of the general succumbing of Victorian architecture to a heterogeneous mass of shapes and styles. What is most important is to see in this period not a discarding of the past; rather the formation of new canons from the past, for example in literature with the attempt to find a 'home-grown genius' which could stand for all in British culture over against the domination of the classics.

We can add that many of the greatest artists of the period were concerned with exploring the limits of purity and corruption – Blake would have termed them innocence and experience, but they would be differently phrased by Dickens. We can trace the notion of corruption through from the Revolution and the fear of being contaminated by foreign influences, to the high Victorian belief that contact with the lower classes, despite all one's philanthropy, might somehow tarnish one's morals and character. And through it all we can sense the troubled and shifting taboo in the area of sexuality; all that went with Regency libertinism, all that was signified by the life of Byron, became one pole of this contrast.

The other pole became the great norm of respectability, heavily bolstered by the Oxford Movement. As Blake had foretold in *The Marriage of Heaven and Hell* (*c*.1790–3), there are 'two classes of men' on earth. There are angels and there are devils; from his own point of view, Blake much preferred the devils, but the point here is that in saying this he foreshadowed precisely the duality which was more or less forced on the Victorians by the heterogeneity of the society they were trying to manage.

In fact, seen as a whole, the period traces a change in, and an intensification of, the conception of social responsibility. It is this process of change which culminates in the bowler-hatted, corsetted image of the Victorians; and we may ask what this notion of responsibility is supposed to protect. What is certain is that it was Wordsworth's reliance on socially responsible individual enlightenment which led to Tennyson's concept of the societal role of the poet; and in this transition a great deal of the period is summed up. What, however, is also symbolically important about that transition is this: when Wordsworth wrote in the *Prelude* about his encounter with the mountain he can now be seen to have demonstrated a very revealing attitude towards his own parenting, but we may justly doubt whether Wordsworth himself saw it this way. When Tennyson wrote his poems of mourning and loss, of the disasters which had overtaken the world he knew best, he too had an understandable wish to clothe these nightmares and fantasies in garments which were not their own. But he was uneasy about doing so, for he *knew* that there was a problem here, a question about the relationship between a disturbed society and the accompanying instability of the psyche, and thus he participated in the general increase in psychological awareness which characterised the period.

But this collocation is symbolic also in another way; for both Wordsworth and Tennyson were great soloists, plunging upwards into the peaks or downwards into the depths of melancholy. They were, to put it mildly, and despite some of the imagery of Victorianism, not convivial or clubbable men; neither were Blake, Constable or Turner. So the early norms of the Victorians have this hard divide to cross: how to maintain a notion of community when what one finds is shards and fragments.

And this process of continuous negotiation of difficulties, which is how we may best perceive any culture, went on during these years most visibly in terms of the written word. Though the masters of the visual arts, if not of music, were indeed there, the years 1785–1851 are most importantly recorded in words. We may seek to explain this imbalance in two ways. First, we are dealing here with a period when the expansion of education was largely focused on issues of literacy, and the word is easily the most accessible form of communication. Second, we may hypothesise that it is the written word which most resonantly encapsulates national aspiration and national discord, for the simple reason that we are here dealing with language, and language is the substance of national identity.

And certainly the period was one in which definitions of the national identity were crucial. What is it, people were asking from the Napóleonic Wars through to Crimea, that we are doing, or being, by owning to our Britishness? And, as a subtext, is being British enjoyable? Or does it involve being virtually swallowed by notions of responsibility and duty? What is to happen to the maverick, the difficult soul, the individual, in this world of increasing organisation?

Thus a dialectic existed: on the one hand, notions of symmetry and order, on the other visions of chaos and excess. Within this there was an important debate about the notion of freedom, about British freedoms and the freedoms of mankind, and it is one which endures to the present day. Do we best exercise our freedom by taking up our right to diverge from social norms? Or do we best exercise it through a defined democracy where we have choices, but they are circumscribed by a prevailing texture of political debate? The arts in Britain during this period were dominated by such concerns, and by the very different positions the artist might take up vis-à-vis the social norms. The artist was at once the harbinger of triumphs and chaoses to come, and the creative mind attempting to give shape and coherence to these competing forces.

Part II
Studies in the Individual Arts

Two views by J.M.W. Turner. (Above) Edinburgh from Calton Hill, *with the Castle greatly magnified dominating the scene; on the left is the early nineteenth-century gaol, now demolished. (Below)* The High Street, Edinburgh, *looking east to Holyrood. St Giles and the seventeenth-century market cross, on the right, now removed. Both engravings for Sir Walter's Scott's* Provincial Antiquities and Picturesque Scenery of Scotland *(1819–26).*

1 Edinburgh: City of Reason and Nature

ALEXANDER YOUNGSON

When Dr Johnson made his journey to the Highlands of Scotland in 1773, he observed of Edinburgh merely that it was 'a city too well known to admit description', but added that it contained 'men of learning whose names want no advancement from my commemoration'. Thomas Jefferson, co-author of the Declaration of Independence, founder of the University of Virginia, designer of Monticello and President of the USA, writing from Paris in 1789, remarked that where science was concerned – and in his day science included all branches of philosophical and experimental learning – 'no place in the World can pretend to a competition with Edinburgh'. Benjamin Constant, in later life the author of *Adolphe* and intimate friend of Madame Récamier, was a student at Edinburgh University in its greatest years, and this is how he describes the intellectual atmosphere of the place:

I arrived at Edinburgh on 8th July 1782 . . . I set myself to my studies with enthusiasm, and thus began the most agreeable year of my life. Work was taken seriously by the young people of Edinburgh. They formed a number of literary and philosophic societies; I was a member of some of these, and I gained distinction as a writer and speaker, although in a foreign language. I made close friends with men who, for the most part, became well-known in later life . . . Among all these young men, the one who seemed to show most promise was the son of a tobacco-seller, named John Wilde. He exercised an almost absolute authority over all his friends, although most of them were much his superiors in birth and fortune.
(Benjamin Constant, *Journal Intime précédé du Cahier Rouge et Adolphe*, ed. Jean Pistler (1945); my translation)

Observations like these were not unusual. It was a commonly accepted fact of the time that for science, philosophy, literature and literary criticism the place to go was Edinburgh. And by those who knew the city it was equally well understood, as Constant shrewdly observes, that the young were fired by an earnest enthusiasm for knowledge, which would bring fame to many, and that Edinburgh, the ancient capital of Scotland, was in some respects a more aristocratic but also a more democratic community than could then be found in either France or England.

Scotland was a small country with a passion for three things: fighting, education and religion. The first of these took numberless Scots overseas to seek their fortune as mercenary soldiers. Many of them became senior officers in foreign armies. (The story goes that, during one of the numerous wars between the Russians and the Turks which took place in the eighteenth century, a truce was called and the Russian commander went out to meet the Turkish pasha. The conversation began with the words, 'Weel Sandy, and hoo's a' yer folks in Aberdeen?'). This capacity to make good in foreign lands was due in part to the national system of education. Education in Scotland was for virtually the whole population. At the time of the Reformation the proposal was made that henceforth there should be a school in every parish, and this situation was more or less reached and maintained. The laird's son, although he might go farther, began with the cottar's at the parish school. There were grammar schools, but no public schools as understood in England.

As for religion, the great body of the people were members of the Protestant Church of Scotland, founded during the Reformation. This national Church – the Kirk – was imbued with a spirit that often seems singularly unjoyful, severe and narrow – the spirit of Calvin and Knox. Yet it was the Kirk that proposed and supervised the school system, and for over two hundred years the Kirk dominated the life of the nation. Towards the end of the eighteenth century its hold began to weaken, but it remained enormously important. It had a strong egalitarian influence, partly because in its life and management small regard was paid (at least by the usual standards of the time) to differences of wealth or station. Also, the number of aristocratic families in Scotland was relatively large, which reduced their exclusive superiority. Several thousand persons in the middle and lower income groups could claim to be related to noble lords, so when the wealthier families crowded into Edinburgh for the winter, they found themselves in a small town (the population in 1800 was only 85,000) where they had many relatives as well as many friends, and the rest of the people were not strongly disposed to treat them as superior and unapproachable persons.

This peculiar social structure was reinforced by the physical structure of the Old Town of Edinburgh. Set along the ridge of a hill that descended from the Castle at the top to Holyrood Palace at the bottom, it consisted chiefly of lofty stone tenements, 'built to a height that is almost incredible', which housed nearly the whole population. Every tenement had its own miscellaneous collection of citizens. In each of them there might be found lords and ladies, judges, judges' clerks, apothecaries, doctors, tavern keepers, tailors, stone masons, ministers of religion, grave diggers – all were under one roof and shared a common stair. Until the end of the eighteenth century much business was transacted in the High Street, where all these persons necessarily met; and for several years after that everyone had to do most of their shopping at the various open-air markets – the fish market for example,

in Fish Market Close, a steep, narrow, stinking ravine. The fish were generally thrown out on the street at the head of the close, whence they were dragged down by dirty boys or dirtier women; and then sold unwashed – for there was not a drop of water in the place – from old, rickety, scaly, wooden tables, exposed to all the rain, dust and filth;

(H. Cockburn, *Memorials of His Time*, 1910)

Edinburgh from the Mound; *lithograph by J.D. Harding after W.L. Leitch (c.1854)*.

or the vegetable market, which was

entirely in the hands of a college of old gin-drinking women, who congregated with stools and tables round the Tron Church . . . There was no water here either, except what flowed down the gutter, which, however, was plentifully used.

These conditions began gradually to pass away in the last quarter of the century. The Town Council had resolved to build a New Town, 'a splendid and magnificent city', on the fields to the north of old Edinburgh. There were to be no markets in the town, no business premises, no crowds. Even more remarkable, each family was to have a house of its own, instead of only a part of one. This new town was to be a city of repose, of contemplation; of 'learning and the arts', as it was put in the *Proposals* of 1752; dissociated from the Old Town by physical separation and, to some extent, by intention. Building began in 1766 and continued, with brief interruptions, for seventy years. Several large landowners made successive plans which kept development orderly and spacious; among them was Henry Raeburn (1756–1823), perhaps Scotland's most famous portrait painter.

The Old Town of Edinburgh; *coloured aquatint by J. Clark after A. Kay (1814),
showing the Old Town from Princes Street with Salisbury Crags and Arthur's Seat in the
background.*

As Edinburgh grew, its leading citizens – 'gentlemen of taste' – showed an
increasing concern for the look of things, for architecture, townscape and
distant views. On several occasions they had to fight to preserve them.
Princes Street, the grandest street of the New Town, looked for its whole
length across the Nor' Loch to the Old Town and the Castle, a magnificent
prospect with a wonderful sense of space, so essential to the whole feel of
Edinburgh as we know it; yet a prolonged struggle was needed to prevent
building on the south side of the Street and so save this grand visual
conjunction of the old and the new. There was a row over new buildings at
the turn of the century when it was discovered that some 'glorious prospects'
looking westward from the Calton Hill would be spoiled. There was trouble
about a proposed railway line through Princes Street gardens in the 1830s.
Time and time again this question of how the town would look and what its
citizens would look out on, was raised; and on every important occasion (until
the railway finally invaded Princes Street gardens in the 1840s) those who
were in favour of scenic advantage won. Sacrifices, sometimes considerable
sacrifices, were made for the sake of how things would look. And it is because
of this continued concern for appearances that Edinburgh today is a beautiful
and inspiring city.

Yet the architecture of Edinburgh is not its greatest claim to fame. There
are some splendid public buildings – Register House (1774–88) by Robert
Adam, and the University (1789–1834) by Adam and Playfair, and Playfair's
Royal Scottish Academy building (1832–6) and National Gallery of Scotland

Register House (1774–88). Robert Adam.

The Royal Institution (now the Royal Scottish Academy), showing Princes Street and the Castle. Lithograph by S.D. Swarbeck (1837).

(1850–7). The palace fronts of many streets are also very fine, especially Robert Adam's handsome elevations in Charlotte Square and Gillespie Graham's Moray Place. There is excellent architecture in Edinburgh, but the strong effect of a singular character rests more on the orderly planning of the town as a whole and on the bringing together of man's work and nature's.

The first plan, by James Craig, bears a quotation from Thomson's *Seasons*:

Drawing room, No. 6 Charlotte Square (1798).

See long Canals and deepened Rivers join
Each part with each, and with the Circling Main
The whole enlivened Isle.
(*there was to be a canal where the railway line now runs*)

Advice on planning the New Town was given by William Starke, who argued
that the practice of Claude and Poussin, in repeatedly combining trees and
architecture in their paintings, showed that there could be no beauty where

either of these was wanting; therefore town planners should also combine them. This reference is suggestive, for there is in the paintings of Claude a Virgilian element, a feeling, as Lord Clark put it, 'of a Golden Age, of grazing flocks, unruffled waters and a calm luminous sky, images of perfect harmony between man and nature'. Perhaps it is not going too far to suggest that the New Town of Edinburgh is, as it were, a realisation of an ideal landscape of this kind, combining the intellectual order of classical architecture and regular planning with a prospect of nature, of fields and trees and hills, laid out for man's enjoyment like a gentleman's park. Certainly it is the total effect that impresses. As Blanqui said, 'the most interesting of all these beauties . . . is the view of Edinburgh as a whole, amid its splendid encircling mountains'.

The success of the New Town, as of any other speculation, depended on finding customers, and these soon appeared. Among the first was David Hume (1711–76), one of the world's greatest philosophers, abominated by many of his countrymen as a sceptic or even perhaps an atheist; South St David Street, it is said, was satirically named after him. Raeburn came on his return from Rome in 1787, Creech the bookseller moved from the Old Town (although he kept his shop in the High Street) early in the nineteenth century, and by that time most of the lawyers in Edinburgh had likewise 'flitted' across the Nor' Loch.

What the lawyers did was crucial, in this as in many other matters, for Edinburgh was a city of the law. Before 1750 Scots Common law was already a flexible and harmonious system, and in the latter part of the eighteenth century it was developed and applied by several remarkable men. Many of them, the judges especially, exhibited memorable force and eccentricity of character. Lord Braxfield, effectively head of the criminal court through the 1790s, 'was like a formidable blacksmith. His accent and his dialect were exaggerated Scotch: his language, like his thoughts, short, strong, and conclusive'. Political repression brought work to the courts, and Braxfield, who like his fellow judges was as Tory as the government in London, presided at several political trials. 'Let them bring me prisoners and I'll find them law' was a remark openly attributed to him; and political feeling ran so high that his friends, instead of decrying this scandalous observation, 'spoke of it as a thing understood, and rather admired it as worthy of the man and of the times'. The coarse and savage humour of the eighteenth century stood out in many of his utterances. During one political trial the prisoner ventured to say that all great men had been reformers, 'even our Saviour himself'. Braxfield replied (it is said *sotto voce*), 'Muckle he made o' that, for he was hangit.'

Another of the Scottish judges of the day, Lord Monboddo, is chiefly remembered for his belief that the orang-utang is a class of the human species and that human infants were born with tails. But he wrote *Of the Origin and Progress of Language* and *Ancient Metaphysics*, each work in six volumes, and his 'learned suppers' were a notably pleasant feature of Edinburgh life. He regarded coaches as effeminate, and travelled everywhere on horseback, even to London, until he was eighty. James Boswell (1740–95), for many years a practising advocate in Edinburgh, possessed no dramatic habits of thought or

North side of Charlotte Square (1792–8). Robert Adam.

behaviour like these, and seemed to many 'a little man', dissipated,
improvident, and self-complacent. But his achievement is one of the most
singular in literature, the product of almost thirty years of study and revision.
Francis Jeffrey began his law career just as Boswell's ended. He was an
advocate, a Whig politician, a judge, and finally a reforming Lord Advocate.
Yet in addition to all this he was one of the small group who founded the
Edinburgh Review in 1802, and he ran it for many years as a spare-time
occupation.

It may well be asked how working lawyers could find the time to write
histories, biographies, critical reviews, books on language, morals,
metaphysics, or scientific agriculture. Part of the answer is that the old
Scottish Courts enjoyed what can only be described as lengthy vacations.
When this agreeable scheme of life came to an end in 1836, an eminent judge
wrote in his journal as follows:

Our vacation is encroached upon; our two months in spring, and the long glories of
the four months in summer and autumn, are no more. The vernal blackbird, the
summer evening, the utter cessation of business, the long truce, the mind's recovery of
itself, the relapse into natural voluntary habits . . . it is this abstraction from legal
business which has given Scotland the greatest part of her literature that has adorned
her. The lawyers have been the most intellectual class in the country. The Society of
the Outer House had given them every possible incitement, and the Advocates'
Library has furnished them with the means and the temptation to read.

(*Journal of Henry Cockburn 1831–1854* vol I., 1874)

These privileges set the lawyers apart.

1. J.M.W. Turner, Shade and Darkness - the Evening of the Deluge *(1843). (See p.121)*

2. *J.M.W. Turner,* The Bay of Baiae, with Apollo and the Sybil *(1823). (See p.135)*

3. *John Constable,* Scene on a River *(c.1830–7). (See p.169)*

4. *William Dyce,* The Judgement of Solomon *(1836). (See p.138)*

5. *Sir Edwin Landseer,* The Old Shepherd's Chief Mourner *(1837). (See p.171)*

6. *John Constable, The Hay Wain (1821). (See p.123)*

7. *Cane ware morning tea set with tray, engine-turned to emulate the appearance of bamboo (1792). Josiah Wedgwood. Teapot height 45cm.* (See p.278)

8. *Saloon at the Reform Club, Pall Mall (1837–41). Sir Charles Barry. (See p.206)*

9. *The Elizabeth Saloon at Belvoir Castle (1824). B. and M. Wyatt. (See p.277)*

10. *Royal throne and canopy in the House of Lords Chamber, designed by A. W. N. Pugin and Sir Charles Barry (made by John Webb of Bond Street, London; 1846–7). (See pp. 208, 275)*

But the law was not everything in Edinburgh, and it is fair to add that the University (where most professors lectured, unlike their counterparts in Oxford and Cambridge) performed at least as well. The Medical School had come into existence in the 1720s, founded by a small group of professors who had studied at Leyden, then the foremost centre of medical learning in Europe. Progress was rapid, and by 1800 Edinburgh and Glasgow had become 'undoubtedly the greatest medical schools in Britain, and probably in Europe'. Both enjoyed an international reputation. Of those who graduated from Edinburgh as doctors in the first half of the nineteenth century, approximately one half came from Scotland, one third from England, and the remainder from 'the colonies'. The most famous of these graduates entered the School in 1827, a poor boy from the country; this was James Young Simpson, who twenty years later, now an Edinburgh professor, announced his epoch-making discovery of chloroform anaesthesia.

The Faculty of Arts was likewise progressive, and distinguished. The first chair of English Literature in the world was established by the Faculty in 1760. Adam Ferguson, whose *Essay on the History of Civil Society* appeared in 1767, is recognised as one of the founders of sociology, and his *History of the Roman Republic* went into many editions both in Britain and abroad. (He, too, was a character. When Chaplain to the Black Watch he charged with the troops at Fontenoy. In later life he suffered what must have been a stroke, but recovered, and generally wore a coat with a fur-lined greatcoat on top, and fur-lined half boots, even within doors. He kept a large thermometer in the house, and his life 'was regulated by Fahrenheit'. But in 1793 he set off 'in a strange sort of carriage, and with no companion except his servant James, to visit Italy for a new edition of his history. He was then about seventy-two, and had to pass through a good deal of war; but returned in about a year, younger than ever' (Cockburn, *Memorials*). Ferguson resigned from his chair in 1785, and became joint professor of mathematics in the University (although he now devoted most of his time to farming, twenty miles from Edinburgh). He was succeeded by Dugald Stewart, whose course in philosophy during a period of over twenty years was described by one of his students as 'the great era in the progress of young men's minds'. Lord Cockburn, an eminent judge and author of a brilliant volume of *Memorials*, declared that Stewart's excellence as a lecturer was so great 'that it is a luxury to recall it':

His ear both for music and for speech, was exquisite; and he was the finest reader I have ever heard. His gesture was simple and elegant, though not free from a tinge of professional formality; and his whole manner that of an academical gentleman. Without genius, or even originality of talent, his intellectual character was marked by calm thought and great soundness . . . Everything was purified and exalted by his beautiful taste; not merely by his perception of what was attractive in external nature or in art, but by that moral taste which awed while it charmed, and was the chief cause of the success with which he breathed the love of virtue into whole generations of pupils.

(Cockburn, *Memorials*)

James Mill, Henry Brougham and Walter Scott were perhaps the most famous of all his auditors, but there were many others of note, and it has

been said without exaggeration that here in Edinburgh, in the early
nineteenth century, 'the embryonic great crowded and jostled in profusion'.

Students came to Edinburgh University because it was so obviously, in
modern jargon, 'a centre of excellence'. But another reason for their coming
was the war. War in Europe was all but continuous from 1792 to 1815, and
travelling or studying abroad during all these years was well nigh impossible.
As a result, families as well as students arrived in Edinburgh in large
numbers, some for the education and 'improvement' of their children, and to
enjoy the society of the place. The means for enjoyment and culture were not
wanting. There were balls at the Assembly Rooms (the old Rooms in or
beside the Old Town before 1800, the new Rooms in the New Town
afterwards) and concerts in St Cecilia's Hall, elegant and delightful, or in the
New Town. Painting was taught by Alexander Nasmyth (1758–1840), 'the
father of Scottish landscape painting', who is nevertheless especially famous
for his portrait of Burns, done from a pencil sketch made in 1787 when the
poet visited Edinburgh. A few months' residence in the Scottish capital, with
access to education and 'refinement of every kind', conferred all the graces
upon young ladies from the country, who then 'came out'. Such a one was
Miss Williamina Belscher, who in 1792 raised a romantic passion in the heart
of Sir Walter Scott.

With Scott we are back once more to the law. Scott published *The
Minstrelsy of the Scottish Border* in 1802 and 1803 and *The Lay of the Last
Minstrel* in 1805. Almost at once his way was clear; as he himself put it, 'The
success of a few ballads had the effect of converting a painstaking lawyer of
some years' standing into a follower of literature'. The popularisation of
romance had begun. *Waverley* appeared in 1814, and made an instant
impression:

The unexpected newness of the thing, the profusion of original characters, the Scotch
language, Scotch scenery, Scotch men and women, the simplicity of the writing, and
the graphic force of the descriptions, all struck us with an electric shock of delight.

(Cockburn, *Memorials*)

Yet Scott concealed his authorship. This course he explained by saying that
he was 'not quite sure that it would be considered decorous in me as a Clerk
of Court to write novels . . . clerks are a sort of lay brethren from whom
some solemnity of walk and conduct may be deemed proper'. There was a
real difficulty, for Scott was and remained essentially a man of law. As
another distinguished lawyer has pointed out,

Scott was not like Stevenson, whose practice at the Scots bar consisted of one petition
and whose knowledge of the Civil law of Rome just enabled him to know that
stillicide was not a crime nor was emphyteusis a disease: he was a practising lawyer
familiar with the world in which life and law made contact in so many differing ways
and with so many often curious consequences.

(Lord Cameron, 'Scott and the Community of Intellect'
in *Edinburgh in the Age of Reason* 1967)

As a result, what Scott wrote is imbued with the law of Scotland. *Waverley*
involves the law of entail of land, *Guy Mannering* recalls two current *causes
célèbres* of the day involving missing heirs, *The Heart of Midlothian* is about

the Porteous riots of 1736 as well as the law of concealment of pregnancy and child murder. These historical romances recalled to Scott's contemporaries times and scenes and characters so near as almost to linger in the memory, and yet so remote that they could be freely remodelled and reinterpreted. Many of Scott's works were illustrated by Turner, notably the collected edition of Scott's poems. The vision of each great Romantic appealed to the other, and Edinburgh to both of them. Turner visited Edinburgh on five occasions, and produced several marvellous drawings and watercolours of the city, including the dexterously distorted 'Edinburgh from Calton Hill'.

In a sense, Scott wrote for his friends. In a sense, everyone who wrote in Edinburgh in those days wrote for his friends, because Edinburgh was a metropolitan city and yet also a small town where the network of friendship and personal acquaintance was very fine, and where specialisation and the segregation of knowledge had as yet made little progress. Much of the style of life of the eighteenth century continued into the nineteenth, at least for a decade or two – there continued to be eighteenth-century clubs (of which Edinburgh had a great many), eighteenth-century formal dinners, eighteenth-century formal balls. Duels were still occasionally fought by gentlemen (a relative of James Boswell was killed in a duel in 1822) and ordinary misdoers were still occasionally hanged in the Grassmarket. But the end of the war in 1815 brought great changes. The constant excitement of military preparation (so greatly enjoyed by Scott) disappeared, as did military idleness. Paris and Geneva became as popular with those who travelled for their education or general enlightenment as Edinburgh once had been, and Rome was only a little further away. Fear of revolution subsided, and little children no longer went to bed frightened by what they had heard their parents say at dinner about the atrocities that would follow any change in the existing political system. George IV visited Edinburgh in 1822 – the first visit by a reigning monarch since 1617 – and thereby drew Edinburgh more closely and more familiarly into the ambit of English life. Ten years later Scott died. In 1839 a competition took place for the design of a monument to perpetuate his memory. The winning design was by George Meikle Kemp, a self-taught artist and architect who even in his native city was almost unknown.

Six years were required to build the Scott Monument, and no one who visits Edinburgh can fail to notice it. In a classical city it is fantastically Gothic; and yet it is more Victorian than Gothic, an affair of niches, statues, pinnacles, gargoyles and flying buttresses. In the year that it was completed trains began to run through Princes Street gardens. The transition from the eighteenth century to the age of Victoria was swift and decisive. By 1850 Edinburgh was far larger, far more sanitary, and a good deal more orderly than it had been seventy years before; it was also less innovative, less cosmopolitan, and above all less personal.

Francis Towne's A View from Rydal Park *(c.1786) showing the area near Rydal Mount, where William Wordsworth spent the last 37 years of his life. In the distance is Lake Windermere.*

2 Literature

JOHN BEER

Literature after 1785: genius, sensibility and 'divine chit chat'

While there were many British writers after 1785 whose work would now be referred to as 'Romantic' there was no Romantic movement, as such, in England. Whereas on the continent of Europe A.W. Schlegel, lecturing successively in Jena, Berlin and Vienna between 1798 and 1809, was able to attract audiences who were first invited to align themselves with a tradition of romance which included the Nibelungen, Arthurian literature and *Don Quixote*, and then to approve of art which was 'organic' and 'plastic', rather than 'mechanical' and 'picturesque', there was no figure of equivalent authority in the British Isles. If there was a particular writer to whom most others related it was Samuel Taylor Coleridge (1772–1834); but he was not a leader with a formulated message or programme, rather a man of unusual gifts and intelligence who provoked the thinking of others and who had a decisive influence on a number of young writers during their formative period. What we see when we look at the period as a whole is rather an extraordinary flowering and richness of creativity, involving individual writers who were drawn to think and write in new ways, and who sometimes enjoyed collaborative relationships with other individuals. It is only in retrospect that each can be seen to be pressing to an extreme some element in what would eventually be seen as a larger pattern of 'Romantic' thinking and writing.

As we now look back on the literature of the mid-eighteenth century, similarly, it is easy to discern 'pre-Romantic' elements, but the original authors would not have seen them so. It is we who now notice the increasing number of scenes in nature, or the growing emphasis on liberty, or the tendency to investigate states of the human sensibility. The 'proto-Romanticism' of such writings lies rather in their appeal to the first Romantics themselves.

Thomas Chatterton (1752–70), for example, a young and prolific poet who had died by his own hand before his eighteenth birthday, leaving an extraordinarily large quantity of writing including the Rowley poems, which were written in a pseudo-medieval style, fascinated them. His unusual promise had been acknowledged by Horace Walpole, Joseph Warton and Samuel Johnson, who described him, respectively, as a 'masterly genius', a 'prodigy of genius', and 'the most extraordinary young man that has encountered my knowledge'. For the next age he would be the prototype of thwarted genius, as in Wordsworth's lines 'the marvellous Boy,/The sleepless Soul that perished in his pride'. Keats's dedication to him of *Endymion* would be followed by Shelley's *Adonais*, where he would be the first of the dead to rise in acknowledgement of Keats. The fact that his suicide took place in London, where he had gone in hope of achieving poetic recognition, made him the exemplary victim of an unfeeling establishment. Wordsworth's phrase was closer to the truth; it was less the neglect of others than his own pride that had led to his fate. The image of neglected genius fitted the expectations of the new age too well, however, to be easily dislodged.

Chatterton had passed off his pastiches by presenting them as recently discovered originals. In this he was following a path recently pioneered by James Macpherson (1736–96), who had ministered to the age's interest in antiquity by producing prose poems which he offered as translations from manuscripts of Ossian. Younger poets, ignoring the controversies thus set in motion, would find in them pointers to a new kind of poetry. William Blake (1757–1827), for example, found a model in Macpherson's rhythmic sentences, with their sad rise and fall, for his loose seven-foot lines in *The Book of Thel*. He also wished to rewrite such poetry in a more positive mode, however. Macpherson's heroine Oithona, raped by a tyrant, left disconsolate and then slain in the battle to avenge her honour, he replaced by his Oothoon, a young woman who refused to recognise that she had been dishonoured when she was raped and abandoned by a tyrant, and who found her belief in the spirit of delight thwarted only by her young lover, who could not accept so affirmative an attitude. Similarly, when Chatterton's lines

> How dydd I know that every darte
> That cutt the airie waye,
> Might not find passage to my heart
> And close my eyes for aie?

were rewritten by Blake in *The Marriage of Heaven and Hell*, they converted latent fear into potential optimism:

> How do you know but ev'ry Bird that cuts the airy way
> Is an immense world of delight, clos'd by your senses five?

Other models were available for young poets. William Wordsworth (1770–1850), whose earliest writings show a similar predilection for revived medievalism, was soon turning to more reflective writers such as Mark Akenside (1721–70), who came from the same part of the country as himself and shared his feeling for the wilder workings of nature. A passage in Book iv of 'The Pleasures of the Imagination' has been singled out for its remarkable resemblance to the verse which Wordsworth was to be producing a generation later.

O ye Northumbrian shades, which overlook
The rocky pavement and the mossy falls
Of solitary Wensbeck's limpid stream;
How gladly I recall your well-known seats,
Beloved of old, and that delightful time
When, all alone, for many a summer's day,
I wandered through your calm recesses, led
In silence by some powerful hand unseen.
Nor will I e'er forget you; nor shall e'er
The graver tasks of manhood, or the advice
Of vulgar wisdom, move me to disclaim
Those studies which possessed me in the dawn
Of life, and fixed the colour of my mind
For every future year . . .

The young Wordsworth was drawn also to James Beattie (1735–1803), and particularly his poem 'The Minstrel, or the Progress of Genius', which had appeared in 1770–4. His sister Dorothy found some lines in it strangely close to his own nature:

In truth he was a strange and wayward wight,
Fond of each gentle, and each dreadful scene . . .

Edwin, the young poet so described, was, like Wordsworth himself, 'of the north countrie' – the region which had recently been denominated by Thomas Percy the true home of 'minstrels'. Of humble origins, Edwin had been drawn from an early age to leave his fellows and visit the 'lonely mountain's head' or 'deep untrodden groves', where he found himself drawn naturally to feelings of rapture or pity.

The emphasis among poets of the 1770s on the cultivation of genius in solitude drew their successors to follow a similar course. It was for this reason that a poet such as Wordsworth did not merely turn aside from the writing of fashionable satire but resisted the attractions of writing a local dialect poetry in the manner of Robert Burns (1759–96) – a course which must have been attractive to someone growing up near the area from which the Border Ballads had originated. Burns's direct passion and straightforward humanity, coupled with strong lyric gifts, were to have no notable English counterpart, however. The cult of solitude which Wordsworth adopted, followed by exposure to the classical and mathematical stringencies of Cambridge, was to produce a different kind of poetry.

Coleridge looked back to similar antecedents. His earliest long poem, which he continued to revise for many years, was his 'Monody on the Death of Chatterton'. He also shared the previous generation's enthusiasm for poetic genius itself. In a letter of December 1796 he spoke of the degree to which he had been 'inspired' and 'whirled . . . along' by the last part of Collins's 'Ode on the Poetic Character', which concluded by enshrining Milton, the inspired poet, in a paradise like the one that he himself had created. The image of such a Milton, more heady than the text he created, was attractive to the new generation. When Coleridge turned in the same letter to particularise further, it was to express his admiration of 'the *head* and fancy of Akenside, and the *heart* and fancy of Bowles'. Akenside he liked because he had shown how one could write 'metaphysically' in poetry; the choice of William Lisle Bowles (1762–1850), which is more unexpected, was, as it turned out, shared by Wordsworth who, discovering the *Sonnets* in London when they were first published in 1789, had been so struck that (to the annoyance of his companion) he had stopped in a niche of London Bridge to finish them. Coleridge's own poem to Bowles suggests what they both found valuable: 'My heart has thanked thee, Bowles!' it begins, this tribute of 'the heart' being directed to one who speaks with a sweet sadness which awakens the reader's own sympathies towards others.

For young poets such as Wordsworth and Coleridge at this time 'genius' and 'sensibility' were words of power. Genius was the more difficult. Although usually intended to convey, specifically, either responsiveness to the spirit of a place or an invocation of one's inward powers, it could easily suggest that one thought one's own powers to be unique, or at least well above the average. It was most discreetly to be explored by aligning oneself with past poets or adopting some other mode of distancing. Wordsworth, in his first long poems, pays tribute to the 'genius' of the places he is describing, while Coleridge finds it easiest to convey his idea of genius in the persons of the Ancient Mariner, a man cut off from the reader both in time and in space, or of the inspired poet at the end of *Kubla Khan*, set in a context which includes the imperfect 'commanding' genius of the Khan himself, Apollo with his magic music, the intoxicated (and half-ironised) poet of Plato's *Io* and other far-off figures of the kind.

Sensibility, the quality to be found pre-eminently in Bowles, was less controversial and ran with the grain of the age. Many contemporary poems written for drawing-room readers directed their emotions to small birds and animals or to beggars and outcasts. The inducing of human sympathy was believed to have become more necessary in an age which cried up the virtues of freestanding independence.

Both genius and sensibility were vulnerable ideals, however: the appeals to fear and pity on which both were partly based were during the same period giving rise to a proliferating fashion for the 'Gothic' – a mode which encouraged writers to play upon such emotions in their readers with little seriousness of purpose. Many early examples were absurd and sensationalist, but by the 1790s the elegance of Ann Radcliffe's writing in novels such as *The Mysteries of Udolpho* (1794), along with the power of Lewis's *The Monk* (1796), had made the fashion so respectable that Jane Austen's satire in *Northanger Abbey* (begun in 1798 but not published until 1818) was opportune.

In his letter of 1796 Coleridge invoked another pair of qualities which suggest a wariness of extravagance: 'the solemn Lordliness of Milton, & the Divine Chit chat of Cowper'. This view of Milton corrects his earlier, more excited recollection by presenting him now as majestic rather than godlike, serious rather than ecstatic; ideals which are more easy of emulation. This tempering of aspiration with humility was accompanied by a growing recognition that Milton's political principles were relevant to current problems. By 1800, indeed, when the ideals of the French Revolution were at a low ebb, he would have become for Blake, Coleridge and Wordsworth a timely figure, to whom they could point a bewildered generation for guidance. When they felt themselves forced back on to the defensive by those who scorned their poetic experiments, similarly, they were likely to look back to him as one who had followed a path of exemplary humility. A still better and more recent model was William Cowper (1731–1800) who could be appealed to the more readily because his political principles were basically acceptable across the range of contemporary attitudes.

Cowper's career illustrates well the opportunities and problems which poets were facing in the late eighteenth century. While the materials for poetry were in one sense expanding as never before, the possible points of focus were shrinking. If one were writing a long poem one might feel drawn to range into many fields; one might also draw heavily upon one's own thoughts and feelings; but where would the centre of such a poem be found? A sense of lack, rather than of plenitude, becomes pervasive: Wordsworth begins his drafts towards an autobiographical poem with the telling question 'Was it for this?'; and for the only full length poem that he chose to publish in his lifetime selects a title, 'The Excursion', which has a deliberate casualness, suggesting something other than the great events or purposeful travels of which epics are made. If this journey is to be an odyssey it will be on the smallest scale.

Such modesty finds a predecessor in Cowper's longest poem, *The Task*, for which a subject was found when his friend Lady Austen suggested the sofa in his room. This still point in his turning world proved a particularly apposite point of departure, since the intimacy which it suggested, the opportunities for personal conversation directed to one or two chosen companions, fitted the poetic style in which he excelled. Yet the larger world is strongly present to his mind in his rural retreat. The current growth in communications has brought with it the regular newspaper, making it possible for him to range widely over current political and social issues.

The Task, published in 1785, a year after Johnson's death (and the opening date of this volume), marks with some accuracy the point of transition from the neo-classicism of the eighteenth century to the Romanticism of the new age. Cowper's attitudes set his insistence on the importance of liberty within a highly traditional framework, while his assumption that the poet might be best licensed to speak from a position of retirement looked back to a long succession of similar assertions in the previous age. What he had also achieved, however, was a method of providing a framework for, and a way of writing a 'meditative blank verse' which would provide a valuable model for his successors. Coleridge's term 'Divine Chit chat' is well founded: Cowper writes with a winning informality but does not lose an ultimate seriousness of purpose. Weighty passages, such as that which begins with the line 'By ceaseless action, all that is subsists', co-exist with lighter touches, providing one potential model for Romantic modes. His informality of approach, similarly, looks forward to their conversational style. One need only juxtapose Cowper's description in Book Four of *The Task* of fireside musings beside a grate where a film of soot sometimes appears – portending, in country lore, the arrival of a stranger – with Coleridge's treatment of a similar scene in 'Frost at Midnight' to see how much the later poet has learned from the former, yet how much further and more delicately he has developed the idea.

In turning back to *The Task*, one finds, more often than one expects, the groundwork for developments in the next generation: Cowper's lines 'I would not enter on my list of friends/ . . . the man/ Who needlessly sets foot upon a worm' expresses a sentiment that is basically present (along with more subtle intricacies and riddles) in *The Ancient Mariner* and resurfaces in Wordsworth's 'Hartleap Well'; his description of gypsies sparks an expression of equally mixed feelings in Wordsworth's poem 'Gypsies'. Cowper would provide points of security for writers in the next generation, and for some, such as Jane Austen, would continue to be centrally important. By 1810, on the other hand, poets could afford to be more adventurous. And even the earlier Romantic poets, though less critical, were never wholly at ease with him, for his melancholia and periods of mental suffering signalled covert warnings that the poise·of his attitude was not so stable or invulnerable as it at first sight appeared. If they probed too deeply, they might find themselves simply looking down into what was least secure in themselves.

Blake's energy and vision

Blake once said that Cowper had come to him in a vision expressing a wish that he could be permanently insane, adding 'You retain health and yet are as mad as any of us all – over us all – mad as a refuge from unbelief . . .'. In writing that, he not only indicated how he viewed the difference between himself and poets such as Cowper but established terms for judging his own condition. Readers of Blake are likely to notice signs of manic extravagance and something very like paranoia from time to time, yet his work, unlike that commonly associated with mental patients, also has a remarkable degree of control and pungency. Suggestions of disturbance often occur, indeed, when he is most intent to act, think and create positively. To the end he abhorred 'the divinity of yes & no too'; his most fervent rejections of a universe constructed entirely upon reasoning turned immediately to positive assertion:

'What,' it will be Questioned, 'When the Sun rises, do you not see a round disk of fire somewhat like a Guinea?' O no, no, I see an Innumerable company of the heavenly host crying 'Holy, Holy, Holy is the Lord God Almighty'.

From an early stage Blake had differed from his contemporaries, believing that the world of Bacon, Locke and Newton, far from providing a reassuring foundation, must ultimately deliver its adherents into a universe of despair and meaninglessness. In his earliest poems, published in 1783 as *Poetic Sketches*, he had lamented the lack of inspired poetry among many of his contemporaries and predecessors, appealing rather to earlier figures such as Edmund Spenser and William Shakespeare. By about 1788 he was producing, in his plates 'There is no Natural Religion' and 'All Religions are One', the basis of the philosophy by which he was to live for the rest of his life, including the assertions that 'Man's perceptions are not bounded by organs of perception' and that what is bounded is 'loathed by its possessor': 'The same dull round, even of a universe, would soon become a mill with complicated wheels'. When Blake later wrote of 'dark Satanic mills' the statement went far beyond a criticism of current industrial conditions: human beings constructed mills, and allowed them to be constructed, because they had been taught to see their own minds as no more than machines with complicated wheels. To show others the infinite in everything that they looked at was the chief aim of his poetry and art. At his most characteristic he reinforced the endeavour by bringing both modes together in plates combining text and designs.

That last decision was particularly paradoxical, since it automatically denied him a large audience for things that he felt needed saying urgently and widely; yet he was prepared to accept that limitation to preserve his own independence. He was above all a fighter for liberty: the spirit that had made Cowper declare, ''Tis liberty alone that gives the flower/ Of fleeting life its lustre and perfume . . .' and declare that England's happiness lay in her freedom, was intensified in Blake's mind to a vision where all human beings might achieve a common liberty. Yet this outgoing flame of liberty in the man was matched by an equally stubborn structure at his core needing to contract itself at times into hard independence. The near-contradictions in his work were a direct result.

The conflicts that were threatened by such contrary assertions were normally evaded by a mediating imagination that was also quite unusually vivid. While this could sometimes develop his fears of negation into menacing nightmares, it gave him at best a sense of unusual inspiration; between the extremes it provided some of his most characteristic and successful modes of imaginative expression. In his designs flowers can turn into flames, flames into flowers.

Although Blake had little formal schooling, having been apprenticed to an engraver at an early stage of his career, his writing carries evidence of voracious reading in his youth. He was moved not only by the Elizabethans but by the whole seventeenth-century tradition of imaginative enlightenment, whether in the metaphysical poets or in poetic metaphysicians such as the Cambridge Platonists – who had helped provide an intellectual tradition for the supremacy of the human imagination. If Plato's writings attracted him, Plato himself seemed too much of a geometrician; it was the humane Socrates of Plato's presentation or the vivid neo-platonists who drew him most. Mystical writers such as Paracelsus and Jacob Boehme ranked in his mind with visionary Old Testament prophets such as Isaiah and Ezekiel. Above all, he saw it as his task to do for a new age of revolution what Milton had done for the seventeenth century, extending the sway of freedom from the political sphere to include the social as well: this would be achieved not by following the puritan Milton, who could too easily appear as 'clothed in black, severe & silent', but by releasing the energies and imaginative powers that had been most evident in Milton's early poetry.

During these years the political failure that had resulted in the loss of the American colonies seemed to him of a piece with the sexual failures between individual men and women. His prophetic book *America* opens with a frontispiece showing a failed male angel, wrapped up in himself, while a woman and child nearby suffer emotionally from his self-isolation. In a

Blake's etched frontispiece for his book America: a Prophecy *(1793).*

contemporary work, *Visions of the Daughters of Albion*, the corresponding political dimension of sexual tyranny is opened to view when Bromion tells his female victim, Oothoon, 'Thy soft American plains are mine'. In Blake's eyes such sadistic relationships were characterised by a mistaken possessiveness which bespoke a false consciousness: human beings dominated by the laws of reason quantified pleasures, as they quantified everything else, not perceiving that a different kind of law applied to delight. In *The Book of Thel* the marigold sees the world differently:

> Pluck thou my flower, Oothoon the mild!
> Another flower shall spring, because the soul of sweet delight
> Can never pass away.

The same philosophy informs Blake's well-known couplet,

> He who binds to himself a joy
> Doth the winged life destroy;
> But he who kisses the joy as it flies
> Lives in Eternity's sun rise.

Rejecting the binding, bounding possessiveness of the analytic eye, Blake appealed to a spirit of more generous vision which he believed to be latent in all human beings, but left to sleep along with the imaginative powers which eighteenth-century art discouraged.

A sense of this hidden power pervades the lyrics of his *Songs of Innocence and Experience* (1789–94) and the more complex *Marriage of Heaven and Hell* (*c*.1790–3), a work which (unlike Nietzsche's not dissimilar writing) is concerned not with the death of God but with the sleep of man – a sleep which leaves him no longer able to apprehend what the divine life is like. The ironic and even sardonic element is very Nietzschean, but at its most rhapsodic the writing is more like a hymn to the creation:

> The pride of the peacock is the glory of God.
> The lust of the goat is the bounty of God.
> The wrath of the lion is the wisdom of God.
> The nakedness of woman is the work of God.
> Excess of sorrow laughs, Excess of joy weeps.
> The roaring of lions, the howling of wolves, the raging of the stormy sea, and
> 　　the destructive sword, are portions of eternity, too great for the eye of man.

The various modes of affirmation, irony and the sardonic in *The Marriage* are a sign of the vitality of Blake's mind at this time, but a work that alternates between them sets up problems that he does not fully face. 'Everything that lives is holy' writes Blake the rhapsodist; Blake the sardonic humorist declares: 'As the catterpiller chooses the fairest leaves to lay her eggs on, so the priest lays his curse on the fairest joys'. A detached and sceptical reader might comment that if 'everything that lives' includes 'religious caterpillars', caterpillars too must be holy. Why then are they held up for condemnation? Blake's doctrine overrides such objections – but only by giving even the separate statements in his work individual lives of their own. He appeals, in other words, to the living, responsive psyche rather than to the analytic mind which weighs one affirmation carefully against another.

When Blake's Urizen saw that 'all life feeds on life' he wept; Blake himself, however, does not.

It was easier to express so positive and versatile a spirit by way of song and illustration than in words. Much of Blake's narrative writing was devoted to describing a humanity in which, once the larger humanising imaginative power had been lost, a state of sterile and self-perpetuating contention between reasoning power and free energies ensued. The worshippers of reason (often shown as aged) tried desperately to retain an order which they felt to be in danger of disintegration, while those who strove for freedom produced only destructive acts against the restraints imposed on them. At the climax of his unfinished manuscript poem *Vala*, or *The Four Zoas* (*c*.1795–1808), the political emphasis of the earlier writings gives way to an affirmation that release comes through restoration of vision:

> The Sun has left his blackness & has found a fresher morning,
> And the mild moon rejoices in the clear & cloudless night,
> And Man walks forth from midst of the fires: the evil is all consum'd.
> His eyes behold the Angelic spheres arising night & day;
> The stars consum'd like a lamp blown out, & in their stead, behold
> The Expanding Eyes of Man behold the depths of wondrous worlds!
>
> (ix, 825–30)

This transition from physical freedom to liberation of the imaginative powers corresponds, among other things, to a changing situation in the culture itself. About 1790, when the ferment created by the French Revolution was still at its height, Blake had been one of a number of writers, all associated with the publisher Joseph Johnson, who were breaking new ground. Erasmus Darwin's *Botanic Garden* (1789–91), an attempt to bring scientific knowledge into poetry, Wordsworth's earliest long poems and the *Political Justice* of William Godwin (1756–1836) were all published by Johnson, who also befriended Mary Wollstonecraft, author of works such as *Original Stories from Real Life* (1788), illustrated by Blake in 1791, *A Vindication of the Rights of Woman* (1792) and *The Wrongs of Woman*. Godwin went on to produce a novel, *Things as they are, or the Adventures of Caleb Williams* (1794), which raised questions about the state of the prisons, and of justice more generally, in England at the time. The questioning mode was taken further by other novelists, including Robert Bage, whose *Hermsprong, or Man As He is Not* (1796) displayed the trials of a bluntly truthful hero.

Already, however, such books were becoming difficult to publish, the inauguration of *The Anti-Jacobin* in 1797 marking a movement in favour of the status quo which looked back to works such as Eliza Parsons's *Woman As She Should Be* (1793), and in which the evangelical writings of Hannah More (1745–1833) played a central role. Blake could not be untouched by such changing pressures. In 1793, with Europe in turmoil as a result of the French Revolution, the political prospects for mankind had looked at once exciting and fearful. If the European powers were to persist in their hostility to revolutionary freedom, Blake feared that the resulting violence would be totally devastating; even so, however, the prophetic voices in the works of those years offered a way of transformation which would liberate not only political captives but all those human beings who wore 'Mind-forged manacles'. By the end of the decade the fact that a worldwide revolutionary movement had not after all happened changed his perspective. If, as it now seemed, the current political institutions would always find ways of reinforcing themselves against the threat of revolution, human beings needed to find ways of living with them while not submitting to their barren ideology. Humanity could be renovated, in other words, only by changing its image of itself.

So Blake went back to his original critique of contemporary philosophy, calling for a humanity that would not only use its senses for observation and analysis but learn how to contract and expand them so as to bring them into accord with the visionary rhythms of the universe, a pulsing core of light and music which he believed gave it its true significance. In his later writing his character Los, the artist, is the hero of civilisation because he continues to create, and so to 'keep alive the divine vision'. By continuing to make forms, provided that they are living and energetic, not dead and geometric, the artist is bound to be on the right side so far as humanity and its interests are concerned. At the climax of *Jerusalem* (*c*.1804–20) the visionary way of perceiving has been recovered:

All Human Forms identified, even Tree, Metal, Earth & Stones: all Human Forms identified, living, going forth & returning wearied Into the planetary lives of Years, Months, Days & Hours; reposing, And then Awaking into his Bosom in the Life of Immortality.

(99.1–4)

Such was Blake's vision at its height; but he knew by now that he could not easily convey it to his contemporaries in an extended form. His later writing is often at its most successful, in fact, when he returns to an aphoristic way of writing closer to that of *The Marriage* and the *Songs*, as in his 'Auguries of Innocence', where his vision re-emerges in its simplest form:

> To see a World in a Grain of Sand
> And a Heaven in a Wild Flower
> Hold Infinity in the palm of your hand
> And Eternity in an hour.

Although the prophetic books seem at times wholly given over to descriptions of cruelty and suffering, his own sense of things was basically joyful:

> Man was made·for Joy & Woe
> And when this we rightly know
> Thro the World we safely go.
> Joy & Woe are woven fine
> A clothing for the Soul divine
> Under every grief & pine
> Runs a joy with silken twine.

('Auguries of Innocence')

Old age did not affect what Blake believed to be essential in himself – 'the Real Man The Imagination which Liveth for ever'. Confronting death in a letter of April 1827, he saw it simply as a means of 'Leaving the Delusive Goddess Nature & her Laws to get into Freedom from all Law of the Members into the Mind, in which every one is King & Priest in his own House . . .'.

No English writer has so completely demanded to be taken on his own terms; no writer more fully rewards those who are prepared to do so.

Wordsworth: loss and consolation

At first sight Wordsworth's achievement might appear diametrically opposed to that of Blake. Blake, as we have seen, was not concerned with making his meanings explicit, preferring often to speak in riddles and so produce writings whose obscurity defied contemporary canons of clarity; Wordsworth's characteristic method was to describe simple incidents, or even commonplace sentiments, and hope to bring out their special significance. There is a closer relationship between the two poets than might at first appear, nevertheless, for both had in their childhood enjoyed exceptional visionary powers. Whereas Blake continued to affirm their importance, however, maintaining to the end that all human beings possessed them but they were lost by not being cultivated, Wordsworth believed that they must necessarily fade and that the art of being properly human consisted in learning how to live with that fact.

For Wordsworth the loss of such powers was akin to the fading of the ideals of the French Revolution among his contemporaries. In each case the loss was to be accepted but the significance of what was lost must not be disregarded; instead, a way of mediation must be found which should keep alive the values of the lost vision. Wordsworth eventually found his central mediating virtues in the observance of duty and the cultivation of affection. In addition to devoting much of his later writing to these twin themes, he regrouped and revised his earlier poetry in the light of that perspective. In certain poems, such as 'Michael' and 'The Brothers', humble people were presented with a dignity and a tragic quality that made them emblematic for the rest of mankind; their grief over the breaking of intimate bonds was an eloquent reminder that (to quote his words in 'The Old Cumberland Beggar') 'we have all of us one human heart'.

Wordsworth had begun by writing poetry in modes more readily recognisable to contemporary readers, dealing with familiar themes of sublimity and pathos, each set against an appropriate landscape. But even as he wrote them experiences in revolutionary France, such as his love-affair with Annette Vallon, which produced a child, and the friendship with Michel de Beaupuy that made him for a time consider throwing in his lot with the Girondiste cause, were changing his sense of things profoundly. When this period of passionate commitment was followed by the shock of war between England and France in 1793, he was left with deeply divided loyalties. For some years he wrote poems and plays with solitary figures at their centre; it was not until 1797, when the impact of his sister's direct human feelings was reinforced by encounters with Coleridge's ebullient intelligence, that he began to find a way of writing which did not simply return him to isolation and despair.

When he did, the first product was a series of distinctive poems, many following the pattern of popular contemporary verses as found in the magazines and journals of the time, but marked in each case by some further quality. Published in 1798 as *Lyrical Ballads* they were presented as having been written chiefly 'to ascertain how far the language of conversation in the middle and lower classes of society is adapted to the purposes of poetic pleasure' – a statement much explored by subsequent critics. The quality that renders them unusual by comparison with the drawing-room pieces of the time emerges more clearly, however, in the Preface written two years later:

The principal object . . . was to make the incidents of common life interesting by tracing in them, truly though not ostentatiously, the primary laws of our nature: chiefly as far as regards the manner in which we associate ideas in a state of excitement.

This more fugitive aim helps to explain some unexpected features in the poems, such as their preoccupation with unusual states of mind. The obtuse narrator of 'The Thorn', drawn back repeatedly to observe the strange behaviour of a woman whose simple repetitive grief he cannot understand; the alternating concern and delight of the mother of the Idiot Boy who in his strange nocturnal adventures responds to the world as if for the first time, hearing owls as crazed cocks and seeing the moon as a cold sun; or the stubbornness of the small girl who is so closely bonded to her brothers and sisters that she cannot conceive how the deaths of two could make any difference to the number of her family; these and other elements in the poems evidently sprang from discussions with Coleridge concerning the nature of human unconscious processes and the kinds of law that they might be obeying – laws very different from those based on pure rationalism. The later emphasis in the Preface on the question of diction has proved somewhat misleading, for it is all too easy to feel that the use of the language of conversation in the middle and lower classes of society – if that is all that is going on – is bought at the price of banality or bathos.

At the end of the 1798 volume Wordsworth re-established his poetic credentials by way of a meditative poem in the tradition of Cowper. In 'Lines written a few miles above Tintern Abbey . . .' he took stock of what had happened to him between the emotional days of 1793, when the sound of waterfalls haunted him 'like a Passion' and the present, when his pleasure in nature was more reflective. The strange contrast between his current state of mind, which imposed its stately rhythms on his experience, and the remembered passions of the past, stretching back to a time when mind and nature were so united that he could not be sure whether external objects had a separate existence at all, was to provide much of the impetus for subsequent poems, including the 'Ode: Intimations of Immortality from recollections of early childhood', in which he tried to come to terms with the loss of the splendours of the world as seen through the eyes of childhood wonder and 'Resolution and Independence', a poem which gives a new valuation to those who, like the leech-gatherer encountered on a lonely moor, display simple endurance. It is explored most subtly and fully in the autobiographical poem which he began writing shortly after concluding *Lyrical Ballads* and which, having remained in manuscript for the rest of his life under the title 'Poem, Title not yet fixed upon . . . Addressed to S.T. Coleridge', was published shortly after his death as *The Prelude*.

From one point of view the early books of *The Prelude* suggest the existence in nature of spirits, or a spirit, to which as a boy he had been particularly responsive. This idea (a natural development from eighteenth-century notions of the 'genius of place') had continued to haunt him: they had been present in the references to 'a motion and a spirit, that impels / All thinking things, all objects of all thought,/ And rolls through all things' in 'Tintern Abbey'. This set of beliefs, which at its height was explored with Coleridge under the general theme of the 'one Life', could be exciting to poets who felt oppressed by the limitations of a mechanised universe, offering a sense of the universality and indestructibility of life. But that reassuring sense was liable in turn to be undermined, disastrously, by reminders that even if life on the grand scale is immortal individual lives are not. That contradiction was never better – or more succinctly – conveyed than in a brief two-stanza poem which juxtaposed the trance-like sense which could be experienced in moments of love with the workings of a universe which negated it:

> A slumber did my spirit seal;
> I had no human fears;
> She seemed a thing that could not feel
> The touch of earthly years.
>
> No motion has she now, no force;
> She neither hears nor sees;
> Rolled round in earth's diurnal course,
> With rocks, and stones, and trees.

As Wordsworth worked out his larger philosophy, therefore, he came to stress consolation rather than assured vision. There was a similar problem with the question of morality: it was pleasing to picture the existence of a universal life-spirit rolling through all things, but such a spirit, if supposed to have full and dominant sway over human beings, relieved them of the need to make moral choices. Wordsworth, with his massive sense of responsibility, could not have missed such an implication. On the other hand, childhood and youth were not times of full responsibility: it was possible therefore to argue that the workings of nature might play an important part in those years in providing a full human education – and, indeed, that without them the moral growth of a child might be stunted.

This, after all, is one of the main underlying arguments in the 'Lines written above Tintern Abbey', where the animal pleasures of boyhood and the young man's passionately ambivalent relationship to nature are seen as both contributing to his psychic good – perhaps even to his moral resources as well.

Wordsworth set forth teachings of this kind increasingly in his later writings and deferred publication of *The Prelude*, which, as a poem about the conditions that had favoured his growth as a poet, had a circumscribed moral value. Wordsworth believed it to have been a special privilege to have grown up in a countryside where he was allowed to run wild: 'fostered alike by Beauty and by fear'. By comparison with the pursuit of reason which had led him into endless contradictions in his youth until he 'yielded up moral questions in despair', his adventures among the fells of Cumbria had taught him about the mystery of things, giving him an inner vision, a permanent psychoscape against which he could set the meaningless and shifting pageants exhibited by mankind in large towns. Most significantly of all, there had been times when some state of excitement, particularly if suddenly arrested, had left him open to unusually profound sensations, where nature seemed in some way to reveal the unity that lay at her centre and impress it permanently within his own being. Such experiences had for him a 'renovating virtue'. Looked back upon, they could seem like oases in a desert, though their value could be experienced only in solitude.

Wordsworth was aware that to describe such experiences as significant for others was to risk charges of an inhuman arrogance. Only if he could demonstrate that what he himself had gained was available to all human beings in like circumstances could he feel confident that he had something to say to a wider audience. The main work that he addressed to his contemporaries at this time, *The Excursion*, had as its central figure an ordinary travelling man, a pedlar, who had yet been fortunate enough to be brought up among the hills of Scotland where he read some of the greatest classics – Milton, the Bible – while living in a wild landscape. The wisdom he acquired, owing nothing to the agencies of eighteenth-century polite civilisation, could be presented as a test case for Wordsworth's basic philosophy concerning the true resources of human beings.

The writing of *The Excursion* took place during the later events of the Peninsular War, a time when the need for strong action against France was matched by a growth of moral enquiry. By the time that it was published in 1814, however, the dominant mood had been lifted by a succession of English victories and the new élan associated with the Regency. As a result, there was not at that moment a fashionable audience for what Wordsworth was saying. The religious found it dangerously unorthodox and Jeffrey in the *Edinburgh Review* ridiculed it for its constant attention to people of low degree: 'the wife of an unprosperous waiter – a servant girl with her infant – a parish pauper . . .'; even the radical William Hazlitt, who might have been expected to praise just those features of the poem, was incensed at its stigmatising of the French Revolution.

To critics of a more reflective turn of mind *The Excursion* was a major work of the time. But Coleridge put his finger on an important truth when he pointed out that Wordsworth's aim of renovating great central truths might well appear, to those who had not followed the same complex paths as he, no more than a restatement of commonplaces. Readers who do trace that strange and strenuous process sympathetically find *The Excursion* a distinctive and memorable achievement. Nevertheless, it remains true that its best passages, poetically, are those which date back to his most creative period. The story of Margaret in Book One, one of the finest pieces he ever wrote, was originally a separate poem, 'The Ruined Cottage'. Coleridge, to whom Wordsworth read the poem in 1797, was immediately impressed, particularly by the conclusion describing Margaret's obsessive concern for news of her husband and her decay, recorded in that of the cottage itself:

> Meanwhile her poor hut
> Sunk to decay, for he was gone whose hand,
> At the first nippings of October frost,
> Closed up each chink and with fresh bands of straw
> Chequered the green-grown thatch. And so she sate
> Through the long winter, reckless and alone,
> Till this reft house by frost, and thaw, and rain
> Was sapped; and when she slept the nightly damps
> Did chill her breast, and in the stormy day
> Her tattered clothes were ruffled by the wind
> Even at the side of her own fire. – Yet still
> She loved this wretched spot, nor would for worlds
> Have parted hence; and still that length of road
> And this rude bench one torturing hope endeared,
> Fast rooted at her heart, and here, my friend,
> In sickness she remained, and here she died,
> Last human tenant of these ruined walls.

Coleridge's comprehensiveness

Although Coleridge wrote poetry throughout his life, it was only for a few years that he could be regarded primarily as a poet. At other times he combined such activities with researches and writings in many fields – political, scientific, critical, moral, theological. Above all he thought of himself as a metaphysician: one who, in his own words, 'feels the riddle of the world, and may help to unravel it'. What he termed his 'inquiring spirit' was active in all these concerns. So far as his poetry was concerned it informed some of his most delicate descriptions and vivid images; even more, it played a part in his emergence as a major literary critic of his time.

At first sight one is tempted to make a comparison with Goethe. But unlike Goethe, who was adept at concentrating his energies towards one purpose at a time, Coleridge was a man whose unusually wide-ranging consciousness was matched by an equally active conscience, keeping him aware of the value of the old even as he found himself attracted to the new. The very contradictions which were inherent in the new phase of civilisation were fully operative in his own psyche, so that the work he left was often fractured or fragmentary.

These contradictions were evident from his very earliest years. As the youngest son of a scholarly country clergyman who represented much that was best in the eighteenth-century Church he was given a strong conventional moral upbringing, yet his unusual imaginative and intellectual powers caused him to be cosseted as an infant prodigy. From this happy condition he was uprooted by the sudden death of his father and plunged into the stark world of a London school, Christ's Hospital, where he protected himself against the pangs of isolation and the dangers of hostility by voracious reading. To be allowed to wander the streets of London and explore some of its libraries at a time when new ideas were in the air was also an exciting experience; he was much drawn to the new ideas of reform and renovation which were abroad – not only from the writings of Voltaire, Rousseau and their followers but in the rediscovery of ancient vitalist ideas such as those of the neoplatonist philosophers. At Cambridge and after, alternation between this delight in intellectual speculation and guilt at the infirmity of purpose induced by his highly active consciousness (a combination which gave him, as he himself put it, a 'smack of Hamlet') continued.

All this is well caught in his first major poem, *The Aeolian Harp*, where, in the long first part, nature at her most peaceful and harmonious is pictured as replicating the work of the creator, creating myriads of animated beings that are wakened into their fullest life by the blowing of an 'intellectual breeze' (which presumably operates on and in the human psyche as well); in the second part such speculations are rejected as impious, affording potential licence for immorality. In poetic terms the transition is from the descriptions of the notes of the Aeolian harp itself,

> Such a soft floating witchery of sound
> As twilight Elfins make, when they at eve
> Voyage on gentle gales from Faery Land;
> Where *Melodies* round honey-dropping flowers,
> Footless and wild, like birds of Paradise,
> Nor pause, nor perch, hovering on untam'd wing

to the poet's dismissal of

> These shapings of the unregenerate mind,
> Bubbles that glitter as they rise and break
> On vain Philosophy's aye-bubbling spring.

There is no doubt which side of the argument Coleridge's own poetic imagination favours. The poem is validated as an entire statement, on the other hand, by Coleridge's efforts to reconcile himself both with the workings of that imagination and with the requirements, moral and political, of the society about him.

Coleridge's feeling for the subtler energies of life was intensified a year or two later by his friendship with William and Dorothy Wordsworth, his power for sensitive description being particularly evident in meditative poems such as 'This Lime-tree Bower my Prison', 'The Nightingale' and 'Frost at Midnight'. The deeper struggle continued, however, being dramatised in *The Ryme of the Ancyent Marinere* (1798), where the strength of the imaginative achievement makes the final moral ('He prayeth best, who loveth best / All creatures great and small') seem strangely inadequate to the effects of the poem as a whole. At times the sense of a central harmony at the centre of creation is magically evoked:

> Around, around, flew each sweet sound,
> Then darted to the sun;
> Slowly the sounds came back again
> Now mix'd, now one by one.

Yet this central harmony, if true, would render only more perplexing the significance of a universe that can so effectively hide its meaning. Much of the poem's power comes in fact from complex movements between opposites such as terror and peace, between

> Like one that on a lonesome road
> Doth walk in fear and dread,
> And having once turned round walks on,
> And turns no more his head . . .

'The Mariners', an engraving by David Jones from the 1929 edition of Coleridge's The Ryme of the Ancyent Marinere.

and

> This seraph-band, each waved his hand:
> No voice did they impart –
> No voice; but oh! the silence sank
> Like music on my heart.

Coleridge had here discovered what amounted to a new way of writing poetry, a play of mind which liberated his poetic powers to perform at their finest. He reached a similar level in the first part of the poem begun immediately afterwards, *Christabel*, where the problem of allowing innocence to survive and flourish in a world where nature's energies act ambiguously and amorally is personified in the encounter between the innocent Christabel and the enigmatic Geraldine, who at times is 'most beautiful to see / Like a ladie of a far countree' yet who hides a nameless horror beneath her fine clothes. This complex idea was even more hard to work than that of the *Mariner*, however, for here the plot demanded a resolution: the poem remained tantalisingly incomplete, a piquant fragment which would prompt such different kinds of reworking as Keats's 'The Eve of St Agnes' and Byron's 'Parisina'. In the third 'supernatural' poem of that time, *Kubla Khan*, the wished-for completion was in a single final stanza presented as simply accomplished: the ambivalent nature of the Tartar ruler, projecting beautiful landscape gardens yet riven by his knowledge that the destructive powers in nature were imaged in himself ('A woman wailing for her daemon lover', 'ancestral voices prophesying war') evanesced into the reconciling and eclipsing power of the inspired Apollonian poet, effortlessly enforcing his vision on all who saw and heard him.

Kubla Khan, which remained in manuscript for nearly twenty years, raised questions concerning the status of the visionary imagination that did not cease to agitate Coleridge's mind. Soon after writing it he spent a winter in Germany, where he learned at close quarters of major developments in subjects such as philosophy, physiology and biblical studies. On his return he alternated between London journalism, commenting on the immediate political issues of the day, and recondite researches into psychological matters. His growing suspicion that his poetic powers were declining, or at least in abeyance, along with the advent of a hopeless love for Wordsworth's sister-in-law Sara Hutchinson, resulted in the verse letter to her which he later abridged and etched into 'Dejection: An Ode' – addressed now to Wordsworth and published on his wedding-day.

In 'Dejection', Coleridge takes stock of his poetic powers and their current decline. They are not failing him completely, of course; the very poem he is writing displays skills operating at a very high level. What he feels to be 'suspended' is, explicitly, his 'shaping spirit of imagination' – that spirit which would give overall form to what he is doing. But if his habit of analysis and investigation has now taken over his whole mind, instead of being a valuable tool for his larger powers to employ, that is, he believes, the result of his domestic unhappiness and resulting decline of joy.

The problems could be stated but not resolved in the poem, as in Coleridge's own life, so that resort to his analytic powers would become, whether he liked it or not, his most available mode. After the break with Wordsworth in 1810 he relied still more on such resources. In future he would become remarkable among his contemporaries not only for his poetry but for his literary criticism.

Coleridge's Shakespearean lectures first established his reputation in this sphere, being notable among other things for his use of psychological comments on the actions of the characters and on the role of the audience. It was in *Biographia Literaria* (1817), however, that he endeavoured to set forth at length his principles as a critic and to provide some justification for his career so far. Characteristically, he presented this autobiography in a mixed form, veering between discursive anecdotes of his early life and abstruse philosophy. His dilemma was by now a familiar one: on the intellectual plane he wished to reconcile the aesthetic with the moral, by suggesting that what was most deeply true of our emotional response to literature was a key to our appreciation of the moral universe; yet while such a reconciliation called for almost superhuman powers, he knew himself to be – more than most, perhaps – a fallible mortal. Accordingly the work ranges between self-deprecating reminiscence and high aspiration.

The key, if there is one, lies in the divine supremacy of imagination, but that is precisely what he cannot demonstrate: after some intricate philosophical discussion, therefore, he breaks off to present a brief and portentous pair of paragraphs at the end of chapter 13 which are at once dazzling and riddling. Imagination he distinguishes from fancy in terms of the kinds of powers that are invoked by each; he also distinguishes between different levels within imaginative activity. Readers are left to make what they will of these subtly worded and pregnant hints, while Coleridge moves on into a more readily accessible mode with his long and detailed analysis of Wordsworth's poetry, its qualities and its defects.

In later life Coleridge became a strangely haunted figure, turning increasingly to theological questions. Here his emphasis was still the same: how far could his readers get towards the truth by exploring their own faculties? Coleridge remained convinced out of his own experience that those who looked deep into their own consciousness while also committing themselves to the Christian faith would find doubt disappearing in a new assurance of their truth. To many in his age this was welcome news; others, however, were to try the experiment themselves only to find that their scepticism had not after all dispersed.

The final stages of his life saw Coleridge in a double role: on the one hand increasingly looked up to as a Christian sage, pointing the way forward to those who found themselves in religious doubt, on the other an elderly poet writing plangently but memorably about his condition in old age. Titles such as 'Work without Hope', 'The Pang more sharp than All', 'Duty surviving Self-love' and 'Love's Burial-place' tell their own story, which is perhaps best summed up in another poem, entitled 'Love's Apparition and Evanishment', where the poet, sitting in a garden that reminds him of his lost love, imagines himself visited first by lost Hope:

> And then came Love, a sylph in bridal trim,
> And stood beside my seat;

> She bent, and kiss'd her sister's lips,
> As she was wont to do; –
> Alas! 'twas but a chilling breath
> Woke just enough of life in death
> To make Hope die anew.

This theme of 'life in death', which had been at its most active when he wrote *The Ancient Mariner* and which had realised itself in unforeseen ways in his later life, survives even into his final 'Epitaph' (1833), where he solicits a prayer for himself,

> That he who many a year with toil of breath
> Found death in life, may here find life in death!

Even here the seeking for eternal life in the Christian sense carries echoes of earlier thinking, when his sense of the 'one Life' had not only stimulated the writing of some of his finest poems but had caused him to look at the stirrings of life in nature and human consciousness in a new way, seeking out the relationship between them. In the search for that elusive connection had lain the germ of his greatest achievements.

Jane Austen: pleasures and principles

Like Coleridge, Jane Austen (1775–1817) was brought up in a country parsonage. Although her range of intellectual abilities did not show the extraordinary breadth of his (in that respect George Eliot was to provide a better parallel) she was similarly precocious, her sharp powers of observation prompting her to a good-tempered comedy seasoned, at times, by merciless perceptions of human weakness.

In her lifetime the star of the English gentry was at its zenith. That class, consisting primarily of military and naval officers, landowners and clergy, had established its ascendancy at the time of the 1688 Revolution and had been consolidating its position ever since. Among other things, it defined itself by an unwillingness to assimilate those who were engaged in trade. The progress of Jane Austen's brothers, two of whom became admirals, bore witness to the social mobility that was possible within her own class, on the other hand. She also had connections – though not close ones – with the nobility.

Current events in France had a strong significance for the gentry as a whole. So long as the ideals of the French Revolution were presented as offering an enlargement of 'liberty' they could accept them with equanimity. The aims of 'equality' and 'fraternity' were more dubious, on the other hand. The Napoleonic wars, still more threatening, soon affected the gentry in other ways. Military and naval men were in great danger, yet might also achieve unusually rapid promotion. Religious observance became increasingly important to a class which believed that the disastrous course of events in France had been precipitated by the failings of the French aristocracy, with their absenteeism, their lack of social responsibility and their disregard for the moral teachings of religion. The appropriate lessons must be learnt if England was not to suffer the same fate. The static nature of the agricultural economy made it hard to believe that any general economic improvement (as opposed to the relief of hardship enjoined upon Christians) could take place, and this view was reinforced by the writings of Malthus, who saw attempts at economic betterment as doomed to exacerbate the very problem they sought to solve by increasing even more rapidly the number of mouths to be fed. On this view of the matter all that could be prescribed was a combination of morality and self-restraint among the well-to-do, along with measures that might make and keep the lower orders content with their lot.

This reading of the social state, though not to be ratified in later history, appeared logical enough at a time when the full implications of industrialism were not fully understood. Accordingly, the dominant classes lent their support to the calls for an increased sense of social responsibility and religious devoutness from Evangelical Christians such as Hannah More and Wilberforce. The small part played by religion in most of Jane Austen's novels is at first sight surprising, therefore, particularly as their satires on the clergy might be thought to encourage an irreverent disposition. Such things can be explained partly by her known tendency to reticence, no doubt; the fact is, however, that her attitude to religion also shifted with the times. Whereas she had written in 1809 'I do not like the Evangelicals', by 1814 she was saying 'I am by no means convinced that we ought not all to be Evangelicals'.

From the first her prime instinct led her to a kind of wit that was peculiarly suited to the written page, calling for a leisured lingering over the ironies of particular phrases. It is not for nothing that she has become supreme among authors to whom readers turn back. Her wit has much in common with Pope's ('There has been one infallible Pope in the world', she once wrote), particularly where he shares her aim of reconciliation. The serious point of her novel *Pride and Prejudice* is to show these two human characteristics, so often the means of separation between people, being transposed into more humane versions of themselves, principle now matched by right judgement. These are older and more traditional failings; in *Sense and Sensibility*, where she scrutinises qualities more germane to the eighteenth century, the aim is slightly different: she follows Johnson in upholding the superiority of sense over a cult of sensibility that could too easily become self-enclosing, but is sufficiently a child of her age to intimate that the enhancement of sensibility and sympathy is not to be undervalued.

The experience of reading these novels is not what such a diagrammatic account might suggest. Very often the reader's admiration comes, locally, from the exact placing of words, a mastery which she again shares with Pope. There are times when the spirit of comedy takes over almost completely, times also when the mordancy of the commentary is breathtaking, as when she records that Mrs Bennet 'was a woman of mean understanding, little information, and uncertain temper'. Sometimes, indeed, she allowed her wit free rein in a manner which might seem to contravene the Christian bidding to charitableness. But when in her private letters her vein of satire ran into cruelty, she could offer the excuse that the letters were intended for one person alone, who would understand the spirit in which they were written.

Although Jane Austen makes comparatively few direct references to current political issues, she evidently knew well what was going on in England at the time. Accustomed as she was to read newspapers and journals she could not have totally ignored the political sections, particularly when many of her relatives were serving in the armed forces. In her society women were expected not to discuss politics and she seems to have honoured the embargo – perhaps not without wry amusement that feminine minds of the calibre of her own were being thus barred. Her own comments, when they come, tend to be general, but should not be discounted on that score. When she writes to her sister on 31 May 1811 about the battle of Albuera, 'How horrible it is to have so many people killed! – And what a blessing that one cares for none of them!' the second part of the sentence is not a callous retraction of her feelings, rather an intensification ('How terrible it is to have so many killed, and how finally unbearable it would be if someone one cared for personally were among them').

The actual dates of composition of her novels (as opposed to the dates of their publication) make it clearer still that she was in tune with the dominant currents of the time. The contemporary call to religious seriousness by Evangelicals, which acquired further urgency from the events of wartime, influenced the composition of *Mansfield Park*, begun in 1811, where the adherence to principle that Wordsworth and Coleridge were also encouraging at the time is a paramount issue. In this novel the heroine Fanny Price is presented as a girl without immediate attractiveness who is also looked down upon by the inhabitants of Mansfield Park (where she is a poor relative); yet she slowly wins her uncle's favour by her seriousness and her insistence on propriety during his absence from home. The novel has divided critics: some admire Fanny Price for her integrity, reading the novel as a fine and subtle moral statement, while others find the life of the novel to be with the Crawfords, the gay and worldly brother and sister whose irruption into Mansfield Park sets events in motion and who might be seen as bringing a breath of fresh air into a shrine of staid and sterile forms. Current concerns of the time had left their mark here more firmly than elsewhere.

No such dilemmas greet the reader of *Emma*. By the time she began this in 1814, the climate in England had changed dramatically. The anxieties of the Peninsular War had given place to decisive victories, while at home the Regency had brought a spirit of relaxation. The extraordinary flowering of English literature in the subsequent years owed a great deal to the atmosphere thus created. Although *Emma* is demonstrably a novel in which moral concerns figure, they have not the same weight as in *Mansfield Park* – nor, for that matter, is there a formal pairing of qualities on the model of the earliest novels. The juxtaposition here, which is of a subtler kind, is between the human failings of someone who is still growing up and the right judgement of an older man who seems morally faultless. The fact that Emma's failings are so forgivable and she so vital a presence means that the moral conventions of society press less hard on the reader, who is drawn in to the subtle but more rewarding exercise of a judging sympathy. It is a process akin to Coleridge's divergence into criticism: the atmosphere of *Emma* witnesses to a new kind of freedom – an unjarring atmosphere of comedy and even indulgence – which is yet quite without moral capitulation.

The critical spirit, once given rein, could not in future be completely subdued. *Persuasion*, her last completed novel, presents a situation more complex than any of the previous ones; the heroine has suffered years of unhappiness through being persuaded by her counsellor, Lady Russell, to relinquish the man she loved. The judgement of the woman to whose opinions she owed the deepest respect proved fallible. Happily the novel's events finally bring her to marriage with the same man and she is able to reconcile herself to her wasted years with the reflection that if she had not submitted, 'I should have suffered more in continuing the engagement than I did even in giving it up, because I should have suffered in my conscience'. She admits, nevertheless, that she would never herself give such advice. The divergence between ordination and right judgement is thus exposed openly to the reader's questioning.

There is a similar ambiguity in her last novel, *Sanditon*, which was left uncompleted (and probably unrevised) in manuscript. The strongest and clearest topic in the book is Sanditon itself, a village being newly reconstituted as a seaside resort and so the precise opposite to the kind of rooted and established place which Jane Austen herself valued. The characters who bustle through her pages, 'improving' here, planning a 'Waterloo Crescent' there, are wide open to satire. Yet there is a crucial hesitation, for Jane Austen also displays a feeling for the energy of these creatures; there is an innocence about their busybodying, and even about their valetudinarianism, which might have heralded further subtleties. At one point in her manuscript she allowed herself the judgement 'this disease of activity', only to cancel it in favour of the more ambiguous 'this strange restlessness of activity'. Blake held that a true artist was of the devil's party, even if unconsciously, for he was on the side of creative energy. Was there an element in Jane Austen's literary creativity, too, which found itself in complicity with new making – even if the result was no more than a seaside resort?

The point may be pursued a stage further. When Catherine Morland attends her first ball only to find her pleasure countered by the anonymity of the company, so that 'she could not relieve the irksomeness of her imprisonment by the exchange of a syllable with any of her fellow-captives', or when Maria Bertram echoes Sterne's sentiment in her words 'I cannot get out, as the starling said', how far do the echoes extend in their author's mind? At a self-conscious level, perhaps, she would contend only that liberty is not to be found in ballrooms or in the heedless world of the Crawfords. True liberty she would have located in a well-appointed room, and like George Herbert she would have believed not in escaping from one's cell but in finding the right way to illuminate it. In the end all was contained and where necessary modified by the work of what more than one critic has called her 'loving intelligence'. The attractions of energy were all about her, however, and as an artist she could hardly escape their implications altogether.

Hazlitt and the logic of liberty

Like Coleridge and Jane Austen, William Hazlitt (1778–1830) came from a 'clerical' family – but with a crucial difference. Whereas they were both born into the Anglican Church, and so into a social establishment which included the local gentry, he was brought up among the dissenters, and the academy he attended, Hackney New College, was at that time (1793–5) in a turbulent state, with various supporters of the principles of the French Revolution in its midst. Where such enthusiasts had been checked by news of the violence in France, moreover, they now found a new rallying point in Godwin's *Political Justice*, published in 1793, which turned those principles to non-violent purposes by proclaiming the importance of benevolence as an under-rated human resource.

Years later, Hazlitt was to look back on the heyday of Godwin's influence with nostalgia. In an essay on him which he placed, pointedly, at the beginning of his collection *The Spirit of The Age* (1825), he recalled in rhapsodic tones how young men had given up their prospects in the professions for the sake of the new disinterestedness. 'Is this sun of intellect blotted from the sky? . . . Or is it we who make the fancied gloom, by looking at it through the paltry, broken, stained fragments of our own interests and prejudices?' Hazlitt himself gave up the prospect of an assured living as a unitarian minister, and never relinquished the generous view of human nature which he had imbibed during those years. Instead, he opened himself to any powerful and humane experiences that might offer themselves. The acting of Mrs Siddons and the writings of Rousseau, for example, seized his emotions and imagination. Less predictable was the effect of Burke, whose eloquence struck him as indisputably great, however profoundly he might disagree with him politically. Early in 1798 the personality of Coleridge made its first, ineffaceable impression when, after hearing him preach at Shrewsbury, he seized gratefully on an invitation to visit him in Somerset and met Wordsworth as well. To that visit we owe the best account of the two poets at the height of their creative powers, the essay 'My First Acquaintance With Poets'. He later claimed that he owed to Coleridge the awakening of his creative powers.

Yet it was not to literature that he had immediately turned for a vocation then. His journey of self-discovery took him naturally to Paris – attracted not primarily to the Paris of politics, but to the Paris of art. During the fragile peace of 1802–3 he spent the daylight hours studying and copying the treasures – especially from Italy – that Napoleon had brought to the Louvre. Despairing at succeeding in art he then turned to philosophy and produced an anonymous *Essay on the principles of human action* (1805), in which, following Godwin, he argued for the 'natural disinterestedness of the human mind'.

This idea runs through the whole of Hazlitt's writings, providing a line of consistency in what might otherwise seem a strange melange of jostling ideas. It explains his preoccupation with egotism – a human characteristic towards which he could, in harmony with his principles, show understanding but which he could not condone, and which he noted in writers as diverse as Rousseau and Wordsworth.

The failure of his *Essay* to attract attention was a source of disappointment; it was only gradually that he discerned in the essay form itself, shortened and transformed, a medium perfectly suited to his gifts, allowing him at one and the same time to indulge his altruism and to delight in memories of his own past. His most impressive pieces have a strong autobiographical element, combining elements of self-deprecation with a desire to share his enjoyment of life. If he enjoyed the cultivated pursuits of reading and painting, he also delighted in popular pleasures, such as watching Indian jugglers or going to see a fight in the country.

Pedestrianism, which had been one of the enterprises of equality in his youth, is praised in a piece entitled 'On going a journey'. Yet there is an important qualification to this apparent taste for the demotic, conveyed in its first sentence: 'One of the pleasantest things in the world is going a journey; but I like to go by myself'. At this point the Romantic solitary separates himself decisively from the radical who would not only delight in all human society but accept all human company at its own valuation. Hazlitt's ill-starred passion for Sarah Walker, the daughter of his landlady, recorded in his *Liber Amoris* (1823), displays the contradictions inherent in such a position. On the one hand he could congratulate himself on a genuinely classless love, yet that attachment was based on an idealising of its object, a making of Sarah something other than she would ever be. Hazlitt, the apostle of liberty, had not, in other words, perceived the need to allow another individual to choose her own form of independence.

One of the most fascinating features of the book is its unashamed element of self-exposure, Rousseauian but still rare. His approach is captivating in a quite different way from Jane Austen's, where the art lies rather in concealing emotions while hinting at full cognisance of their existence. The key term in his aesthetic vocabulary was 'gusto', an idea which sprang from his belief (which he regarded as a major discovery) that the association of ideas, then so popular as a means of explaining human behaviour, tended to be traced within one sense at a time, whereas the kind of association which he found truly memorable was that involving more than one sense. Everyone might admire a sunset, but a particular individual would be enabled to summon up that sunset more vividly by remembering the touch of dew on the hands and the fact that he or she had been reading Rousseau at the time. The importance of this for Hazlitt was that it helped deliver the individual from subordination to an abstract philosophy which nourishes itself thinly on the isolation of sense-experiences.

His essay 'The Fight' brings out an element in Hazlitt which shows him still more decisively the member of a new generation: his delight in intensity. During the fight itself the two combatants proved their heroism by their willingness to come back from near defeat and to take further punishment until one of them 'was not like an actual man, but like a preternatural, spectral appearance, or like one of the figures in Dante's *Inferno*'. His appreciation of such intensity, where energy turned into an essence of itself, was responsible for his delight in Edmund Kean's acting – indeed, it was an account of his that seems first to have made Kean's reputation. The general impression was of one who could be, on stage, 'all passion, all energy, all restless will'. But the energy of passion was not the most terrific part: 'it is the agony of his soul, shewing itself in looks and tones of voice'.

If asked to define his values for himself Hazlitt would probably have chosen the two that he ascribed to his own father: truth and liberty; these, rather than social justice, were his guiding lights. But his delight in energy extended to his political views as well, and particularly to Napoleon, where the belief that the French Revolution had initiated a crucial new phase in human affairs coloured his view so strongly as to excuse all the excesses of his career: the defeat of Napoleon, generally an occasion of rejoicing in England, was for him a disaster. In time some other progressive thinkers would reach similar conclusions as they surveyed post-Napoleonic Europe in the cold light of day, but in the immediate aftermath of Waterloo Hazlitt's attitude was unacceptable to his contemporaries and responsible for his vilification in rival journals. One result was that to this day he has always enjoyed something of a subterranean reputation.

Keats's disinterested intensities

The temporary decline of London as a literary centre which took place at the turn of the century was accompanied by a division along social and political lines. While the Whig Holland House set and the associated group around Samuel Rogers regarded themselves as arbiters of taste, other and younger men believed themselves entitled to look for a new kind of art to meet the demands of a new age. Far from assuming that the only possible response to the violent events in France was to return to older principles, they saw that calamity as a false departure from noble ideals, which now cried out to be fulfilled in other, non-violent ways.

John Keats (1795–1821), son of an ostler and born into a family with mixed social connections, exemplified the new kind of writer. His first literary discoveries were made at school and in the company of the schoolmaster's son Charles Cowden Clarke, with whom he kept up his friendship when he became apprenticed to a surgeon. At this time his enthusiasms, like those of the young Blake thirty years earlier, were for writers such as the Elizabethans and the early Milton, with Spenser a particular favourite.

By the time he began writing, reading of his contemporaries had reinforced the hope that a decisive change was at work in the culture. In 1816, his sonnet 'Great spirits now on earth are sojourning . . .' closed with lines in which (breaking the sonnet form) he tried to seize the new spirit of the age:

> These, these will give the world another heart
> And other pulses. Hear ye not the hum
> Of mighty workings? —
> Listen awhile ye nations, and be dumb.

The three major figures of the sonnet – delineated without being named – were Wordsworth, Leigh Hunt and the painter Benjamin Haydon. Leigh Hunt (1784–1859), then coming into prominence for his radical political and literary views, influenced Keats strongly for a time, and published some of his first writings. The friendship did not assist Keats's reputation, since Hunt was under fire not only for his political views but for what were seen as vulgarisms in his verse, and the appearance of similar lines from Keats led to the two poets being grouped together as 'the Cockney School'. Keats's

pleasure in physical sensuousness went further than Hunt's, leading to forms
of expression which, while attractive in their openness, were vulnerable to
ridicule. Class-associated attacks on Hunt ('He talks indelicately like a tea-
sipping milliner girl') could in 1818 be directed still more virulently against
one who was known to have been a surgeon's apprentice: ' . . . so back to the
shop Mr John, back to "plasters, pills, and ointment boxes" &c.'.

In spite of the crassness and unfairness of such criticisms, which, as several
correspondents were quick to point out, ignored the emergence of an
uncommon poetic talent, some of the criticisms were not altogether unfair.
The unfortunate effect of being bracketed so firmly with Hunt, however, was
to subject Keats to blanket condemnation just at the time when his own
powers were developing and expanding to an extraordinary degree. His
writings in the intervening period – and particularly his letters – had already
displayed an intelligence outsoaring anything that he had learnt from Hunt.

A new and potent presence in this process had been Hazlitt, admired by
Keats for his 'depth of taste'. Keats read his contributions to Hunt's
Examiner, attended his lectures and met him personally; his letters show him
exploring Hazlitt's ideas and extending them. The importance of liberty was
so obvious to him that it hardly needed arguing; but although in September
1819 he declared a wish to contribute something to 'the Liberal side of the
Question' before he died, he recognised from an early stage that to be
politically free was not the same thing as to 'feel' free. This had more to do,
perhaps, with the images of life that he set out in his poem *Sleep and Poetry*:

> The light uplifting of a maiden's veil;
> A pigeon tumbling in clear summer air;
> A laughing school-boy, without grief or care,
> Riding the springy branches of an elm.

(ll.92–5)

Equally relevant were his question and answer in *Endymion* (1818):

> Wherein lies happiness? In that which becks
> Our ready minds to fellowship divine,
> A fellowship with essence, till we shine
> Full alchemized, and free of space. Behold
> The clear religion of heaven!

(i, 777–81)

Such passages develop Hazlitt's 'liberty and truth', taking in his other ideas.
His 'Gusto' becomes 'relish', focusing more upon the sensuous and
particularising its qualities with loving care. Keats's object was not simply to
dwell on the pleasure of the senses but to trace and try to capture in that
pleasure what was 'essential' – in the literal sense of the word.

Keats also showed Hazlitt's feeling for intensity of experience. Commenting
on one of Benjamin West's pictures in December 1817 he wrote:

It is a wonderful picture, when West's age is considered. But there is nothing to be
intense upon; no woman one feels mad to kiss; no face swelling into reality. The
excellence of every Art is its intensity, capable of making all disagreeables evaporate,
from their being in close relationship with Beauty & Truth . . .

He then went on to cite *King Lear* as a work exemplifying this principle throughout, which for Keats meant something precise – a certain kind of focused energy that was valuable in guiding one to the essences of things.

This train of thought is important for the understanding of the concepts of Beauty and Truth, which were for a time at the centre of his thought. In April 1818 he asserted that he had no feeling of humility towards anyone or anything – except 'the eternal Being, the Principle of beauty, – and the Memory of great Men'. The point of the last phrase had already been clarified in a letter: 'Men of Genius are great as certain etherial Chemicals operating on the Mass of neutral intellect – . . . they have not any individuality, any determined Character'. In 1820 he looked back over his brief career: 'I have left no immortal work behind me . . .but I have lov'd the principle of beauty in all things, and if I had had time I would have made myself remember'd'. This degree of intentness on a particular aim took Hazlitt's feeling for energy to a new level. He could also share Hazlitt's more general feeling for the intensities of common human experience. 'Though a quarrel in the streets is a thing to be hated,' he wrote in 1819, 'the energies displayed in it are fine; the commonest Man shows a grace in his quarrel'. In the same letter he maintained that 'there is an electric fire in human nature tending to purify'. He wanted to tease out this perception still further, however. In his 'Ode on a Grecian Urn' (1820), for instance, he was to puzzle future critics by its concluding message:

> 'Beauty is truth, truth beauty' – that is all
> Ye know on earth, and all ye need to know.

The lines offer themselves to be turned round in the mind as one might turn the urn itself, seeing it from different points of view. If it is taken simply to mean that beauty and truth are interchangeable, however, its value as a message to mankind is questionable. Keats, who felt more than most for human suffering, would hardly have lent himself to such a general interpretation. The lines need to be read rather in the light of the poem as a whole, which begins with quiet contemplation of the urn itself ('foster-child of silence and slow time') yet reaches an early climax by entering into the very energies of the scene that is depicted on it, where the pursuit of maiden by lover is held at a moment near consummation:

> Bold lover, never, never canst thou kiss
> Though winning near the goal – yet do not grieve:
> She cannot fade, though thou hast not thy bliss,
> Forever wilt thou love, and she be fair!

The tension between the relishing of such ardour and the pleasure of seeing it made permanent dominates the final 'Beauty is truth, truth beauty', a statement not about the nature of the universe at large but about the ideal to which human experience should aspire. 'I never can feel certain of any truth but from a clear perception of its Beauty', he wrote elsewhere: it was in the ardent pursuit of the essences of things that one might hope to reach a state where 'all disagreeables evaporate, from their being in close relationship with Beauty & Truth'. The last lines of the ode itself can be properly read only by

'What pipes and timbrels? What wild ecstasy?' The Borghese Vase, a Roman replica in Pentelic marble, 1st century BC, *of a Grecian urn.*

way of response to the poem in its entirety – which includes entering imaginatively into the energies of the 'mad pursuit'.

Even so the silent urn retains its enigma. Keats once acknowledged that he carried 'all matters to an extreme'; he also knew that reaching the extreme would not necessarily produce summation of pleasure. In the ode human passion can leave no more than

> . . . a heart high-sorrowful and cloyed,
> A burning forehead and a parching tongue.

> (11.29–30)

The pursuit of the extreme of luxury, similarly, was likely to produce a state not of satisfaction but of melancholy. Keats could be relaxed about pleasure, as with his love of claret ('the only palate affair that I am at all sensual in'), but he also believed that, as he put it in the 'Ode on Melancholy' (1820):

> in the very temple of Delight
> Veiled Melancholy has her sovran shrine . . .

This reflection, coupled with his belief in ardour, led on to a fascination with death itself, the experience in which the union of beauty and truth might be finally experienced. Writing to Fanny Brawne, with whom he was hopelessly in love during the last period of his life, he said on one occasion, 'I have two luxuries to brood over in my walks, your Loveliness and the hour of my death. O that I could have possession of them both in the same minute'. A month or two earlier, in March 1819, he had written the sonnet beginning 'Why did I laugh tonight?' which ended with the couplet

> Verse, fame, and beauty are intense indeed,
> But Death's intenser – Death is Life's high meed.

Such statements take to a logical extreme Keats's desire for an intensity of experience that would not be negated in the sequel. In the 'Ode to a Nightingale' (1820), a poem as intense in its passiveness as was the 'Ode on a Grecian Urn' in its projection of activity, his delight in the bird's song leads on to numbness and an aching of the heart – an experience such as to make death within such a setting seem a luxury. The reflection that while human beings die the nightingale's song does not diverts him to a different train of thought, however, in which the full enchantment awakened by the bird is evoked only to end with the word 'forlorn', tolling the poet back to a sense of his human isolation (like that of Milton's Adam 'In these wild woods forlorn'). The poem ends not in rapture but in a question:

> Was it a vision or a waking dream?
> Fled is that music . . . Do I wake or sleep?

Once again Keats finds himself teased out of thought – a state which is, nevertheless, 'like eternity'.

In these ways Keats took Hazlitt's delight in energy, gusto and intensity to new extremes. Hazlitt's belief in 'disinterestedness', similarly, was echoed and developed in his extraordinary power of empathy with the person to whom he was talking or writing – or with other living beings for that matter: 'The setting sun will always set me to rights', he wrote in 1817, 'or if a Sparrow come before my Window I take part in its existence and pick about the Gravel'. It could even extend into the world of objects: Richard Woodhouse reported how he could 'conceive a billiard Ball to be soothed by a sense of its own smoothness & feel pleasure from a consciousness of its own smoothness – & the rapidity of its Motion'.

If Keats could 'intensify' his consciousness to an extreme, in other words, he could also 'extensify' it by entering into the being of others. Intensity is not absent from the letters, at least when he is writing to those whom he knows will appreciate what he is doing; but such passages are embedded in writing notable for the display of a debonair insouciance and a power to look at himself humorously from the outside. In a letter of March 1819 a self-description containing germs for the 'Ode on Indolence' ('Neither Poetry, nor Ambition, nor Love have any alertness of countenance as they pass by me . . .') is preceded by this description of the state itself:

. . . a delightful sensation about three degrees on this side of faintness – if I had teeth of pearl and the breath of lilies I should call it langour – but as I am I must call it Laziness . . .

Keats's ability to match intensity of emotion with disinterested play of mind sometimes undermined his endeavours towards a coherent whole. His long poem 'Hyperion' worked towards a climax in which the young Apollo would realise his own essence in the act of 'dying into life'. This soaring beyond the human was abandoned by Keats, however, to be replaced by a new version, entitled 'The Fall of Hyperion' (1819), in which human sympathy was paramount, the poet's role being defined not by aspiration but

by the ability to enter into and feel the sufferings of others. As the prophetess
Moneta warns him,

> 'None can usurp this height ...,
> But those to whom the miseries of the world
> Are misery, and will not let them rest.'

(ll.147–9)

This poem too remained unfinished, foreshadowing the final intensity of
Keats's subsequent illness and death. The play of his mind, as shown in the
great Odes, emerged more extensively in the peaceful 'Ode to Autumn'
(1820), which is united by a rhythm corresponding to that of the earthly
seasons which it vividly evokes, and the late poem 'Bright star', where the
state of the human body in a trance-like state is matched with features of the
external world, the movement of the sea and the mask of snow on moors and
mountains being the predominant linking images. Keats's fascination with the
relationship between stillness and movement, evident in the 'Ode on a
Grecian Urn', here reaches a marvellous culmination in which steadfastness
and change, chastity and passion, constantly move in and out of one another.

Keats's response to ebbings and flowings in nature was closely related to
his belief in the importance of the human heart, which by its rhythmic
control of the bloodstream performs a function similar to that of the tides on
a cosmic scale. This sense of the heart as centre (echoing Wordsworth's 'We
have all of us one human heart', a line he quoted approvingly) gave him in
turn both resting-place and a point of reference. It was one of his misgivings,
on the other hand, that his outgoing nature seemed at times to deprive him of
his identity as a person. The experience of being in a room where the
identities of everyone else pressed upon him so hard that he found it hard to
realise his own was familiar to him, and led to a shift of emphasis in his
thought.

While 'Bright star' is in continuity with Keats's early poetic aspirations,
'The Fall of Hyperion' shows the extent of this shift. In 1817, he had
produced an 'innocent' version of his ideas which still came home to essence:

I am certain of nothing but of the holiness of the Heart's affections and the truth of
Imagination – What the imagination seizes as Beauty must be truth – whether it
existed before or not – for I have the same Idea of all our Passions as of Love they are
all in their sublime, creative of essential Beauty . . .

By 1819, however, his further reflections on human identity, and the
pressures laid on human beings by their circumstances, had led him to
formulate his own version of identity by way of questions about the
relationship between the human soul and the world in which it was forced to
live:

. . . what was his soul before it came into the world and had These provings and
alterations and perfectionings? – An Intelligence – without Identity – and how is this
Identity to be made? Through the medium of the Heart? And how is the heart to
become this Medium but in a world of Circumstances?

In the journey from the first affirmation to the second series of questionings,
made in the world of 'experience', can be found the central story of Keats's
career as a poet during those years.

Shelley's search for correspondences

While Keats had to make his way largely through his own literary efforts, Percy Bysshe Shelley (1792–1822) had enjoyed a childhood environment like Jane Austen's and then been sent to Eton College, where he became an example of a breed not extinct to this day, the Etonian radical.

Like Keats he grew up when the belief in human liberty seemed to call only for further definition and refinement. In this context, the growing contemporary interest in science proved a heady brew during his years at Oxford, his enthusiasm for the kind of rapprochement between various kinds of knowledge that Coleridge had sought in his early poetry being unqualified by Coleridge's respect for Christian orthodoxy. Thomas Taylor's translations from the Platonists joined in his mind with the new discoveries in electricity and chemistry to suggest a new and more optimistic view of man. The philosophy of necessity, handled cautiously by those who wished to retain a belief in the Will of God, presented no such obstacles to Shelley, who firmly called his early pamphlet, published while he was still at Oxford, *The Necessity of Atheism*. The fact that he was using the word 'necessity' in its strict philosophical sense did not save him from expulsion.

From early youth Shelley was a rebel in politics, totally possessed by the ideal of freedom that had for a time captivated the previous generation. Throughout his career he wrote in favour of the radical view, making himself unpopular with the governing classes but protected by his own wealth from disaster. Chartists and others who pursued the rights of the labouring classes later in the century would remember with gratitude verses such as his 'Mask of Anarchy', composed soon after the Peterloo massacre in 1819, including its mordant portrayal of contemporary statesmen:

> I met Murder on the way —
> He had a mask like Castlereagh —
> Very smooth he looked, yet grim;
> Seven bloodhounds followed him . . .
>
> Next came Fraud, and he had on,
> Like Eldon, an ermined gown;
> His big tears, for he wept well,
> Turned to mill-stones as they fell.
>
> And the little children, who
> Round his feet played to and fro,
> Thinking every tear a gem,
> Had their brains knocked by them.

Those who read Shelley purely for his politics, however, are bound to be somewhat disappointed. From the beginning, like Coleridge, he alternated between a desire to influence current events and a more wary conviction that such an impact, to be effective, could come about only through a change in his contemporaries' view of their own nature. Study of electricity and chemistry convinced him that the universe was a more mysterious place than eighteenth-century thought had allowed for. His aim was to investigate the subtleties of nature along with the subtleties of the human mind in search of points where they might be in harmony. Restoring to people a sense of their unity with nature might encourage them to act from more benevolent motives.

In this respect his poetry takes its point of departure from his immediate predecessors. Coleridge, standing on the cliffs above the sea and invoking the spirit of liberty which, though betrayed by the French, was still active in the movements that stirred both the pines above him and the distant surge of waves out at sea, or brooding on oppression in 'a green and silent spot among the hills' ('O'er stiller place/ No singing sky-lark ever poised himself') was a forerunner, at least obliquely, of the poet who finds powerful emblems of liberty in wind and soaring skylark. Coleridge, indeed, described in Shelley's 'Letter to Maria Gisborne' as

> he who sits obscure
> In the exceeding lustre and the pure
> Intense irradiation of a mind,
> Which, with its own internal lightning blind
> Flags wearily through darkness and despair —
> A cloud-encircled meteor of the air,
> A hooded eagle among blinking owls —

a man who suggested that the light of the mind might be in correspondence with a light at the heart of nature, was a talismanic figure. The idea of the 'correspondent Breeze', used explicitly by Wordsworth in the opening of *The Prelude*, advanced to the status of a major symbol in the 'Ode to the West Wind' (1820), where it does not simply indicate a harmony between mind and nature but is identified with his own aspiring spirit. The autumn wind which helps prepare the ground for new birth in the spring becomes the correlative of the poet's work – needing, like that, to be complemented by illumination.

The brilliance of the writing is at its most intense, in fact, when Shelley is evoking effects of light and reflective clarity:

> Thou who didst waken from his summer dreams
> The blue Mediterranean, where he lay,
> Lulled by the coil of his crystalline streams,
>
> Beside a pumice isle in Baiae's bay,
> And saw in sleep old palaces and towers
> Quivering within the wave's intenser day . . .

The poet's skein of imagery mirrors its subject: quivering in the mind while remaining essentially still, it displays Shelley's more general gifts for clear if etherial imagery and his unerring mastery of poetic movement.

In 1817, offering some criticisms of Shelley's drama *The Cenci*, which he had just received, Keats asked to be forgiven for suggesting 'that you might curb your magnanimity, and "load every rift" of your subject with ore'. It was a shrewd comment, bearing on Shelley's particular habits as a poet while throwing even more light on Keats's own. Shelley's aims were purposively different, however; while Keats sought to seize tangibilities and evoke the sensuous, Shelley looked to the translucencies of things and the operation of subtle energies. A profitable reading of Shelley's poetry will avoid exclusive concentration either on the verbal text as such or on the objective world that the poet is trying to convey; the mind must be tuned, rather, to the pitch of Shelley's – a difficult and unusual task in the twentieth century, when poets and critics alike look for more tangible criteria of judgement. T.S. Eliot could not explain why it was that he had been 'intoxicated by Shelley's poetry at fifteen' yet now found it unreadable.

The fact was that, like Keats, Shelley cultivated a condition of mind in which he believed it could penetrate Nature and discover her secrets. The wonder is not that he failed, but that he succeeded to such an extent. In doing so he lighted on various natural phenomena which conveyed to him elusive correspondences between nature and his own inner feelings. Here again he followed Coleridge, who had been drawn to the inner quality of light that he felt to be revealed best at the moment of sunrise. Shelley's search led him also to the processes of spring, renewing life as the sunrise renews light. The exquisite delicacy of vegetative life in the moment of its renewal was a favourite theme. In the case of *Prometheus Unbound* (1820), Shelley's longest and greatest experiment in educing the subtler forces of nature and showing them to be on the side of human benevolence, he explained that spring itself had been a major power in its composition:

The bright blue sky of Rome, and the effect of the vigorous awakening spring in that divinest climate, and the new life with which it drenches the spirits even to intoxication, were the inspiration of this drama.

Another, more unexpected symbol was the snake, a creature which fascinated more than one Romantic poet, partly because its form and freedom of movement presented a vivid contrast to the eighteenth-century ideal of geometric fixities, partly because it prompted suggestions about the subtle relationship between energy and evil. For Blake, the serpent was a fine emblem of energy at its purest, an essential element in all true humanity but always potentially destructive and liable to work in corruption if not allowed its part in the full life of the human being. Coleridge's sense of the serpent's ambiguity was expressed in his character Geraldine in *Christabel*, at her best a beautiful woman, but at her worst prompting an imitative shrinking of the eye, a hissing, redolent of some hardly to be named evil. Keats, finally, had expressed the elusive beauty of the serpent in his character Lamia, beautiful and glittering, yet withering and disappearing under the cold eye of reason.

Shelley was by no means unresponsive to the suggestions of malevolence in *Christabel*; when he heard it read aloud he rushed from the room, declaring afterwards that he had seen eyes in the breasts of Mary Godwin. But so far as snakes were concerned he delighted particularly in the fact that they sloughed their skins each spring, emblematising beautifully the renewals that were taking place about them. It was his innocent delight in such energies, perhaps, that won him the nickname 'Snake' among his intimates.

Shelley's feeling for nature had nothing of Wordsworth's tentativeness. In his great rhapsodic poem-drama *Prometheus Unbound*, Earth utters her emotions at the rise of Prometheus' free spirit:

I am the Earth,
Thy mother; she within whose stony veins,
To the last fibre of the loftiest tree,
Whose thin leaves trembled in the frozen air,
Joy ran, as blood within a living frame,
When thou didst from her bosom, like a cloud
Of glory, arise, a spirit of keen joy!

Throughout this drama the freedom of the human spirit is aligned with the freedom of nature. The state of the mind, however, is the ultimate key: for the price of physical resistance to tyranny is likely to be further tyranny of one kind or another. When Demogorgon, the mysterious prophetic figure of the poem is asked who made the world, including thought, passion, reason, will and imagination, he replies 'God'. But when he is asked who is responsible for such things as terror, madness, crime and remorse the only answer vouchsafed is 'He reigns'. The power underlying such phenomena has no namable identity; it is simply an energy, to be conquered not by an equivalent force but by the power that works through 'Gentleness, Virtue, Wisdom and Endurance'. Only when Prometheus revokes the curses he has poured out against Jupiter, replacing them with the words 'I wish no living thing to suffer pain', can his unbinding begin.

Shelley, like Blake, saw the creative artist as the figure who worked most surely in the interests of humanity. In his *Defence of Poetry* (1821) he tried to vindicate the forces of love and imagination at a more direct level by showing how they acted in the mind of the true poet. His famous assertion 'Poets are the unacknowledged legislators of mankind' takes eighteenth-century reliance on law and reinterprets it in terms of an imaginative power that works for mankind; while his elegy on the death of Keats, written in the same year under the title *Adonais*, presses the point home. In this poem the mysterious forces of eternity and energy appear in their more familiar forms as light and fire, emerging in the imagery of the concluding twin visions of 'That light whose smile kindles the Universe' and

that sustaining Love
Which through the web of being blindly wove
By man and beast and earth and air and sea,
Burns bright or dim, as each are mirrors of
The fire for which all thirst.

Nowhere does Shelley come closer to finding imagery for the elusive workings he believes to be at the centre of the universe. He concludes his poem with the complementary image of himself as voyager in a bark which draws him away from the human crowd and into a region where the only guide is 'the soul of Adonais, like a star'.

The subtlety and consistency of Shelley's vision are slighted by those who find in his language only vague shapings and impotent yearnings. At the same time it must be acknowledged that he himself was alive to the vulnerability of his views. The disastrous effects of his beliefs on some of those close to him questioned the validity of his vision of the poet as a disregarded prophet who was in touch with the deepest profundities of human nature, impulses to renewal which were bound in the end to surface and issue in human improvement. Something of this uncertainty can be traced in his last, unfinished poem, 'The Triumph of Life', which breaks off not in affirmation but in a question: 'Then what is life? I cried'.

Shelley's death at sea shortly afterwards, sailing into one of the tempests that from time to time rise up in the Mediterranean, was – whether deliberately undertaken or not – a highly emblematic act, putting to the universe the questions he had been wrestling with increasingly during his later career.

Byron: an identity of action

While Keats and Shelley both found themselves moving against the fashionable currents of the age in working out their individual poetic visions, George Gordon, Lord Byron (1788–1824) existed in a more provocative relationship with his audience, testing to the limits his power of flouting contemporary presuppositions about respectability while appeasing his readers with appeals to their sentiments or sense of humour. From the first he spoke to certain kinds of Englishmen and Englishwomen – particularly those who enjoyed the pleasures of sport. More than anywhere else in the poetry of the period we sense physical energy governing the writing and influencing its movement. The skills which his poetic hero Pope had employed in maintaining a conversational flow across the heroic couplets of his Epistles were a chief resource, but he went further, eschewing some of Pope's verbal delicacies in favour of a running stanza that could less afford to linger.

The fact that he was himself a member of the aristocracy assisted the excitement he created, the sense of a man walking the tightrope of public favour while executing gestures of disdain. And since, if Byron allowed himself sexual freedoms in his poetry, these were slight compared to the obscenities in some of the writing and art that flourished just below the public surface in his society, he could also be seen as challenging its hypocrisies.

The Whigs, particularly, found in him a figure to admire. While Samuel Rogers (1763–1855) along with George Crabbe (1754–1832) had always been their favoured poets, Byron was recognised immediately as a genius – the more readily because of his ability to continue where Pope had left off. It was not until 1811 that he was received at Holland House, the centre of Whig fashionable taste, since a hostile review in the *Edinburgh* had stung him to attack those who he thought had instigated it: 'Illustrious Holland! hard would be his lot/ His hirelings mentioned, and himself forgot.' Others who were attacked in *English Bards, and Scotch Reviewers* harboured hostility more permanently.

In 1812 Byron published the first cantos of *Childe Harold*, the poem in which he found a persona for himself as a lonely Romantic hero, travelling through the world and reflecting on what he saw. The first cantos were redolent of the Spenserean stanzas of Thomson and Beattie, but Byron's use of them for a European travelogue marked a new development, corresponding to the growing fashion for travelling. In canto iii (1816), where he brought his writing up to date with long reflections on the field of Waterloo, fought the previous year, Byron perfected this persona, writing openly in the first person as a solitary and haughty exile who could find satisfaction only in the contemplation of sublime European scenery or in pilgrimages to the graves of great and independent figures ranging from ancient Romans to modern thinkers such as Gibbon and Rousseau. In the conclusion, love of Nature is associated with love of Man but in a mode differing sharply from Wordsworth's. After expressing a desire to live in the desert 'with one fair Spirit for my minister', he moves in the direction of pantheism with lines beginning 'There is a pleasure in the pathless woods,/ There is a rapture on the lonely shore . . .' and concludes with an aspiration to 'mingle with the universe'. He makes it clear, nevertheless, that it is by the sea that he entertains such feelings, and the sea, with its powerful energies, is finally identified with himself: 'thou goest forth, dread, fathomless, alone'.

The Byronic hero was to appear in several of his other poems and to win particular approval on the continent of Europe, particularly as he participated in the various contemporary movements for freedom. He won most acclaim, however, for his satirical later verses, including *Don Juan*, begun in 1818, and *The Vision of Judgement* (1821), a satire on Southey's poem of a similar name in which he lambasted the current Laureate for his turn-coat politics. In both he employed a new verse-form which allowed him to conclude with a couplet of elegant disdain or ridicule that could yet be lightened by a touch of the ludicrous, as with the stanza describing the meeting between Satan and Michael in *The Vision of Judgement:*

> . . . Michael and the other wore
> A civil aspect: though they did not kiss,
> Yet still between his Darkness and his Brightness
> There passed a mutual glance of great politeness.

In the years before his death during the Greek War of Independence Byron explored more serious issues – still with his own lonely poetic identity at the centre – in poems such as *Cain* and *The Deformed Transformed*. Meanwhile cantos of Don Juan continued to appear regularly. In due course the story's events took the hero to London, giving Byron a series of opportunities to satirise contemporary English society, and then to 'Norman Abbey', a thinly disguised version of the Newstead Abbey where he himself had been brought up and the scene for some farcical events before the story was broken off by his death.

That death, and the cause for which Byron was fighting at the time, gave the final impetus to a reputation on the continent of Europe which has lasted to the present day. But in any case the dash and verve of his writing, coupled with his cynicism concerning the ultimate value of human life, were likely to make him more readily available internationally than other great English poets of his time. As a lonely noble individualist he was a figure comparable in his own way to Napoleon. Such qualities did not endear him so readily to his own countrymen, who might prefer Wordsworth's appeal to the human heart and his values of duty and affection. Yet the fascination with energy that was increasingly being felt in the culture meant that he would not easily be forgotten. Arnold, who placed Wordsworth first among the poets of the time, was to see Byron as a necessary complementing presence, taking over Algernon Swinburne's praise of him for 'the excellence of sincerity and strength'; John Ruskin began his autobiography by pronouncing himself 'a violent Tory of the old school; Walter Scott's school, that is to say, and Homer's', but before long he was singing the praises of Byron at length and recalling his determination from an early stage that 'Byron was to be my master in verse, as Turner in colour'. The eighth chapter of *Praeterita i* is an eloquent tribute to Byron's significance for those who succeeded him: their sense that his supercilious cynicism was redeemed by a grasp of reality superior to anything in his contemporaries – or indeed his predecessors. Although Byron's delight in energy may have aligned him more naturally with Milton's Satan than with the angels – may, indeed, have rewarded him at times with an equivalent fare of bitter ashes – his feeling for thrust and action made him a natural patron for the cult of chivalry that Ruskin and others were to invoke to counter the utilitarian philosophy of the new age.

The image of a meteor came naturally to those who contemplated his career in retrospect. He himself saw the meteoric forces of life differently, however, as he showed in *Don Juan*:

> O Love! O Glory! what are ye who fly
> Around us ever, rarely to alight?
> There's not a meteor in the polar sky
> Of such transcendent and more fleeting flight.
> Chill, and chained to cold earth, we lift on high
> Our eyes in search of either lovely light;
> A thousand and a thousand colours they
> Assume, then leave us on our freezing way.

'*What*, after all, are *all* things – but a *show*?' he concluded; but even in that brief exposition he had displayed something that might normally escape the superficial reader: a sense of vision that constantly sought to burn through the shams and hypocrisies of his time. It was something that Coleridge, for one, had immediately perceived at their first meeting:

. . . He has the sweetest Countenance that I ever beheld – his eyes are really Portals of the Sun, things for light to go in and out of . . .'

Allowing something for poetic hyperbole, this still suggests what it was that fascinated Byron's contemporaries, creating, in spite of his outrageous behaviour, the sense of a charm which was, in the end, not darkly Satanic but brilliantly illuminating.

A tradition of the heart?

Most of the figures discussed so far believed that a new spirit was abroad, which called for a new kind of writing. Other writers of the time, hardly less important, believed that if a shift was called for it need not be so radical. When George Crabbe (1754–1832) produced works such as *The Village* and

The Borough he was attempting to bring his readers back from the pastoralism of eighteenth-century verse with its idealisation of rustic scenes, to the actualities of places such as Aldeburgh in Suffolk, where he was for a time rector.

> There thistles stretch their prickly arms afar,
> And to the ragged infant threaten war;
> There poppies, nodding, mock the hope of toil,
> There the blue bugloss paints the sterile soil . . .

Such writing directed attention to the conditions of the poor in England, but without implying a need for change. More than anything Crabbe wished to open the eyes of his readers to things as they were (a very different kind of realism from that which Ruskin was to discern in Byron) and for that the verbal exactitude of Pope, latched like his in the heroic couplet, sufficed. Crabbe's is still the vision of an eighteenth-century naturalist attempting to provide an exact record; he cannot avoid a mournful note, however, his most characteristic mode being the elegiac contemplation of a complete career and its significance, as in 'The Vicar' or 'Peter Grimes' in *The Borough*.

Crabbe's vocation as a clergyman took him to a series of livings around London and he would sometimes visit the metropolis itself for society. John Clare (1793–1864) was more intimately bound to his locality, being happiest in the one place, Helpstone, where he had been brought up. His devotion to its landscape amounted in fact to a bonding. He deplored the enclosures of the time for their economic effects but even more because they violated the configurations of the countryside he loved. While he could on occasion speak out against the injustices suffered by the labourers he still felt himself an isolated figure among them, suspected of setting down their affairs in his writings. Whereas Crabbe could draw comfort from the dignified separation which his life as a clergyman ordained, Clare was thrown back on the life of the countryside itself, described with a touching lyricism which could sometimes be unexpectedly pointed in its political implications, as in his poem 'Remembrance':

> Inclosure like a buonaparte let not a thing remain
> It levelled every bush and tree and levelled every hill
> And hung the moles for traitors – though the brook is running still
> It runs a naked stream cold and chill.

(lines 193–6)

In his own way Clare was one of the more extreme English Romantic poets: his poems were published by John Taylor, who also published Keats, and those who opened his volume would have found poetry which was moving far from traditional forms. This was Romantic independence in its purest form, a degree of isolation which he shared only with Blake.

So far as other Romantic writers were concerned there were constant mutual encounters. Wordsworth might seem to be living aloof in the Lake District but he had Coleridge, Southey and Thomas de Quincey living nearby for long periods and was visited by Charles Lamb and Hazlitt, who in turn knew Hunt and Haydon. Keats was in touch with the latter group and was present on the 'glorious evening' when they entertained Wordsworth and drank confusion to the memory of Newton – perhaps the closest England ever came to a declaration in favour of Romanticism. Southey knew Coleridge and Walter Landor; Shelley went to the Lake District in the hope of meeting Coleridge but met Southey instead; Byron encouraged Coleridge and became intimate with Shelley. This widespread network of casual acquaintance had its part to play in diffusing Romantic ideas and practices.

There were also those who were fascinated by the new ideas without being drawn into full participation. Robert Southey (1774–1843), who shared Coleridge's interest in the mythologies of other countries and cultures, and wrote long poems such as 'Thalaba' and 'The Curse of Kehama' which then provided a springboard for more openly Romantic writers such as Byron was one, Thomas Love Peacock (1785–1866), a close friend of Shelley, another. Peacock's view of human nature, though antithetical to Godwin's, was no less kindly: he could not help noticing how self-interest entered into the actions even of those who seemed most unworldly, nor could he resist the comic implications of some of their beliefs. Himself a lover of 'tea, Greek and pedestrianism', he resisted the more soaring motions of his friends and acquaintances. Much as he might enjoy Shelley's platonism he developed his own, un-Socratic, form of the dialogue, delighting in setting off one extravagant opinion against another. Nor was it only contemporary Romanticism that drew his eye: he was even more taken by the absurdities, when taken to an extreme, of pre-Romantic cults such as that of the picturesque. Given also his own delight in language, the idiosyncrasies of which he handled with a meticulous mastery, the way was open for a series of novels such as *Crotchet Castle* (1831) and *Gryll Grange* (1860) which have remained a pleasure to subsequent readers, extravaganzas in which one ludicrously over-developed idea is played off against another within the setting of an eccentric country house.

Charles Lamb (1775–1834), whose acquaintance with Coleridge at school had made him his deepest admirer and his most quizzical friend, had a comic sense to rival Peacock's; but the bounds of Lamb's writing were more irregular, his humour occasionally betraying the stresses to which he was subject. Having been present on the dreadful occasion when his sister Mary murdered their mother in a fit of insanity, Lamb took on himself the responsibility of looking after her and collaborated with her in some works, including the celebrated *Tales from Shakespeare*.

It is not to these that one looks for his distinctive contribution to literature, however, but to the *Essays of Elia*, contributed to the *London Magazine* from 1820 onwards, which in turn reflect the gifts already shown in his private letters, where humour and inventiveness pervaded. His play of mind exercised itself in the literature and ideas of the past rather than those of the present day. Coleridge's enjoyment of the 'lazy reading of old folios' was developed by Lamb into a positively sensuous pleasure:

. . . I seem to inhale learning, walking amid their foliage; and the odour of their old moth-scented coverings is fragrant as the first bloom of those sciential apples which grew amid the happy orchard.

Sir Thomas Browne, with his frank scepticism in matters of religion, was a particular favourite with Lamb, since his particular way of writing (which amounted to a love-affair with language itself) provided the context for a view of humanity combining love and imagination yet rooted in a tolerance for the failings of mankind. For many Victorians Lamb's work was a living fulfilment of the values of duty and affection propounded by the later Wordsworth. But where Hazlitt aims at ardour and frankness Lamb is more circumspect, teasing both the reader and himself. Even the name 'Elia' which he chose for his pseudonym and which, taken from a fellow-clerk, aligned him with the new breed of anonymous workers in the city, may have concealed a further esoteric joke, since it combines two of the Hebrew names for God, El and Yah. At all events, the persona thus created enabled him to play in and out of his own identity.

The country of remembered experience, always at hand for Hazlitt, was a still more readily available resource for Lamb. His eagerness to enter into the past and reinhabit it was assisted by his deliberate use of archaisms. From the opening of the first essay, 'Reader, in thy passage from the Bank – where thou hast been receiving thy half-yearly dividends (supposing thou art a lean annuitant like myself) . . .' the tone is set by the use of the formal/informal 'thou', the assumption of the reader's complicity with a persona which is in fact fictitious, and the skilful use of 'lean annuitant' to suggest not only the source of a meagre income but a figure touched by the passing of the years. Lamb's archaisms are not allowed to become a purely escapist device. While they signal an old-world courtesy to the reader, they also recall Browne's serious mannerist style, which had been able to draw on Latinisms as a linguistic resource. Lamb's use of such locutions is necessarily more eccentric, yet it is vivified by his sympathy with Browne's reasoned case for tolerance.

At the same time, Lamb's self-awareness led him to argue (in an essay of that title) that one must allow for 'imperfect sympathies'. Yet even as he is acknowledging his prejudices frankly, what he is evidently demanding from those he fails to sympathise with is some sign of an equivalent sympathy and play of mind on their part. The strictures sometimes levelled against him are more properly to be directed against those who take over his attitudes and mannerisms as the model for a comfortable conservatism. To do that is to miss what is hidden behind Lamb's reserve – a reserve half-broken in his 'Confessions of a Drunkard', where he speaks of his own weakness in a more moralising and self-condemnatory tone than customarily, but never fully broken to reveal the self-sacrifices that his devotion to his sister had led him to make, with all its losses and benefits. In his intertwining of love and reticence, an uprightness beneath whimsicality that is also crossed by sharpness of perception, Lamb links himself directly back to Cowper. His distinctive combination of affection and imagination was recognised by Coleridge, who wrote:

. . . he has an affectionate heart, a mind sui generis, his taste acts so as to appear like the unmechanic simplicity of an instinct . . . Lamb every now & then *eradiates*, & the beam, tho' single & fine as a hair, yet is rich with colours, & I both see & feel it.

Another early admirer of Coleridge and Wordsworth, Thomas de Quincey (1785–1859), read *Lyrical Ballads* while still at school and even, on running away, thought of going to the Lake District. The Coleridge he actually met in 1807, however, was a man whose eloquence seemed more like that of a somnambulist. Nevertheless, de Quincey took up residence near Grasmere for a few years and was one of the first to be permitted to read *The Prelude*.

Before meeting Coleridge he had already become addicted to opium and the acquaintance did nothing to lessen his interest in its effects. While Coleridge allowed himself only very rare mentions of the drug in his published works and tried repeatedly to rid himself of the habit, de Quincey's fascination triumphed more often over self-loathing. When in 1822 he published anonymous reminiscences of his career under the title *Confessions of an English Opium-Eater*, the identity of the author was soon an open secret. The *Confessions* were followed by further autobiographical accounts of his earlier life, including reminiscences of Wordsworth and Coleridge which made it clear that his attitude to both had become, like Hazlitt's, deeply ambiguous. He could not escape the sense of a debt to their poetry (which is to be traced in many verbal reminiscences), yet he also felt in some sense betrayed. Wordsworth, despite his affirmation that 'we have all of us one human heart', had not been willing to acknowledge the Grasmere girl whom de Quincey had married; and he could not be sure whether Coleridge's intellectual legacy to him, which had included an idiosyncratic reading of Kant, had been a blessing or a disaster. His greatest achievement lay in the production of prose dream-visions which were memorable for their faithful rendering of the circularity, repetition and unexpected emphasis characteristic of dream experience.

For his deepest mode, however, de Quincey looked to Wordsworth, who from an early point in his career had believed that human beings learned most from the experience of suffering, which opened out their spirit to a sense of infinity that was blocked or inhibited at times of action. By the time that de Quincey came to know him personally, he had passed into the penumbra of his long reaction to the death of his brother John. The kind of insight produced by his human sorrow corresponded to states of mind which de Quincey recognised from his own experiences under laudanum, and which he personified in a figure called 'The Dark Interpreter'. 'There is in the *dark* places of the human spirit – in grief, in fear, in vindictive wrath – a power of self-projection . . .,' he wrote: the Interpreter was 'the *dark* symbolic mirror for reflection to the daylight [of] what else must be hidden forever'. What he showed de Quincey could be of extraordinary beauty, as in his vision of Savannah-la-Mar, the city which had been removed to the bottom of the ocean. Yet his feeling for such scenes of timeless immobility is matched by his delight in energy. His was a different delight from the 'railway mania' of his contemporaries, one of his most impassioned essays, 'The English Mail-Coach' (1849), being an elegy over the animal spirits powering the form of transport that had dominated the earlier years of the century.

De Quincey's writing can move naturally between energy and stasis, between consciousness and the unconscious: a modern – and even more a post-modern – mind finds much material for exploration in his labyrinthine processes. In his own time, however, a final question can be seen to lurk behind them, that of a providence whose motives and purposes were riddling (a riddling actualised during de Quincey's own infancy in the behaviour of a mother whose love for her children could never be demonstrated by any gesture more physical than the sprinkling of lavender-water and milk of roses over them at their stern morning parades). During de Quincey's lifetime the question of providence was pressing hard, as writers turned from affirmation of God's law to stress rather his love.

Methodism, the founding experience of which had been John Wesley's moment of 'heart-warming', had contributed strongly to this new emphasis on heart rather than head, on the New Testament as opposed to the Old. But for some this affirmation made the workings of divine providence only more mysterious. Blake put the matter vigorously:

I cannot help saying 'the Son, how unlike the Father!' First God Almighty comes with a thump on the Head. Then Jesus Christ comes with a balm to heal it.

One of the attractions of de Quincey's writing, then as now, was the sense it gave of a man perpetually questioning providence – and finding an answer, if anywhere, only in the strange fidelities of the human heart.

London, the scene of early trials which were ineradicable from de Quincey's memory, continued to fascinate him, but he made his final home in Edinburgh, the lost capital which was at one and the same time the most regressive and progressive of European cities. Deprived of its earlier central importance, it cherished local Scottish traditions all the more jealously, while reaching out – over London's head, as it were – to other European cultures. The disappearance of its governing power made it a city of lawyers and merchants, relying on the old university traditions of the community to provide an intellectual impetus which English universities lacked at this time and increasingly dwelling on its own potentialities as a cultural centre.

The figure who best united these forces, and particularly the links with the past, was Sir Walter Scott (1771–1832). The Scottish Enlightenment gave him the sense of a firm base from which a writer could work, while the independent links which had been established with the continent gave him early news of literary innovations, including the potentialities for developing traditional ballad forms offered by writers such as Bürger, two of whose ballads he translated.

Living away from the main centre of the new commercial life (the 'halloo and humbug' of London, as he called it), while constantly aware of its influences, he was ideally placed to contrast the new kind of civilisation that was being imported from the south with the older way of life which survived virtually untouched in the Scottish countryside. Although a sense of this contrast lies behind much of his writing, it is not often centrally treated, however. It is responsible rather for Scott's belief in the strong and valuable qualities which he finds in such older forms of culture, and particularly the humane qualities which he traces in the individuals brought up within them.

Scott's extraordinary popularity in his own century also had to do with the international situation at the time. His championing of a society that had lost its separate nationhood but still retained a strong national identity found an immediate echo in other European countries struggling for independence. From Italy to Ireland, those who succeeded found it necessary to promote two kinds of literary hero: a national poet (for whom Robert Burns provided an obvious exemplar) and a historical novelist who could bring out what was special to their particular society. Manzoni's *I Promessi Sposi*, written between 1821 and 1827, is the most prominent among the many national novels which owed such a debt to Scott.

The exact political import of his novels has proved more difficult to determine. Those who know Scott to have been a Tory and feudalist are surprised to discover the breadth of his historical vision, particularly if their own political allegiances lie elsewhere. This has always been evident; as early as 1834 a radical writer, William Howitt, wrote

Genius, when it retires from the consideration of everyday subjects . . . is too noble to see anything but the broad light of everlasting truth, to feel anything but the majestic presence of nature, and the quickest sympathies with struggling humanity.

Georg Lukács, similarly, in a chapter on Scott that has been widely influential, set him among the writers who manifest a depth which they do not understand themselves, 'because it has sprung from a truly realistic mastery of their material in conflict with their personal views and prejudices'. The two statements differ importantly: Lukács's contention that anyone who tries to render what he or she finds in history with sufficient regard for what is there is bound to benefit subsequent writers, whatever their political complexion, is very different from Howitt's discernment in Scott of nature's presence and sympathies with struggling humanity, which he finds to proceed from the 'glorious visions and emotions' of genius itself.

Neither, perhaps, points with sufficient exactitude to the elements in Scott that made him such a universal favourite in his own century; for that, George Eliot is a better guide:

When Scott takes us into Luckie Mucklebackit's cottage, or tells the story of *The Two Drovers*, more is done towards linking the higher classes with the lower, towards obliterating the vulgarity of exclusiveness, than by hundreds of sermons and philosophical dissertations.

What she valued in him was a reconciling power, an ability to look across the classes of human society and indicate what human beings might be seen to have in common. To Victorian England, with its more complex aim of preserving the class-system intact – and even elaborating it further – while allowing also for social mobility and for qualities which might cut across such divisions, the novels of Scott, coming from outside that particular system, had a particular value. The old Scottish tradition of bettering oneself by education could be honoured without needing to be taken fully into the English way of life; this kind of egalitarianism was as appealing to conservatives of the 'One Nation' school as to liberals.

Scott's regard for the moral qualities of the sturdy individualist, wherever they might appear, was matched by his feeling for homely and warm-hearted affection. This never emerges more clearly, perhaps, than in *The Heart of Midlothian* (1818), a novel the concerns of which are indicated by the play of words in the title. 'The Heart of Midlothian' was the joking name for the jail in Edinburgh; Scott gave it serious point by showing where the true heart of Midlothian was to be found: in the individual heroism of Jeanie Deanes, with her singlehanded fight to secure justice for her sister.

In ways such as this Wordsworth's high valuation of the universal human heart found its way into the nineteenth-century mainstream. Keats's cultivation of the heart might seem hectic, Lamb's a trifle mannered, de Quincey's obscure and labyrinthine; but that which such writers had figured out in more subtle forms was meanwhile being given flesh and blood by Scott, promoting a heroism of the heart that was to appeal most directly to the Victorians. As the later Waverley novels were appearing, moreover, a new figure, for whom the theme was to be even more important, came on the scene. A feeling for the universal human heart was, in fact, the hallmark of the work of Charles Dickens (1812–70), matched only by his fascination with the extraordinary variety of human nature.

In his childhood he read widely in eighteenth-century fiction, including Smollett and Fielding, and the results are apparent everywhere, particularly in his comedy. But perhaps the works that affected his writing most deeply were the oriental tales, including *The Arabian Nights' Entertainments*, with their stress on the unexpected. Where the inhabitants of traditional English fiction lived under the eye of providence the 'oriental' world was one where the wanton operations of earthly powers could produce situations of nightmare. Dickens's plotting owed much to this further dimension. In his novels things will normally turn out providentially but on the way there will be many incidents where the presiding 'purpose' seems sinister rather than benevolent. He also draws on, and enriches, the current fashion for the grotesque.

At the age of twelve Dickens began working in a blacking warehouse while his family removed to the Marshalsea debtors' prison. Later, in the city, his imagination was caught by the effects of the rules of commerce – the ultimate laws, it seemed, by which the city lived. Those who manipulated such rules to their advantage – whether they were lawyers extending a case and exacting more and more fees or business men looking for advantage – seemed far removed from the world of simple humanity.

The most important literary development of the time in cultural terms was that of the drama. Formerly a licensed pleasure for those who were not inhibited by religious objections, it was now more readily acceptable to the middle classes. Dickens, who had seen stage performances from childhood onwards, retained an intense fascination, sometimes himself taking part in stage performances into which he threw himself with intense energy. In his public readings from his novels, similarly, he believed himself capable of achieving a greater rapport with his audiences than could be hoped for from the printed page alone, conveying a piquant dramatic situation or a sharp dialogue while also suggesting elements in a situation that could not be enacted directly on the stage. Dickens's method of serial publication enabled him to exploit such effects further by holding readers in suspense as they waited for the next month's instalment.

The novels are also notable for personages presented with leading characteristics that would make them memorable on the stage. Such characters may be strictly subordinate so far as the plot is concerned. Sarah Gamp, for instance, appears in no more than nine chapters of *Martin Chuzzlewit* (1843–4), yet this professional nurse who 'went to a lying-in or a laying-out with equal relish' has her own individual form of speech ('leave the bottle on the chimbley piece, and let me put my lips to it if I am so dispoged'), along with an extra dimension given by her imaginary friend 'Mrs Harris'.

Samuel Pickwick, victim-hero of *The Pickwick Papers* (1836–7) was conceived primarily in comic terms, inhabiting one of the pockets of innocence which were being created within new urban environments, where a man of independent means could occupy himself blamelessly in the fields of natural observation or sport. Like Fielding's Parson Adams, Pickwick finds himself in improbable situations where he is the victim of comic misunderstanding, while the protection he receives from his worldly-wise manservant Sam Weller is a genial version of the relationship between Don Quixote and Sancho Panza. The novel shifts its mood in the middle, however, when Pickwick, refusing to accept a court's unjust decision, finds himself flung in jail and sees something of the city's darker side.

In the other great work which established his early fame, *Oliver Twist* (1837–9), Dickens took a figure as innocent as Mr Pickwick but gave him, instead of affluence, the pathos of neglected childhood poverty. Plunged unwittingly into a set of London criminals, Oliver's extraordinary resistance to participation in the unlawful leads him to constant victimisation until eventually (in the tradition of romance) he is rescued and discovered to be of gentle birth.

In this work, Dickens's power of evoking feeling is fully displayed for the first time. The old man, Fagin, who presides over a gang of child-criminals draws some of his power from the language of affection with which he addresses them – a language which, though ironic, is not entirely without basis. The relation between the robber Bill Sykes and his mistress Nancy evokes pathos of another sort in her loyalty towards him and the cruel violence which turns his love for her to murder.

These early novels also display Dickens's striking ability to move between the animate and inanimate. There is, for example, a moment when Mr Scrooge in *A Christmas Carol* (1843), looks at the knocker which he has seen on his door every day of his career and sees instead the face of his dead partner, Jacob Marley:

Marley's face. It was not in impenetrable shadow as the other objects in the yard were, but had a dismal light about it, like a bad lobster in a dark cellar. It was not angry or ferocious, but looked at Scrooge as Marley used to look; with ghostly spectacles turned up on its ghostly forehead. The hair was curiously stirred, as if by breath or hot air; and, though the eyes were wide open, they were perfectly motionless. That, and its livid colour, made it horrible; but its horror seemed to be in spite of the face and beyond its control, rather than a part of its own expression.

Later, in *Dombey and Son* (1846–8), a long passage would be devoted to the life of a room in a deserted house, where signs of life interact with the stillness of covered forms still more eerily:

Within doors, curtains, drooping heavily, lost their old folds and shapes, and hung like cumbrous palls. Hecatombs of furniture, still piled and covered up, shrunk like imprisoned and forgotten men, and changed insensibly. Mirrors were dim as with the breath of years. Patterns of carpets faded, and became perplexed and faint, like the memory of those years' trifling incidents. Boards, starting at unwonted footsteps, creaked and shook. Keys rusted in the locks of doors. Damp started on the walls, and, as the stains came out, the pictures seemed to go in and secrete themselves. Mildew and mould began to lurk in closets. Fungus-trees grew in corners of the cellars. Dust accumulated, nobody knew whence nor how; spiders, moths, and grubs were heard of every day. An exploratory black-beetle now and then was found immovable upon the stairs . . ..

Although not an 'intellectual' novelist, Dickens increasingly favoured the adoption of a 'strong idea' to provide a centre for each novel's concerns, which often had to do with the life of the great city. In the earliest years he was more interested in the workings of commerce and the law than in the effects of the Industrial Revolution. The world of *Pickwick Papers* was that of the coach rather than the steam-train and the approach to Birmingham in that novel was described in impressive but even tones. But when Little Nell and her grandfather enter a manufacturing town in *The Old Curiosity Shop* (1840–1) the industrial scene has qualities of nightmare animations:

. . . On every side, and as far as the eye could see into the heavy distance, tall chimneys, crowding on each other, and presenting that endless repetition of the same dull, ugly form, which is the horror of oppressive dreams, poured out their plague of smoke, obscured the light, and made foul the melancholy air. On mounds of ashes by the wayside, sheltered only by a few rough boards, or rotten pent-house roofs, strange engines spun and writhed like tortured creatures, clanking their iron chains, shrieking in their rapid whirl from time to time as though in torment unendurable, and making the ground tremble with their agonies.

This atmosphere had something to do with contemporary fear of the human violence that industrialism was thought to be breeding; the vision of industry as primarily a disruptive force came out more fully in *Dombey and Son*, where the creation of a railway in London has an effect like that of some great natural disaster:

There were a hundred thousand shapes and substances of incompleteness, wildly mingled out of their places, upside down, burrowing in the earth, aspiring in the air, mouldering in the water, and unintelligible as any dream. Hot springs and fiery eruptions, the usual attendants upon earthquakes, lent their contributions of confusion to the scene. Boiling water hissed and heaved within dilapidated walls; whence, also, the glare and roar of flames came issuing forth; and mounds of ashes blocked up rights of way, and wholly changed the law and custom of the neighbourhood.

Although Dickens's extraordinary powers of imagination resembled those of Coleridge he was not subject to the same religious guilt. Despite his feeling for the grotesque he resisted a view of human beings which stressed their inherited propensity to sin. Such beliefs led in his view to the dismal sabbath-restrictions of English life and a zealous busybodying all too often associated with pious hypocrisy. His own leanings were in the direction of a broad religion of humanity which he believed could be found in the Jesus of the Christian gospels.

This view brought about problems of its own, however, since he was all too aware of the prevalence of wickedness in his society, which on his terms had to be explained either by that human stupidity which could on happier occasions be the stuff of his comedy, or by deeply-rooted hardness of heart.

The latter theme is explored powerfully in *Dombey and Son*, where (as the title hints) a wealthy city merchant's love for his son is dominated by his desire for self-replication in his own, commercial image; his daughter, Florence, being meanwhile rejected. The action comes to a climax in a battle of wills with a wife (his second) as proud and obstinate as himself, who elopes with his own manager – a development which initiates the fall of his business. In his final ruin, however, he is sought out by Florence, whose love for him has remained constant: his cold hauteur melted, he ends his days a better man, devoted to his little grand-daughter – of whom it is said 'he hoarded her in his heart'.

That phrase is a telling one, however, for in the act of proclaiming the heart's triumph it still hints at an ambiguity. Has Dombey's nature changed totally for the better, even in this dénouement?

For the moment Dickens could escape such issues by unfolding more optimistically the development of a human heart in relation to another that remained constant. In *David Copperfield* (1849–50) the hero's affection is increasingly reinforced by way of growing attachments, including that of the aunt whose affection is no less powerful for being harshly expressed. Suspense is supplied by the love for him of his childhood friend, Agnes Wickfield, which must, under the conditions of Victorian decorum, remain totally hidden until it is known to be reciprocated, creating in his mind an equivalent dam of affection which is all the more powerful in its final breach. Yet Dickens's growing awareness that the faith of the heart was always liable to be betrayed, or to betray itself, is suggested even in this novel, where the kind of confidence in love that is expressed at the end requires the record of a lifetime's testing for its authentication.

A new sense of the past

The deaths of Keats, Shelley and Byron overshadowed English poetry for many years afterwards. By contrast with the ambiguous and complicated achievements of Coleridge and Wordsworth these poets had seemed to be striking boldly into new paths and exploring new forms; yet their experiments proved hard to follow, and the sombre scene in England in the 1820s made their appeal to the senses appear to some self-indulgent and lacking in social responsibility. The initiative passed to the novelists and poets were left on the defensive.

Alfred Tennyson (1809–92), as a young man struggling for recognition, had reason to sympathise with the increasingly loud voices of protest. In 'Locksley Hall' his narrator attacked contemporary obeisance to expedience:

> Cursed be the social wants that sin against the strength of youth!
> Cursed be the social lies that warp us from the living truth!'

(lines 59–60)

He even fantasised about retreating to a tropical island which might provide more enjoyments than were to be found at home –

> . . . in this march of mind,
> In the steamship, in the railway, in the thoughts that shake mankind.

From one point of view discontent with the utilitarian presuppositions of the age might seem to license a development of the lyrical vein that the recent Romantic poets had been opening up, yet Tennyson could not ignore the sense of grievance that existed in society. In his poem 'The Palace of Art' he painted sensuously appealing pictures of the scenes which might adorn a building created for the pleasure of the eye, only then to reject the whole conception as intrinsically immoral and requiring the purgation of guilt. While his gifts as a lyrical poet made him more attractive to many readers than he could ever be as a social commentator, he could not turn his back on the issues of the time.

Current intellectual movements, particularly those in Germany, were contributing to the mood of enquiry. In the older English universities, scientific facts were still regarded as a part of the divine order and those who taught them were usually members of the clergy. But while the main impetus for diffusion of new ideas came for the time being from outside them – notably from the University College of London, founded in the spirit of Jeremy Bentham and opened in 1828, the new developments could not be ignored, even if their full implications were not seen. In Cambridge the elections of Adam Sedgwick and John Henslow to the chairs of geology and botany brought to those subjects clergymen of vigour, who were determined to work for the advancement of knowledge, while still evidently believing that what was being discovered would further disclose God's purposes. Even when the geological studies of Charles Lyell and others challenged the traditional chronology of the Bible there was a corresponding increase in awe at the length of the processes that were being revealed. By comparison with a creation story that could have happened yesterday, the field of the past was seen to stretch back over aeons, covering extraordinarily slow processes of growth and change. If the past were contemplated on that scale, the sense of grandeur must inevitably be enhanced; but if, with a colder eye, one looked into the significance of individual human lives they must begin to seem irrelevant to such vast and complex processes. While from one point of view this might be salutary and humbling, disturbing questions were raised about the foundations of human values.

Another effect was to foster a literature of memory. There began to emerge that looking back into the past in search of security that was to mark a good deal of Victorian literature, music and art, with the result that even a major event such as the Great Exhibition of 1851, though dominating the press and conversation, was little reflected in literature of the day, the major works that had appeared in the preceding year having been more concerned with the past than with the current wave of enthusiasm for British invention. Chance had a certain amount to do with this: it was an accident that Wordsworth's death in that year released for publication *The Prelude*, his great autobiographical work. It was less fortuitous, on the other hand, that Dickens should in the same year have produced his reminiscent novel *David Copperfield*, where autobiographical structure combined with fictional exploration induced a basic affection for the past. In 1850, also, Tennyson found it finally possible to publish the collection of poems that had accumulated around his feelings of grief for the loss of his friend Arthur Hallam seventeen years earlier.

In Memoriam is a complex work. At its most direct level it is a long poem about grief and time. For Tennyson, pierced by the new sense of the past that the geologists were bringing to bear, the adage that time heals all wounds was less comforting than disturbing. As he wrote in section 78, 'O sorrow, then can sorrow wane?/ O grief, can grief be changed to less?' The pain he had felt at Hallam's death had been an earnest of the intellectual and emotional debts he had owed to him living. In the poem as a whole it emerges as a comfort when he discovers that his grief is not destroyed through time but can rise up again just as sharply many years later.

That is perhaps the deepest note in the poem as a whole; it is certainly the most plangent. Yet it is equally important to Tennyson to learn that life can continue in its constant rhythmic movements of ebb and flow, of systole and diastole; and this is reflected in the distinctive metre and form of the poem, where the last line of each stanza rhymes with the first, rounding it – while a rhythmic impulse from the central couplet moves each stanza forward to the next. But there are also moments of stasis, producing unforgettable vignettes, as when the poet stands in the street where Hallam lived and finds in the knowledge of his loss a ready link with the impersonality and lack of significance in modern city life:

> He is not here; but far away
> The noise of life begins again,
> And ghastly thro' the drizzling rain
> On the bald street breaks the blank day.
>
> (sect. 7)

In happier times the break of day was the time of hope and promise that it had been for Coleridge and Shelley. But Tennyson, who knew that dawn itself might be to dying eyes the moment when 'the casement slowly grows a glimmering square', and so be 'sad and strange', felt more at home with the twilight glimmerings of evening and morning, more appropriate settings for his alternations between elegy and tentative affirmation.

A visit to Cambridge brought back memories of the time when he had attended meetings of the Apostles, the small group of idealistic young men who had met weekly to discuss ideas which could range from metaphysics to the play of market forces. Their ebullience came vividly to mind as he saw the door of the room

> Where once we held debate, a band
> Of youthful friends, on mind and art,
> And labour, and the changing mart,
> And all the framework of the land . . .
>
> (sect. 87)

It was again a moment of loss: another name was on the door.

The concern with public affairs that was to remain with Tennyson takes

second place in this poem to the personality of Hallam, who had seemed not
only to introduce a new note but even to be a new kind of man. At all times
his memories take a darker tone from the intervention of that death, which
has changed their colourings, yet the very activity of coming to terms with
what has happened is therapeutic – and to this also the memory of earlier
discussions contributes. One of the most memorable sections of the poem is
the one that describes the Tennyson family moving away from the landscape
that Hallam shared on his visits there: a countryside that they had always
known and which had become saturated for them with the affection they all
bestowed on it. 'Unwatched', 'unloved', 'uncared for' are the words that come
to Tennyson's mind as he imagines the landscape without them —

> As year by year the labourer tills
> His wonted glebe, or lops the glades;
> And year by year our memory fades
> From all the circle of the hills.

(sect. 101)

This idea of a landscape that had been in one sense sustained by their loving
perception of it, witnesses also to the new consciousness that was being
fostered by geological investigations, rendering its thoughtful inhabitants
more attentive to the local and particular landscape even as they became
increasingly aware of its temporary and passing nature.

In Memoriam is a central poem in that liberal tradition which, in the act of
pursuing freedom, demanded that individuals prove their independence by
coming to terms with a world that granted them no appeal to an external
moral authority. Tennyson attempted this by making the yearning and
aspiration that are felt in human love the test and earnest of his relationship
with the universe at large. In the face of Hallam's senseless death the main
hope he could offer lay in the fact that if such a man could exist once there
was no reason why he should not again. Perhaps he was 'a noble type /
Appearing ere the time was ripe'. A key word here is 'noble'; at the very
moment when Tennyson was postulating a 'crowning race' that should fulfil
Hallam's promise he looked back to older feudal and chivalric ideals in order
to suggest what that race might be like. The past was to be invoked once
again, this time to make his redeeming concept of love an effective agent of
progress.

The rectory home of his childhood and youth and the affections which
revolved around it played a strong part in Tennyson's work; further north,
meanwhile, a drama of a more intense kind was unfolding in a parsonage set
against a bleaker landscape. At Haworth in Yorkshire the three daughters of
Patrick Brontë, the perpetual curate there, Charlotte (1816–55), Emily
(1818–48) and Anne (1820–49), together with his son Branwell (1817–48),
proved to have literary gifts of the highest order. In their childhood they
produced the 'Chronicles' of Angria, an imaginary country they had invented
together. As they grew older Branwell disappointed the hopes of his family,
falling into habits of dissipation, but his sisters fulfilled their promise in
works of sharp wit and depth of feeling.

It is hard to appreciate their novels fully without perceiving the extent to which the authors were rooted in Romanticism, yet were developing some of its themes at the expense of others. Charlotte Brontë pursued the Romantic ideal of reconciling the head with the heart, and in trying to be true to both exposed the tensions involved. She also turned away from the cultivated sentimentalities of contemporary literature, showing how the heart's truth might subsist most fully in people of a caustic disposition. The shrewdness of her observing eye led her not only to see other people – and herself – clearly but to appreciate the limitations of a life lived too prudently – however worthy one's moral character might be. William Crimsworth, the hero of her first novel *The Professor*, is a professor in more than one sense, for the term was used at the time for someone who made his principles known and tried to act upon them. Crimsworth keeps a clear head and acts well at all times, and eventually wins a young woman whose rationality is matched by the workings of a heart more expressive than his own; yet the final chapters of the novel make the reader aware of limitations to which he himself is blind as he brings up his son to develop the same self-restraints that he has exercised.

Having escaped from the enclosure of her parsonage home by working as a governess in a Brussels still in the afterglow of Waterloo, Charlotte Brontë was drawing on her own experience of self-liberation: she was indeed to be condemned by some contemporaries (inexplicably, it might now seem) for her outspokenness. Her essential moral seriousness is best seen in her concluding novel, *Villette* (1853), where in a subtle plot the governess-heroine, while never quite breaking the spell of the attractive male character with whom she first falls in love, is drawn increasingly to the human profundity of the more sardonic Paul Emmanuel. Her fascination with the Byronic hero, natural enough in one of her generation, found its expression in the creation of other characters who refuse to fall neatly into the patterns offered them by society, her greatest creation in this mode being that of Mr Rochester in *Jane Eyre* (1847). Even Rochester, however, was thrown into the shade by her sister Emily's portrayal in *Wuthering Heights* (1847) of Heathcliff, the outsider rejected by the society in which he is brought up who dominates the events of the novel by the power of his passion for his childhood love Catherine Earnshaw.

Both sisters were also concerned with the question of human identity and its establishment – particularly with the extent to which love might be impossible without a degree of identification between the lovers. When Paul Emmanuel begins to establish his claim on Lucy Snowe it is by voicing his belief in their affinity:

Do you hear that you have some of my tones of voice? Do you know that you have many of my looks? I perceive all this and believe that you were born under my star.

It is a presumption of inescapable attachment that finds its apotheosis in Catherine's pronouncement in *Wuthering Heights*: 'I am Heathcliff' – which was in its turn an extreme version of the impulse towards self-identification with another being that had characterised Tennyson's mourning over Hallam.

Although *In Memoriam* was composed over many years, its publication in 1850 chimed with a strong elegiac mood among English poets of the time. The events which had made 1848 a year of revolutions on the continent had

had a far less violent counterpart in the Chartist movement. Increasing awareness of what was happening across the Channel, on the other hand, made writers conscious of the fragility of the concordat between religion and science that had preserved a unity in English culture. The Alpine peaks of France and Switzerland emblematised the point, presenting a severer challenge to human beings than the hills of Wordsworth's Cumbria. In the autumn of 1849 Matthew Arnold (1822–88) wrote his 'Stanzas in Memory of the Author of "Obermann"', commemorating the life of Senancour – of all writers, in his opinion, 'the most perfectly isolated and the least attitudinizing'. Senancour's achievement focused Arnold's current problem: whether to follow him into isolation, or, if not, how to heed the demands of the world:

> Ah! two desires toss about
> The poet's feverish blood.
> One drives him to the world without,
> And one to solitude.

Of the two great models that came naturally to his mind, Wordsworth, with his elected solitariness, could not help, while Goethe had had the advantages of a peaceful youth denied to those who, like Arnold, had been 'reared in hours / Of change, alarm, surprise':

> . . . Wordsworth's eyes avert their ken
> From half of human fate;
> And Goethe's course few sons of men
> May think to emulate.

In the following year Wordsworth's death prompted a continuation of this vein in Arnold's 'Memorial Verses', where another name was added to those who had most inspired his generation: Goethe's diagnostic power and Wordsworth's supreme healing ability were now complemented by Byron's energy; among these gifts, however, it was Wordsworth's that seemed the least replaceable. Arnold's sense of his own potentialities as a poet involved the development of a similar healing power which must in turn be harmonising. Aware of all that was happening in the European mind, including the growth of biblical criticism, Arnold knew that the old order which Wordsworth had tried to uphold and reinterpret in his withdrawal from the new intellectual movements of his time could not easily be sustained as a whole view. From this time forward he would turn his thoughts increasingly to contemporary culture, seeking to educate and to animate those to whom it belonged by making them better aware of their roots. By the same token he would write increasingly in prose.

In this and other respects 1850 proves to have been a surprisingly sensitive date, marking a shift to themes that were to dominate the second part of the century. In the 1840s Ruskin was confining himself mainly to writings such as the first two volumes of *Modern Painters*: the voice of Ruskin the social reformer belonged to the future. The dominant voice of that decade was in fact that of Thomas Carlyle (1795–1881). When Carlyle came to London in the 1820s, he had already responded to the German literature that was being translated into English. While he might find fault with Goethe for his immorality, he found in his writings, and particularly in *Wilhelm Meister* (which he himself translated) a power, a forthrightness and a vision of humanity which he missed in contemporary London. The brilliance of Coleridge, whose writings he had read with respect, seemed to him on a brief acquaintance to be vitiated by a damaging desire to have the best of all worlds, producing a philosophy which he summed up scornfully as 'the sublime secret of believing by "the reason" what "the understanding" had been obliged to fling out as incredible'. John Stuart Mill (1806–73) took a more sympathetic view, seeing further into Coleridge's purposes. Comparing his mind with that of Jeremy Bentham (1748–1832) as the two most seminal of the age he distinguished their respective strengths:

By Bentham, beyond all others, men have been led to ask themselves, in regard to any ancient or received opinion, Is it true? and by Coleridge, What is the meaning of it? The one took his stand *outside* the received opinion, and surveyed it as an entire stranger to it: the other looked at it from within, and endeavoured to see it with the eyes of a believer in it; to discover by what apparent facts it was at first suggested, and by what appearances it has ever since been rendered continually credible – has seemed, to a succession of persons, to be a faithful interpretation of their experience.

Carlyle, however, believed that the age demanded a more positive message. The devotion of the age to mechanism, rightly denounced by Coleridge, needed to be attacked directly and vigorously – a purpose to which he brought his concept of 'The Eternal Powers', working out their way whether or not human beings chose to heed them. The turning-point for himself had come in a moment of conversion mirrored in the experience of his character Teufelsdröckh in *Sartor Resartus* (1833–4). From the sense of the world as a world of death, a 'huge, dead, immeasurable Steam-engine, rolling on, in its dead indifference', a world which had pervaded, as an 'Everlasting No', the whole of his being, Teufelsdröckh had found himself coming to recognise the alternative view which would prompt an 'Everlasting Yea'. Even while he was adeptly and ironically presenting his vision through the persona of an extravagant German thinker who might seem far from the common-sense scepticism of his English contemporaries, Carlyle was revolving the irony further so that the vision of this strange figure could emerge as offering the true remedy for the age's problems.

Like others he turned to the past for the presentation and development of his vision, but it was a recent past, which he could bring up to date still further by skilful appeal to the present. In *The French Revolution* (1837) he took the most portentous event in contemporary memory and wrote about it in the grand style. This was history presented more dramatically than ever before, perhaps: the contrast with the cool, urbane, distancing approach of Gibbon was evident enough. Against a history that was there to be appraised and considered rationally Carlyle was offering a version in which the immanent workings of the Eternal powers glimmered and glared through a narrative working always in the present tense.

Carlyle's rhetoric – the use of 'lo!' and 'ah!', of 'dost thou' and 'art thou' – may look dated to modern eyes, but to his contemporaries it revived the tones of Biblical prophecy. Even today it can still exert its original power, as when he tries to restore sublimity to a great industrial city:

Sooty Manchester, – it too is built on the infinite Abyssess; overspanned by the skyey Firmaments; and there is birth in it, and death in it; – and it is every whit as wonderful, as fearful, unimaginable, as the oldest Salem or Prophetic City. Go or stand, in what time, in what place we will, are there not Immensities, Eternities over us, around us, in us . . .?

Dickens was deeply affected. He took over some of Carlyle's rhetorical devices and in the preface to *A Tale of Two Cities* (1859) acknowledged his debt to that 'wonderful book', *The French Revolution.*

Carlyle was impatient with those who were trying to restore and uphold the Roman Catholic faith, yet he believed that in its time it had embodied elements vital to humanity. The Abbot of St Edmundsbury in *Past and Present* (1843) was a hero because of the life-stance in which he had existed: 'Wonder, miracle encompass the man; he lives in an element of miracle; Heaven's splendour over his head, Hell's darkness under his feet'. But it had been his unconsciousness of his religion that gave him his true integrity: 'The Unconscious is the alone Complete'. There is a dangerously thin boundary, nevertheless, between Carlyle's attempt to restore that kind of unconscious respect for the Eternal Powers and the advocacy of an unthinking obedience to authority generally, between the kind of exemplary heroism for which he was calling and autocratic leadership. Carlyle would eventually find his ideal contemporary ruler in Frederick the Great of Prussia. His earlier elevation of Oliver Cromwell, who combined authority with righteousness, had been less controversial.

Carlyle's writing, with its strong historical dimension, was contributing to a far-reaching preoccupation, associated with the interest in memory already noted. As new social questions arose the nature of their solutions was seen to depend partly on one's interpretation of the past. So in the 1830s members of the English Church, perceiving that Biblical scholarship was making the Word of God an unstable foundation for their faith and disturbed by the State's interference in their affairs, enquired with new urgency into their Church's authority. The initiators of the Oxford Movement sought to found the Anglican Church more fully in a Catholic tradition and so regain a longer historical continuity. The first fruits of this new vision of the Church were to be found in John Keble's popular collection of verses entitled *The Christian Year* (1827), but the issues emerge more extensively in the twin accounts by John Henry Newman (1801–90) of the events preceding his decision to enter the Roman Catholic Church: his evocation of the emotions involved, in the novel *Loss and Gain* (1848), followed by his account of the logical processes which led him to see Anglicanism as a heresy in *Apologia Pro Vita Sua* (1864). The reverberations of the larger struggles involved spread far into the fiction and memoirs of the time.

Attempts to find the right historical context of interpretation for political ideas, similarly, can be found everywhere, ranging from the work of Benjamin Disraeli (1804–81), who in his novels *Coningsby* (1844) and *Sybil* (1845) sought to set the contemporary industrial and social situation against a tradition of aristocratic responsibility, to that of Charlotte Brontë, who in her novel *Shirley* (1849) tried at a more direct level to balance the legitimate grievances of the workers against the need to keep order in society. At the time when she was writing the Chartist movement was at its height and a major topic of discussion; in a remote Yorkshire town, with poor communications, the threat of violent insurrection was not to be taken lightly. Following a familiar nineteenth-century pattern, she set her novel more than thirty years before, basing its action on the Luddite movement and in particular the attack on Rawfolds in Yorkshire in 1812, where the Luddites were repelled by the military with many casualties. Despite her strenuous efforts to be fair, the case of the workers was not always adequately represented, since she did not always allow them to speak fully on their own behalf. Charlotte Brontë entered into collusion with her readers – presumably imagined as belonging to the middle class – allowing her prose to be whimsical as well as indignant.

Yet this was an effective mode, as with the closely observed and even acerbic picture of the oppressions suffered by the working class in a novel by Charles Kingsley (1819–75) published in the following year. In *Alton Locke* the tailor-hero is seen passing through contemporary society, with its injustices, and looking for a just way of life. The novel also contains a biting picture of Cambridge which displays Kingsley's bent of mind further when the narrator turns to a panegyric of the young men who are rowing on the river. Kingsley emerges here as another of the great Victorians who cultivated the heart – the devotion being expressed in his case by way of physical exercise and open-air observation of nature. He too was trying to counteract the attractions of Chartism by recalling the upper classes to a feeling of their responsibilities.

The more radical kinds of argument that appeared in Friedrich Engels's *The Condition of the Working Class in England* in 1844 had made little headway by 1850, the most potent force at work in the culture being that of liberalism. The most characteristic fictions of these decades are in fact to be found in the poetry of the somewhat anarchistic liberal Robert Browning (1812–89) who, having first taken his bearings from Shelley – called 'The Suntreader' in *Pauline*, his earliest long poem – had begun to develop his gifts more distinctively in poems such as those in *Dramatic Romances* (1845), where the poetry was poised between simple story-telling and use of narrative and lyric art to make some point about human nature generally. By 1850 Browning was embarked on the poems which would finally make his name when they appeared five years later in the collection *Men and Women*: a series of dramatic monologues in which each character was given the opportunity of telling his or her own story – often in such a way that the reader might by one means or another discern a further narrative beyond. This is another version of Romantic benevolence, since it is implicit in the venture that the poet gives his characters a space wherein to express their individual identities, each of which then turns out to be unique.

At the same time the reader is conscious that the freedom of these characters is itself limited. 'When we read a dramatic poem by Browning', wrote T.S. Eliot, 'we cannot suppose that we are listening to any other voice than that of Browning himself'. This is not altogether fair, for one is aware of a very distinctive personality in each case; yet it is true that each statement seems to be contributing to a philosophy of humanity which will bind the poet's vision into a unity. There is, for instance, the sense of a divine being guiding human events, however obscure their significance may seem to be. The humble church organist, working away at the 'mountainous fugues' of Master Hugues of Saxe-Gotha in his organ loft, sees a possible interpretation of human existence as well as of the music he is playing, 'God's gold just shining its last' through the 'zigzags and dodges' of life as they weave in and out, when he turns his eyes up to the roof:

> What with affirming, denying,
> Holding, risposting, subjoining,
> All's like . . . it's like . . . for an instance I'm trying . . .
> There! See our roof, its gilt moulding and groining
> Under those spider-webs lying!

(xix) *Men and Women*

This attempt to render the mind in the very act of its straining after explanation witnesses also to the new psychological bent in the nineteenth-century mind. Although it had been fostered by earlier Romantic poets, they had tended to describe or suggest the processes (as in Coleridge's meditative poems) rather than enact them dramatically. Browning's experiments look back to Shakespearean drama and across to the variety of dramatic voices in contemporary novels such as those of Dickens.

The play of mind encouraged by such writing was not altogether to the taste of the age, however, and after the middle of the century sterner and more strenuous modes came increasingly to the fore. The tone was again set by Carlyle, who in his *Life of John Sterling* (1851) attacked Coleridge for his failure to direct the spirit of the age in a more decisive manner. Sterling himself he saw as having suffered from a similar malady: in spite of his 'sleepless intellectual vivacity' he had not been properly a thinker at all:

I likened him often, in my banterings, to sheet-lightning: and reproachfully prayed that he would concentrate himself into a bolt, and rive the mountain barriers for us, instead of merely playing on them and irradiating them.

Ch.1.

To many Victorians, conscious of great problems and the urgent need to deal with them, this was a damning comment. If such minds produced imaginative literature, that must be consigned to the nursery. The play of the mind was for children.

The role of women was particularly open to question. Women writers had been at work long enough to merit serious and equal consideration with men, and the value of the feminine had been brought into prominence by Romantic idealisations. These were kindly and gentle versions; there was also a wild and untamed one, yielding such diverse forms as those in Wordsworth's *Joanna* or La Motte Fouqué's *Ondine*. Shelley's *Witch of Atlas*, written at the end of his life, showed him under the spell of a femininity totally at play, a manifestation of the free spirit which was to the male eye at once attractive and tantalisingly frustrating.

The freedom of women was, as such, a difficult, almost impossible theme. In *The Princess* (1847) Tennyson wrestled between two possible versions of the female role within current society: the one invoking woman as full partner to the male in all human activities, the other as presiding over a domesticity which guarded her husband's values and provided repose when he returned from doing the world's work. Tennyson found a solution by making the poems 'a medley' (a medley which he added to in 1853, when he included some of the best lyrics he ever wrote) and in making the action of the poem basically farcical. William Makepeace Thackeray (1811–63), on the other hand, constructed his *Vanity Fair* (1847–8) around alternatives closer to those just mentioned: on the one hand Amelia Sedley, who 'had such a kindly, smiling, tender, gentle, generous heart of her own, as won the love of everyone who came near her', on the other Becky Sharp, witty, heartless, sarcastic, irreverent and fascinating to men. In Thackeray's novel there can be no resolution into a fully satisfactory third mode; if a mode does emerge it is the sardonic, sounding a note that is to echo through much succeeding fiction. In such a society as England was becoming, devoted to the exploitation of technological inventions and to expansion overseas, there was no means of circumventing the affirmation of male domination; but the fact that society afforded unprecedented opportunities for women to exercise power if they knew how to use the right techniques could be acknowledged by a novelist skilled in wry comedy. (Trollope's Barsetshire novels, with the redoubtable Mrs Proudie, followed only a few years later.)

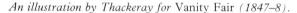

An illustration by Thackeray for Vanity Fair *(1847–8)*.

If Victorian society had proved more adept at incorporating the element of play, some of the brilliant elements in the work of Blake, Coleridge, Lamb, Keats, Shelley and Jane Austen might have been taken up more fruitfully in late nineteenth-century literature. Like Carlyle, however, the age was becoming less interested in the play of sheet-lightning than in finding thunderbolts to rive mountain-barriers. Not everyone followed suit, nevertheless. In the late 1840s, years which produced an extraordinary crop of memorable books, a particularly great one was produced by one of the very women who were being marginalised by Victorian society and who lived (as several of the greatest Romantics had done) away from the metropolis. Emily Brontë's *Wuthering Heights* stands in silent condemnation of the slighting of feminine powers that was implicit in contemporary attitudes; it also reverses the compliment paid by male writers to female daemonism.

She was not the first to do so. In 1818 Mary Shelley had found a matrix for the various ideas which were contending for dominance in her mind by writing her novel *Frankenstein*, its central character a human created by a scientist. The monster thus made was so hideous as to cause fear in all who encountered it, yet it was also intelligent enough to understand the principle of benevolence and to expect to be treated according to it. Maddened by its inability to discover the love which it needed, it turned instead to vengeance and hounded its own inventor to death. The tale immediately turned into an archetypal myth, but it has more often been employed as a cautionary tale concerning the presumptuousness of scientific investigators than as a morality tale about the failure of love in human society. A story which was avowedly Promethean is commonly read as Faustian.

Mary Shelley's story had strong elements of the fantastic, not only in the creation of the monster, but in the superhuman powers ascribed to it in its later career. Emily Brontë, by contrast, sets her 'monster', Heathcliff, in the midst of a known and familiar setting: the Yorkshire moors. Apart from one or two supernatural hints in the opening events the action is naturalistic. During the course of the narrative Heathcliff behaves more and more villainously, and is indeed seen as a villain by the narrator, Nelly Dean; but his own version of things is that his actions were undertaken because he had been barred from the society of the only woman he had ever loved, Catherine Earnshaw, with whom he was brought up from childhood. The focus, once again, is upon the universal human heart, even if Heathcliff's increasingly violent and calculating behaviour, like that of the monster in *Frankenstein*, so masks this that the narrative as it runs out may leave a different impression.

The novel also contains a powerful new enactment of the theme which had informed the portrayal of the devil in Blake's *Marriage of Heaven and Hell* and Coleridge's Geraldine in *Christabel*: that of the moral ambiguity of energy. From the start Heathcliff's attraction lies in a daemonic power which is more a natural force than a human. Catherine, similarly, has an element of the wild and the untamed in her and is never more happy than she was as a young girl when she roamed the moors together with Heathcliff. The strong implication of their story is that such male and female daemonisms are at once realer and closer to the earth itself than the human emotions bred more tamely in society; there is also a suggestion that such daemon-lovers can now only wail for one another. Just as Jane Austen had given a renewed and an intenser life to some of the ideas inherent in Augustanism, so now, years after the main Romantic writers, those ambiguities of energy around which Blake, Coleridge and Wordsworth had constructed their works and which had been brought to a fine point in Byron's career had found a renewed expression.

As de Quincey had pointed out, however, the focus of energy itself was shifting, even as Emily Brontë wrote, from that which was vital and animal to that which was driven by steam. In developments which were increasingly seizing the Victorian imagination the energies of wild life, which could now be traced back over aeons to the very fossils that were disturbing contemporary thought, were being displaced, paradoxically, by an energy generated from even older fossils. After Newman's secession to the Church of Rome, a contemporary recalled, there was a great calm in Oxford, to be broken only by a new fever, when 'speculative theology gave way to speculation in railway shares'. The uses of the past were proving to be strange indeed.

Thomas Lawrence, Richard Westall, *pencil drawing (c.1795)*.

3 The Fine Arts

MICHAEL ROSENTHAL

Introduction

In the *Discourse* of 1788 commemorating Thomas Gainsborough (1727–88), Sir Joshua Reynolds (1723–92) spoke of the British School having yet to come into being. By 1851 painting and sculpture in Britain had developed and changed in ways which could not have then been anticipated. The Pre-Raphaelites were exhibiting oil paintings of extraordinary colouristic brilliance and apparent truth to appearance, aiming to represent a particular nature which Reynolds could only have understood as appealing to sensual and therefore debased tastes, but which they believed to embody in great and little the truths of God's creation. They had taken much from John Ruskin (1819–1900), who in Volume I of *Modern Painters* (1843) had attempted to vindicate J.M.W. Turner (1775–1851) from the charges of extravagance and gratuitousness which, late in his career, were customarily levelled at him, by presenting him as the supreme naturalist, the man who, more than any previous painter, had perceived the essential truths of natural appearance. Yet Turner's own ideas had been formed on the teaching of Reynolds (among others) and we are now beginning to appreciate the complexity of the content of his pictures, themselves one response to the demand for a serious national art which Reynolds had articulated. That it was in landscape rather than history that he attempted to supply this need is itself worthy of comment. Reynolds might have accepted that a great landscape painting was better than a mediocre *istoria*, but at comparable levels it was, for him, always history which must occupy the highest rank, for only history could communicate the ethics of civic public life.

That both Turner and John Constable (1776–1837) were able to take over practically everything from Reynolds, save for the notion of public art being by definition history paintings, points to a general characteristic of this period: the way that received aesthetic theories were being modified and attacked, and their substitutes suffering similarly, to the extent that, by the 1820s, it is hard to discern any commonly held standard at all. Reynolds died in 1792. In 1851 the Pre-Raphaelite Brotherhood went public. The intervening years saw the careers of Turner, Sir Thomas Lawrence (1769–1830), John Flaxman (1755–1826), Constable, Benjamin Robert Haydon (1786–1846), John Sell Cotman (1782–1842), Sir Francis Chantrey (1781–1841), William Blake (1757–1827), Sir David Wilkie (1785–1841) and many others. Just glancing through their works will show the striking formal dissimilarity characteristic of the period, more particularly its earlier part. Blake's paintings could never be mistaken for those by anyone else. Constable and Turner shared common ends but their means could be very different. The portraits of Lawrence and Thomas Phillips (1770–1845) were popular among the aristocratic and upper middle classes, but individual in their styles. A 'natural' style, coexisting with many others, became apparent only towards the 1830s.

A problem in presenting an inevitably incomplete overview of this period is that historical research has been highly selective, paying scant regard to the rank artists were accorded in their own time. Some whom we have chosen to single out, obviously Blake, would have appeared but as peripheral figures to the contemporary view. In the 1830s Constable's reputation, at its highest in the 1820s, was so uncertain that the then-respectable *The Times* described him as an 'amateur' artist, and he never was thought the near-equal of Turner and never gained the professional and public recognition of his fellow landscapists Sir Augustus Wall Callcott (1779–1844) or William Collins (1788–1847), who, in 1825, sold his *Prawn Fishers at Hastings* (Royal Coll.) to George IV for 300 guineas.

Collins we have practically forgotten. The reputation of Lawrence survives, that of Phillips does not. Turner was thought of, as we do, as a giant, but, by the later 1820s one who had fallen into wilful eccentricity. Thereafter he never failed to attract notice, often as something of a freak in view of what else was taking place. Our habit of imposing our own aesthetic values on the art of the past accordingly distorts any historical account of it. Until very recently Constable's oil sketches were privileged over his large easel paintings (despite his 'I do not consider myself at work without I am before a six foot canvas') because they were erroneously valued as 'anticipating' Impressionist paintings. To inspect Constable's brilliant oil sketch of *Barges at Flatford Lock* (*c*.1810–12, Victoria & Albert Museum) shows it has nothing formally in common with an Impressionist painting, while the functions of each work were also entirely different. Constable's sketch acted as particular study to inform a larger conception of naturalism to be realised on exhibitable works, an Impressionist painting was finished study from nature based on the approximate transcription of optical perceptions – while France in the later nineteenth century provided artists with an environment rather different from that in England earlier.

With Turner the problem is different and more acute. His extraordinary qualities were recognised by contemporaries – 'Turner has some golden visions – glorious and beautiful, but they are only visions – yet still they are art – & one could live with *such* pictures in the house', wrote Constable in 1828 – and modern historians have concentrated on him to an extent that our knowledge of his work far exceeds what we know about other paintings, and those whom we have decided were less outstanding suffer by comparison.

John Constable, Barges at Flatford Lock *(c.1810–11)*.

Turner dominates through the sheer extent of his output, which ranges through antiquarian watercolours of architectural subjects, through subject pictures, through historical landscapes and re-workings of classical subjects, to, eventually, the late and extraordinary mythologies, like *Shade and Darkness – the evening of the Deluge* (1843, Clore Gallery, colour plate 1). Indeed, his paintings can be so complex that it is impossible to do them justice in a survey. For instance, of the continuing themes which demand exploration we might consider the relations his works bore to those of the old masters. These were complex and long-lived, so that in *The Festival upon the Opening of the Vintage at Macon* (1803, Sheffield City Art Galleries) he employed a Claudean compositional formula to historicise a modern pastoral subject, while placing his own imagery within an esteemed tradition in order to lay claim for the high pretensions of his own landscape. This painting, now dark and cold, surveys from high ground a valley in which the Rhône lies in a fat serpentine, and established relations of topography abstracted through composition, which would recognisably reappear in different contexts, as in

J.M.W. Turner, Dido Building Carthage *(1815)*.

England. Richmond Hill. The Prince Regent's Birthday (1819, Clore Gallery).
In these we survey a like valley from a like eminence, to connect the specific
with the general landscape type, and to remind us that in works like *Dido
Building Carthage* (1815, National Gallery) and *The Decline of the
Carthaginian Empire* (1817, National Gallery) Turner used Claude's seaport
composition to structure historical landscapes of startling luminescence, in
which the eye is constantly taken by details like the handling of tree-tops in
the distance or reflections near to, and in which the subjects bore a
contemporary meaning in their connection with the political ethics of the rise
and fall of empires in a newly post-Napoleonic age.

The fate of empires and their cultures was a theme which Turner would
also turn to in his Venetian scenes, for Venice served as a paradigm of an
imperial maritime state comparable to Britain but whose fortunes had been
suddenly and irrevocably reversed by the dictat of a conqueror. In 1843 *The
Sun of Venice going to Sea* (Clore Gallery), accompanied in the Royal
Academy exhibition catalogue by verses which spelled out the grim fate
awaiting the vessel: the 'ship of state', the *Sol de Venezia*, the principal object
of the painting, (and named on its canvas sail on which we can also discern a
painting like one of Turner's) returned to the theme of the fates of empires
and the arts. The brilliant colour must refer to the Venetian tradition further

to contribute to its content, and we must wonder what role was played by the watercolours he made in that city, works where through sparing, often vermilion outline and judicious washes, he rendered views of that city in an atmosphere of opalescent clarity.

Turner's range was astonishingly wide and his mastery of media idiosyncratic, and sometimes dubious, as with the oil paintings which would gradually disintegrate on gallery walls . Although 'colour beginnings', in which nature was refined to areas of blue, yellow, white, pink and red paint and which were then worked up into the evanescence of *Noreham Castle Sunrise* (1835–40, Clore Gallery) or *The Fighting Temeraire* (exhibition, 1839, National Gallery) tempt us to consider their relations to finished works as well as 'studies' such as the ones Turner made in Italy in 1828, this cannot be the function of an historical survey of this kind.

Our prospect over the art of this period can only be partial. General tendencies, are, however, apparent. Portraits still formed the mainstay of many artists' practices, although, with the exception of socially exalted sitters, they abandoned much of the formal language of civic grandeur instituted by Reynolds in favour of more intimate representations. History painting remained the ideal which few achieved and to which many paid lip service, and manifested itself in many and unlikely forms during the entirety of this period. Genre, or subject painting, had been a constant in British art which came to dominate by the 1830s, superseding landscape painting, which had been enjoying unprecedented popularity.

With those who formed the market for pictures travelling in increasing numbers, and with a growing familiarity with the theories of the Picturesque propounded intially by the Reverend William Gilpin, (1724–1804), and elaborated less influentially by Uvedale Price (1747–1829) and Richard Payne Knight (1750–1824), there was a constant demand for landscape painting. Turner, the dominant figure of the age, was a landscapist. It is also significant that it is landscapes that we associate with the provincial schools of artists founded first in Norwich and then in Bristol. And the legend is that Eugene Delacroix learned fundamental lessons from Constable's *Hay Wain* (1821, National Gallery; colour pl. 6) on its exhibition at the *Salon* of 1824.

In sculpture, artists continued to supply demands which changed little in kind. Patrons required busts and tombs and works of edifying subjects for domestic interiors. Architectural sculpture became increasingly important, and public sculpture, monuments to the worthy or statues in urban spaces, continued to be erected. Sculpture manifested a stylistic development which can be roughly paralleled in painting. Early in the period it showed some variety: individual masters had distinctive manners, while working in a neo-classical idiom. By the later 1810s it was possible to distinguish two principal styles. Some sculptors, pre-eminently Sir Francis Chantrey (1781–1842), were concerned to reproduce appearance as accurately as possible. Others adopted neo-classical conventions of forms which could, as the work of John Gibson (1790–1866) demonstrates, sit rather uneasily with their rather more sensual handling of textures.

Painting took longer to evolve any formal homogeneity, and was more tentative in displaying it. But by the 1830s certain artists, Edwin Landseer

(1802–73), Charles Robert Leslie (1794–1859) and William Mulready (1786–1863) among them, all produced fluently drawn compositions where paint, clear and pure in colour, was applied with conspicuous skill. Such mastery over media now came easily to British artists; the expert instruction in the Royal Academy Schools must have contributed to this advance in practical expertise. And although artistic output was still noticeably variable, a taste for genre subjects taken either from literature (scenes from *The Vicar of Wakefield* were so common in exhibitions as to be satirised) or from everyday life was now evident, and a type of painting which fits those criteria we could consider as typical of 'Victorian' art had clearly emerged.

Artists were also supplying work to the engravers. They produced discrete prints – reproductions after portraits of the famous or infamous, or after pictures of general interest – or as some other form of illustration. Book illustration was hugely popular, and artists like Thomas Stothard (1755–1834) or Richard Westall (1765–1836) derived considerable income from producing designs. The Academician William Hamilton painted and exhibited oils from which the engravers Bartolozzi and P.W. Tomkins later engraved fine prints for a 1797 edition of Thomson's *Seasons*. Turner (who was astute in making large sums after prints of his own works) is well known for having done the watercolours for the vignettes to Samuel Rogers's poem *Italy* (1830), and landscape prints were generally popular, either as book illustrations, or independently, or published as a series of illustrations of some interesting locality, or as plates in the ever-popular drawing manuals which no genteel young lady would be without.

Circumstances of the times

Art is not produced in a vacuum. A society must express some need for it, and that society's character will determine what painting, drawing or sculpture is produced. In the early nineteenth century British society underwent a spectacular and unprecedented transition. By 1850, as plans for the Great Exhibition showed, Britain was a highly industrialised country, with a population of some 21 million people. As only around 2½ million of these had been alive in 1800, this was a developing and young society. Where 23 per cent of the populus had lived in towns in 1801, the figure had risen to 34 per cent in 1851, and not only London, but the great industrial centres of Birmingham, Manchester and Leeds, and trading ports like Bristol and Liverpool developed at an unheard-of rate. Where travel had been geared to the horse in the 1800s, by the 1840s it was possible to traverse the country on railway trains.

Besides the dramatic changes associated with industrialisation – the rapid augmentation of the middle classes, the growth of professional self-consciousness, the appearance of an urban proletariat with its attendant problems – political transformations were also wrought. With the Repeal of the Test and Corporation Acts in 1827, the Emancipation of Roman Catholics in 1828 and the passing of the first Reform Bill in 1832 an *ancien régime* founded on a landed interest at last gave ground to the new wealth created by commerce and industry and allowed it a modicum of political power. Attacks on the Corn Laws, leading ultimately to their repeal in 1845, were a politically symbolic climax to the apparent decline of the landed interest, and it is of import here that during this decade the new Palace of Westminster, being built to replace the medieval original destroyed in a fire of 1834 (an event recorded in paintings by Turner) seemed an appropriate symbol for the way a political system originated by the Normans had been overtaken by events.

These social transformations did not provide stable conditions for the creation of the fine arts. The increase in their constituency (for material wealth necessitated the acquisition of culture) was attended with increasing confusion as to the function of the arts and how they should be perceived to be fulfilling it. This was manifested not only in increasingly complex relations between artists themselves, but also in a steady growth of art criticism of various descriptions. Such criticism presupposed that some needed a literary bridge to assist their comprehension of the pictorial, while acting as an outlet for opinions on taste so various as to attest to a rapidly developing social instability among the classes which presumed to cultivation.

Artists' working circumstances became rapidly more complicated. In the early 1800s there were clear signs of an increase both in the market for painting and among those who served it. Various societies and institutions concerned with promoting the arts were founded. Trevor Fawcett has written that

In 1803 the Norwich Society of Artists was founded and in 1805 held its first annual exhibition. Edinburgh and Bath followed suit in 1808. In 1809 the Northern Society's exhibition was inaugurated at Leeds. Liverpool made a new start in 1810.

Norwich was home to fine painters like Cotman and John Crome (1768–1821), while in Bristol first the noted genre artist Edward Bird (1772–1819) and then the landscape painter Francis Danby (1793–1861) thrived. In the metropolis the most significant event was the founding of the British Institution.

In June 1805 the founding Governors of the British Institution established a gallery for the exhibition of works by native artists, along with a few select specimens by other European painters. Their aims were to

encourage and reward the talents of the Artists of the United Kingdom; so as to extend and improve our manufactures, by that degree of taste and excellence which are to be exclusively derived from the cultivation of the Fine Arts; and thereby to increase the general prosperity and resources of the Empire.

A desire to see the British School flower was inspired partly through a conviction that one knew great nations through their cultural legacy – hence Turner's concern with Rome in his *Forum Romanum* (1826, Sir John Soane's Museum) as well as with Venice, France and Britain. Yet the national achievement must have seemed wanting against the works of the European masters, which could still be seen despite the war with France, for many pictures from dispersed collections were coming to London auction houses, and the Peace of Amiens in 1802 had allowed many British artists to visit the Louvre and contemplate the plundered masterpieces with which Napoleon

John Crome, Poringland Oak *(c.1818–20)*.

had filled it. In London Hazlitt was astounded by the riches of the Orleans Collection in 1798 and wrote of a 'mist' which 'passed away from my sight'. Turner, Joseph Farington (1747–1821) and many others worked hard in the Louvre – Turner, in particular, seeking to divine the principles on which Titian, Poussin and others had operated. Reynolds had persistently urged British painters to surpass the masters: this was an aim now given added impetus.

At first the British Institution maintained cordial relations with the Royal Academy; but it was principally conducted by the wealthy connoisseurs. It contained a study collection, and its first annual exhibition in 1806 not only caught the popular imagination but also provided a further and welcome space for painters to show their work (it soon became normal to exhibit there pictures unsold at the previous year's Royal Academy). Until 1817 the Institution offered premiums for works in various categories, historical or poetical compositions, or landscapes, but thereafter purchased any picture felt to be distinguished by its excellence. Soon the Institution appeared intent on reminding the Academy of its own traditions. It followed a retrospective exhibition of the paintings of Reynolds in 1813 with one of Wilson, Hogarth and Gainsborough in 1814, and then, in 1815, one of Flemish and Dutch painters. Lawrence is supposed to have exclaimed 'I suppose they think we want teaching'.

Of other exhibiting societies, The Society of Painters in Watercolour was inaugurated in November 1804 and held its first annual exhibition in 1805. Its rival, The New Society of Painters in Miniature and Watercolours, became the Associated Artists in Watercolour in 1808, the year of its first exhibition, but disbanded through financial problems in 1812.

Watercolour, an inferior medium in the Academic view, was beloved of amateurs and ladies, and fared badly in competition with oils. Hence the first exhibition afforded an opportunity to show watercolours by Robert Hill (1769–1844), John (1778–1842) and Cornelius Varley (1781–1873), John Glover (1767–1849) and William Havell (1782–1857), all respected masters and mainly landscapists. From an aquatint of the 1808 exhibition we see that many exhibits were large. Watercolour, originally a system of washing and tinting drawings, was attempting technical effects 'not inferior in power to oil-paintings, and equal in delicacy of tint, and purity and airiness of tone'. These effects had been pioneered by Turner building on the example of Paul Sandby (1725–1809), Gainsborough and Thomas Girtin (1775–1802) in large watercolours of mountainous and other subjects of the 1800s, and these other artists were quick to follow suit in producing watercolours of a solidity and richness more usual in oil paint. But Turner was also beginning to create effects analogous to those of watercolour in oil painting. This laid the ground for aesthetic confusion. The consensus had been that drawings, and such were watercolours considered, were for private contemplation not public display, but it seemed that this no longer applied.

The watercolourists' relations with consumers were always volatile. Cotman who swore he never would become a drawing master did, and stayed poor. Collins spent the 1810s assiduously building up a circle of regular patrons to give him future professional security. By the 1820s the provincial societies of artists (for instance in Norwich, Plymouth and Exeter) tended not to fare well. By the 1830s the provinces were welcome recipients of loan exhibitions of works by noted London artists, and the art press was expanding to accommodate the real interest of the growing middle-class public.

Though relations between painters and the British Institution had worsened, its Governors offered a selective patronage in their private dealings. Sir George Beaumont bought from Wilkie, who painted modern genre subjects with extraordinary technical facility and also made an unambiguous formal homage to seventeenth-century genre painters like Teniers by inserting his own work in their Old Master tradition. More generally it seemed that the connoisseurs favoured modern work reminiscent of old art, and the cry that such a slavish respect hampered the development of a native school was heard once more. Matters were exacerbated by the way the Institution awarded premiums. In 1814 Turner unsuccessfully submitted *Apullia in search of Appullus vide Ovid* (Clore Gallery) for one. This close pastiche of Lord Egremont's Claude, *Jacob with Laban and his Daughters* made the point about the connoisseurs and modern art by a pictorial joke. Beaumont had long been campaigning against Turner (for he detested both his painting on light grounds and confusion of media) and would not have appreciated it. Beaumont failed to damage Turner, but his follower, Callcott felt that the abuse hurt him commercially, and for this reason chose not to exhibit at the 1813 Royal Academy. In 1815 and 1816 an anonymous (but probably artistic) writer published two *Catalogues Raisonnés of the Pictures now exhibiting at the British Institution*, which were blistering indictments of those who 'set themselves up as Arbiters in art, whilst coming to the judgement seat unprepared with any information at all drawn from the contemplation or study of nature . . .Their ONLY standards are old pictures'.

This conflict indicated a profound confusion about the role of the artist in a rapidly transforming Britain. Turner had real respect for the old masters, but wished to work within their tradition to develop a distinctly modern art. Connoisseurs like Beaumont or Payne Knight seemed so blind to this that in 1824 Constable feared for the malign spell they might cast through the proposed founding of a National Gallery:

Should there be a national gallery (as is talked) there will be an end to the Art in poor old England, & she will become the same non entity as any other country which has one.

The reason is both plain & certain. The manufacturers of pictures are then made the criterion of perfection & not nature.

At issue was economic survival. The artists felt justly threatened. Cotman's patron, Dawson Turner, reminding him in 1826 that 'You have lived long enough to know that your present style will not succeed, and you have talent enough to adopt any other. The public is a body that cannot be forced . . . such among us who have to live by it, must be content to follow its taste', pointed up the precariousness of their position. Yet precisely such formal singularity as Turner complained of was essential if artists were to attract attention by marking their productions distinctly from those of rivals.

This uncertainty declined in the 1830s, when more settled political and social conditions fostered a corresponding stabilisation in the art world.

Corporate patronage began to assert itself and the great early Victorian collections began to be formed. Yet the Royal Academy itself came under repeated attack. Various non-academic artists, pre-eminently Haydon but also John Martin (1789–1854) and George Clint (1770–1854) later expressed their antagonism to the Academy to a Parliamentary Committee of 1836, but the new President, the amateur artist Sir Martin Archer Shee and his colleagues were successful in temporarily defending the institution. After moving to the National Gallery in 1837 further attacks came from radical politicians, notably Joseph Hume (who wanted free entry to the annual exhibition on particular days, since it was held in a public building). Shee again counter-attacked, but attacks were maintained into the 1840s, with politicians seeking to make the Academy accountable to Government and the Academy resisting this as a Public Institution which must enjoy a liberty impossible under the jurisdiction of those fired by particular political motives. Exhibitions in the meantime continued to be increasingly popular, as the 1830s and 1840s saw a rapidly-growing public concern with the fine arts.

This showed up in the increase in the volume of art criticism – a medium which attracted writers like Thackeray – and in the market itself. Private patronage remained crucial to painters: characters like Robert Vernon and John Sheepshanks (1787–1863), who gave some 233 paintings and numerous sketches to the nation, playing an active part. But the State now became involved, too. In 1836 a Select Committee on Arts and Manufactures had called for the encouragement of fresco painting in Britain. In 1841, another, called to consider 'the promotion of the fine arts of this country in connexion with the Houses of Parliament', recommended their decoration in that medium. A Fine Arts Commission chaired by Prince Albert mounted a competition of cartoons for the proposed decoration, which attracted young artists, amateurs, and Haydon, and proved extremely popular with the public.

By 1837 the State had also founded a Government School of Design, overseen by artists. This signalled a changed view of the rôle of art in national life. Around 1800 it was automatically assumed that improvement in the fine arts automatically led to a corresponding improvement in other areas of design. Now the country had developed a 'manufacturing population', and William Dyce, the Director, felt that the School of Design should inculcate the specialisations necessary to the tasks in hand. Yet, in 1851, *The Art Journal* asked 'When will England learn that even for the purposes of commerce Art is useful – and that where the higher and nobler Arts are assiduously cultivated the inferior ones are also sure to flourish?' These views were contradictory because society had assumed so complex a character so swiftly that there was little hope of critical consensus over the virtues, vices, or functions of the fine arts. Ruskin may have adopted so forceful a tone to allay this confusion.

Criticism in confusion

It is illuminating to review attitudes to the fine artists. The latent disagreement manifested in reaction to William Etty's (1787–1849) paintings of nudes in the 1820s reveals a breakdown in any critical consensus. *Cleopatra's Arrival in Cilicia* (taken from Plutarch's *Life of Anthony*) drew this from *The Times* when shown at the 1822 British Institution:

> . . . we take this opportunity of advising Mr Etty, who has some reputation for painting *Cleopatra's Galley* not to be seduced into a style which can gratify only the most vicious taste. Naked figures, when painted with the purity of Raphael, may be endured: but nakedness without purity is offensive and indecent, and in Mr Etty's canvas is mere dirty flesh.

This critic, ignorant of *istoria* necessitating the idealised presentation of the nude, perceived Etty as pandering to the sensual not the intellectual faculties. He and Constable were rival candidates for election to Academician in 1828. Lawrence backed Etty and delegated Shee and Phillips to canvas votes for him. They bearded Constable himself at the British Institution. 'I was "pounced" on by Mr Shee at the Institution on Saturday, and came in for my share of castigation. I have heard so much of the higher walks of the art that I am quite sick.' For Lawrence it was straightforward. A history painter must have the preference over a landscapist. Subject alone had come to indicate *istoria*, and in January 1829, Constable, again having to canvas the Academicians, wrote of his coming confrontation with 'highminded members who stickle for the "elevated & noble" walks of art – i.e. preferring the *shaggy posteriors of a Satyr* to the *moral feeling of landscape*'.

William Etty, Cleopatra's Arrival in Cilicia *(1822)*.

Constable believed that content, not subject, elevated art. The teaching of Farington and Beaumont and the decisive influence of Reynolds committed him to the ideal that painting should aspire to communicate high moral ideals; which, perversely, he believed could be realised in landscape. Reynolds, in his *Discourses*, a powerfully influential statement of traditional theory, understood the nation ideally to comprise a commonwealth of disinterested citizens who cultivated their intellectual faculties and were therefore able to promote a painting of an abstracted moral idealism; necessarily *istoria*, for only this could have no tendency to sensual gratification, a pleasure available potentially to any viewer. In the 1770s Reynolds may still have been able to distinguish a commonwealth of citizenry in the landed aristocracy into whose hands the government of Britain was entrusted. But by the 1790s such a view was no longer practically tenable, although many retained it.

The many opinions expressed on the proper formal characteristics of the art of a national school attest to the volatility of society. Johan Heinrich Fuseli (1741–1825), as Professor of Painting in the Royal Academy, published his first three lectures in 1801. In his view of art history, painting declined as 'public grandeur gave way to private splendour', and 'the Arts became the hirelings of Vanity and Wealth'. In a privatised society painting could no longer expect to communicate ideas of a moral or any other kind. Payne Knight, in his *Analytical Inquiry into the Principles of Taste* (four editions 1805–8) claimed that painting was simply 'colour, light and shade and all those harmonious and magical combinations of richness and splendour which form the charm and essence of the art'. And it was open to all to assess the sensual appeal of art. Payne Knight was not unopposed, but ideas like his were beginning to take hold. Yet despite his expressed sentiments, Payne Knight, along with fellow connoisseur Thomas Hope (1774–1831), encouraged Richard Westall (1765–1836) in a shift from genre to historical subjects, paying the enormous sum of 1000 guineas for a *Grecian Marriage* in 1811. Payne Knight approved of 'the utmost purity and dignity of heroic character, embellished and not impaired by the most rich and splendid colouring'. But despite its historical subject the painting was not in the Grand Style. It was illustrated on the small scale, and emphasised the charm and elegance of the figures. In other classical subjects painted for Payne Knight, *Flora unveiled by Zephyrs* (1807) or *Vertumnus and Pomona* (1809), Westall produced richly-coloured cabinet pictures, evolved from the tradition of Watteau, and destined for private contemplation, pictures which took historical subjects but did not present them as *istoria*.

These failures of communication were important. In the catalogue to the collection of Sir Abram Hume there is nothing on the subject of Titian's *Death of Actaeon* (National Gallery), which was historically central, but much on the technical quality of the painting of 'the water ruffled by the wind, and the bush in the foreground'. Yet, to Constable in the 1830s, Titian's greatest achievement was his representing landscape in *St Peter Martyr* also to communicate meaning, and thus to endow landscape itself with a potential for an elevated moral content, which art appeared to be losing. In Volume I of *Modern Painters* Ruskin vindicated Turner's art for its hyper-naturalism: a capacity to recognise natural appearances was all he could be confident of finding common to the new and vast audience for art.

History painting

Accordingly, history painting showed little consistency, and the circumstances of the time explain why Haydon's career was disastrous, why its most complex art was produced by Turner. Old ideas died hard. The Governors of the British Institution offered large premiums for history paintings. William Hilton (1786–1839) who could find it hard to sell works gained £122.10s. for the *Entombment of Christ* in 1811, and the Directors later paid 1000 guineas for his *Christ crowned with Thorns* (1825, Royal Academy). The idea persisted that the artist should aspire to be a history painter. In 1812, Bird, generally popular for his genre scenes, showed *The Day after the Battle of Chevy Chase*, a scene of carnage, considered by Payne Knight 'the highest style of historical composition' at the British Institution. It earned him both his Associateship of the Royal Academy in 1813, and the prestigious appointment of Historical Painter to Princess Charlotte. Even though he was a portraitist, Phillips submitted *Venus and Adonis*, an unfortunate pastiche of Titian, as his Diploma Piece in 1808. And in 1811 the animal painter and landscapist James Ward (1769–1859) sent as his Diploma Piece 'a scene of two naked Bacchanalian Children, a performance much inferior in merit to his pictures of Horses. He said he did not like to be admitted into the Academy as a *Horse Painter*'.

The creation of true history painting was impossible. Without public patronage or large public wall spaces, private attempts to patronise it were tried and failed. The bookseller Macklin's successful Poet's Gallery in Pall Mall prompted Alderman Boydell's scheme, initiated in 1786 and realised in 1798, for a gallery of Shakespearean subjects by the most notable artists. The commissions were recouped from visitors to the Gallery and by selling prints after the works. Shakespeare, central to national culture, was thought to communicate a natural universality of sentiment. The Gallery opened with 34 canvases by Barry, Northcote (1746–1831), Reynolds and others, commemorated by Gillray with a print entitled *Shakespeare Sacrificed; – or The Offering to Avarice*. The engravings after the pictures (few of which were in an appropriate Grand Style) instituted a new role for *istoria* as a kind of illustrative imagery.

Macklin's Bible (for which there was also a Gallery) was published between 1791 and 1800 with engravings after some 71 paintings, many by Philip James de Loutherbourg (1746–1812). This French-trained artist was competent with figural subjects, and in *The Creation* (1800, Private Coll.) acknowledged the Grand Style. Amongst the clouds an imposing figure of God gestures towards a bursting light, while angels with stone tablets, apparently representing the active and contemplative life unhelpfully related the subject to Moses receiving the Laws, which de Loutherbourg's basing God on Michelangelo's Moses suggested anyway. Other artists, including Reynolds, Fuseli, Hoppner, Stothard and Hamilton contributed to the project, and West's *Moses showing the Brazen Serpent* (engraving 1793), the Bible's frontispiece, also sets a Michelangelesque figure in a barren setting. The picture galleries were short-lived. Boydell's was dispersed in 1805. In 1813 the young American painter Leslie wrote 'I find that pictures from modern poets do not take. Even Shakespeare, Dante and Milton are scarcely sufficiently canonised to be firm ground'.

Fuseli had instituted his Milton Gallery through the sponsorship of friends as a means of promoting his own attempts at *istoria*: it lasted until 1801. His *Sin intervening between Satan and Death* (1793–6, Los Angeles, County Museum of Art), rooted both in Hogarth's *Satan, Sin and Death* and Barry's fine engraving of the same subject, made less of it than they by burying everything in obscurity. And despite their deep learning, Fuseli's works, while sharing a particular synthetic formal vocabulary with other artists' works, are usually more personal in content, which itself reveals something of the communicative potential *istoria* now had.

Fuseli's style amalgamated a neo-classical simplicity with Florentine mannerism. His shapes were flattened and linear, his anatomy stylised and emphatic, characteristics apparent to a greater or lesser degree in pictures by, among others, Romney, Westall, Flaxman, or Guy Head (1762–1800), whose *Echo flying from Narcissus* was in the 1800 Royal Academy. Echo, face on, realised almost on a solid-geometric basis, stretches across the picture at a slight diagonal, practically cocooned in carefully composed flying robes, and highlit against a mountainous landscape background (now dark and obscure) to force attention onto the semi-naked figure, an invention related to the similar ones of William Blake – in Plate 2 of *The Book of Urizen* (*c*.1795) for instance – and a type of funerary sculpture, notably Flaxman's Cromwell Monument of 1800, where the departing soul is portrayed ascending to heaven.

In this idiom of representation form was simplified and the lessons to be learned from a study of Michelangelo and the antique were plainly displayed. Adam, in an engraving after Westall's *Raphael with Adam and Eve* (1795) is muscular, and seated cross-legged with elbow on knee and chin in hand to denote intense thought, listens to a beautiful and androgynous Raphael. In physical realisation he is like the Adam which Blake would place with his back turned to an Eve entwined by the serpent and receiving the apple from its mouth into hers in 1808 (Boston, Museum of Fine Arts). Here the subject, with a dual relation to the Bible and Milton, is accessible, but Blake used this vocabulary indiscriminately, thus connecting compositions, such as the frontispiece to 'Europe' (?1824) to both *Urizen* and *Newton*, to infer that it was significant within his private cosmology. Paradoxically Blake wanted this private imagery, the true heir to the Grand Style but now confined to the printed page, to enter the public sphere.

The Catalogue title to Blake's one-man exhibition of 1809 at his brother Robert's house stated that the pictures were *Water Colours, being the Ancient Method of Fresco Painting Restored . . .*. In the Catalogue itself Blake extolled the true art of Michelangelo, Raphael, Giulio Romano and Dürer against the meretricious painting of Titian, Correggio, Rubens and Rembrandt; thus appearing to conform with traditional ideas as to the proper means of

William Blake, The Spiritual Form of Nelson Guiding Leviathan *(c.1805–9).*

rendering *istoria*. Two of the exhibits, both in tempera on small canvases, represented *The Spiritual Form of Nelson guiding Leviathan* (c.1805–9, Tate Gallery) and *The Spiritual Form of Pitt Guiding Behemoth* (?1805, Tate Gallery), Blake wanting 'a national commission to execute these figures on a scale that is suitable to the grandeur of the nation . . . in high finished fresco'. Pitt was the earthly destroyer, and Nelson directed Leviathan against figures of those nations warring with Britain, a black slave slumped under his feet pointing to the consequences of patriotism as it was then understood.

Historical imagery was now to be seen by few and understood by fewer, and this was the only form the Grand Style could now take.

Blake's work was ignored. Deviating iconographically from all the other numerous representations of these subjects, his imagery, like Fuseli's, demands learned elucidation. If this means of regenerating *istoria* were rejected, its only resorts were either to enter the private realm as the illustration of texts, as with Flaxman's influential designs after Homer and Dante, where the linear rendition of the subjects implies that they no longer had substance, or to appear in a different form. Turner persistently painted historical landscapes. *The Goddess of Discord choosing the Apple of Contention in the Garden of the Hesperides* (1806, Turner Bequest), a mythological subject based on actual terrain, embodied an alchemical allegory within an imagery of moral uses of knowledge, which critics missed, although they spotted how central to the performance was the paraphrase of Poussin which was unambiguously made. Turner returned to mythological themes with *Mercury and Herse* (Private Coll.) and *Apollo and Python* (Turner Bequest) in 1811, while Carthage began appearing in his work as a moral paradigm. He steadily produced such subjects. The glorious azure and golden *Bay of Baiae with Apollo and the Sybil* (1823, Turner Bequest; colour pl. 2) dissolved and reworked a Claudean composition to communicate Turner's assimilation of Mediterranean light and colour in a subject of the fall of great imperial nations through the decadence attendant upon luxury. Critics thought the picture 'gorgeous' but missed its meanings, until Ruskin in 1857 explained the sybil as 'the type of the ruined beauty of Italy' (a content which was also carried by some of Turner's Venetian subjects). His range was enormous and such historical subjects as *Regulus* (1828, reworked 1837, Turner Bequest), where we, like Regulus, gaze into an unremittingly glaring sun (although unlike him we can close our eyes) or *Bacchus and Ariadne* (1840, Turner Bequest), appeared regularly at the Royal Academy. *Shade and Darkness – the Evening of the Deluge* (Turner Bequest) in 1843 and *Light and Colour (Goethe's Theory) – the Morning after the Deluge – Moses writing the Book of Genesis* (Turner Bequest) adapted colour and tone polarities comparable to Titian, in such works as the *Pietà* (Venice, Accademia), to boost an imagery of death and regeneration which *The Spectator* saw as 'daubs' and *The Athenaeum* as 'Mr Turner's flagrant abuse of his genius'.

Traditional history painting was produced by Northcote and by West, who also displayed his works to full advantage in a custom-built Gallery (other artists, obviously Turner, were also resorting to this useful means of showing work to potential patrons). West's earlier works displayed pedestrian learning. Later ones appear uncertain in drawing, colouring and scale: his *Venus lamenting the Death of Adonis* (1803 RA; Rutgers University Art Gallery) (a small variant on a theme attempted previously) was presumably inspired by Titian's pictures in the Louvre. Venus, disproportionately long, has dislocated her left thigh. Behind her, an equally peculiar Cupid, is surmounted by some small-scale nymphs with features out of fashionable portraiture, while Adonis could be a very large garden statue. West was not always this incompetent, and his election to President of the Royal Academy indicates less grudging contemporary appreciation of his gifts and reveals something of the level of popular taste. *Death on the Pale Horse* (Pennsylvania Academy of the Fine Arts, Philadelphia) was enormous, and caused a sensation on exhibition in 1816. Yet although the subject is clearly apocalyptic, it is the fragmentation of the composition or the anatomical eccentricities which strike the eye now but did not then. West was attempting to revive what never had been a British tradition.

That the age was demanding paintings of a size suited to domestic display was ignored by Haydon, who, isolated from society, constantly in debt and paranoiacally egomaniacal, set himself to produce grandiose compositions, often after long labour in extreme privation. The subject of *Christ's Entry into Jerusalem* (St Mary's Sanctuary, Norwood, Ohio) perhaps acknowledged that the only public knowledge one might presuppose was of the Bible. It took Haydon between 1814 and 1820 to paint and was exhibited at the expense of others in the Egyptian Hall, Piccadilly, netting the artist a profit of £1298 in entry fees. The painting was rhapsodised by newspapers, and the venerable actress Mrs Siddons's approval of its 'supernatural' look allayed the disquiet expressed about the head of Christ, who indeed looks a bearded and flat-headed contemporary figure. The composition itself was not unskilled, and the crowds of figures served to set off the principal figure dramatically. As was the tragi-comic way with Haydon's career, a bid of £1000 made for the painting in his absence was turned down on his behalf, and it then did not sell. Yet, *Blackwoods*, on seeing the picture exhibited in Edinburgh – a public art now had to travel to its public – concluded that Haydon was 'already by far the greatest historical painter that England has yet produced'. As befitted a painter in a privatised society, Haydon himself believed that great history painting would be the result of individual genius and not social circumstances.

Istoria was a fragile ideal. In 1831 Daniel Maclise (1806–70) won the Royal Academy's Gold Medal for historical painting with *Hercules at the Crossroads* (Dublin, National Gallery of Ireland). This time-honoured subject, painted by Annibale Carracci and assimilated into the British canon by Shaftesbury, should present a stern lesson on the moral necessity to follow Virtue. But Maclise, while attempting to sustain this content – Vice involves us in the picture through eye contact and a winning leer – paints so as to destabilise it. Virtue is unyielding and in plain clothes. Vice inhabits a delightful bower, bordered round with *putti* (like the ones in the then-popular fairy paintings, which Maclise also produced). Hercules does not meditate on his choice but reaches instinctively towards the figure of Virtue, although Vice, a nude painted for display to the extent that her pubic hair is visible through her flimsy drapes, holds him effortlessly. The simple message gets lost in the ambiguities of its presentation and the lush richness and colouristic density of the painting itself. On winning his prize, Maclise did not take up the travelling scholarship to Italy which went with it, for he was less interested in history painting in the old sense, than in paintings of literary or theatrical scenes, and those historical events illustrative of events in the national past, rather than redolent with the imagery of public virtue.

With other artists there are comparable ambiguities. Etty was obsessed by painting naked women, principally because of his own inadequacy when confronted by real ones. In a *Venus and Cupid* of around 1833, the content

Benjamin Haydon, Christ's Entry into Jerusalem *(1814–20).*

Daniel Maclise, Hercules at the Crossroads *(1831).*

was transmitted by pictorial cross-connections, here with Titian, also meant to protect the imagery from pornographic readings. Contemporarily the Scots artist William Dyce (1806–64), painting with greater austerity and impressive skill, was also attempting *istoria*. His tempera rendering of *The Judgement of Solomon* (Edinburgh, National Gallery of Scotland; colour pl. 4) was by Raphael out of Veronese, a Renaissance manner proving the most suited for communicating this subject. Dyce had travelled to Italy in the 1820s and was probably familiar with the work of the Nazarenes whose influence appeared in his Madonnas of the late 1820s, painted in a manner also respectful of the early Raphael, and therefore pictures again imbued with content through association. Yet in clarity of design and deceptively simple colour, they were quite unlike work being done by anyone else, so while their meanings are clear to the initiated, nothing indicates that they were the expression of a common body of belief. *Istoria* was again the realm of the private.

And, tellingly, David Scott (1806–49), Dyce's co-winner for a prize in 1836, painted completely differently to completely different ends. *Russians burying their Dead* (1832, Glasgow, Hunterian Museum) was extraordinary in painting and composition. Scott eschewed the description of minute materiality common by then, indicating background figures loosely with thin paint and allowing the canvas texture to show, even in the foreground. In the

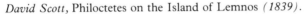

David Scott, Philoctetes on the Island of Lemnos *(1839).*

left background, a sinister fence of three ranks of soldiers leaning on bayonetted rifles have the crescent moon to their right. Exhibited at the Scottish Academy, it did not sell. Scott's later *Philoctetes on the Island of Lemnos* (1839, Edinburgh, National Gallery of Scotland) shows greater attention to surface in the painting of Philoctetes himself, arched in grief on barren rocks as his fellows sail into the distance under a startlingly-streaked sky. But Scott still maintained stylistic flexibility and rendered the water simply by means of sweeping brushstrokes, loaded at one end, and thinner through their length.

Scott was one of the failures in the competition for cartoons for the fresco decoration of the new Palace of Westminster. The Commission assumed from the outset that to promote painting would have a 'beneficial and elevating' influence on the people, and called for the depiction of subjects from British history, Shakespeare, Spenser, or Milton (who proved the most popular choice). Fresco, intimately associated with the great decorative schemes of Renaissance Italy, announced the high civilisation of the society which now presumed to use it, even though it was unsuitable because of the damp. The cartoons themselves were to be either chalk or charcoal on paper, between ten and fifteen feet long, and the winning entries were reproduced lithographically, E. Armitage's *The Landing of Caesar*, an impressively drawn scene of confusion with violently contorted, Michelangelesque bodies, quotes from many other paintings, including Géricault's *Raft of the Medusa*. Save for the directing figure of Caesar, it can be hard to tell Britons and Romans apart. It gained the first prize, while G.F. Watts took the second with *Caractacus led in Triumph through the Streets of Rome* and C.W. Cope the

E. Armitage, The Landing of Caesar *(1843); lithograph by W. Linnell.*

third with *The First Trial by Jury*, intelligible through recalling a *Judgement of Solomon*. Despite the relevance of these subjects to a particular historical mythology of Britain, they chiefly function as imaginative illustration, and even then contemporaries needed instructing, through the catalogue. Although Eastlake thought that the vast throng of visitors to their exhibition showed up 'the love of the lower orders for *pictures*', those pictures demanded literary elucidation. Even those pictures eventually frescoed in the New Palace were unclear. Thus Dyce's *Baptism of King Ethelbert* actually reveals itself as only the baptism of a royal figure, for Ethelbert still wears his crown, and background architecture, which could be either Moorish or Byzantine, is of little help in elucidating the content of the painting. Maclise's frescoes of *The Spirit of Chivalry* and *The Spirit of Justice*, subjects appropriate to the ideal parliamentary ethos, are composed as Renaissance *Sacra Conversazione*, and staffed by personifications whose contributions to any iconography are unclear. Pictures such as these defeat their own purpose.

Contemporary subjects and genre

Genres besides *istoria* communicated profound meanings simply by being the product of their culture. In the 1850s Maclise embellished the Houses of Parliament with frescoes of *The Meeting of Wellington and Blücher* and *The Death of Nelson* (oil painting in the Walker Art Gallery, Liverpool). The latter is instantly identifiable as a scene demonstrating the patriotism and selflessness so strongly promoted at this period. The dying Nelson fitted the convention for the figure, and the naval setting was knowable through vicarious or actual experience. Such art, related to *istoria* in being concerned

Daniel Maclise, The Death of Nelson at Trafalgar *(1861)*.

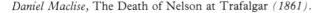

to inspire elevated sentiments, attempted this through the heroic presentation of scenes from contemporary life.

Perhaps as an American less restrictively conscious of the European tradition, Copley John Singleton (1737–1815) was, in his enormous *Death of Chatham* (1779–81, Tate Gallery) to mythologise a contemporary hero. He showed the picture privately, charging entrance, and augmented this considerable revenue by selling an engraving after the painting. A print was also taken after West's *Death of Nelson* of 1806 (Liverpool, Walker Art Gallery) (an obvious prototype for Maclise's picture) but showing just the portrait heads, with a numbered key assisting their identification. Nelson proved a popular subject. Constable made a watercolour of the *Victory* (Victoria & Albert Museum), Turner's *Battle of Trafalgar* (1806, Clore Gallery), a *tour de force* of sails, smoke and rigging, was admired, particularly after its repainting in 1808.

De Loutherbourg painted *istoria* and 'contemporary history' which, as with *The Battle of Valenciennes* (1794, Lord Hesketh, Easton Neston) was sometimes commissioned by market-wise engravers, here V. & R. Green. Both this picture and its companion piece, representing Lord Howe's momentous victory over the French fleet in 1794 had significant patriotic importance and became great attractions. The wars produced numerous such incidents as the British fought to protect their unwritten constitution from democracy. De Loutherbourg was an enterprising person who in the 1780s had invented his Eidophusikon, a mechanical apparatus which exhibited dramatically-lit and very convincing moving representations of such scenes as *Shipwreck of the Halsewell, East Indiaman*, in a forerunner of the various panoramas which were to become so popular in the 1800s.

De Loutherbourg's genre scenes, landscapes and comic representations of contemporary events, suggest that 'genre', the picturing of everyday scenes,

embraced several categories of painting. These included literary subjects –
Wilkie would paint scenes from Burns as readily as from actuality, and saw
no need to adjust his style to do so; theatrical representations (a sub-species
in which Clint specialised); and pictures of the populations of foreign lands.
Sometimes the staffage (the figures painted into a landscape) dominated
enough to transform a landscape painting into a subject picture, with artists
like Collins, who sought to exploit the popularity of both genre and landscape
painting becoming involved in a fine balancing act. Collins secured his fame
with *The Disposal of a Favourite Lamb* (1813, RA), where the rustic setting
was an essential support to the pathetic scene of the 'sturdy urchin
indignantly pulling away the butcher's boy, who reluctantly and good
humouredly pressed forward to lead the dumb favourite of the family to the
greedy slaughterhouse; the girl tearfully remonstrating with her mother . . .
yielding to the iron necessities of want'. The picture was not only a hit at
exhibition but a small engraving of it sold some 15,000 impressions, which
indicates just how far this kind of imagery could be considered common
property.

There were prints like this or the many mezzotints which William Ward or
J.R. Smith produced after Morland, the dissemination of Francis Wheatley's
(1747–1801) inventions (like his *Cries of London*, 1793) by the same means, or
Thomas Rowlandson's (1756–1827) comic prints or rustic subjects. Then
those various popular annuals which began to proliferate in the 1830s were
frequently embellished with reproductions after new or favourite pictures,
and genre scenes were characteristic of book illustrations. *Olivia's return to
her Father*, a roundel, one of Stothard's designs for an edition of *The Vicar of
Wakefield* of 1792, is conceived as a genre scene. Stothard, skilfully
miniaturising his figures, retained sufficient marks of age or facial difference
to save them from the blandness of contemporary work by others. Stothard, a
consistent and popular artist (the famous engraving after his *Canterbury
Pilgrims* was found in many houses) also worked effectively on the large scale,
as with the fine and richly-coloured *Othello and Desdemona* (Stratford-upon-
Avon).

The miniaturisation of genre and its widespread dissemination through
various media, including watercolours, exempted it from the restraints which
so undermined the feasibility of *istoria*. If novels, plays and poems were the
bedrock of the culture acquired by all classes, book illustrations could
eventually create an expressive vocabulary of pictorial representation, an
imagery which also communicated meaning simply through being familiar.
What eventually developed was a painting which embodied elevating ideas in
a rendering of the known and the particular.

The dominant genre painters of the early part of the period include
Wheatley, Morland, Westall and William Redmore Bigg. Bigg was sufficiently
well thought of to become a Royal Academician in 1814. His expositions of
the simple and virtuous poor living exemplary lives, widely disseminated
through engravings, were characteristic of much of this sort of painting:
effectively composed, competently drawn, and pleasingly coloured, qualities
also prominent with Wheatley. In Wheatley's scenes of rural genre the charm
was partly implicit in the way his colouring – pinks, blues and other hues –

and handling were developed from the French rococo. *The Fisherman's Wife* (1796, Private Coll.) is set by her cottage, embowered in trees to refer to Gainsborough's Fancy Pictures. The left third of the picture is taken up with a view across the water on which her absent (and therefore industrious) husband makes his living. She shows herself the ideal partner. Young, buxom and pretty, she glances towards us while mending the nets where her bonny infant plays, while by her feet are hens (an emblem of proper domesticity) and to her left a wicker bird cage, perhaps pointing to the reward of industry being the leisure to enjoy its occupant's song. This woman is deserving because she is neat and busy. Wheatley overlays the image with the common theme of waiting for the fisherman's return, perhaps to suggest that this absent one may be serving his country. Although he made no good living, his *Rustic Hours* or *Four Times of Day* (1796, Yale Center for British Art) maintains the unexceptionable proletarian imagery, where labour is attended with neither dirt nor physical effort, and its rewards are to be seen in a brood of healthy children and the right to fall asleep over the kitchen table of your neat and spartan cottage. These paintings were preceded in their exhibition at the Royal Academy in 1801 by the publication of mezzotints in 1800.

Mezzotint, a favoured and typically British print medium, was also used by Morland. Morland, a spectacular alcoholic, preferred the company of low-life friends to the social betterment his sales might have bought. His rural genre pieces compare superficially with Wheatley's. In *The Benevolent Sportsman* (1792, Cambridge, Fitzwilliam Museum) a slickly-painted and pleasing lightly coloured landscape, there features a gypsy encampment, presumably on common land. The males' dark complexions make the association with 'Egyptians', and they would seem threateningly alien, save for the figure touching his forelock while accepting alms from a sportsman (whose white horse contrasts with their dark and resting donkey) to defuse the scene, for the indolent poor were not then viewed with much approval. As John Barrell has demonstrated, disturbed reactions to Morland's imagery pointed to the constraints on how real life might be pictured. In Ward's mezzotint after the *Door of a Village Inn* (1793) the faces of the serving-girl and her children are smiling. Morland had painted them miserable and blank. A viewpoint which saw the poor as content in their station (the Revolution in France had sharpened up attitudes considerably) and industrious enough to clothe themselves decently found difficulty in accommodating the possibility that the poor themselves might not concur.

They must be painted as by Wheatley or Bigg, or in the comic mode perfected by Rowlandson. His imagery ranged from the pornographic, to rural scenes, to the seriously satirical. His genre subjects connected with experience, but his line, which moved almost independently around or past what it designed, distanced the scene from direct documentation. This shift was helped by the subtle exaggerations of features; he utilised these techniques consistently. In *Gaffer Goodman* from *The English Dance of Death* (1815–16, San Marino, Henry Huntington Library and Picture Gallery) the gaffer, with his grossly distorted features, shares a pipe with death, while his young wife, busy at her spinning, flirts with a swain through an open window, neither incidentally being in caricature. The cauldron boiling over

Thomas Rowlandson, 'Gaffer Goodman' from The English Dance of Death *(1815–16)*.

the fire by which sits the gaffer points to the rewards of a dissolute life, even
Industry flirts, and only the dog reacts to Death with any real terror. The
proper vehicle for this moral content should have been the Grand Style.

Rowlandson enhances the irony through communicating it in the inferior
medium of drawing (there is a parallel with Blake here). The eventual
elevation of genre subjects in oil painting was stimulated by Wilkie's *Village
Politicians* (1806, Earl of Mansfield). This subject was risky and potentially
seditious, for proletarian drinking in ale-houses was frowned upon, but
Wilkie laundered it in a variety of ways. The picture title referred to Hector
MacNeil's *Scotland's Skaith*, a poem about the tribulations of a family where
the father is addicted to politics and whisky, thus relating the canvas to a
literary fiction. Then the residual element of caricature sets the image within
that comic tradition which Rowlandson had developed, and, through the
exaggerated grimaces, recalls those seventeenth-century Flemish tavern scenes
to which the picture was deliberately stylistically related. This scene of
Scottish boors arguing over their newspaper is reassuring as well as amusing.
Moreover, Wilkie seemed capable of developing that seventeenth-century
genre painting so valued by connoisseurs like Beaumont or Payne Knight. So
sensational was Wilkie's success with *The Blind Fiddler* (1807, RA),
commissioned by Beaumont, that Turner riposted with the comparable *A
Country Blacksmith disputing the Price of Iron, and the Price charged to the
Butcher for shoeing his Horse* (1808, RA, Turner Bequest). The title parodies
the particularity of Wilkie's pictures, and Turner carefully filled the canvas
with hens, tools and vegetables to maintain the joke: contemporary critics saw
humour in subject alone. In that year he exhibited another genre scene in *The
Unpaid Bill* and in the mid-1830s extracted genre from the realm of the

Sir David Wilkie, The Village Politicians *(1806)*.

everyday in the pictorially sophisticated and chromatically splendid and ambiguous renderings of interiors at Petworth.

There were other reactions. Bird's *Country Choristers rehearsing an Anthem for Sunday* (1810, RA, HM The Queen) referred to various works Wilkie had so far exhibited (he thought Bird's picture deficient in painting and colouring). Bird nevertheless claimed massive popular attention – his *The Reading of the Will concluded* attracted large crowds in 1811 – perhaps because he made few demands on spectators. Wilkie, however, was developing in breadth of style and sentiment. *Distraining for Rent* (1815, Edinburgh, National Gallery of Scotland) was topical in years of agricultural depression. It depicts a farmer's family in various attitudes of despair as the bailiffs inventorise their possessions. Extremely subdued colour, mostly shades of brown and restrained chiaroscuro, boost the sombreness of this tragic *drame bourgeois*. Wilkie was elevating genre and an onlooker would appreciate his skill in characterising the typical, and reflect on the very serious issues which underlay the scene.

Some learnt more than simply to pastiche Wilkie. Mulready, initially a painter of landscapes and surburban scenes, moved towards genre in the 1810s. *The Village Buffoon* (1815, London, RA), his Diploma Piece, apparently baffled the Academicians, until Wilkie explained the subject: a relatively well-off (his cane is silver-topped) but silly old man paying court to a young village girl, slumping embarrassedly against the door post. Mulready understood how, if people learned to read his imagery, subject could be

William Mulready, The
Village Buffoon *(1815–16)*.

communicated by facial expression, gesture, and composition, and how it was
appropriate publicly to present a painting on the theme of *Vanitas* in this
manner. He was another exceptionally able artist, who experimented in
expanding the range of his subjects. The very fine *Interior of an English
Cottage* (1828, HM The Queen) connects thematically with Wheatley's
Fisherman's Wife except that here it is a gamekeeper, whom his wife (with
their daughter lying tired against her knee) has not so far seen approaching,
who might not have survived the dangers of his occupation. Mulready had
learned too about colouristic propriety, for the predominant earth colours
communicate a sombre mood.

Wilkie meanwhile was inventing further means of celebrating modern life.
*Chelsea Pensioners receiving the London Gazette Extraordinary announcing the
Battle of Waterloo* (1821, Apsley House), commissioned by the Duke of
Wellington in 1816, catalogues the moment as the end of a debilitating war is
announced. Géricault, ignorant of the subject, perceived this as an abstracted
celebration of Victory itself. All classes, ages, sexes and races are seized by
the euphoria of the moment. The fluid handling, with accents of colour over
the canvas, created a brilliance of pictorial effect, continuing with a fine
ability to manage facial expression, to engage the beholder's interest. Yet
Wilkie painted the climaxes of contemporary life small scale, proper to the
place of this public art within the domestic apartments where the life of a
privatised society was conducted.

Wilkie's later style became looser and, influenced by Spanish painting (he
had visited mainland Europe in 1825–6 for the sake of his health), far darker.

Sir David Wilkie, The Irish Whiskey Still *(1840)*.

Sir Edwin Landseer, The Highland Whisky Still *(1826–9)*.

The Irish Whiskey Still (1840, Edinburgh, National Gallery of Scotland) recalling an 1835 visit to Ireland, is in a tradition of low-life scenes in portraying a rough interior with an old man assessing the poteen. It should be contrasted with Landseer's *Highland Whisky Still* (1826–29) commissioned by the Duke of Wellington. Landseer had a good line in Scottish subjects, and here, for bootleggers were often poachers too, he tells a poignant tale of how criminality must corrupt the young. Only the lurcher which (typically of Landseer) gazes with beseeching sadness at the poacher, whose coarse features, stubble, black hair and scowl confirm his villainous character, seems to perceive, along with us, the catastrophic effect that this environment must have on these still-innocent children. All is sentiment and clever illusionism, and the canvas was admired at the Royal Academy in 1829. Wilkie, however, presented a meditation on the nature of civilisation. He had found the Irish existing in a 'state of primeval simplicity' under 'the most simple and pastoral conditions'. The wisdom of the old man (the complex forms of the still have alchemical connections) is put to no useful end, the bearded young man represents raw but undirected strength, while the naked child stoking the fire is reminiscent of the *putti* one might find in earlier depictions of the forge of Vulcan.

Few attempted so elevated a sentiment. Mulready (who also painted literary illustrations or pictures of childhood of fascinating interest) centred the narrative of *The Widow* (1823, Sir Richard Proby) on a recently bereaved widow succumbing to the blandishments of a suitor, to the disapproval of her maid, which Ruskin thought risqué. Because the later *Choosing her Wedding Gown* (1843) was from *The Vicar of Wakefield*, a transaction between men and women could be pictured without attracting adverse comment. In *The Sonnet* (1839, Victoria & Albert Museum), a small painting of humble courtship, the beautifully lit and depopulated landscape suggests an Arcadian setting fit for figures so sturdy and finely proportioned as practically to recall Renaissance models. Danby's earlier *Disappointed Love* (1821, Victoria & Albert Museum) is a comparable picture, where the solitary young girl sits with head bowed, the torn pages of a letter floating away on a gloomy stream, and a miniature of her lover on the grass between her and her fine red scarf.

Literary and theatrical illustration was always popular, and Clint specialised in this. *Mr. Young as Hamlet and Miss Glover as Ophelia* (1813, London RA) was in that convention codified by Zoffany where the painting commemorated the stars in performance. *Falstaff relating his valiant Experiences at the Boar's Head, Eastcheap* (1835, Petworth) detailed the wry amusement Falstaff's bragging excites, to contrast with its companion-piece, showing the duel between Sir Toby and Sebastian from *Twelfth Night*, an exterior scene on a terrace emphasising the distress created by combat. The extremely skilled Leslie often pictured well-known incidents from favourite books. *Uncle Toby and the Widow Wadman in the Sentry Box* (1830, Tate Gallery), featuring the old soldier from behind, militarily erect and concentrating on the plan, while the young and pretty widow pays attention to him, was typical of these well-painted and undemanding pictures and connects with Mulready's *Choosing the Wedding Gown* or E.M. Ward's *Dr Johnson in Lord Chesterfield's Ante Room* (1845, Tate Gallery). Of other artists' versions of the national heritage, Maclise's *Merry Christmas in the Baron's Hall* (1838, Dublin, National Gallery of Ireland) is a Jacobean scene of unstinted bounty and radiant good humour. The increasing numbers of pictures concerned with recreating a national past indicated, perhaps, how separate it was now felt to be.

Genre painting had expansive boundaries. Maclise had also dabbled in scenes from the supernatural in his *Scene from Undine* (HM The Queen) which he exhibited in 1848 at the Royal Academy as, obviously enough, did Landseer in his *Scene from a Midsummer Night's Dream* (1848–51, National Gallery of Victoria, Melbourne); and there is the famous *Fairy Feller's Master Stroke* by Richard Dadd (1817–86). Equally peculiar were foreigners, and pictures of the customs and costumes of other countries proliferated, connecting with landscape paintings of exotic regions by J.F. Lewis (1805–76), William Daniell (1769–1857) or David Roberts (1796–1864). C.L. Eastlake produced *banditti* pictures, or, in 1827, an *Italian Scene in the Campo Santo: Pilgrims arriving in Sight of Rome and St Peter's Evening* (Woburn Abbey) where female and male pilgrims of different characters and ages react in varying ways to the hazy vista of Rome and the Campagna. Popish imagery then had a particular charge as the established Church reeled under first the Repeal of the Test and Corporation Acts, and then the Emancipation of the Catholics. The real market for Italian scenes was signalled by Collins painting them after his Italian journey of 1837–8.

Genre paintings had a wide appeal. Even Haydon in *Punch, or May Day* (1829–30, Tate Gallery), following Wilkie, painted a colourful, everyday scene more successfully than *istoria*: compare his *Curtius leaping into the Gulf* (1836–42, Exeter, Royal Albert Memorial Museum) with its expressive terror on the face of the horse and blankness on that of Curtius. Wilkie, or Mulready in *Train up a Child* (1841, Forbes Magazine) which not only engaged with the actual problems of Lascar beggars but also concerned itself with complexities of social interrelationships, led to the asking of serious, complex, and ultimately moral questions. Richard Redgrave (1804–88) was keen to concern his art with real social issues. Genre painting was the best medium for communicating them, and now satisfied the need for a serious public art in a privatised society.

Sculpture

When Lord Elgin showed those Parthenon sculptures he had removed in a house in Park Lane in 1809, their reception was mixed, with artists generally very enthusiastic and some connoisseurs not. From 1809 Elgin's attempt to arrange their sale to the nation was hampered by Payne Knight's wrong but influential low opinion of them. This dispute again points to the characteristic contemporary lack of consensus in matters of taste. Sculpture was perhaps the last true public art to survive, with much of it displayed in public buildings like churches, or in public spaces. Yet it was not immune from historical pressures.

In 1799 Flaxman conceived a plan to erect a giant statue of Britannia at

Greenwich. Judging from Blake's print this would have stood behind the Queen's House and dwarfed both it and the Observatory. Flaxman presumably had antique precedents in mind. Greenwich, notional maritime heart of Britain (as it was painted both by Turner and de Loutherbourg) was an ideal location: the statue would be visible from the sea, and 'as Greenwich Hill is the place from whence the longitude is taken, the monument would, like the first milestone in the city of Rome, be the point from which the world would be measured'. This scheme came to nothing, but significantly in the 1840s, comparable ones did. In 1838 a competition – in a commercial society competitions let artists compete for commissions and allowed for some corruption in the way of nobbling the judging committees – was held for a monument to Nelson in Trafalgar Square. William Railton took first prize for his submission of a Corinthian column. This was controversial. The *Art Union*, by then influential, wholly opposed it, even after Railton had won a second competition in 1839 with the same design (this time, recalling Flaxman, Peter Hollins submitted another for a 120-foot high statue of Britannia). The column, up by 1845, was eventually topped with E.H. Baily's Nelson – Landseer's lions took longer.

It was in this decade, too, that Matthew Coates Wyatt (1777–1862) and James Wyatt the younger (1808–93), again in the face of some critical vitriol, cast a 30-foot tall equestrian statue of the Duke of Wellington, destined for Decimus Burton's triumphal arch at Hyde Park Corner. Even though the government decided, once it was up, that it must come down, it was in place between 1846 and 1883. That such sculpture flourished only now is one phenomenon among others, like the unprecedented decision to insist that the New Palace of Westminster be in an imitation of an earlier architectural style, and lavishly embellished with sculptural decoration as in actual medieval buildings. Here the sculpture was supervised by John Thomas and the decoration of the Royal Exchange after 1844 with work by, among others, Richard Westmacott (the younger) suggests that it exercised a potent example. By then the British had a sense of nationality of a different order from that at the beginning of the period.

Sculpture had a distinct market and was a complicated process. Bronze needed casting. Marbles were often based on models, whose dimensions were transferred by pointing machines before assistants cut out the statue in rough. It was therefore expensive, and it was imperative that sculptors attract clients. A hardly foolproof way of doing this was by exhibiting at the Royal Academy. Benedict Read writes that when 'Musgrave Lewthwaite Watson died in 1847, aged forty-three, the common refrain was: "he was a lost man – what might he have been if encouraged".' He had spent long years as a journeyman for others and never had the money to initiate major independent work. But there was also a nexus of highly regarded artists – Chantrey, Flaxman, Sir Richard Westmacott (1775–1856), Gibson – which was patronised and enjoyed financial independence.

In 1802 Chantrey broke his indentures as an apprentice carver and gilder to begin portrait painting, first in his native Sheffield, then London. He started sculpting in 1805, becoming famous through his bust of Horne Tooke at the 1811 Royal Academy exhibition. This, he claimed, secured some

£12,000 worth of commissions. Flaxman began working for Wedgwood, and after a trip to Rome in the late 1780s and early 1790s, gained Academic honours and a high reputation, which accordingly attracted those (including George IV) anxious to be seen to patronise merit. Sir Richard Westmacott called Flaxman 'the greatest of modern sculptors', a high compliment for a contemporary of Canova. Whereas Chantrey mostly produced monuments and busts, Flaxman specialised in monumental sculpture. A different approach was taken by Mrs Eleanor Coade (fl.1769–1820) who in 1769 set up a manufactory of artificial stone at Lambeth. Indeed, in mass-production of *objets d'art* Mrs Coade was astute enough to employ such artists as Flaxman, Bacon and Thomas Banks (1735–1805) as modellers. The most famous Coade project was to fill the West Pediment at Greenwich between 1810–13 with large figures after designs by West. Coade's stone sculpture also serves to remind us how necessary a part of the environment sculpture was.

Portrait busts stayed popular as tokens of vanity and as commemorative souvenirs to display dynastic pride or embellish public spaces with reminders of the worthy; as well as occasionally augmenting tombs. In a long career Joseph Nollekens (1737–1823) produced numerous busts and massed an enormous fortune. His *Charles James Fox* (1792, Earl of Leicester), a head and shoulders, refers to the antique in the drapery, while the face appears to represent the original, with heavy features and unruly hair. This is a public image to be balanced against popular satirical representations of Fox. Nollekens was stylistically eclectic. *Charles Burney* (1802, British Museum), fleshy in features but recognisable as an older version of the musician painted

Sir Francis Chantrey, Reverend Horne-Took *(1811)*.

Joseph Nollekens, Charles James Fox *(1792)*.

by both Gainsborough and Reynolds, is in his daily wear. In 1814 the brewer Samuel Whitbread (London, Drury Lane Theatre) was Roman, even down to his haircut and costume. Of busts by others, Banks's *Warren Hastings* (1799, Commonwealth Relations Office) also hints at the antique through dress, a means of which Reynolds would have approved for ridding the sculpture of specific temporal reference while admitting the need to communicate the realities of appearance through the detailed modelling of facial planes, drilled eyes, and apparently actual hairstyle.

This 'realism' came to dominate. Chantrey's bust, *Horne-Tooke* (1811, Cambridge, Fitzwilliam Museum) had to attract attention for representing the notorious radical, but is also superior sculpture, as Nollekens acknowledged by having an exhibit removed to give it a better place at the Academy. There is nothing classical here. The plainness of Tooke's buttoned coat sets off the head, carved with extreme sensitivity to illusionism. There is a real impression of bone under skin. The set of Tooke's jaw and gaze reinforce an impression of particularity, and the novelty of the conception must have been extraordinary. The age demanded distinction in all fields, and Chantrey came to rank as highly as Turner, Wilkie or Lawrence. Chantrey apart, the demand for busts was steady enough to keep others employed, working in the same type patterns.

Whole-figure statues also represented notable people, either contemporary, dead, or fictional (as with much of the sculpture for the new Palace of Westminster). Flaxman based the head of his William Pitt (1812, Glasgow Art Gallery) on Nolleken's bust, and adopted that pose from Roman magisterial statuary earlier used by Reynolds for *Commodore Keppel*, to insist that, despite modern dress and a peculiarly elongated form, Pitt was, appropriately to his posthumous reputation, the latter-day equivalent of one of the great public figures of antiquity. Chantrey's *Pitt* (1831, London, Hanover Square) was proportionately more convincing, and signified Pitt as statesman through his grasping a scroll and a large cloak of indeterminate fashion. In a contemporary statue of *Canning* (1832, London, Parliament Square) Westmacott also utilised the scroll, and added a toga, while giving the head a very contemporary appearance. These alternatives remained viable. Gibson's *Robert Peel* (1852, London, Westminster Abbey) was (as one would expect from a Rome-based artist trained by Canova and Thorvaldsen) togate and fitted with the obligatory scroll. In 1845 the ill-fated Musgrave Lewthwaite Watson had carved *Major Aglionby* (Carlisle, Assize Courts) as a completely modern figure.

These statues could also serve for monuments. Funerary sculpture, important for a clientele sharply aware of its individual self-importance, were very variable and inventive, ranging from plain plaques set in walls to large and complex schemes. The former sort admitted different types. The inscription to Henry Westmacott's (1784–1861) monument to Edmund Escourt (d.1814, Shipton Moyne) is on a sculpted cloth draped over a headstone, a pattern John Rossi (1762–1839) elaborated in his monument to Catherine Whalley (d.1817, Eaton, Northamptonshire) where the inscribed circular plaque was held by two angels. In 1818 the freemason John Postlethwaite was commemorated by T. MacDermott (St Michael's, Ashton-

John Gibson, Robert Peel *(1852).*

under-Lyne) with an eccentrically lettered tablet between two columns, recording his having 'attained the highest orders of *Masonry* without becoming PROUD', the whole surrounded with various masonic insignia.

The traditional full-scale memorial still flourished. In Rossi's Dryden monument (post 1797, Canons Ashby), a female figure mourns, an arm round the funerary urn, backed by the traditional pyramid of eternity. In Sir Richard Westmacott's Fox monument (1810–23, Westminster Abbey) a toga-clad Fox is raised from his bier while a half-kneeling African, hands clasped, gazes at him with respect for his humane attainments.

The numerous other tomb types made can only be glanced at. In Flaxman's severely classical Cromwell memorial the deceased ascends heavenwards, assisted by angels, in a serpentine design. This was a popular invention, with Thomas Farrell's (1798–1876) monument to Countess de Grey (d.1848, Flitton, Bedfordshire) being an interesting late variant. Here the angel raises the deceased in relief, set against the pyramid of eternity, family and friends, sculpted in the round, displaying a carefully composed scene of grieving on the earthly plane. Other types had one or two female figures mourn over a portrait medallion, or featured deathbeds, like

Sir Francis Chantrey, The Sleeping Children *(1817)*.

Chantrey's monument for David Pike Watts (1817–26). The philanthropist rises from reading the Bible to bless his daughter and her three children (educationalists of the time favoured the exposure of children to the dying), the elder two finding the sight intriguing, the youngest turning to clutch his mother. Sir Richard Westmacott combined this with the ascending soul type in a monument to the Duchess of Newcastle (Clumber Chapel, Nottinghamshire) who died after the birth of twins, one still-born, the other not long surviving her, in 1822. The Duchess, her infants appearing to sleep, raises herself from her deathbed as if to answer the call of an angel set in a relief plaque in the wall above her.

When Banks's monument to Penelope Boothby (Ashbourne, Derbyshire) who died aged six was exhibited in the Royal Academy in 1793, it was openly wept over by Royalty. The child apparently sleeps on a mattress on a neo-classical sarcophagus, a conception developed in Chantrey's *The Sleeping Children* (1817, Lichfield Cathedral), a comparable sensation at the Academy. Chantrey commemorated the two daughters of a Mrs Robinson, working from a death mask for one of the faces. They sleep in each other's arms, the bunch of snowdrops held by the younger a touching symbol of the death of beauty in the springtime of life. The monument inspired poems, pottery imitations sold well, and the idea proved popular. A variant is the monument to John Fane, the infant son of Lord Burghersh, who had died in 1816 (Applethorpe, Northamptonshire), represented in his nightcap, half out of the bedclothes, in the way of sleeping children.

Some monuments were intimate, others severe. Some impressed their subject's saintliness, others their earthly achievements. Flaxman, at University College, Oxford, showed William Jones studying among the Indians, with the inscription 'He formed a digest of Hindu and Mohammedan Laws'; and at Christchurch Priory Lady Fitzharris (d.1813) reading quietly to her children. In 1841 Westmacott the younger had Lady Ann Fitzpatrick (Grafton Underwood, Northamptonshire) dispensing charity. Busts remained popular. The major innovation occurred around 1840, partly influenced by the Gothic Revival and the intolerant aesthetic of A.W. Pugin. We begin to find medievalising recumbent effigies, often realised as sleeping figures. Raffaelle Monti dressed Lady de Mauley (d.1844, Hatherop) in medieval costume, clutching her rosary, and lying on a tomb chest embellished with Gothic mouldings, guarded on each side by a pair of praying angels.

The various free-standing groups set up in St Paul's Cathedral (*c*.1800–20) to commemorate the heroic dead of the Napoleonic Wars, commissioned by a 'Committee of Taste' including Charles Townley, Beaumont and Payne Knight (amateur was preferred to professional judgement on matters of taste throughout the period) are intermediary between tomb and public sculpture. Flaxman set Nelson (1808–18) on a plinth inscribed with the names of his victories. At its base were appropriate allegorical reliefs, and to one side Britannia points out his example to a couple of lads while to the other a British Lion crouches and snarls. Bacon the Younger's monument for General Moore had him being lowered into the tomb, to suggest that private and public imagery could coexist.

Commemorative sculptures changed over the period, the later years seeing grandiose constructions like the Scott memorial in Edinburgh. In Sir Richard Westmacott's 1809 monument, the Duke of Bedford (London, Woburn Square) leans on a Rotherham plough, reliefs around the plinth reinforcing the imagery of agricultural reformer. The analogy would be with Flaxman's Nelson. Chantrey's bronze equestrian statue of George IV, in Trafalgar Square, adapted an esteemed pattern which retained its vitality. But now Sir Richard Westmacott had attempted a large-scale tribute to the Duke of Wellington as Achilles (London, Hyde Park); an allegory which would not have communicated, for most would not have understood it. With Nelson's column or John Graham Lough's (1798–1876) megalomaniac Lord Collingwood (1847, Tynemouth) we realise how much things had changed. The latter is a 23-foot high statue on a 50-foot plinth above rising steps with parapets embellished with canons. The state always could supply recognisable heroes, but their less allusive and more bombastic representation was significant.

Society now valued individual achievement, hence the commemoration of the triumphal individual. Earlier works communicated sentiment, or information about the virtues of the person represented; busts or free-standing statues accommodated public men in a fictive community. That ethos vanished as the enterprise culture took over. The Pike Watts monument communicated an abstract virtue. Dr Arnold's tomb by Thomas dogmatically communicated the Christian goodness of the schoolmaster by referring to the 'Christian' middle ages through its Gothic surround. Its expressive language

Sir Richard Westmacott, The Duke of Wellington as Achilles *1814–22).*

was simple. Gothic was good. And the free-standing subject-pieces which
sculptors also produced to demonstrate their powers changed perceptibly in
character, too. Flaxman's *Fury of Athamas* (1790–4, Ickworth) illustrates a
ghastly tale from Ovid, familiar to cultivated people. It attempts, in the
complex arrangement of the group and the obvious references to the
Laocoon, to set its sculptor within a great and continuing tradition. Gibson
would try to maintain this. His *Mars and Cupid* (1821, Chatsworth) was
decisively in the modern neo-classical idiom, with a soft surface polish not
found in actual classical sculpture, although by now in *Cupid and Psyche*
(1822, Woburn Abbey) Sir Richard Westmacott demonstrated subjects
lacking in point save as providing the opportunity to carve the naked figure
with propriety. Patrick Macdowell's (1799–1870) *Girl Reading* (1838, Dublin
Society), a figure in early adolescence, wears flimsy drapes, off the shoulder,
while gazing with heavy-lidded eyes at a book. With an Etty this
pornographic display would have meant censorious criticism. Sculpture
justified it through referring to a content it no longer had: unlike architectural
sculpture.

Like classical pediments, modern ones were often filled with sculpture. Sir
Richard Westmacott carved various figures indicative of the progress of
civilisation for the British Museum, itself considered to mark an important
stage in this, from 1841 to 1847. But the work was arcane and unintelligible.
It was the medieval and other personages carved for the Houses of Parliament
and later public buildings, always with care, but seldom with distinctive style,

which indicated the view the 1840s had of a past which it had appropriated, and had formed, as in the paintings of Ward, Maclise and others, to fit its present purposes.

Portraiture

Portraits, from watercolour miniatures to full-length oils, were always in demand. There were both developments and the end of the Grand Style portrait initiated by Reynolds and later prosecuted by John Hoppner (1758–1810) or Sir William Beechey (1753–1839) into the 1800s. After them, sitters were painted in their daily apparel or occasional fancy dress which, after the mid-1830s, tended to be medieval. Artists like Lawrence and Sir Henry Raeburn (1756–1823) developed tricks of lighting to suggest an air of mystery, often adapted to representations of creative individuals. Haydon's fine *Wordsworth musing upon Helvellyn* (1842, National Portrait Gallery) features the poet from a low viewpoint, arms crossed and head bowed, as clouds lour around the mountain tops.

Then there was the 'keepsake' portrait, which developed around 1830. Often head and shoulders only and of a glamorous woman, these early pin-ups stand apart from those numerous portraits which, through their insistent emphasis on domesticated settings, make us aware of the increasingly private character of life. The public man as Reynolds had sought to create him survived largely in sculpture. Significantly, one portrait type which began proliferating in the 1790s was the carefully-finished drawing (Dance the architect specialised in finely rendered profile heads). Drawings had been for the contemplation of family and intimates; only caricatures previously were generally displayed.

Reviewing the 1829 Royal Academy exhibition *The New Monthly Magazine* noted the 'inordinate number of portraits . . . a general fault in every exhibition in England'. We have since paid proportionately less attention to portraiture, and know little of the work of respected artists like John Jackson (1778–1831) or William Owen (1796–1825). Yet, despite the quantities of hack work, there was such demand that even in the 1820s Constable painted excellent portraits, and artists like Lawrence or Raeburn were high calibre. Like Haydon's *Wordsworth*, Landseer's *John Gibson* (c.1850, RA), although painted indoors and apparently dressed in a blanket, gazes downwards with a similar gaze, signifying 'creative' introspection.

Earlier comparable figures had been isolated, their intense looks directed past any onlooker. Thus John Linnell (1792–1882) painted Collins, and a print of 1848 included Collins's signature to anticipate later cigarette cards of sports stars. Raeburn used these devices for *Scott* (Edinburgh, National Gallery of Scotland) and in his painting of the same tartan-clad sitter, painted for Murray the publisher in 1818, Phillips highlit the face which stared out of the top left-hand corner of the picture. Lawrence's very fine chalk portrait of Westall (1790s) had initiated something of this. Westall, looking to the lower right, has seemingly tense features which draw our attention, something helped by the face being the only properly finished part. None of these

Thomas Lawrence, Elizabeth Farren, later Countess of Derby *(1790)*.

creative people smile, as they might have in the eighteenth century. Phillips's rather wooden *Byron* (who had a sense of humour) in Albanian costume (1813, National Portrait Gallery) is without expression.

The exceptionally gifted Lawrence gave something of this mystique to men, but not to women or children. He produced some memorable drawings, comparable to Ingres in fluency and accuracy. With the tonally realised *Isabel Smith* (Tate Gallery) the frame of a bonnet emphasises a face accentuated by a precise gaze, sharp nose, and thin-lipped scowl. In contrast, in a drawing of the Duchess of Wellington (1814, Duke of Wellington), the ringlets and large soulful eyes impressing her glamour shift the image towards the keepsake. Lawrence was also keen to flatter in paintings of women. The full-length *Elizabeth Farren* (1790, New York, Metropolitan Museum) appears to glance out of the picture plane, as she glides across an extensive landscape, clutching a fur-lined cloak to her neck with an ungloved hand, her lips slightly parted, and her hair the same colour as her frock. Lawrence characteristically utilised the brilliance of oil paint to suggest brilliance of character here. Otherwise he saw women as dutiful mothers or respectable matrons. Children were represented as charming in a sweet way.

Men could think, or take action. Lawrence was comfortably melodramatic with *John Philip Kemble as Coriolanus* (1789, RA, Guildhall Art Gallery), where the hands, head and one foot are highlit to isolate him in a way comparable to the amazing *John, Lord Mountstuart* (1795, RA), who died after falling from a horse in 1794. Lawrence portrayed him swarthy and dramatic in the half light, with a gloomy Spanish landscape streaked yellow to suggest water reflecting sky, stretching behind him. A silver and red cloak lining set off Mountstuart's face, looking characteristically and introspectively into the distance. Even with the traditional format of the seated male figure in an interior, Lawrence eschewed those customary props which had defined social role or particular activity. *The Prince Regent* (1818 RA, The City of Dublin) struck a compromise, maintaining the conventions of royal portraiture by picturing the Prince in Garter robes, hand on a paper to impress the commitment to duty, with the traditional curtain as backcloth. Yet the gaze mimics Kemble's to portray the public man as private individual – the *British Press* wrote of 'a little flattery'. And Lawrence's *Pope Pius VII* (for the prince) in 1819 was a study in papist scarlet of a small seated man lost in thought.

Raeburn's portraits compare with those of Lawrence. Based in Edinburgh, save for briefly after 1810 when he went to London to check on the opportunities opened up by the recent death of Hoppner, Raeburn did dispatch works for exhibition, and was elected Royal Academician. Yet, as he wrote to Wilkie in 1819, he felt isolated, knowing little of what was going on in the art world, and wanting news. Raeburn handled paint as fluently but differently from Lawrence, laying it in block-like touches. *Sir John and Lady Clerk* (*c.*1790, Dublin, National Gallery of Ireland) is an exceptional variant on the theme of the married couple in a landscape. In intimate contact, his pointing out something to his wife allows them to participate and not pose in landscape. The scenery is hills, trees and valleys and, through beautifully painted effects of backlighting, the artist relates man to nature not as its

Sir Henry Raeburn, Sir John and Lady Clerk *(c.1790).*

owner, nor in self-congratulatory contemplation of it, but as held in some kind of momentary harmony with it through light and colour, for their clothes partake of the hues of their surrounds.

Until the 1830s pictures seldom informed much on the relations of the sitter with her or his fellows. Instead they tended to impress how every man had become an island. Maclise's fine pencil and watercolour portrait of an anonymous man in his study (*c.*1831, Edinburgh, National Gallery of Scotland) shows him refined and modern, surrounded by elegant furniture, an environment expected to communicate meanings and recuperate that eighteenth-century convention Lawrence had abandoned. When Mulready pictured the collector Sheepshanks in his study (*c.*1832–4, Victoria & Albert Museum) rather than showing the public man in contemplation, as would earlier have been the case, he represented the private man engaged in those private activities which establish his cultivation. Sheepshanks, who has been looking over some prints, addresses the maid who brings a cup of coffee and the mail (perhaps a reminiscence of Chardin to allude to the honourable character of domestic virtue). And in Maclise's celebrated *Charles Dickens* (1839, National Portrait Gallery) Dickens wears his everyday clothes, in a domestic interior, lost in thought as befitted a novelist.

Confronted by young and elegant women, both Alfred Stevens (1817–75) with *Emma Pegler* (*c.*1833, Liverpool, Walker Art Gallery) and Etty with *Mrs. Vaughan* (*c.*1835–40, Cardiff, National Museum of Wales) showed their sitters with fashionable, off the shoulder gowns, and a matter of factness comparable to Lawrence's drawings more than his paintings. Likewise,

Sir Edwin Landseer, Windsor Castle in Modern Times *(1841–5)*.

Landseer's *The Viscountess Fitzharris* (1844, Earl of Malmesbury) was a beauty, seated at an open window with a brace of appealing dogs, calmly sewing. The domestic portrait had again become the norm.

Landseer continued this. *Windsor Castle in Modern Times* (1841–5, HM The Queen) shows Albert greeted by Victoria in the green Drawing Room, which he has littered with the dead birds (including a kingfisher, held by the Princess Victoria), the bounty of a hunting expedition from which he has emerged spotlessly clean. This is as domestic, private a couple (albeit living in a house with very extensive grounds) as any of their respectable subjects. Landseer's nearest approach to a state portrait commemorated a fancy dress ball when the couple had donned medieval costume. And Albert's effigy at Windsor was also carved as a medieval figure to suggest that Royalty abstracted might only thus be realised, as medieval architecture appeared appropriate to the Houses of Parliament. Otherwise portraits were firmly of the present.

Landscape

Landscape painting was also concerned with the contemporary. Like genre it grew to unprecedented heights of popularity in a wide variety of forms. Turner dominated. His earliest efforts date from 1789, when he was 14 years old; and he lived until 1851. From near the beginning to the end, his work was dignified by a serious interest in content meant to instate it on the level of *istoria*, an ambition which immediately points to the complex nature of the history of landscape painting over this period.

Landscape appeared in many media. The most exalted were in oil paint, but they were used too as decorations on furniture. Watercolour and graphic media were popular, particularly with amateurs. Landscape prints gave artists a regular income because of various demands for views, instruction manuals, illustrations to books, or prints after notable paintings. Turner's *Liber Studiorum* mezzotints published after 1808 demonstrated the range and scope of landscape. Other artists issued prints independently; Crome took a chance with etchings, Cotman attempted to make a living through antiquarian illustrations.

Links between painted, drawn and reproductive media were often close. Thomas Hearne's (1744–1817) watercolours and drawings were engraved by W. Byrne for *The Antiquities of Great Britain*. Forty watercolours by Turner plus work by William Westall (1781–1850), Samuel Owen, Peter de Wint (1784–1849), William Havell (1782–1857), William Collins and others were delivered to W.B. Cooke for publication in 16 parts as *Picturesque Views of the Southern Coast of England* between 1814 and 1826, when the completed set was bound for issue in two volumes. In prints of antiquarian scenes the inspiring remains of buildings could interact with landscape. The standard views of country houses were always popular. And the pictures of coastal towns Turner did for Cooke ask questions about the pictorial sophistication of their market, for their complex iconographical references to a notional 'Britain' would have been more normal in oil paintings.

The United Kingdom afforded a variety of scenery. Mountainous regions were increasingly popular with tourists, themselves evidence of the increase and social distillation of the leisured classes, so that the Lake District was considered infested with visitors, and pictures of it stood a real chance of selling because of their souvenir value. Ironically the region came to be perceived as representing an area of traditional values, unspoiled by the progress so evident in nearby industrialised Lancashire; an element also behind attitudes to Scotland or Wales, although mediated by established ideas about those countries. Otherwise, Hereford or Shropshire were envisaged as loci of agricultural plenty, Kent was always thought pleasing, and Devon was reputed to supply the English equivalent to Mediterranean light.

Artists like Constable, or less extremely the Norwich painters, concentrated on regions otherwise frequently ignored; the Valley of the Suffolk Stour, the flatlands around Norwich. Landscape expanded to include coastal views and, after 1815 (although Turner had reached Switzerland during the Peace of Amiens), European ones, as painters like Cotman and Richard Parkes Bonington (1801–28) discovered Normandy and others went beyond. Italy held a peculiar fascination, the scenery of Africa, the Near East and Asia became popular, and the British were becoming familiar with representations of their colonial territories. Lycett was sending back views in New South Wales, Hearne had made views in Antigua, Thomas and William Daniell travelled extensively on the Indian sub-continent and published *Oriental*

Scenery in six parts between 1795 and 1808, Thomas exhibiting at the Royal Academy until 1828. This geographically indiscriminate imagery was a cultural analogue of the range of British imperial, political, trading and touring interests.

Landscapes varied. Sporting pictures, scenes of horse-racing or fox-hunting, were designed for a particular clientele, a social sub-grouping whose identity became more distinct as the century progressed, and were not much approved by the non-sporting world. These pictures changed little, recreating an imagery established at the beginning of the century. At its least elevated, sporting painting simply recorded the lineaments of favourite animals in some fitting environment, and artists like Sawrey Gilpin (1733–1807) (controversially elected Royal Academician in 1797) attempted to distinguish themselves from painters of meat by picturing scenes from *Gulliver's Travels* or other reputable sources. The other extreme showed imaginative landscape, an expansive category encompassing Martin's paradisical confections, and some of Turner's works, ranging through visualisations of classical scenes, the recreations of literary settings, to the earlier pictures of Samuel Palmer (1805–81). There were landscapes of sublime or picturesque scenery, rustic scenes, farming landscapes, and numerous other sub-divisions.

Drawing was considered a polite accomplishment, and drawing masters proliferated. Cox moved from London to Hereford in 1811 to teach at a girls' school, and published one of the many instruction manuals where the subjects to be copied were chiefly landscapes. The aesthetic theories of the Reverend Gilpin, Price and Payne Knight were widely disseminated, assimilated to a popular notion of the Picturesque, and discussed and argued over. Until landscape became less dominating in the 1830s, so much was produced the market could hardly bear it, as Cotman's career or Cox's various moves through the Midlands (pragmatically inspired by his resignation to regular employment as a drawing master) attest.

British landscape painting enjoyed unprecedented popularity between 1790–1830, developing in a rich variety of ways, before a period of consolidation during which less experimentation, with the exception of the work of Turner and Constable, was apparent. By 1800 there was already a good market for picturesque scenes, whether in watercolour or oil. The contemporary picturesque appears in works by Morland, or de Loutherbourg, who, in *Tintern Abbey* (1805 RA, Cambridge, Fitzwilliam Museum) virtually created a manifesto of such imagery. On the far side of his river banks, which rise with fictive steepness, rural figures engage in typical occupations. The composition otherwise comprises a depiction of the rough woodland and interesting rocks characteristic of the Wye Valley, with no violent extremes of colouring. Tintern Abbey itself is to one side, at a distance. Although medieval architecture, being redolent of historical and national interest, was a proper landscape subject, Gilpin thought Tintern Abbey pictorially disappointing. The regularity of the gable ends 'hurt the eye'; he thought a mallet 'judiciously used (but who durst use it?) might be of service in fracturing some of them'. To be picturesque, de Loutherbourg chanced losing antiquarian content.

Artists studied more than the picturesque. Mountains had once been a

feature for distances, to reduce their intimidating character. After his 1802
Swiss trip Turner pictured them from close vantage to emphasise their
frightening grandeur. On a tour to the Lake District in 1806 Constable partly
ignored the standard views to concentrate on fixing effects of light and
weather in watercolour. Girtin had liberated the medium from filling in local
colours in pictures like *The White House, Chelsea* (Tate Gallery), where tones
and washes revealed expressive possibilities to be exploited by Crome,
Cotman, Varley and many others. This lively experimentation happened
during a period of war when native scenery represented what would be lost
should the French prevail. This, with the nominal closure of the European
continent, partly explains why landscape became so popular a national art. In
the 1800s there was an upsurge in oil sketching from nature. This practice
was thought to have originated with Claude, and, associated with the French
Academy in Rome, had been transmitted into Britain by Wilson and his
pupils.

Turner oil-sketched along the Thames from 1804, and Linnell, William
Henry Hunt (1790–1864) and Mulready, all closely connected with John
Varley, experimented with the practice, as did Constable, Cox, and William
Delamotte (1775–1863).

Turner painted both large and small oil sketches, capturing a plethora of
detail and effects. *Willows beside a Stream* (1806–7, Turner Bequest), on a
medium-sized canvas, was probably painted from a punt on the Thames and
details a group of boughs only, otherwise indicating colouristic and tonal
relations broadly and summarily. The smaller *Windsor Castle from Salt Hill*
(*c*.1807, Turner Bequest) is more thickly painted on panel and describes a
distance where the horizon is varied with the grey silhouette of Windsor
Castle and the darker ones of trees. These sketches were the basis for those
Thames landscapes of the 1800s which showed its various agricultural

J.M.W. Turner, Thomson's Aeolian Harp *(1809).*

activities, or the splendour of Windsor Castle, to signify that precious national culture commemorated too in paintings of Pope's Villa, dilapidated, and *Thomson's Aeolian Harp* (1809, Manchester City Art Galleries). Here Turner's view of the Thames Valley from Richmond Hill, taken by Thomson to exemplify 'Happy Britannia', was composed as a Claude to consolidate the Arcadian associations and define this scenery as the stage for that exemplary civic and political life (realised in such virtuous terms as paintings like this) which must be saved from the French. Constable and those others who had taken up oil sketching began from about 1810 to paint working British landscapes which celebrated daily life in moral terms. Constable in particular impressed how this productive relationship with their countryside resulted in those beautiful agricultural landscapes denoting the social harmony and political stability unique to the British (granted that this was a particular view). This kind of painting peaked in 1815 with several harvest pictures: de Wint's fine view of the Lincolnshire open fields (Victoria & Albert Museum) or G.R. Lewis's (1782–1871) *Hereford from the Haywood Lodge* (Tate Gallery), a painstaking painting of an actual view in that county.

These scenes apart, de Loutherbourg painted scenes of avalanches or with *banditti*. Mountain landscapes proliferated in the work of artists like Julius Caesar Ibbetson (1759–1817). James Ward for a while painted landscapes deeply marked by the example of Rubens, for Beaumont had bought the *Château de Steen* for his wife, before going on to an ambitious rendering of the native scene. This huge *Gordale Scar* (1814, Tate Gallery), commissioned

James Ward, Gordale Scar *(1814)*.

by Lord Ribbesdale, was exhibited at the British Institution in 1814. *The Monthly Magazine*, sensitive to Ward's aims, wrote of a

vast dell formed by perpendicular cliffs of limestone strata . . . A chasm in the rocks, down which falls a cascade, enlightens the gloom on a plain at the bottom, on which Mr. Ward has introduced groups of wild animals peculiar to this country, and among others, the bull.

That the *Sporting Magazine* in 1815 called the picture a 'coarse, dark, ostrogothic piece of mosaic painting' reminds us of how uncertain opinion on taste then was. Ward's canvas was of a size more properly used for *istoria* to imply that his landscape was its latter-day equal.

Others were less ambitious. In the 1800s Callcott painted landscapes reminiscent of Dutch prototypes to please the connoisseurs, before angering them by basing his manner on Turner's. Collins made his name with rural genre scenes, where the landscape, neatly painted and not perceptually demanding, was a vital component. In Norwich Crome rendered the local scene in a manner derived from a study of Ruisdael, Hobbema and Gainsborough; Cotman's style was different enough to inspire public antagonism. His *Durham Castle and Cathedral* (*c*.1809–10, Norwich Castle Museum) possibly appeared at the Norwich Society Exhibition of 1809, and making no concession to the antiquarian illustration expected with such a subject, was realised in simplified colouristic and tonal planes.

These artists were still practising in the 1820s, when, perhaps, the reputation of landscape was highest when a group of painters, Bonington, Thomas Shotter Boys (1803–74), Samuel Prout (1783–1852) and Cox among them, began to work in a loosely comparable way. Prout, established as a teacher and writer of drawing manuals in the 1810s, was a skilled draughtsman. In *Durham from the North West* (*c*.1816) he shows himself,

John Sell Cotman, Durham Castle and Cathedral *(c.1809–10)*.

unlike Cotman, to have been willing to communicate the desired picturesque effects of detail and chiaroscuro. In the 1820s, often painting buildings, he emphasised the broad plasticity of form and striking effects of light and shade, frequently accented by clear sweeps of colour which in due course would be rendered in lithography. Boys and William Callow (1812–1908) painted similarly, supplying the market with the pleasing and striking landscape imagery perfected by Bonington. Bonington used oil paint as easily as Lawrence and created brilliant souvenirs of French or Italian scenes. In watercolour he shared the taste for firmly drawn outlines filled out with washes and prominent colour, and this luminous style, in his hands or those of Cox, developed along with a type of landscape which was often tonally light, and concerned to impress a sensation mainly of flickering light and shade, subject having become of secondary importance.

Meanwhile the Shoreham-based Palmer's complex and highly wrought sepia drawings had as much to do with the prints of Van Leyden and Dürer as with local scenery. In the foreground of *The Valley Thick with Corn* (1825, Oxford, Ashmolean Museum) a bearded patriarchal figure reads while reposing against a tree stump. The corn, with impossibly heavy heads, grows in a landscape conceived as an agglomeration of fecund organic forms. Something of this artistic vocabulary was taken over by Palmer's friends Edward Calvert (1799–1883) and George Richmond (1809–96), but it was he who perpetuated the fiction with greatest conviction. This transformation of reality was a reaction against it during a time of rural social unrest which culminated in the 'Swing' riots of 1830. Palmer's incapacity to find meaning in the present was comparable to Boys and those other painters resorting to

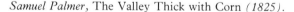

Samuel Palmer, The Valley Thick with Corn *(1825).*

formulae and pleasing patterns to picture scenes which were valued as souvenirs, illustrations, or some generally recognisable 'naturalism'. After marrying in the 1830s, Palmer had for financial reasons to adopt a tight, colourful and representational style to picture sites in Italy or Wales, a type of watercolour drawing not unlike Myles Birket Foster's, which Andrew Wilton considers to have evolved from 'the precisely measured hatching and stippling in bright colour that Turner developed'.

While genre painting flourished in the 1830s, landscapes seemed to settle, Linnell produced full-blown rural scenes, often including harvests, far from the meticulous 'realism' of his work of the 1810s, Callcott continued painting expansive landscapes, and Clarkson Stanfield (1793–1867) land or seascapes often reminiscent of earlier work by Turner. In 1833 his *Venice from the Dogana* (Earl of Shelbourne) so exasperated Turner that he painted *Venice from the Dogana . . . Canaletti painting* (Clore Gallery) actually on the exhibition walls to show Stanfield how it ought to be done. In different ways Turner and Constable were becoming marginalised, suffering critical opprobium because people failed to comprehend their art. Ann Bermingham has suggested that the view of landscape had become predominantly that of the suburbanite. It was to be looked at but not understood. Thomas Creswick (1811–69) or Frederick Richard Lee (1799–1878) created pleasing rustic scenes which a visitor from town might appreciate through the 1840s.

Yet Turner's abstract and grand compositions must remind us that landscape had pretensions to high art, if society no longer believed it. Both he and Constable were ambitious to supply the public painting they knew Britain required. Constable, early convinced this must be his goal, was forced to adjust the means by which he thought he might achieve this, but never lost his conviction that achieve this he must. He knew from Reynolds that one learned the mechanics of painting by studying the masters, but this must be refined by working from nature. He attempted this in various ways before embarking from 1808 on a long campaign of sketching around the family house at East Bergholt. Possibly following Turner, around 1810 he began to paint working scenes, after 1814 directly from nature, with, despite their unpretentious dimensions, a serious moral iconography, sympathetic to the ideology of the rural professional classes whence he had originated. His *View of Dedham* (1814, Boston Museum of Fine Arts) includes a dunghill, with the distant village, and pictured the Stour Valley as the productive result of industry; in the ordered and harmonious disposition of its parts, this represented a paradigm of the superior character of British society, here 'naturalised' through the studious verisimilitude with which its appearance was rendered.

This idea of landscape was transformed in the 1820s under the impetus of the different scenery and conditions Constable experienced, first at Hampstead (where he began taking his family in 1819) and then Brighton (where he was going from 1824). He began seeing abstracted light effects as a natural factor which might, if transferred to painting, unify representations of particular places by a more general naturalism. In East Anglia social disturbances combined with this apprehension to change his landscape, so that with *The Leaping Horse* (1825, RA) he invented a scene, realised in a rough and picturesque style, which suggests without describing appearances. By the 1830s, as Constable mourned the England the radicals had wrecked, he refined landscape to colour and chiaroscuro and in these sought eternal truths. He claimed to have found in Titian a unity of landscape and *istoria* which justified exalted claims for the moral potential of landscape. In a world being so dramatically transformed by man, only nature appeared not to change.

Constable translated these perceptions into an expressionistic imagery as in *Scene on a River* (c.1830–7, Washington, Phillips Collection; colour pl. 3) which few could have tolerated and fewer understood. He stayed fired by the old humanist conviction that society evolved into civilisation only when it produced great moral art. Turner shared this ideal, perhaps because of respect for the Academy and Reynolds. But his attempts at embodying it were far more varied and ambitious, although they too ended in a species of abstraction, the colour beginnings (canvases on which he laid out areas of white and primary colours). Given the circumstances of the 1800s, with the Watercolour Society claiming elevated status for watercolours, or the Sketching Society gathering to make historical landscapes in pencil and watercolour over a convivial evening, some artists understandably felt that landscape had real potential to become the public art Britain so sorely lacked.

Turner always aimed to rival the old masters and to imbue his pictures with a high moral content. *Thomson's Aeolian Harp* was followed in 1812 with *Snow Storm, Hannibal and his Army Crossing the Alps* (Clore Gallery) to which he attached lines from his manuscript poem, *The Fallacies of Hope* in the Royal Academy Catalogue. In this landscape of terrible Alpine scenery, realised in the throes of a storm creating a white cortex against which elephants are silhouetted, Turner embedded a rumination on the fates of ambition and empires, which he would continue in 1815 with *Dido building Carthage* and in 1817 *The Decline of the Carthaginian Empire*; these pictures were painted with an unprecedented knowledge of perspective and ability to create the illusion of looking into light, to deliver a moral warning to Britain at the end of the Napoleonic Wars and the beginning of agricultural depression. Critics missed his content, although, with the exception of Beaumont and Holwell Carr of the British Institution, they were united in their praise of his stupendous naturalism.

Turner also showed an unprecedented mastery of watercolour, and there are stories of how *A First-Rate taking in Stores* (1818, Bedford, Cecil Higgins Art Gallery) was begun

. . . by pouring wet paint onto the paper till it was saturated, he tore, he scratched, he scrabbled at in a kind of frenzy and the whole thing was chaos – but gradually and as if by magic the lovely ship with all its exquisite minutiae came into being . . .

and in this way exemplified an exercise in making 'a drawing of the ordinary dimensions that will give . . . some idea of the size of a man of war'. He used watercolour in many ways, for paintings like this, or for recreations of the Venetian skyline losing itself in subtle atmosphere with red outlines and washes. The range of his output has been mentioned. In the 1831 RA alone *Caligula's Palace and Bridge* (Clore Gallery) was an extraordinary golden

Italianate confection hinting at connections with Claude and Watteau and concerned again with the decline of States. *Lucy, Countess of Carlisle, and Dorothy Percy's Visit to their Father, when under Attainder upon the Supposition of his being concerned in the Gunpowder Plot* (Clore Gallery) is an exercise in historical genre; *Admiral Van Tromp's Barge at the Entrance of the Texel* (Sir John Soane's Museum) reworks seventeenth-century Dutch seascape in order to represent an historical event; *Watteau Study by Fresnoy's Rules* is an irritated demonstration to critics who complained of his overuse of white (as well as yellow) and *Fort Vimieux* (Private Coll.) a desolate scene of a shipwreck lit by a red declining sun.

Turner's capacities were extraordinary and he might create form from chaos. In 1828 he painted *Lake Nemi* (Clore Gallery) directly onto raw canvas in broad masses of primary colour, featuring the lake as a white mass and the cliffs as blue, colours he tried out in scrapings onto the canvas. Here he apparently painted a canonical classical landscape directly from nature. On this same Italian campaign *Fishing Boats in a Mist* (Clore Gallery) is remarkable for its startling yellow sail against a pale blue sky and dull water, and in the corner of the canvas patches of pure colour which form themselves into the shapes of people. At this point in his career his pictures could baffle spectators, but not always. *The Fighting Temeraire tugged to her last Berth to be broken up* (1839, Clore Gallery) was easily understood as representing the decline under industrialisation, itself celebrated by Turner in *Rain, Steam and Speed* (1844, Clore Gallery) of that Britain which had vanished with the political reforms of the 1820s and 1830s. But as we have seen, a concern with the proper conduct of empire stayed with him. Even his tribute to Wilkie, *Peace – Burial at Sea* (1842, Clore Gallery), where the coffin is lowered into the sea in a blaze of red light against the blackness of the hull, may refer to Wilkie's 'Spanish' blackness, and, in showing the scene at Gibraltar, relate the subject to British imperial pretensions.

By this time the columns of adverse criticism revealed that the values of the 1830s and 1840s were not Turner's. This was an uncomprehending world that wanted the simplicities of Pugin or Ruskin to guide their confrontations with art.

From Turner, John Martin learned to paint the terrific, and he produced canvases of subjects he might expect people to recognise. *The Destruction of Herculaneum and Pompeii* (*c*.1822, Private Coll.) had a storm out of *Hannibal*, a vast landscape, enormous architecture and histrionic staffage, in order to explain itself clearly. Martin's imagery changed little. In *The Great Day of his Wrath* (1852, Tate Gallery) which is almost ten-feet wide, there was an abundance of scarlet, and dark falling rocks (as in the avalanche pictures of *c*.1810 by Turner and de Loutherbourg), lightning, lava and terrified people. Francis Danby had moved from the tranquil sentiment of *Disappointed Love* to mining the same seam, granted that he varied his production. Although Turner in *Shade and Darkness – the Evening of the Deluge* and *Light and Colour – the Morning after the Deluge* showed himself to be rather more profoundly concerned with comparable subjects, he was 'universally' condemned by the critics when the pictures were exhibited in 1843. For reaction to Turner's paintings to move from adulation to incomprehension in

Sir Edwin Landseer, Coming Events Cast their Shadow Before *(1843); also known as* The Challenge.

so short a time points to the amazingly rapid change in British society during his lifetime.

By Turner's death, Edwin Landseer had become one of the most popular artists. Like Mulready or Maclise, Landseer was a skilful technician, able to paint with a suggestive fluency and mastery, manifesting that colouristic brilliance common to many of the artists who came to prominence in the late 1820s. As we have seen, his range was wide. He could, particularly in comic scenes with dogs, descend beyond the mawkish, and some of his paintings are sadistic. But there were exceptional works. *The Challenge* (1843, Duke of Northumberland) shows a barrenly dramatic Highland landscape, snow-capped peaks rising against the moon-lightened sky, where the bellowed challenge of a stag is answered by another, swimming across a lake to join in combat. The inferred element of heroism in conflict is no longer human, and the setting is not fit for the social existence of men. It is extremely interesting to consider Ruskin's sentiments on *The Old Shepherd's Chief Mourner* (1837, Victoria & Albert Museum; colour pl. 5). A collie rests its chin on the coffin of its master, and Landseer has expressed the scene in a language which is 'clear and expressive in the highest degree'. The dog's 'rigidity of repose . . . marks that there has been no motion nor change in the trance of agony since the last blow was struck on the coffin lid', as though this were a scene from the Passion of Christ, which as Ruskin describes it must rank 'as a work of high art'. A representation of a simple room containing a coffin and a sheepdog had become elevated to *istoria*.

James Gillray, The Apotheosis of Hoche *(1798)*.

4 Graphic Satire and Illustration

JOHN HARVEY

It is not surprising that English graphic satire – that boisterous world of hand-coloured prints, sometimes savage and sometimes anarchic, with its Rowlandson gluttons and Gillray ogres – had its heyday in a period of huge social upheaval: the last years of the eighteenth century and the first years of the nineteenth, the years that saw the French and the Industrial Revolutions, and Britain divided and all Europe at war. The prints certainly were potent propaganda, they could laugh at nightmares or engender and swell them, as in their crude visions of brutish revolutionaries. In their calmer moods, the prints lampooned everyone: the professions, royalty, the services, dustmen, so that, taken together, the massive picture-show they make seems the tireless self-contemplation and self-mockery of a society exploding with wealth and pain.

That is perhaps the chief impression the prints give: of an art that for all its moralising embodies the often brutal vitality of the time. We see it not only in the activities shown, the preening and whoring, the gaming and money-grubbing, the drinking and revelling and above all, enormously, the eating – prelates gourmandising on a Fast-day, Nelson grossly devouring ships, a dyspeptic Pitt and ravenous Napoleon carving big slices of a plum-pudding world. We see it in their compositions, which are multitudinous, tumultuous, a tumbling crowd poured straight into the prints from the jam-packed London streets. We see it in the etched lines with which the prints are drawn – lines which, in the masters, in Rowlandson and Gillray, flow and spike and weave in a powerful rippling current. The piety of the age, and its refinements of sensibility and introspection, are not represented; but its appetites and pleasures and passions are. It is carnival art for the robust carnival life of the late eighteenth century.

The vitality shows at its most attractive in Thomas Rowlandson (1756–1827), who, even if he draws with a satiric inflection, still warms involuntarily to every pleasure. His line is gregarious, it wants to loop and curl, and for each new curve to be a new person, together with others in some activity – crowding to see the King or soldiers, promenading in Vauxhall or Bath – which becomes a dance, with one rich rhythm whirling through it.

Thomas Rowlandson, 'The Dram Shop', an illustration for The English Dance of Death *(1815–16)*.

People's clothes bulge plumply round fit plump forms; he can caricature beauties so they keep their beauty – fat but upright, handsome, fertile. His colouring is delicate, beautiful, with clear washes in the foreground, a lustre in his distances.

He still is a satirist, exposing appetite and snobbery, alert to jealousy. What he leaves out are the fears of his age: he has no demons, no large group is suffering, he doesn't want blood. When he illustrates *The English Dance of Death*, it is a dance; his forms bulb, there is no anxiety: even the skeleton, causing havoc in each plate, is all supple mobile springy line, alive and active, more rubbery than bony.

James Gillray (1757–1815) is the age's other mood. He is dry on pleasure if not scathing. His work has a vehemence which made him the doyen of English satirists, and also brought him international fame. It is a vehemence which can shock. In her pages on Gillray in *Romantics, Rebels and Reactionaries*, Marilyn Butler complains of the 'ugly pessimism of his images', of his 'coarse-grained, chauvinist and misanthropic art'. His compositions can be magnificent – in the language of the time, 'sublime' – but also terrifying in the apocalyptic (and xenophobic) exaltation with which they imagine suffering and war advancing through earth and sky. In *The Apotheosis of Hoche* there are flying garlands of decapitated heads, while the headless themselves, in legions, bow down before the god Equality, who proclaims a gruesome new Ten Commandments. 'Denounce thy Father & thy Mother', say the tablets, 'Thou shalt Murder . . . Thou shalt Steal . . . Thou shalt bear false witness.' The sky is filled with ape-faced and skull-faced French Revolutionaries. In coloured versions of the print the corpse-filled river at the bottom is crimson.

Such visions are one aspect of Gillray's art. He can also be quiet and firm and human, as in his satire of *The Fashionable Mama*: a plate executed with elegant irony, criticising unnaturalness among the elegant. A young mother sits gowned and coiffeured for the assembly rooms. She can feed her child without disturbing her toilette since there are holes in her dress which allow her to give her breast to the baby – held at a safe distance by a servant. The mother may be following a fashion in preferring to breast-feed, rather than use a wet-nurse; but she is also devoted to fashionable socialising and keeps to a minimum the embarrassment of contact.

Gillray's politics, moreover, are not a simple constant of conservative chauvinism. Intensely topical, seizing new subjects from day to day, he works in different prints from different levels of himself. One print may be rancorous invective, another a caprice and *jeu d'esprit*. Even when expressing the great fear of revolution – the nation's theme in the 1790s – he can be now direct and shallow, and now searching, penetrating.

French-Telegraph making Signals in the Dark is an intense but simple quantity. It was made in 1795. France had declared war on England in 1793, and the print plays on what for many was the ultimate double nightmare: a French invasion, and an English revolution, combined. We see a semaphore-machine, with the face of the Whig orator Charles James Fox, raising a lantern to France (the semaphore was a recent, and French, invention). The 'Dark' is the darkness by which evil deeds are done, the darkness of England's peril: on the right of the print the French fleet has set sail, from a fortress with a banner saying 'République'. Indeed, the fleet is nearly here, and the distance between London and the coast has been elided so as to

James Gillray, French-Telegraph making signals in the dark *(1795)*.

FRENCH-TELEGRAPH making SIGNALS in the Dark.

make the capital frighteningly exposed. As well as being a semaphore, Fox is also a sort of Martello Tower, and through an arch in its base we see axes and pikes. These weapons cannot be for the French soldiers who would already have arms, so they must be provided for the English populace, who will rise in a mutiny, given French support. Such a rising would be murderous, and impious too. London, in her vulnerability, is represented by St Paul's Cathedral: it is specifically at this church that the rigid hand of Fox is pointing.

It is a picture of the anxieties of the privileged and the prosperous at a time when both reformist agitation and the harsh suppression of it were at an extreme. The print does not crudely say that Fox is plotting treason. The shape of the semaphore fits the gesticulations of an orator, and the print's point is that Fox's public speeches, and his rhetoric in the House, are so dangerously radical they are an invitation to the French to invade. It is, in other words, a political smear: it shows Gillray grinding the reactionary axe.

In other prints we find subtler politics and deeper care. A work like *John Bull and his Dog Faithful* is a window onto the troubled English conscience of the 1790s.

This print, made in 1796, is oblique in its approach, taking its start from a relatively trivial parliamentary debate. Mr Dent of Leicestershire had proposed to help the strained Exchequer by imposing a tax on dogs. The poor in particular would benefit, by having made available to them 'those broken victuals which come from the tables of the affluent, and which at present are consumed by dogs'. He seemed as much concerned with killing dogs as with taxing them, and recited to the House a catalogue of canine crime, noting for instance that 'a dog had been seen killing two sheep, which having done, he went and washed himself in a pond, so that there were no marks of blood upon him'. The motion was supported by William Wilberforce, who argued that the ensuing slaughter of dogs would help the poor by saving them from hydrophobia.

In the course of the debate it was pointed out that the poor kept dogs, and might both need and love to keep them, and that therefore a dog-tax was not the best way to help. The bill was principally opposed by Richard Brinsley Sheridan, the dramatist, a Whig. He closed with an apostrophe to the trained dogs then used by the British army, and deplored the proposed

decree of massacre against these useful animals, at the very time when their brethren form a part of that combined army in Jamaica, which is fighting successfully against the Maroons, and supporting the cause of social order, humanity, and religion.

At the close of the debate the prime minister, William Pitt, proposed a tax 'on the dogs of the opulent'. As a result the dog-tax was introduced – though confined to dog-owners whose houses were large enough to be assessed for tax – and became, duly modified, the dog licence as known until recently.

The debate was a news item of the day, and the best-known participants are represented in the print – as dogs, with William Pitt on the left and Sheridan on the right. The arguments of the debate are also illustrated: that dogs can guide and help, but also harrass and worry, and in particular that they can be both the enemies, and the saviours, of the poor. Play is made

JOHN BULL & his Dog Faithful; — "Among the Faithless Faithful Only found."

James Gillray, John Bull and his dog Faithful: among the Faithless Faithful only found *(1796).*

with the new invention, the licence, by inscribing on Pitt's collar 'Licenc'd to Lead' and on Sheridan's 'Licenc'd to Bite' (in the background is Charles James Fox, with 'Licenc'd to Bark' on his collar). The print does not, however, take up the debate in the simple satiric spirit one might expect – by mocking the odd ideas of helping the poor, or by reciting the list of canine crimes. Rather, Gillray makes this in some ways obnoxious and in some ways comic debate the pretext for a general political allegory.

The basic suggestion of the print is clear. Gillray, by this date, worked regularly in the Tory cause, and so, starting from the fact that Pitt had exempted the poor from tax, he represents William Pitt as the guide-dog of England, leading John Bull to safety through the barking and biting of the Whigs. John Bull here is not stout John Bull: he is ragged and maimed and burdened with debt. He needs guiding because he is blind, and might stumble down the precipice at the front of the print. The precipice we may take as representing revolution – that is, a momentous social upheaval like that in France. Pitt is supported by a quotation from Milton: 'Among the Faithless, Faithful only found'. The line refers to the angel Abdiel among Satan's host, thus casting the Whigs as the rebel angels plotting to overthrow Heaven. Behind and over Pitt is the British Oak, and beyond it, in its shelter, is London, again represented chiefly by St Paul's. The implication perhaps is that Pitt can save the nation not just because he is the heaven-born minister, but because he represents – he 'has behind him' – a natural order, rooted, civilised, devout.

Seen in this light, the print seems propaganda, on behalf of a conventional Tory vision. It is not, though, so simple. The British Oak, for instance, seems intended to naturalise John Bull in his present misery and depletion, and to dissociate him from anything that could suggest chopping the tree down. For the tree too has lost limbs: but still it puts out new shoots and new leaf. But if that is the intention, it is hardly fulfilled, since Gillray disrupts his own caricature-convention by making John Bull so real. He is an actual blind cripple, larger, more solid and more imposing than anything else in the plate. Everything in the way he is drawn says he is not a branch of a tree – and of course he cannot see the tree anyway, or anything there that is meant to give him comfort, and that is a great poignancy of the picture. It is an extraordinary vision of the representative Englishman and the national tree: they are the upright presences that balance the composition, and also generate its political division. They both are, and are not, metaphors for each other. They approach and won't meet, blind to each other.

Again, there is the disparity between John Bull, in real plight, eloquently drawn in an emphatic line with a jagged rhythm, and the caricature-slightness (in comparison) of Pitt. The Pitt-dog has a bone in its mouth, and thus in an odd way is linked with the dog Sheridan on the right, sinking its teeth into the wooden leg of John Bull. The wooden leg is drawn with a cruel visual equivocation so that it looks also like a bone – like, in fact, the bared bone of John Bull. It is a pun perhaps on being reduced to the bone, to a walking skeleton; it is a touch of appallingly harsh visual poetry, of a kind that is the signature of Gillray's genius.

As Draper Hill has pointed out, the artist has given his own face to John Bull: it is a self-portrait, blinded. Gillray, it seems, was like many who may initially have sympathised with the French Revolution – it is recorded that he drank to the Jacobins – but who then failed to see their ideals fulfilled, and had, after the Terror of '92 and '93, no optimism: revolution was an abyss. Yet the conservative answer seemed insecure, and its picture of society insufficient and doubtful. Many must have felt blind. The print is a subtle political poem that takes one inside the mind of its time – a critical period in English history when many fears crystallised in political attitudes that are still there today.

The fact that John Bull's face is Gillray's self-portrait makes the picture, further, a satire on satire, an expression of unease about his service to the dog-politician. It is a picture that alters one's understanding of his art. Satire is frequently visually vivid, even when the picture it paints is in words – Pope is one of the most visual of poets – perhaps because the satirist stands apart from his subject, observing it with, among other feelings, hostile interest. What Gillray shows in this print is not a destructive but a troubled eye, that mainly sees that it does not see, and in suffering its failure finds truth, and poignancy, and a power to move.

What happened to the art of caricature after Gillray? In part it lived on in the pages of *Punch*, in the political satires – but how tamed by Victoria – of Sir John Tenniel (1820–1914). But also it travelled, and found a new vigour in the illustrations of novels. This move can be seen in the career of George Cruikshank (1792–1878). He began as a caricaturist – he was the son of a caricaturist, and was early employed to finish plates that Gillray, in increasing insanity, could not finish. But as the fashion and market for caricature declined, he quickly moved to books, and became the acknowledged genius of book-illustration of his day – and an illustrator, especially, of fiction. For if caricature was declining, fiction was expanding in just such a way as to incorporate the caricaturist's art. The key material development was the advent of the serial novel, the novel published in monthly parts. This relied on numerous illustrations, displayed in shop windows as the prints used to be, serving both to advertise each new part, and to identify clearly, over a period of months, leading characters and themes. One cannot separate this general development from the impact of the author who inaugurated and sustained the new mode, Charles Dickens (1812–70).

Cruikshank illustrated Dickens's early novel *Oliver Twist*, and the aptness of the collaboration is clear in the classic plate *Fagin in the Condemned Cell*. As in Dickens's writing, exaggeration and theatricality are combined with intensity. Fagin's face is lurid, but with convincing horror. He hunches as if he could hide from death by making himself tiny. He shrinks as if what has sustained him is being sucked out from the centre.

It is not surprising Dickens worked well with the caricaturist Cruikshank. He is himself famously a caricaturist, both in his dialogue, and in the magnifying attentiveness with which he describes how his people look. And there is a more substantial affinity. The caricatures were visible everywhere in Dickens's childhood, and it is arguable that they informed his imagination in

George Cruikshank's illustration 'Fagin in the condemned cell' for Dickens's Oliver Twist *(1837–9)*.

a profound way that shows in his famous 'animism', his habit of giving objects the life of people, and people the character of things. This is the most prominent idiosyncrasy of what critics call 'the Dickens vision', though precisely this kind of animism is practised by Gillray all the time, in his representations of politicians.

In any event, the illustrators with whom Dickens worked best – Cruikshank, John Leech (1817–64), above all 'Phiz' (Hablot Knight Browne, 1815–82) – were artists trained in the caricature school. They and he shared a voracity of eye, a delight in witty exaggeration, and a Hogarthian impatience to let every part of each picture speak. The result is the busy visual signalling that goes on constantly in both the texts and illustrations of the Dickens novels: there is scarcely a piece of furniture, or a picture on a wall, that does not pass some comment – often ironic – on what the people are doing. In this respect, an illustrated Dickens novel may be seen as a prodigiously rich development of graphic satire, and I want to close by discussing one novel in that light.

Bleak House might well be called a political satire. The title itself, Graham Storey has suggested, is a thrust by Dickens at the glassy hollowness of the Great Exhibition. The novel's strength is not in creating individuals – none of Esther, Ada, Rick, Jarndyce, Lady Dedlock are given much depth. Its great power is in its peculiarly moved apprehension, as it were grieving and raging together, of England: the conservative country, the country that has escaped revolution, that stifles still in ancient obfuscation, in an impenetrable petrified jungle of laws, haunted by predators and parasites; the cities harbouring appalling slums, the countryside and country still held by a semi-imbecilic aristocracy whom Dickens names Dedlock. The exaggerations in this novel have a ferocious poetry, as in the warehouse of Krook, with its piled detritus and clawing cat, the whole place an aggressive metaphor for the Court of Chancery and the heartbreaking waste of life it causes. Krook's warehouse is caricature and metaphor and poetry; it is intensely visualised, with something like the rigorous eye of a Gillray.

It is shown in an illustration eloquent with details. There is a gigantic pair of scales, perhaps those of justice, upended and empty on the left. There are bones and skulls, locks and keys, a grimacing mask, a doll hanged by the neck. It is all old rubbish – and the wreckage of lives broken at law. Krook himself is not terrifying: his sharp bespectacled caricature-face could be the face of an elderly attorney or judge. The figure of Esther is the one non-grotesque presence in the picture, a reserved and swathed virtue in a cavern of waste.

Other illustrations, lighter in spirit, are deft satires on social groups. A plate like *The Dancing School* shows what graphic satire had become for the Victorians: the earlier boisterousness has gone, and there is scant suggestion of the sensuousness of Rowlandson. There is, however, graceful rhythm in the grouping, and a touching sense of companionship. Phiz has at the same time an ironic vigilance, a skill in catching the accents of vanity.

There are too the famous six 'dark plates', for which Phiz enlisted a ruling machine, to achieve especially dark and black tones. What is remarkable in them is not their sombreness, which suits the mood of the novel plainly

'The Lord Chancellor copies from memory', an illustration by Phiz for Dickens's Bleak House *(1852–3)*.

enough, but their emptiness – the fact that, extraordinarily for Phiz illustrations, they show almost no people at all. Their function, it seems, was to bring home the importance of place in this novel: and it is very much a matter of political place, of the homes of powerlessness and of power – the disease-ridden slum, Tom All Alone's, and the salons and walks of Chesney Wold. But beyond that the dark plates emphasise, as does the title of the novel, that the places and place this novel depicts are of a heartrending desolation. Such is the burden of *The lonely figure* – a plate that is deliberately ambiguous since the figure could be Lady Dedlock, or Jenny, or any 'poor houseless wretch':

Where is she? On the waste, where the brick-kilns are burning with a pale blue flare; where the straw-roofs of the wretched huts in which the bricks are made, are being scattered by the wind; where the clay and water are hard frozen, and the mill in which

the gaunt blind horse goes round all day, looks like an instrument of human torture; –
traversing this deserted blighted spot, there is a lonely figure with the sad world to
itself, pelted by the snow and driven by the wind, and cast out, it would seem, from
all companionship.

(Chapter LVI)

'The lonely figure', one of Phiz's 'dark plates' for Dickens's Bleak House.

That is the note of the later Dickens: a kind of exalted yet astringent complaining, a sense of blight descended on the heart. It is a blight we may relate to the elements of 'Victorianism' which Dickens hated, and which strengthened inexorably through his lifetime – above all the hard-hearted self-help moralism, mechanical and puritanical, self-policing, which was England's answer to the dangers of anarchy. England, in late Dickens, cries to be caricatured; it is a country busy distorting its lives.

There is a fondness for connecting the caricature part of Dickens's art with a child's vision of the world; but it would be at least as true to say that if Dickens sees adults and governors with a distorting eye, it is because he sees them as the hurt psyche sees them: what he sees is their power, their fearfulness, which he tries then to outwit with laughter. His caricature vision is an inner vision too – emphatically it is a vision, and Gillray's vision of ogres and animated objects and damage is not wholly different. Both Gillray's satiric prints, and Dickens's intensely visual novels, look at the world and see a nightmare: to which they respond with exuberant, exaggerating imaginativeness.

St George's Hall, Liverpool, view of the Great Hall (1840–56). H.L. Elmes and C.R. Cockerell.

5 Architecture

ALEXANDRA WEDGWOOD

Introduction

Between 1785 and 1851, under the combined influences of the Industrial
Revolution and Romanticism, every aspect of architecture in Britain was
transformed.

The Industrial Revolution led inexorably to urbanisation. In 1800 there
were no cities in Britain, except London, with a population of over 100,000.
By 1833 there were four more: Manchester, Liverpool, Leeds and
Birmingham in that order. The population of the country was both expanding
rapidly and moving to the new centres of work. In 1851 only 28 per cent of
Manchester's adult population had been born there. Much urban growth
during the period covered by this volume, especially in the new industrial
towns, was uncontrolled, chaotic and depressing, dominated by the factory
chimneys and without adequate provision of water or sanitation. Only the
middle-class suburbs such as Edgbaston in Birmingham or Everton in
Liverpool are remembered as architecture.

Towns and cities were, however, at the same time centres of progress. New
types of buildings, sometimes using new materials and new technology,
quickly developed to service the new populations. Churches and chapels,
banks and government offices, museums and theatres, schools and libraries,
shops and hotels, exchanges and markets, mills and warehouses were all
provided in numbers, and many survive today. Civic pride found expression
in municipal buildings and public parks. The rapid expansion of the railway
system with its viaducts and embankments was another crucial factor in the
transformation of the appearance of the architecture of Britain by 1851.

As fundamental an influence on architecture as the economic and social
implications of the Industrial Revolution was the effect of Romanticism,
which had two main results. One may be seen in the need for a building to
provide an appropriate emotional response. Thus Fonthill Abbey (1795–1812)
was designed in melodramatic Gothic, the British Museum (1823–47) in
pedantic Greek, and the Brighton Pavilion (1815–21) in exotic Hindoo. The
second was a great extension in the range of architectural styles which

British Museum, entrance front (1823–47). Sir Robert Smirke.

suddenly became acceptable. As with the other arts, the influence of
Romanticism on architecture was spread through literature.

The first, and best known, formulation of Romantic principles as they
apply to the visual arts was Edmund Burke's *Inquiry into the origin of our
ideas on the Sublime and Beautiful* of 1756. Of particular relevance to
architecture was the *Essay on the Picturesque*, written in 1794 by Sir Uvedale
Price. This was followed by *An Analytical Inquiry into the Principles of Taste*,
written in 1805 by Price's friend, Richard Payne Knight. Out of these
writings developed the Picturesque movement, an important aspect of
Romanticism which had a crucial effect on the aesthetics of the period. The
Picturesque was never a precise style. The original idea was to create a
landscape or a building, or, more often, a combination of the two, which
looked like a picture by one of the great seventeenth-century masters of
landscape painting. In both landscape and architecture this emphasised the
characteristics of variety, movement and asymmetry. It could be applied to
cottages, villas or great houses and their surroundings, in styles usually either
Italianate or castellated Gothic.

Romanticism also engendered considerable interest in the study of the past.
In architectural terms this resulted in a large number of beautiful and often
scholarly books, whose splendid illustrations immensely extended the range of
styles known to British architects. Early forerunners were *The Ruins of
Palmyra* (1753) and *The Ruins of Baalbec* (1757) both by Robert Wood;
Designs of Chinese Buildings (1757) by Sir William Chambers and *Ruins of the
Palace of the Emperor Diocletian at Spalato* (1764) by Robert Adam. Of great
importance for the development of the Greek Revival were the three volumes

of *The Antiquities of Athens* which were produced between 1762 and 1795 by James Stuart and Nicholas Revett.

Interest and delight in the medieval world and Gothic architecture began with novels such as *The Castle of Otranto* (1765) by Horace Walpole and anthologies like *Reliques of Ancient English Poetry*, also of 1765, edited by Bishop Thomas Percy, and continued strongly, fed particularly by Sir Walter Scott's writings such as *The Lay of the Last Minstrel* (1805) and *Ivanhoe* (1819). Illustrated studies of individual buildings were made in *The History . . . and Antiquities of Winchester*, two volumes (1798–1801) by the Catholic bishop, Dr John Milner and in *Plans, Elevations, Sections, and Views of the Church of Batalha* (1796) by James Murphy. Then followed the dedicated work of John Carter who published countless drawings of medieval antiquities, W.H. Pyne and his three-volumed *History of the Royal Residences* (1819) and John Britton who published several successful topographical series including *The Beauties of England and Wales* (1800–16), *The Architectural Antiquities of Great Britain* (1804–14) and *The Cathedral Antiquities of Great Britain* (1814–35). In 1817 Thomas Rickman contributed *An Attempt to Discriminate the Styles of English Architecture*, where the terms 'Early English', 'Decorated' and 'Perpendicular' are given for the first time, and finally Augustus Charles Pugin provided architects with careful measured drawings in his *Specimens of Gothic Architecture*, two volumes 1821–3.

Thus by 1830 a very wide range of material was available to the eager architectural student. The effect, however, could be confusing. The heady days of Romanticism were over and more serious attitudes were gaining favour. The young Augustus Welby Northmore Pugin produced a biting satirical 'Illustration of the Practise (*sic*) of Architecture in the 19th Century on new improved and cheap principles' in his book *Contrasts*, which was published in 1836. The plate shows a series of advertisements including 'Designing taught in 6 lessons: Gothic severe Greek and the Mixed Styles', and under the heading 'Designs wanted' are listed 'A Moorish Fish Market with a literary room over; An Egyptian Marine Villa; A Castellated Turnpike Gate; A Gin Temple in the Baronial style; A Saxon Cigar Divan', and so on.

Pugin was a convert to Catholicism and for him Christianity and Gothic were synonymous. He believed in both with equal fervour and through his writings and his buildings made many others believe too. Even Pugin's powers of persuasion, however, could not eliminate all the other styles that had been brought into existence, and the choice of style to be used in any given situation became a problem for the rest of the nineteenth century. Pugin also introduced the concept of morality into architectural practice in 1841 in his book, *The True Principles of Pointed or Christian Architecture*; buildings could be truthful, as long as they were Gothic. Another powerful voice joined this argument in 1849 when John Ruskin wrote *The Seven Lamps of Architecture*. His Seven Lamps were Sacrifice, Truth, Power, Beauty, Life, Memory and Obedience. Architecture had indeed become serious and concerned with fundamental moral issues. Ideas about 'truth' and 'honesty' in buildings, even if no longer tied to the Gothic style, continued to exercise architects' thoughts until quite recently.

The architects who took part in this transformation between 1785 and 1851

were increasingly aware of themselves as members of a profession and a
profession that was growing rapidly. The Royal Academy was founded in
1768 with five architects. A Professor of Architecture was appointed, Gold
and Silver Medals could be won and Travelling Students were nominated.
Most young men learned by working in the office of an established architect
but increasingly they seized any opportunity to travel in order to study
buildings at first hand, usually in Italy, but frequently in Greece and Asia
Minor. In 1819 Charles Barry became the first British architect to make
measured drawings of Egyptian architecture. A.W.N. Pugin travelled in
Europe almost every summer on a sketching tour. What had been part of a
nobleman's privileged education became an essential part of an architect's
expertise.

All members of the Royal Academy saw themselves principally as artists
who exhibited their work, but there were, of course, architects who saw
themselves rather as engineers and they never became Academicians. Canals,
roads, bridges, railways and warehouses did indeed offer some of the greatest
challenges of this period and Thomas Telford, John Rennie, Thomas
Harrison and Isambard Kingdom Brunel were all designers of genius. The
Institute of Civil Engineers was founded in 1818 with Telford, who had
worked as a mason building Somerset House, as President and with eight
members. In 1834 the Institute of British Architects was founded. Architects
then felt in need of emphasising their importance and so they chose as their
President an Earl, Earl de Grey, only an amateur architect. At the opening
meeting of the Institute on 15 June 1835 it was announced that eighty
members had been enrolled. A Charter of Incorporation was granted in 1837
and in 1866 it was given leave to add Royal to its title. The Institute grew
rapidly with 159 members in 1840. This can be compared with a total of 1675
people who called themselves architects in the census of 1841, a number
which undoubtedly included some builders and engineers. A number of
journals supported this new professionalism; Loudon's *Architectural
Magazine* started in 1834, *The Transactions of the Institute of British
Architects* in 1835, *The Civil Engineer and Architect's Journal* in 1837 and *The
Builder* in 1842.

Architects continued to learn principally in the offices of senior architects.
During this period Barry's office was one of the largest, best organised and
most influential, a model for the rest of the century. London was always the
centre but there were important regional architects, such as John Foulston in
Devonport and Plymouth, John Dobson and Richard Grainger in Newcastle
upon Tyne, John Foster in Liverpool, and W.H. Playfair in Edinburgh.

Adam and Chambers, followed by John Nash, all engaged in speculative
building, but gradually this became professionally unacceptable for architects,
and their place was taken by speculative builders. The first important and
best known speculative builder and developer was Thomas Cubitt who
transformed the building industry. In 1815 he took the crucial step of setting
up a firm which employed all the building trades, masons, carpenters,
bricklayers and so on, on a permanent basis. By 1851 quantity surveyors were
regularly employed and all the essential features of modern architectural
practice were in place.

Overview of architects, building styles and types

In 1785 British architecture was still dominated, as it had been for the previous twenty-five years, by Sir William Chambers (1723–96) and Robert Adam (1728–92). Chambers was completing his great work at Somerset House and Adam was working in Edinburgh at the University and in Charlotte Square, but they were both near the end of their careers. At the death of Chambers his official appointments of Surveyor General and Comptroller of the Office of Works were given to James Wyatt (1746–1813), whose superficial brilliance allied to his general unreliability seem to epitomise the architecture of much of the early part of this period.

The son of a Staffordshire builder, Wyatt studied in Venice under the painter–architect Visentini. He made his name immediately on his return in 1770 by winning a competition for the rebuilding of the Pantheon, a place of public entertainment in Oxford Street, with a splendid domed neo-classical design. From then onwards he was inundated with commissions and produced a number of elegant classical houses such as Dodington Park, Avon (1798–1808). He designed in all the current styles and his most famous building was the great Gothic Fonthill Abbey in Wiltshire which was commissioned by that arch-Romantic, William Beckford, and built between 1796 and 1812. The plan was ridiculous: with the arms of an immense irregular cross meeting at a central octagon which was surmounted by an octagonal tower 225 feet high to the top of its pinnacles. In an altogether

Fonthill Abbey, south-west view (1795–1807). James Wyatt; engraving.

appropriate finale to this over-blown folly, the central tower, thanks to the negligence of Wyatt and the dishonesty of his builder, collapsed in 1825. Wyatt's drastic restorations of several English cathedrals, including Lichfield, Salisbury, Hereford and Durham, earned him the nickname of 'Wyatt the destroyer' during his lifetime.

A much more disciplined architect of the same period was Henry Holland (1745–1806). He remained aloof from the all-pervading Adam style with its light and elegant form of neo-classicism, and was more influenced by contemporary French architects. His greatest work was the later destroyed Carlton House in Pall Mall which he rebuilt for the Prince of Wales, later George IV, between 1783 and 1796. The plan and style of this sophisticated building, with its Corinthian entrance portico approached through an open screen to the forecourt which is decorated with coupled Ionic columns, make an instructive contrast to the vapid Fonthill with its weak repetitive details.

Another original and unorthodox architect was George Dance (1741–1825), the son of an architect of the same name. He had studied in Italy for seven years and was aware of avant-garde French work. On his return he designed two remarkable and imaginative buildings, the church of All Hallows, London Wall (1765–7) and the now demolished Newgate Prison (1770–80). He was interested in unexpected spatial effects and deeply influenced his pupil, John Soane. Soane's own style was too personal, eccentric even, for him to have close followers, but he was an architect of genius and by his death he had done much to set the standards for the newly emerging profession of architecture. Soane's legacy to this period will be considered below together with his exact contemporary, Nash, the other great architect of the time. The two men were opposites in character, interests, work and methods and it is therefore illuminating to contrast them. Almost all Nash's buildings, including those in his great town plan for London, are thought of in connection with landscape. It was largely on Nash's partnership with the landscape gardener Humphry Repton (1752–1818) that the development of the Picturesque depended. Following Capability Brown's death in 1783 there was a desire for something that was both more natural and more obviously Picturesque. Repton was an excellent watercolourist and he illustrated his proposed 'improvements' to prospective clients with delightful watercolours which contrasted the 'before' and 'after' condition of the gentleman's estate.

At the turn of the nineteenth century interest in Greek Revival architecture was growing. Thomas Hope, a connoisseur and patron, was important in the growth of this movement. He introduced impressive Greek designs in the interiors and furniture of his own houses, which he also filled with his fine collection of antique Greek sculpture. He pleaded for the Greek style to be used in the new Downing College, at Cambridge. The successful architect was William Wilkins (1778–1839) who did indeed design the buildings in a chaste Greek Ionic order between 1806 and 1820. Wilkins had travelled extensively in Greece and published several scholarly books on Greek antiquities. Most of his public buildings were in the Greek Revival style, as well as a country-house, Grange Park, Hampshire, which he remodelled into a classical temple. His final building was the National Gallery in Trafalgar Square, built between 1834 and 1838. This is now a much-loved building,

Downing College, Cambridge; view of the east range with the Master's Lodge (1806–20).
William Wilkins.

but it was fiercely criticised at the time of its construction and is indeed a
weak design for so commanding a situation.

A slightly younger man, however, Sir Robert Smirke (1788–1867), became
the leading architect of this movement. He had also travelled extensively in
Italy, Sicily and Greece and made his name on his return with the rebuilding
of Covent Garden Theatre from 1808–9. On Wyatt's death in 1813, his
importance was confirmed when he joined Soane and Nash as Architect to the
Office of Works. This appointment brought him several major commissions
for public buildings such as the British Museum (1823–47) and the now
demolished General Post Office (1824–9).

Though grand, with their impressive Greek colonnades, these buildings
were often dull. The most inventive architect in the style was undoubtedly
C.R. Cockerell (1788–1863). He had also travelled in Greece and worked
there as a serious archaeologist making important discoveries, but in his own
designs he combined elements from Greek architecture with a wide range of
other influences. His branch offices for the Bank of England and the
Ashmolean Museum and Taylorian Institute, Oxford (1841–5) show his
strong eclectic personal style. He created his greatest interiors in St George's
Hall, Liverpool, which he completed between 1851 and 1854 after the death
of its designer, H.L. Elmes.

Neo-classicism was generally more popular in the north of England and in
Scotland and the style survived there late into the nineteenth century. It had
started with the powerful works of Thomas Harrison (1744–1829) in Chester
and Lancaster. Edinburgh, as is described elsewhere in this volume, was
called 'The Athens of the North' and ornamented with a series of handsome

Greek buildings designed by Thomas Hamilton and W.H. Playfair
(1790–1857). Alexander, nicknamed 'Greek', Thomson (1817–75) produced a
number of bold and unusual buildings in Glasgow. John Dobson (1787–1865)
laid out the centre of Newcastle upon Tyne with neo-classical streets from
1835. Meanwhile the Gothic Revival established itself in the south of
England.

Cockerell's scholarly and individual style and diffident manner contributed
to the fact that his rival, Barry, achieved much greater public recognition. His
career, with his introduction of the Italian palazzo style at the Travellers'
Club in 1829 and his responsibility for the rebuilding of the Houses of
Parliament from 1836, is of such crucial importance for the second half of
this period that it will be considered at greater length below. Barry's work at
Westminster is always thought of together with that of A.W.N. Pugin, who
designed most of the interiors and fittings. So here too those two architects
will be looked at together. Pugin's brief but frenetic career was immensely
influential and set the Gothic Revival on its serious course for the rest of the
century.

The date with which this volume closes, 1851, is, of course, chiefly
remembered for the Great Exhibition and the building in which it was
housed, the Crystal Palace. The development of iron and glass and the work
of engineers between 1785 and 1851 will form the final section in this
chapter.

As will be obvious from what has been written above, this was a great
period for building country-houses. The landed classes were prosperous and
the acquisition of a country estate remained a major goal for any aspiring
gentleman. Houses became both larger and more comfortable. The country-
house party became a feature of upper-class life during this period. All the
current styles were considered suitable for such buildings, from elegant
classical such as Bowden House, near Lacock of 1796 by Wyatt, to unusual
classical as at Ickworth, Suffolk, also designed in 1796, by Francis Sandys,
and the dramatic neo-Norman of Penryhn Castle, Gwynedd, of c.1825–44 by
Thomas Hopper, to the careful Tudor revival of Scotney Castle, Kent of
1835–43 by Anthony Salvin.

Much work was also done at this time on royal palaces. Improvements at
Windsor Castle were started by George III and continued enthusiastically by
George IV, who used Jeffry Wyatville from 1824 to add to the picturesque
qualities of the castle and yet provide sumptuous but well-planned interiors.
Buckingham Palace, Clarence House, the Marble Arch and the Brighton
Pavilion were all built or rebuilt for royalty at public expense.

During this period church building again becomes important. The
urbanisation which took place as a result of the Industrial Revolution meant
that substantial numbers of people were not served by any churches. In order
to improve this situation the Church Building Act of 1818 was passed. It
provided for one million pounds and led to the building of six hundred new
churches between 1818 and 1856. Many of the first of these new churches
were built in the Greek Revival style. The most memorable is that of St
Pancras, Woburn Place, London, built from 1819 to 1822 by W. and H.W.
Inwood, but planned in 1816 just before the Act. One of the most important

and expensive Gothic churches was that of St Luke's Chelsea, of 1820–4 by James Savage. By the 1840s, however, under the decisive influence of A.W.N. Pugin, almost all churches were Gothic and there were plenty of commissions for the young Scott, Ferrey, Carpenter and Butterfield.

Many municipalities wanted to emphasise their new importance with an impressive building, which often meant a neo-classical one, such as the Greek Doric County Buildings, Perth, built from 1815 to 1819 by Smirke, or the Town Hall, Birmingham, in the form of a Roman Corinthian temple, designed between 1832 and 1834 by J.A. Hansom and E. Welch. Several museums and many schools were built during the latter part of this period. The museums were usually in a neo-classical style to remind their visitors of the pre-eminence of Greece and Rome. Schools, for instance Rugby by H. Hakewill from 1809 to 1816, often chose Gothic, which was intended to instil in their pupils the ancient traditions of their own country.

As the social and economic basis of Britain was transformed between 1785 and 1851, so was her architecture. Though the buildings produced at this time are of very uneven quality, they are of absorbing interest and they have contributed massively to the nation's architectural heritage.

Soane and Nash

John Soane devoted the whole of his long life single-mindedly to architecture, 'the ruling passion of my life', as he called it, and to his ambition 'to be distinguished as an architect'. In spite of his difficult character, and a style so personal and original that he had no close followers, this he achieved emphatically. His position as the nation's most eminent architect was recognised in 1834 when he was offered the presidency of the Institute of British Architects at its foundation. Soane's style aimed for what he called 'the poetry of architecture', and in this respect, though he used neo-classical forms, he was at heart a Romantic. There was never anything obvious about his work and his handling of space and light, the principal tools in the hands of an architect, constantly gave unexpected and subtle effects.

Soane has been unfortunate in that so much of his work has been destroyed. His great masterpiece, the Bank of England, and all his impressive work at the Palace of Westminster for the House of Lords, the House of Commons and the Law Courts, as well as other major works, have gone. He had, however, ensured by an Act of Parliament that his house in Lincoln's Inn Fields and his collections were preserved for the nation as a museum for 'the Study of Architecture and the Allied Arts'. These remain very much in the condition in which Soane arranged them and provide a fascinating centre for architecture as he intended. His work, both in its complication and abstraction, is certainly in tune with architectural interests at the end of the twentieth century.

Soane came from a humble background which explained some of his later sensitivity. He was born in 1753, the son of a bricklayer in Berkshire and in 1768 he entered the office of George Dance junior, who has already been introduced. This association was of crucial importance to Soane. He called

Dance his 'revered master', and many of the other man's ideas were to be taken up and developed by Soane, who continued to turn to Dance for advice long after he was an established architect.

Soane, however, always eager to learn as much as he could, left Dance in 1772 and joined Holland in order to gain more experience in the practical aspects of architecture. Meanwhile in 1771 he was admitted to the Royal Academy schools, where he attended the lectures given by the first Professor of Architecture, Thomas Sandby. In 1772 he won the Silver Medal and in 1776 he won the Gold Medal with a design for a Triumphal Bridge, which derived from a similar one by Sandby. With the support of Chambers he also won the King's Travelling Studentship in Rome. Before he set off in March 1778, Soane was sent a letter from Chambers urging him to study the work of Michelangelo, Vignola, Peruzzi, Palladio, Salvi and Bernini. He advised him to meet Piranesi and to 'Form if you can a style of your own in which endeavour to avoid the faults and blend the perfections of all'.

Soane did meet Piranesi shortly before his death and was given by him four of his engraved plates of ancient Roman ruins. In Italy he studied widely both classical and sixteenth-century work. Equally important for any young aspiring architect, he made the acquaintance of several influential noblemen, who were making a Grand Tour. One of these was Frederick Hervey, Bishop of Derry (and afterwards Earl of Bristol), whose passion for building was well known. In January 1780 Soane received a letter from the Bishop offering definite employment at Downhill, in Ireland, and Ickworth, in Suffolk. He cut short his studentship and followed his patron to Ireland. He remained there for six weeks but, coming to the conclusion that he had no prospects for employment there, he returned to London and an uncertain future in June 1780.

He established himself gradually over the next decade with a series of commissions for small country-houses, particularly in the counties of Norfolk and Suffolk. His unusual treatment of neo-classical forms, which came to be known as 'primitive classicism', was clearly seen already in the dairy that he built in 1783 at Hammels Park, Hertfordshire, for Philip Yorke, later Earl of Hardwicke, whom Soane had met in Rome. His ideas at this time possibly came from Abbé Laugier, whose influential *Essai sur l'architecture* was published in Paris in 1753. Laugier believed that the basic elements of architecture – columns, architecture and pediment – evolved from the primitive hut and were therefore founded on simple nature and reason. Soane made his Greek Doric portico for the dairy out of rough-hewn tree trunks.

Soane's career, however, really began in 1788 with his appointment as Surveyor to the Bank of England. He obtained this through the support of William Pitt, whose cousin Thomas Pitt he had also known in Rome. The surveyorship provided Soane with financial security and professional status, as well as the most important commission of his life. From this date he was regarded as one of the country's leading architects and only Wyatt had a larger practice. The Bank was at this time expanding its activities and Soane was asked both to rebuild earlier work and to extend the premises. The central portion of the Bank had been built in 1732–4 by George Sampson, and was described by Soane as being 'in a grand style of Palladian simplicity'. To this Sir Robert Taylor made extensive additions, principally single storey wings to the east and the west between 1765 and 1770. From 1792 until 1833 Soane rebuilt much of this. The work had to be done piecemeal and, because of the requirements of security, the building had to be surrounded by a solid windowless wall. This requirement necessitated the use of top-lighting, a device which already fascinated Soane. He wrote about the effect of the '*lumière mystérieuse*' coming from unusual light sources, which he admired in French churches such as the Invalides.

Soane's first work at the Bank was to rebuild the Stock Office between 1792–3. Here he was undoubtedly helped by Dance to create an extraordinary room with a central domed square, lit from the lantern above the dome, and to north and south two square bays with groined vaults, each lit from two semi-circular windows under the vault. On the long east and west axis of this room were shallow aisles or passages, with segmental barrel vaults and no windows. In order to make the Stock Office as fireproof as possible, it was built of brick and vaulted with hollow earthenware pots or cones. This lightness of construction is reflected in the slenderness and linear quality of the decoration which showed a further stage in Soane's 'primitive classicism'. Here he used rudimentary grooved strips and a thin string-course carved with the Greek key pattern in place of familiar pilasters, capitals and entablatures. In his next building for the Bank, the Rotunda of 1796, he again used diagrammatic grooved mouldings. Sir John Summerson has suggested that these motives, which became a hallmark of Soane's work, derived ultimately from Piranesi's Egyptian designs.

Soane built several more domed halls at the Bank which were variations of the Stock Office. In the last of these, the Dividend Office, which was completed in 1823, the thin lines of the piers supporting the dome and the space flowing between them were abruptly contrasted with the strong three-dimensional figures of the caryatids (sculptured figures used as columns) from the Erechtheion which were placed in pairs around the lantern of the dome. The Bank was more or less rebuilt between 1921 and 1937 and Soane's masterpiece was thus destroyed. In the words of Sir Nikolaus Pevsner, this was 'the worst individual loss suffered by London architecture in the first half of the twentieth century'. Only the screen wall with which Soane surrounded his building survives. It has very discreet entrances and is built of Portland stone, rusticated, and ornamented with arrangements of Corinthian columns in antis, that is to say, columns which range with the wall, and come to a climax, somewhat weakened in the early twentieth century, at Tivoli Corner.

Soane's first great country-house belongs to the same period as his early work at the Bank. Tyringham House in Buckinghamshire was built from 1793–7 for William Praed, banker and entrepreneur, but it was drastically altered in 1909. It had a noble entrance hall with Greek Doric columns in the corners supporting a shallow groined vault, which led up to a top-lit inner hall. Only the gateway survives unaltered but this is enough to show the monumentality of which Soane was capable. The design is entirely independent of references to earlier styles and depends on a balance between solids and voids, with immensely strong simple shapes articulated by incised lines. It is only comparable with the visionary and largely unbuilt work of Gilly in Prussia and Ledoux in France.

Pitzhanger Manor, Ealing, entrance front (1800–2). Sir John Soane.

By 1800 Soane was rich enough to buy his own country-house, Pitzhanger Manor in Middlesex. He kept one wing of the previous building which had been designed by his master, Dance, but he pulled down the remainder and had rebuilt the main block by 1802. On the entrance façade he again produced a design of monumental grandeur on an astonishingly small scale. He used the motif of a triumphal arch with grand Ionic columns of Portland stone, each with a strongly projecting entablature which carries a Coade-stone statue, set against bare brick walls. The balance between decoration and plainness and void and solid is entirely satisfying. At Pitzhanger Soane started to collect architectural fragments and casts and placed them in 'Picturesque' settings, such as half-buried columns in the garden and the Monk's Dining Room in the basement. Here Soane showed himself in tune with the Romantic need to evoke an emotional response.

Soane intensely desired his two sons to follow him into the architectural profession, and Pitzhanger was supposed to foster this aim. When he realised that it had failed to do so, Soane sold the property in 1810 and moved its contents to his London house in Lincoln's Inn Fields. Between 1792 and 1824 he built three houses in Lincoln's Inn Fields: No. 12 in 1792, No. 13 in 1812 and No. 14 in 1824. No. 13, the middle house of the three, is the

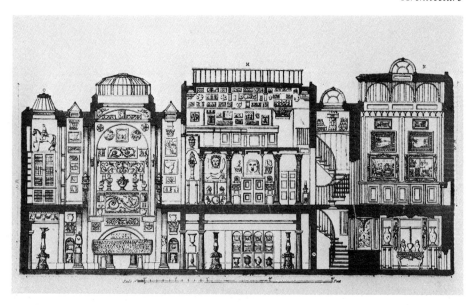

Section through Soane's own house in Lincoln's Inn Fields, London as it appeared in 1827; now the Sir John Soane's Museum; engraving.

Museum proper and connects with buildings at the rear extending behind Nos. 12 and 14. He worked on it bit by bit, adding complicated top-lit galleries over those areas which had been gardens and stables. Into this house-cum-museum Soane fitted his increasingly rich and varied collection of architectural drawings, models, casts and original fragments as well as paintings and sculpture, which ranged from the sarcophagus of Seti I, an important Egyptian monument, to the work of contemporary artists. Soane wanted to demonstrate in this way 'the unity of the arts'. In the architectural settings for these objects, Soane played with subtle spatial effects as in his picture room of 1824, and mysterious sources of light as in his breakfast room of 1812.

While he was living here Soane was asked to design the picture gallery at Dulwich. This was, astonishingly, the first public art gallery to be built in England. It was a most unusual commission. The gallery was to contain principally the collection brought together by the art-dealer Noel Desenfans and originally intended for Stanislas Poniatowski, the last king of Poland. Desenfans left the paintings to Sir Francis Bourgeois who in turn left them to Dulwich College. As well as the gallery, the building had to include a mausoleum to Desenfans and Bourgeois and his wife, flanked by small almshouses. There were, moreover, severe financial restrictions but all this challenged Soane to create between 1811 and 1814 a brilliant building, both austere and complex. As Summerson (who was director of the Soane Museum from 1945 to 1984) has said,

Soane conceived the building in that primitivist style which he had made so readily adaptable to simple brick construction. But the composition, in which each element is detached from its context by some slight break or recession, is intensely original, and unique at that date.

*Westminster Court of Chancery (1820–4; demolished 1883). Sir John Soane.
Watercolour by J.M. Gandy.*

In the interiors, Soane's masterly handling of light is evident throughout,
from drama in the mausoleum to clarity in the galleries.

Soane's originality did not prevent him from holding a number of official
appointments. He succeeded Dance as Professor of Architecture at the Royal
Academy in 1806 and, in 1814, on the reorganisation of the Board of Works,
he was appointed one of the three 'Attached Architects'. In this capacity he
did a great deal of work at the Palace of Westminster in the 1820s. All his
skills as an ingenious planner were called for when he placed the Law Courts,
seven Courts and ancillary offices against the western wall of Westminster
Hall and between its buttresses, and when he created a magnificent royal
route, including a particularly grand staircase, to the House of Lords through
the existing buildings.

Soane, often touchy and neurotic, saw himself as a rival to the self-
confident and adaptable Nash, who was his exact contemporary. They were
opposites in all essential respects, both in their characters and their
architecture. Nash, slick and quick and prepared to try any style; Soane
slowly and painstakingly developing his own. As Summerson has pointed out,
'It is no accident that one always thinks of Nash in terms of *exteriors*, Soane
in terms of *interiors*.' Nash conjures up a picture of artfully placed towers,
stucco, perhaps smooth and painted cream, perhaps dirty and crumbling, seen
against a background of trees. He was the master of the Picturesque and in
Sir Nikolaus Pevsner's words, 'London's only inspired town-planner'.

John Nash was born in 1752 probably in London, the son of an engineer
and millwright in Lambeth. He was employed in the office of Sir Robert
Taylor but by 1777 had set himself up as a speculative builder and architect.
His first houses were remarkable for their stucco fronts. Stucco, a hard
plaster painted to imitate stone but, of course, much cheaper than stone, was
at that period a new material. But in 1783 Nash was declared bankrupt and
he moved to Carmarthen. Here he gradually re-established himself, designing
both public buildings and classical houses for the local squires. By 1796 he
was able to return to London and establish a partnership with Humphry
Repton (1752–1818), the landscape gardener.

While he was still in Wales Nash learned about the theory of the
Picturesque movement, which was then being formulated, as has already been
described, by Payne Knight and Price. In about 1795, he designed a
triangular castellated house for Price on the seafront at Aberystwyth.
Through Price he may also have met Payne Knight, whose seat of Downton
Castle, built between 1774 and 1778, formed the prototype of the
picturesquely asymmetrical country-house, which Nash was to develop in
countless examples.

Nash and Repton worked together until about 1802, satisfying a growing
demand in fashionable society. Repton made the landscape settings of old
estates more deliberately picturesque, while Nash made the existing houses,
or new ones, both more comfortable and more appropriate to their new
surroundings. Nash's houses fell stylistically into two main types, the Gothic
and the Italian. A Gothic example was Luscombe Castle in Devon built
between 1800 and 1804 for the banker Charles Hoare, with the grounds laid
out by Repton. The house is battlemented throughout and grouped
informally around a low octagonal tower. The details of the building are quite
crude, but the plan works well and the enduring attraction is the sensitive
relationship between the house and its site. The best known, and earliest,
version of an Italian type is Cronkhill in Shropshire, which was designed in
1802. Here Nash used a different style to create similar effects of an irregular
silhouette, with a round tower with deep eaves at the corner of the design, a
colonnade and round-arched windows. This style was based on simple
vernacular buildings such as may be seen in the backgrounds of paintings by
Claude. Buildings in such paintings had been specifically recommended to
architects by Payne Knight as having a Picturesque beauty.

Rustic cottages, lodges and other estate buildings formed a further
important element in the Picturesque scene at the beginning of the nineteenth
century. Indeed these small buildings are often the most successful examples
of the style. Designs for cottages were taken seriously by landowners as
'improvements' to their estates and a great deal of care was lavished on them.
Many architects provided designs for this interest, but undoubtedly the most
famous example is that of Blaise Hamlet at Henbury, Bristol which Nash
built from 1810 to 1811 for the retired estate-workers of J.S. Harford, the
Quaker banker. It was all contrived to look as deliberately pretty as possible.
The emphasis is on variety with each stonebuilt cottage different, particularly
in the roofs of pantiles, stone slates or thatch with round, polygonal or
diagonally placed chimneys. An essential ingredient is the landscape, with the

Cronkhill, Shropshire (1802). John Nash.

cottages set around a curving village green which has some well-placed trees. Blaise Hamlet has provided a lasting picture of idealised village life in Britain, and as such has frequently been copied and trivialised. The original has great charm.

A *cottage orné*, as these artfully rustic buildings were called, of 1813 in Windsor Great Park was Nash's first architectural work for the Prince Regent. This was followed in 1813–14 by a suite of new rooms in Carlton House, which was designed by Holland. Holland had also built a Marine Pavilion at Brighton in 1786–7 for the Prince Regent and in 1815 Nash, now established as the Prince's favourite architect, was called in to remodel it. Very large stables had been added to the Pavilion in 1804–5 by the architect William Porden in an Indian style. These buildings, now generally called the Dome, were, together with a house called Sezincote in Gloucestershire, the first buildings in Britain which used Indian motifs, mostly of Islamic origin, like onion domes and scalloped doorways and window-openings. (Sezincote was built by S.P. Cockerell (*c.*1754–1827) for his brother Sir Charles, who had made a fortune in the service of the East India Company.)

The Dome, although it is a heavy building of yellow brick, must have encouraged the Prince to continue his experiments with this brand new exotic style. There was, of course, no question of detailed or accurate copies being made of any actual Indian buildings, which were then known principally through the delightful illustrations in *Views of Oriental Scenery* by Thomas and William Daniell, published from 1795. Nash, however, succeeded brilliantly between 1815 and 1822 in giving the Pavilion an exciting and amusing exterior and lavish interiors, a perfect setting for the pleasure-seeking Prince. He kept the shape of Holland's building and only disguised it.

A cottage orné, Blaise Hamlet,
Bristol (1810–11). John Nash.

The Royal Pavilion, Brighton,
detail of section through the
banqueting room (1815–22). John
Nash; engraving.

He also added two big rooms, the music room at one end and the banqueting hall at the other end of the original building, and a long connecting corridor along the entrance front. On the exterior Nash added Indian colonnades and verandas, with a series of five onion domes and pinnacles to enliven the skyline. The fretwork of pierced stone which appears to hang between the columns at either end and in the centre of the east elevation contributes greatly to the light and shade of the whole composition. The interiors of Nash's new rooms with their shallow domes and convex covings may owe something to Soane, and something to the desire to give the impression of a tent. The gorgeous decoration is mostly Chinese with a hint of Gothic. It was mostly designed and carried out by Frederick Crace.

Nash's greatest achievement, however, was his adaptation of the Picturesque to the urban scene with the creation of Regent Street and Regent's Park in London. In 1806 he had received his first official appointment as an architect to the Office of Woods and Forests, which gave him the opportunity to do this work. In 1811 Marylebone Park, which had been farms and fields, reverted to the Crown. As London was expanding it was obviously necessary to develop the park as a fashionable residential area, which would then require access to Westminster and St James's. In this year, therefore, Nash and another official architect, Thomas Leverton, were asked to prepare plans. In the following year Nash's plans for the park were approved and, at its southern end, the building of Park Crescent began immediately.

Nash's ideas for the park were strikingly original though they derived, ultimately, from the circuses, crescents and terraces which the elder and the

Cumberland Terrace, Regent's Park (1827). John Nash; engraving.

younger John Wood had introduced at Bath between 1729 and 1775. Nash, however, also wanted to preserve much open parkland which would be 'improved' in the best manner of Repton. In this respect, as has often been pointed out, he foreshadowed the garden city of the future and in Park Village he created the ideal suburb for the middle classes. Many modifications were made to Nash's plans. The number of detached villas within the park was substantially reduced, the Prince Regent's pleasure pavilion was never built, and the terraces on the edge of the park were only added between 1821 and 1827. These terraces are designed as monumental classical compositions, grand certainly, but with a theatrical air which extended to careless details and insubstantial construction.

Regent Street, no less than the Park, is a masterpiece both of planning and of the Picturesque, with all its attendant qualities of variety and artfulness. After the necessary legislation had been passed, the plan was adopted in 1813. The street was to begin at Carlton House (where the Duke of York's Column now stands, as Carlton House was demolished in 1827–8), and the first length to Piccadilly Circus, aligned on the house, was the most formal. From Piccadilly, Nash swept his street in a great curve west and north to Oxford Circus, and he emphasised this curve with a colonnaded Quadrant. Practical and economic reasons, including the desire to separate the meaner streets of Soho from affluent Mayfair, determined the route. North of Oxford Circus there were more problems for the alignment. It was decided to use Portland Place as the connection between the new street and the park. This had been built by James Adam in 1773–5 as a private development for the Duke of Portland, who at first objected. The street then had to make a double bend to link with Portland Place, but with a masterstroke in 1822 Nash placed his new church, All Souls in Langham Place, on the outside of the first bend and at an angle. The round portico of the church with its steeple both closes the vista from Oxford Circus and at the same time draws the eye around the corner and prepares the spectator for the final part of the street and its subtle merger through Park Crescent and Park Square with the park.

Nash cared very greatly for his street and, though he was already quite an old man, it was entirely his energy and enterprise which carried the project through to its completion in 1826. He acted as planner, architect, surveyor and speculative builder. The design of the street façades was controlled by Nash, but he allowed a decorative informality except in Waterloo Place, the Quadrant and Oxford and Piccadilly Circuses. Sadly, only the church has survived of the buildings, but the shape of the street and the beauty of the park remain as eloquent as ever.

Nash went on to make other very successful 'Metropolitan Improvements', in the Strand, at Carlton House Terraces and at St James's Park. It was indeed sad that his career ended in disgrace as a result of his unlucky commission from George IV to rebuild Buckingham House as a Palace. The design was inadequate and Nash was accused of excessive expenditure. After his death his reputation remained very low with a generation who believed in truth to materials, so that stucco should not pretend to be stone, and to whom the choice of style mattered. Nevertheless, he provided posterity with some splendid visual effects and his great ability to blend his buildings into their setting has given the British what they instinctively feel to be most appropriate for their country, architecture combined with landscape.

Barry and Pugin

Charles Barry was the epitome of the new professional architect at the beginning of the nineteenth century. Energetic and hard working, he was successful in competitions, then a frequent method of choosing an architect. He ran a large well-organised office, and got on well with his rich clients. He was knighted in 1852 on the opening of the House of Commons, in recognition of his great labours since 1836 as the architect of the New Palace of Westminster.

His training was also significant for the future. He was born in 1795, the fourth son of a Westminster stationer. He was articled at the age of fifteen to an unimportant firm of architects and surveyors, staying there six years and learning the practical basis of his profession. In 1816, on coming of age, he decided to spend a modest legacy from his father on an architectural tour of the European Continent. These travels were in fact crucial to his development. He left England in 1817 and travelled through France to Italy, then from Rome to Athens and on to Constantinople. Barry was about to return home when he was engaged as a topographical artist by David Baillie, an architectural traveller from Cambridge, to accompany him on a visit to Egypt and the Holy Land.

By January 1820 he was back in Rome with a large number of impressive pencil drawings of unfamiliar scenes. Here Barry met J.L. Wolfe, who was deeply interested in architecture and who became a major influence and lifelong friend. Under his influence he concentrated on a serious study of Renaissance architecture, making notes and many measured drawings of buildings in Rome, Florence and northern Italy. Though he never published his Egyptian drawings, the experiences of his travels were to prove invaluable for him and provide him with inspiration for the rest of his life.

On his return to England in September 1820 Barry continued his studies by looking at Gothic buildings. He set up a practice in London and his first works were Gothic churches in and around Manchester, where, having won a competition, he also designed the Royal Institution (now the City Art Gallery) in a straightforward Greek Revival style in 1824. As a result of a win in another competition, Barry produced a charming Gothic design for St Peter's church, Brighton.

It was, however, work in London that mattered. As has already been shown, there was much important building in progress in London, especially the metropolitan improvements of Nash between Regent's Park and St James's Park. In 1826 came the decision to demolish Carlton House, which provided the opportunity of spacious sites for the club houses, which had begun to concentrate in this area. In 1828 the Travellers' Club organised a competition among invited architects for a new building. Towards the end of August, Barry's design was selected.

His proposal marked a new departure in the history of architecture. Barry had decided that the Greek Revivial style was cold and insipid and he turned decisively towards Renaissance Italy. The Travellers' Club, as built from 1829 to 1833, has similarities with the early sixteenth-century Palazzo Pandolfini in Florence and it is recognised as the first 'Italianate' or 'palazzo' style building, a style which was to prove immensely amenable to the British urban scene for the rest of the nineteenth century. The Travellers' Club has no columns on its façades and relies for its effect on its proportions, its great cornice and subtle surface textures like those created by the cut of the masonry blocks.

Barry continued to develop this style when he built the Reform Club, next door to the Travellers' Club, between 1837 and 1841, again as a result of a competition. This larger building has a greater richness and formality and its prototype is a mid-sixteenth century Roman model, the Palazzo Farnese. Italian Renaissance palaces were, of course, designed around open courtyards. In the Travellers' Club this 'courtyard' survives as a substantial, but

The Reform Club (1837–41), with the Travellers' Club adjoining (1829–33), Pall Mall; view of garden façade. Sir Charles Barry.

inaccessible, light well; but at the Reform Club this space is roofed over to make the great central saloon, the focus of the whole design (colour plate 8). Decorated in strong yellows and reds, it rises through two storeys, surrounded by first-floor galleries, to the great concave curve of its glass roof.

Barry adapted his Italianate style for offices for the Board of Trade, 1844–5, for town houses for noblemen, particularly at Bridgewater House, Green Park, between 1846 and 1851, and equally for country-houses which he remodelled and set in terraced landscapes, such as Harewood House in Yorkshire, between 1843 and 1850, and Cliveden House, Buckinghamshire, from 1850 to 1851. He was still altering his Italianate style at the very end of his life. His last work, the Town Hall in Halifax, which he designed in 1859 and was finished after his death by his son, E.M. Barry, is full of references to late sixteenth-century Italian mannerist buildings. His style had thus progressed through all the phases of Italian Renaissance architecture.

Barry's own preferences almost certainly lay with the Italianate style that he introduced, but he was versatile, and his masterpiece, the Houses of Parliament, is, of course, a splendid Gothic building.

The Houses of Parliament at the beginning of the nineteenth century were an inconvenient hotch-potch of buildings. At their centre lay the great medieval Westminster Hall, with the Law Courts clustered in and around it. At right angles to it, the House of Commons sat within the shell of the medieval chapel of St Stephen, the upper part of a two-storied chapel, and beyond it, to the south, the House of Lords from 1800 sat in another refurbished medieval building, the White Hall. From the sixteenth century other offices had been added as the need arose, and by 1800 it was obvious that something had to be done in the interests of efficiency and safety. The job fell to Wyatt and between 1800 and 1808 he considerably tidied up the site in a plain Gothic style. This work was followed by that of Soane, who between 1822 and 1827 rebuilt the Law Courts adjoining Westminster Hall, the royal entrance, gallery and staircase to the House of Lords, the interiors of all this in his own personal brand of neo-classicism, and added libraries and committee rooms.

The real problem, however, lay in the House of Commons itself, which was much too small and awkward, especially after the numbers of Members of Parliament were increased by the union of the Irish and British Parliaments in 1801. But the home of the House of Commons since the middle of the sixteenth century was hallowed by tradition, and in spite of numbers of schemes, no-one could bring themselves to destroy or alter it. Fate, however, took a hand; on 16 October 1834 a great fire, started by the burning of tally-sticks in the furnace of the House of Lords, burnt out the centre of the site, including the chambers of both Houses. Architects were presented with the opportunity of the century.

In 1835 the Lords and Commons committees on rebuilding decided that the best way to find an architect was to have a competition. Anyone would be free to submit an entry so long as it was either in a Gothic or Elizabethan style. This stipulation of the style was unprecedented and was a symptom of the power of tradition at Westminster. Gothic and Elizabethan were equated with nationalism. Soane's splendid and inventive neo-classical interiors, which survived the fire, were all destroyed subsequently, without a second thought.

Barry had seen the fire and was determined from the outset to enter the competition. The entries were submitted in December 1835 and in February 1836 Barry was declared the winner. His design underwent many changes both before and during the long period of actual building, but some features remained constant. These included the incorporation of the major surviving medieval remains into his design, so that the main public entrance to the building included Westminster Hall. Above the surviving lower, so-called Crypt, Chapel, the original home of the House of Commons was re-created as St Stephen's Hall. This public entrance led up gradually to a unified level of the principal floor, on which both Houses and all main rooms were situated. The Houses were placed opposite each other, separated by lobbies and corridors, on the central spine of the building; and, east of them, a further range along the river front contained those facilities most in need of peace and privacy, the libraries, the committee rooms, the dining rooms and the Speaker's House. The long symmetrical river façade was enlivened at either end of the building by the vertical emphasis of a tower. That at the south-west was always to mark the monarch's entrance and provide a home for the records of Parliament, and that at the northern end was to replace the clock tower which had long been a feature of the site.

It was the clarity of this plan, with its excellent provision for logical circulation of the different users of the building, the monarch, peers,

The Houses of Parliament, Westminster (1840–67), view from the Victoria Tower. Sir Charles Barry.

Members of Parliament and the public, plus the imaginative use of the great surviving pieces of medieval architecture, which rightly won Barry the competition. It stood him in good stead during the long years of construction while he had to satisfy endless committees, the Royal Fine Arts Commission, experts in ventilation and commissioners charged with the completion of the building. There was much controversy, including the question of Barry's own remuneration. The scale of the project was unprecedented: the foundation stone was not laid until 1840 and the building was unfinished at his death in 1860.

In spite of all the difficulties Barry believed in his building and was determined that it should succeed. He was a perfectionist and he constantly revised all details to meet his ideals. He was well aware of the difficulties of designing satisfactory Gothic detail in the nineteenth century: the dullness and repetition of, for example, Wyatt's earlier work at Westminster itself and Smirke's at Lowther Castle, Cumbria, were clear warnings. The size and importance of the Houses of Parliament demanded a quality, a quantity and a range of Gothic decoration and fittings which had not been seen before. Fortunately Barry knew whom to approach.

A.W.N. Pugin started to work for Barry on the Gothic details of his King Edward VI Grammar School in Birmingham in 1835, and in the same year he helped draw Barry's competition drawings for the Houses of Parliament. Pugin's brilliant draughtsmanship almost certainly swayed the Commissioners in Barry's favour. Pugin continued to help Barry in the early stages of the design until 1837 when he established himself as an independent architect.

By the end of 1844, however, Barry started to plan the interior of the House of Lords and realised that Pugin was essential to him. Pugin's knowledge of real medieval work was so profound that he could instinctively produce new designs for wooden carvings, metal candelabra and railings, octagonal tables, desks and chairs, tiles, wallpapers and stained glass in a vivid Gothic style, full of richness and variety. Thus, between 1844 and Pugin's death in 1852, were created the major interiors of the Houses of Parliament, with the masterpiece of the two men, the House of Lords, justly described at the time as 'the finest specimen of Gothic civil architecture in Europe', opened in 1847 (colour pl. 10).

Barry effectively refined Pugin's hasty designs and protected his position from committees and the Treasury asking for tenders, enabling him to work with colleagues such as Hardman, Minton and Crace who understood his ways. The two men worked together in harmony, a splendid combination of Pugin's ideas and Barry's judgement. Pugin, however, did not receive the credit that was his due during the nineteenth century and sadly the families quarelled about the respective contributions of the fathers after they had both died. If Barry used to receive all the praise, today it is Pugin's turn and Barry is, equally unfairly, underrated. The building is Barry's, with essential and marvellous contributions by Pugin.

Pugin was indeed very different from Barry. Perhaps the only characteristics that they shared were energy and determination. Barry's official success, his knighthood and recognition by many Academies, had no counterpart in Pugin's life. Pugin's individuality and the speed at which he

The Chamber of the House of Commons (1846–52; destroyed 1941). Sir Charles Barry and A.W.N. Pugin.

worked left no posssibility for an office such as Barry's. 'Clerk, my dear Sir, Clerk?' he is reported as saying, 'I never employ one. I should kill him in a week'. Yet Pugin was immensely influential. Particularly through his writings and illustrations, he set a new course for the Gothic Revival in architecture and the decorative arts for the rest of the century. His life was one of total concentration and his output was phenomenal. Near the end of his short life he said, 'My medical man says I have lived an hundred years in forty'.

His father, A.C. Pugin, has already been introduced as the author of important books which illustrated measured drawings of Gothic details. He was a Frenchman who was established in England by 1792 and subsequently became an architectural draughtsman to Nash. In order to publish his own books he took on pupils and by the 1820s had established a flourishing school of architectural drawing. The young Pugin, born in 1812, was therefore surrounded by architectural subjects and the apparatus of drawing from his earliest days, but did not contribute substantially to his father's publications.

He was intensely precocious and in 1827, at the age of fifteen, started his career grandly with two royal commissions, one for furniture for George IV at Windsor Castle and the other a set of unexecuted designs for church plate. After this glamorous beginning things did not go smoothly for the young, restless Pugin. He was undoubtedly a stage-struck youth, made theatrical friends and worked as a stage carpenter at Covent Garden. Later he was also employed to design stage-sets and in 1831 his work for the ballet, *Kenilworth*, was much praised. At the same time, he was trying to establish his own business, designing and making furniture, metalwork and all sorts of pieces of interior-decoration. These designs had all the impracticality of youthful work. They were exaggerated, aggressive even. It is not surprising that the business failed in 1831.

He also suffered a number of other misfortunes. His first wife died in childbirth in May 1832, in December that year his father died, a few months later his mother died, and finally his aunt, Miss Welby, also died. Pugin was thus left alone in the world, but with a small financial independence. In these circumstances he decided to concentrate on training himself primarily as an architect. He did this by an intensive study of medieval architecture in Britain, France, Belgium, and Germany, and he designed a series of elaborate imaginary buildings, 'Le Chasteau', 'St Margaret's Chapel', 'The Deanery', and 'St Marie's College'.

Through his first publications, his expertise in Gothic design, particularly furnishings, was becoming recognised and he was providing drawings for established architects like Barry and James Gillespie Graham. By 1835 his ideas were crystallising and he converted to Catholicism. In the following year he became both famous and notorious with his book *Contrasts; or a Parallel between the noble edifices of the fourteenth and fifteenth centuries, and similar buildings of the present day; shewing the present decay of taste: accompanied by appropriate text.* This showed Pugin writing in the first flush of his conversion, blaming the Reformation for all the 'pagan' horrors that had entered architecture. In a series of brilliant and witty plates, he showed the Gothic glories of the Catholic past and contrasted them with the poverty and inadequacy of the buildings of his own day, whether they were in neo-classical or misunderstood Gothic styles. The drawings are wonderful examples of Pugin's skill; the Gothic appears rich and solid, the nineteenth-century styles skimped and unpleasant. They clearly revealed the attitude of a generation that was bored with the regularity of late Georgian architecture and was longing for variety and elaboration.

The rest of Pugin's life was devoted to the advancement in Britain of the Catholic faith, to be brought about by the building of churches (and everything else) in the Gothic style. For several years, until about 1844, his aims met with extraordinary success. It was, however, an irony that the Gothic Revival was ultimately much more successful in the Anglican Church, while the Catholics, under the powerful influence of Cardinal Newman, looked once more towards Rome. But that was in the future.

The impact of *Contrasts* was profound, and there was an enlarged second edition of 1841 which sold well. No more could the Gothic style be used altogether lightheartedly or carelessly; its religious connotations had been explained to all. As a result, Pugin's career as an independent architect opened up suddenly and dramatically as the newly emancipated Catholics rushed to employ him on ecclesiastical commissions. He found a platform for his ideas at St Mary's College, Oscott, near Birmingham, through his great patron John, 16th Earl of Shrewsbury, whose seat was Alton Towers, Staffordshire, and his friend and supporter, Ambrose Lisle Phillips, of Grace Dieu, Leicestershire. By the time he came to write his next treatise five years later, he had built or was building more than twenty-five chapels, churches and cathedrals.

Having established the moral necessity for building in Gothic, now in *The True Principles of pointed or Christian architecture* of 1841, he dealt with the practical aspects of the style and it was primarily as a practising architect that he wrote. He proclaimed his two great principles for design:

First, that there should be no features about a building which are not necessary for convenience, construction, or propriety; second, that all ornament should consist of the essential construction of the building.

His beautiful illustrations showed how deep was his understanding of Gothic construction and ornament. He lucidly explained the purpose of drip-moulds, buttresses, crockets and pinnacles, and gave good and bad examples. He ridiculed the mis-use of ornament, as in 'New Sheffield pattern for a modern Castellated Grate'. The liturgical uses for the various parts of medieval churches, which had largely been forgotten, were explained:

An old English parish church, as originally used for the ancient worship, was one of the most beautiful and appropriate buildings that the mind of man could conceive, every portion of it answered both a useful and mystical purpose.

The final development of Pugin's ideas appeared in 1843 with *An Apology for the Revival of Christian Architecture in England*. He not only drew well, he wrote well and powerfully.

His first buildings were in the perpendicular style, which was perhaps the easiest Gothic style to imitate and therefore was where the Gothic Revival began. Examples of these were the Catholic churches of St Mary at Derby, opened in 1839, and St Alban at Macclesfield, opened in 1841. More unusual, both in material and style, was the important Catholic Cathedral of St Chad in Birmingham. Red brick was eminently suitable for that industrial city and the style, that of fourteenth-century Baltic Germany, where brick facing with two west towers with spires and eastern apses are common features, matches the material. Pugin's composition of the exterior of St Chad, with chapels and transepts building up the steeply sloping site, together with the triangular-shaped projection which forms the entrance to the crypt, is excellent and shows his ability to design organically and imaginatively. The interior shows an equally effective handling of space, which is achieved by the most economical means. The steeply pitched roof, painted with stencil patterns and thus an important element in the design, has a continuous slope over nave and aisles.

Pugin built the Catholic Cathedral of St Barnabas, Nottingham, between 1841 and 1844, in a splendid strong Early English style, but, for most of his ecclesiastical work, he came to favour a style based on English examples of the fourteenth century, known as 'Decorated' or, to the Victorians, 'Middle Pointed'. Good examples of these are the Catholic Cathedral of St Mary, Newcastle upon Tyne, the Chapel of St Edmund's Catholic College, Old Hall Green, Hertfordshire, and what is undoubtedly his most famous church, the Catholic church of St Giles, Staffordshire. The reason for its success was that the Earl of Shrewsbury, at whose expense it was built, was persuaded by

Frontispiece to A.W.N. Pugin's An Apology for the Revival of Christian Architecture in England *(1843)*.

Pugin to allow him sufficient funds and a relatively free hand. Pugin worked intensively on the church between 1840 and 1846, an unusual length of time for such a fast worker, and there were many revisions of the plans. It was built of the local red sandstone by Lord Shrewsbury's estate workers and the main feature of the exterior is the beautiful west tower and steeple. The plan is simple, with north and south aisles and chapels, and a projecting chancel, but every possible decorative embellishment and fitting appropriate to a model parish church in the Decorated style has been included.

Indeed, Pugin's churches always consisted of much more than just the building. The fittings, altars, fonts, pulpits, the stained glass, the church plate and other metalwork, and above all a carved screen, usually carrying a rood or crucifix, framing the division between the nave and chancel – all of these were considered essential. Since Pugin was usually working for poor Catholic congregations with limited funds, the results can seem skimped and disappointing, with the money spread too thinly to do anything well. The Catholic church of St Augustine, Ramsgate, built lovingly and slowly at Pugin's own expense and next to his own house, the Grange, is an exception. It was begun late in 1845, opened in 1850 but was still unfinished at Pugin's

Cathedral of St Chad, Birmingham, interior looking east (1839–41). A.W.N. Pugin.

Church of St Augustine, Ramsgate, from the south (1845–52), with the architect's house beyond. A.W.N. Pugin.

death in 1852. The plan is most unusual, with a nave and chancel of almost equal length divided by the central tower, a south aisle almost as wide as the nave, a south lady chapel, a south transept which forms a chantry chapel for the Pugin family, and a south porch. Pugin was generous with his fittings, though sadly several of these have been altered or removed.

Pugin could clearly inspire great devotion, and though he had no office he did have a close group of colleagues and friends who could interpret his designs. They were George Myers, his builder, who also executed his carvings in wood and stone; John Hardman, who based his factory in Birmingham on the production of Pugin's metalwork and stained glass; Herbert Minton, the Staffordshire potter, who developed his range of encaustic tiles under Pugin's influence; and J.G. Crace who manufactured furniture, wallpapers and textiles from the ceaseless flow of drawings which arrived at his Wigmore Street showroom.

Pugin was a designer of genius in two dimensions. He instinctively created satisfying and suitable designs in endless variety. The basis of his patterns was usually stylised natural forms, drawn from his profound knowledge of medieval work, and reproduced in strong flat Gothic colours. Here one feels very close to the enthusiasm and vitality of the man himself. The Medieval Court at the Great Exhibition in 1851 displayed much of this work and, had

Pugin lived, the history of the decorative arts in Britain in the second half of the nineteenth century would have been different.

Pugin, of course, thought of himself principally as an architect. The many implications of his work were carried out by the High Victorian architects, Pugin's contemporaries in years, in the next generation.

Engineers, iron and glass

The immense growth in the number of buildings being constructed in this period led inevitably to a split in the architectural profession, with the more technical aspects being looked after by engineers. It was, however, the work of men like Thomas Telford, George and Robert Stephenson, Isambard Kingdom Brunel and Sir Joseph W. Bazalgette with their roads, bridges, railways and sewers, which brought undeniable improvements to the life of the average inhabitant of the British Isles. Thus engineers were heroes in Victorian times.

Samuel Smiles expressed this feeling of the benefits that had been brought by engineers during the preceding century when he wrote *The Lives of the Engineers* in 1861:

> These men were strong-minded, resolute, and ingenious, impelled to their special pursuits by the force of their constructive instincts . . . .. (Our) engineers have completed a magnificent system of canals, turn-pike roads, bridges and railways, by which the internal communications of the country have been completely opened up; they have built lighthouses round our coasts, by which ships freighted with the produce of all lands, when nearing our shores in the dark, are safely lighted along to their destined havens; they have hewn out and built docks and harbours for the accommodation of a gigantic commerce; whilst their inventive genius has rendered fire and water the most untiring workers in all branches of industry, and the most effective agents in locomotion by land and sea.

Engineers, of course, sometimes collaborated with architects, but often their practical and inventive solutions to particular challenges did indeed produce some architecture of simple but monumental grandeur, originality and spatial excitement. The aqueduct at Pont Cysylltau, the Clifton Suspension Bridge, the Britannia Tubular Bridge, the Crystal Palace and Paddington Station are rightly considered among the glories of their time.

Smiles's earliest engineer was James Brindley (1716–72) who was responsible for constructing the first canals of importance in the country from 1761 for the Duke of Bridgewater. These canals proved to be of great importance in providing cheap bulk transport in the early days of the Industrial Revolution. Some particularly impressive aqueducts for canals were built at the turn of the century by Telford and Rennie. John Rennie (1761–1821) worked on the Lancaster Canal, which he carried over the Lune at Lancaster in 1794–7, and the Kennet and Avon Canal which he carried over the Avon at Limpley Stoke between 1795 and 1800, to both of which he gave classical details. Telford (1757–1834), who had been appointed architect, engineer and surveyor to the Ellesmere Canal in 1793, built two water-tight iron aqueducts at Chirk from 1796 to 1801 and at Pont Cysylltau from 1795 to 1805. Here there are no period details and the nobility of the effect depends on the grand simplicity of the proportions and the daring of the scheme itself.

Soon after the establishment of the canal network, determined efforts were made to improve the roads with techniques pioneered by Telford and John Loudon McAdam. Obviously bridges were an essential part of such a programme and here too new methods of construction were being developed, principally with the use of iron. Iron, both wrought and cast, had been used from the middle ages; but the smelting process, by means of coke introduced by Abraham Darby in about 1709 at his works at Coalbrookdale by the river Severn in Shropshire, meant that cast iron was available in large quantities. It is indeed appropriate that the town is now called Ironbridge after the first iron bridge in the world, which was made by Abraham Darby III from 1777 to 1779. Darby was helped by a Shrewsbury architect, Thomas F. Pritchard, to create this single span supported on a semicircular arch. The result is both bold and light.

Iron became increasingly used as a building material, particularly in mills. By 1800 a system of fire-resistant construction using cast-iron stanchions and cast-iron beams carrying 'jack arches' of tile and brick had been established in English mills. At the same time iron was being used by architects for decorative features in building. The palm-tree columns in the kitchen of the Brighton Pavilion are well-known examples, but also Thomas Rickman, in

The iron bridge at Ironbridge, Shropshire (1777–9). Abraham Darby III and Thomas Pritchard.

Liverpool, working with the local ironmaster, John Cragg, used it for columns and tracery in windows and roofs in a number of churches.

The most notable use of iron, however, remained for some time bridge building. Telford, as has already been mentioned, realised the advantage of cast iron for the aqueducts that he needed for the Ellesmere Canal, in place of the bed of puddled earth that Brindley had used in similar circumstances. At the same period, from 1795 to 1796, he built the Buildwas Bridge in Shropshire, which unfortunately no longer survives. It marked a considerable advance on the Coalbrookdale bridge. It was longer, 130 feet as against 100 feet, used less than half as much iron, and had a segmental, not semicircular, arch. He is said to have constructed over one thousand bridges in Scotland following his appointment in 1803 as surveyor and engineer to the newly appointed Commission for Highland Roads and Bridges.

Telford's most famous bridges, however, came as a result of another major road-building scheme, the road from London to Holyhead via Shrewsbury, which began in 1815. For this he built two great suspension bridges, the Menai Bridge from 1819 to 1825 and the Conwy Bridge in 1826. The

The Menai Bridge, Anglesey (1819–25). Thomas Telford.

Clifton Suspension Bridge, Bristol (1836–64), under construction. Isambard Kingdom Brunel.

principle of a suspension bridge was not new but the scale of these bridges was unprecedented and Telford suspended them from wrought-iron chains. The masonry towers at the Menai Bridge have extremely handsome proportions with very slight and simple details of classical origin. At Conwy the proximity of the great medieval castle prompted Telford to build pairs of castellated turrets at either end of his bridge.

The other great dramatic suspension bridge of this period is that at Clifton near Bristol, which was stimulated by the Menai Bridge. A competition was held in 1829 and won by Isambard Kingdom Brunel (1806–59). Building was extremely slow; it began in 1836 and by 1840 the pylons were ready, but then funds dried up. Work was only resumed in 1861 and finally completed in 1864. Thus Brunel never saw the completion of his masterpiece, which Pevsner has described vividly:

Although not one of the earliest suspension bridges in England, it must yet have appeared a miracle while it was built, owing to the giddy height of the gorge and the daring with which the span was bridged without any intermediate support. The Clifton Bridge might also claim the title of being the most beautiful of early English suspension bridges. That is largely due to the felicitous design of the stone pylons. They are of rubble below but of light ashlar right at the top. The entasis of the sides is extremely sensitively calculated, and the parabolic opening above the square-headed one for the traffic is again a very happy motif. The size and projection of the top cornice matches the rest to perfection. The vertical cables are wonderfully light and so the job of supporting the carriageway safely is done not only with daring but also with grace.   (*The Buildings of England, North Somerset and Bristol*, 1958)

Pevsner did also point out that much more ornate schemes of decoration were contemplated, and so perhaps the much admired effect is due in part to a lack of money.

This brilliant design was Brunel's first independent work. His career was brief but intense, filled with an astonishing number and variety of projects and his character matched his work. As a result he has gained a lasting place as one of the giant figures of Britain's greatest industrial period. The Clifton suspension bridge provided Brunel with influential connections in Bristol, and in 1833 he was appointed engineer for the railway between that city and London. This, with its subsidiary lines, became known as the Great Western Railway and Brunel's conscientious attention to detail produced superb results. His original station at Bristol, built between 1839 and 1840, survives. It has a cantilever wood and iron roof in the form of a hammer beam structure. For the second London terminus built at Paddington between 1852 and 1854, Brunel adapted, as described below, some architectural ideas which he had taken from the Crystal Palace. Bristol contacts also led to Brunel's involvement in ship-building, and the timber-hulled paddle steamer *Great Western* in 1837 and the iron-hulled screw propulsion *Great Britain* in 1843 were built there. The gigantic *Great Eastern* was, however, constructed at Millwall in London between 1854 and 1859. The immense difficulties which Brunel encountered on this project were partly responsible for his early death.

The railways which were being constructed from the 1830s required even more bridges than the canals and roads of the previous generation. One of the most impressive and radical of these is the Britannia Bridge which carries the Chester to Holyhead railway across the Menai Straits close to Telford's Menai Bridge. It was built between 1845 and 1851 and is the design of

Paddington Railway Station (1852–4). Isambard Kingdom Brunel, engineer, and Matthew Digby Wyatt, architect. Painting by W.P. Frith (1862).

Robert Stephenson (1803–59) and the architect Francis Thompson, working in conjunction with Sir William Fairbairn (1789–1874), the consulting engineer. Fairbairn was a great advocate for wrought iron. Following his recommendation the Britannia Bridge was constructed from rectangular tubes made from wrought-iron plates. As with the Clifton suspension bridge, the design is one of simple grandeur, with here a superb balance between the verticals and horizontals. Much of this distinction is due to the subtlety and discretion of Thompson's handling of the masonry. The only extra ornamental features are the magnificent lions at the entrances to the Bridge. These are the work of John Thomas, who was also in charge of the carving at the New Houses of Parliament.

In 1854 Fairbairn published his influential book, *On the Application of Cast and Wrought Iron to Building*. Wrought-iron girders were developed to meet the need for large-span roofs over the platforms in railway stations. The largest made was that for St Pancras station in 1863–5, with a span of 243 feet. In 1855 Bessemer invented a method of making steel in large quantities. Steel was stronger, more durable and cheaper than iron, but, in spite of all these advantages, it was the end of the nineteenth century before steel-frame buildings were erected in Britain.

Glass, of course, has an ancient history, but its use as a substantial building material really belongs to the nineteenth century. Its development had been held back by the expense, the small size of the panes that could be produced and the limited production available. It had, however, long been obvious that glasshouses, or greenhouses, could make a crucial difference to the range of plants that could be grown successfully in the temperate British climate. During the nineteenth century serious plant collecting from all over the world was undertaken by the British. This, allied to the availability of cheap coal for heating, made it the great age for greenhouses. At first timber and masonry were used to hold the glass; an early, and very ornate example of an iron greenhouse, or here more properly conservatory, was the Gothic one with fan-vaulting of 1811–2 by Hopper at Carlton House. That one, however, was *en suite* with the dining room and was designed as much for people as for plants.

Plants certainly came first in the design for the Great Conservatory at Chatsworth, built (1836–40) for the Duke of Devonshire by Joseph Paxton (1801–65), the Duke's gardener, and Decimus Burton, the architect. (It was demolished in 1920, when heating bills became too much, even for dukes.) It was the culmination of a series of greenhouses that Paxton had built for the Duke. Above a low masonry base the whole exterior was covered in glass which rose in two great arches over curved iron ribs, the inner ribs being supported on cast-iron columns. The glass over the iron ribs was set in wooden sashes in a ridge-and-furrow arrangement which was one of Paxton's inventions. Other inventions of his were hollowed out members at the base of the ridge to serve as gutters for rainwater and a machine to cut the sash-bars.

Queen Victoria visited the Great Conservatory at Chatsworth in 1843 and the following year a Palm House was planned for the Royal Botanic Gardens at Kew. This too was designed by Burton, who this time collaborated with the engineer Richard Turner of Dublin. It was of a similar size to that at

The Conservatory.

·CARLTON HOUSE.

The Gothic conservatory, Carlton House, later demolished (1811–12). Thomas Hopper; engraving.

The Palm House at Kew Gardens, (1844–8). Decimus Burton, architect, and Richard Turner, engineer.

Chatsworth but was more beautiful. It had a more interesting shape, with a tall central pavilion, and the continuously glazed surfaces, in place of Paxton's ridges-and-furrows, gave a smooth and hence more bubble-like effect. Both wrought iron and cast iron were used in its construction, and Turner, who had worked on several major conservatories, should be given a substantial amount of the credit for its success.

The buildings, which used iron and glass extensively at this time, mostly greenhouses, markets and railway stations, were built to relatively standard patterns. A building which attempted a much more original scheme was the Coal Exchange in Lower Thames Street in the City of London. It was designed by the City Architect, J.B. Bunning, built between 1847 and 1849 and most sadly demolished in 1962. Behind a conventional masonry exterior lay the Exchange itself, a circular building constructed entirely of cast iron with three tiers of galleries under a glazed dome, which was supported on thirty-two ribs. The structural iron work had elaborate detail, much of it based on a motif of ropes. There was also much painted decoration with particularly interesting panels at the foot of the dome which show tree ferns as they can be studied in coal fossils. A feature, however, which the Coal Exchange shared with less ingenious buildings was an inability successfully to integrate iron and glass with masonry.

By 1850 there was both considerable technical experience and general interest in building in iron and glass and this culminated in the most famous building of its type, the Crystal Palace which housed the Great Exhibition of 1851. The Exhibition grew from a belief in the importance of improving manufacturing design which was deeply held by Prince Albert and Sir Henry Cole, an energetic civil servant, who was also a member of the Society of Arts, of which the Prince was President. It was to be an international exhibition, the first ever, and Prince Albert suggested the site in Hyde Park. A Royal Commission was appointed and in January 1850 the building committee organised an international competition. Two hundred and forty-five entries were received, but none was judged suitable and the building committee produced its own design. This, probably the work of Brunel and T.L. Donaldson, provided a long low brick building, dominated by a great glass dome, which would have been somewhat wider in diameter than that of St Peter's in Rome. It was manifestly impractical because of the expense and the length of time for erection that would be involved, and attracted much public criticism.

One of the critics was Paxton, who scribbled his fundamental idea for the Crystal Palace on a piece of blotting paper during a tribunal of the Midland Railway at Derby which he attended on 11 June 1850. He then made the necessary drawings and the scheme was published in the *Illustrated London News* on 6 July. Its boldness and novelty immediately caught the attention of the public; *Punch* christened it the 'Crystal Palace'; with the support of Prince Albert and Cole it was accepted by the building committee on 15 July. Paxton's concept came from the relatively small Lily House which he had just built at Chatsworth. Those arcaded walls of iron and glass were the prototype for the basic exterior module of a simple arched panel at the Crystal Palace. Both buildings had Paxton's usual ridge-and-furrow roof with the glass held in wooden sashes.

The Crystal Palace, view along the main avenue during the Great Exhibition (1851).
Joseph Paxton. Etching by George Cruikshank.

It was an enormous project and much of the credit must go to Fox and Henderson, the engineering contractors. Both wrought iron and cast iron were used and of course an immense amount of glass, which was supplied by the Birmingham firm of Chance Brothers. The building marked a new era in mass production and methods of pre-fabrication. There was unprecedented organisation both in the manufacture of the structural members, which had to be made both for ease of assembly and disassembly, and in the deployment of the teams of specialised workmen needed. The site was taken over by the contractors on 1 August 1850 and the exhibition opened on 1 May 1851. The building was 1848 feet long and 408 feet wide. It was three storeys high, with the second considerably set back above the ground storey, and the third 120 feet wide. In order to save some great elm trees Paxton modified his original design and added an arched transept just off the central axis. Inside there was a central nave the full height of the building, and aisles with two tiers of galleries to either side. The main structural supports were hollow cast-iron columns which also acted as rainwater pipes. The top tier of columns supported the horizontal wrought-iron girders. The arched principals to the transept were made of wood. The outer skin of glass and wood in its ridges-and-furrows was only intermittently attached to the iron beams. The flooring was of wood.

The total effect which so impressed contemporaries must have been much influenced by the presence of the trees and the colour scheme of red, yellow and blue devised by Owen Jones. A soft blue was used on the girders, which thus merged with the glass and the sky. The same blue was continued with bright yellow stripes and capitals on the columns and there were large patches of red behind the exhibits and in the galleries. The rather monotonous exterior must have been considerably enlivened by the presence of the flags of all the Nations, which was most probably suggested by Barry.

The feel of uncircumscribed space was something new and deeply impressive to most. Thackeray wrote in his Ode on the opening:

> A palace as for fairy prince,
> A rare pavilion, such as man
> Saw never since mankind began,
> And built and glazed.

Donaldson, who had been partly responsible for the building committee's unacceptable attempt, called it 'the most successful edifice of modern times'. To a few, however, it remained a greenhouse. Ruskin wrote:

The quantity of bodily industry which the Crystal Palace expresses, is very great. So far it is good. The quantity of thought it expresses is, I suppose, a single and admirable thought . . . – that it might be possible to build a greenhouse larger than ever greenhouse was built before. This thought and some very ordinary algebra are as much as all that glass can represent of human intellect.

And Pugin thought that it was a 'capital place' in which to exhibit plants but not his stained glass.

The great popular success of the Crystal Palace, however, guaranteed the prestige of iron and glass construction in the early 1850s. An iron ballroom was ordered for Balmoral Castle in 1851 and pre-fabricated iron churches, houses and warehouses were exported all over the world. The most important results were the two new London railway stations, King's Cross built in 1851–2 to designs by the architect Lewis Cubitt, and Paddington constructed in 1852–4 by the engineer Brunel assisted by the architect Matthew Digby Wyatt. King's Cross is particularly remarkable for the successful integration of the two great arched train sheds into the entrance façade by two enormous stock-brick arches. The arches of the train sheds are technically very similar to those in the transept of the Crystal Palace. They were originally made of laminated timbers, but were eroded by the smoke and replaced by iron arches in 1869. At Paddington the collaboration of the engineering and architectural aspects was particularly well managed. There were originally three great parallel sheds crossed by two equally tall transepts. These produced complex spatial effects with which Wyatt's non-period ornament went well.

This enthusiasm for the new building techniques was, however, short-lived and by 1855 was virtually over. (One of the very few exceptions was the interior of the University Museum, Oxford, of 1855–60.) Iron became inextricably associated with cheap utilitarian buildings; bishops refused to consecrate iron churches and the public did not want to look at, let alone live or work in, iron buildings on their streets.

The story of the 'Brompton Boilers' well illustrates the change of attitude. In 1855 Cole had to provide a temporary Museum of Science and Art on the Brompton estate south of Hyde Park, which had been purchased with some of the proceeds of the Great Exhibition. It was designed and constructed by Charles D. Young & Co. of Edinburgh, one of the leading firms which specialised in pre-fabricated buildings. It had a dreary exterior faced with corrugated iron and very meagre details. It was given its nickname of the 'Brompton Boilers' by George Godwin, the editor of *The Builder*, and that title was as effective in damning the building as the 'Crystal Palace' had been in exciting the public so few years before.

The promise of a new style disappeared behind heavy decorated architecture for the rest of the century. The necessary technology to make iron and glass buildings habitable had not been invented. One must remember that the smoke from the heating plant of the Palm House at Kew was carried 500 feet to a chimney in the form of a brick campanile. Iron and glass remained principally shed architecture, really suitable only for trains and plants.

Johan Zoffany, the Sharp family, *shown on their yacht on the Thames (1779–81)*.

6 Music

H.C. ROBBINS LANDON

Introduction

The huge Handel festival of 1784 continued to echo through Britain long after it was over. The 'Account of the Musical Performances in Westminster-Abbey and the Pantheon, May 26th, 27th, 29th; and June the 3rd, and the 5th, 1784 in Commemoration of Handel' (1685–1759) by the British composer and music historian Dr Charles Burney was published in 1785 and it marks a fit opening to this chapter.

Handel's position in Britain at this time, twenty-seven years after his death, was unique in European musical life. In the rest of Europe, some dead composers enjoyed a modest posthumous reputation – Palestrina and Pergolesi are two names that spring to mind – but nothing to rival the Handelian cult in England. By 1785, it was almost only in London that there were trumpeters still capable of playing the great solo parts in Handel's oratorios; Mozart, when arranging *Messiah* in 1789, had to rewrite all the high trumpet parts, because no Viennese trumpeter could manage them. And the Handelian cult extended to other old music as well – Corelli's concertos and Purcell's anthems continued to be played. There were even special societies devoted to the cultivation of old – or as they called it 'antient' – music. It was a uniquely British situation – at least to that broad extent.

New music, especially instrumental, was cultivated side by side with Handel, Geminiani and Corelli in concerts, but at the concerts of 'Antient Music' only old music was performed, and these special concerts were actively supported by King George III, an ardent Handelian. In the opera house, on the other hand, Handel was a dead issue; there, the Italians reigned supreme, and the latest European successes were the rage in London theatres. There was altogether a lively interest in European music, especially of the Austro–German instrumental school – the Stamitz family, Dittersdorf, Vanhal and especially Haydn (1732–1809). Publishers in London were doing a brisk trade in selling Haydn's music, which was known in Britain since the publication of his first string quartets in 1765. Now, Haydn had established a direct contact with a British publisher, William Forster, who began to issue

Haydn's symphonies and chamber music. Haydn's reputation, indeed, was growing with the appearance of each new publication, so that by the time he actually arrived in England in January 1791, he was greeted like an old friend.

All during the final years of the eighteenth century, native British composers produced a variety of music, sacred and secular. While the Handelian influence was paramount in British church music, composers of secular music tended to follow the continental taste, imitating (like Thomas Erskine, Earl of Kelly) the Mannheim school of the Austrians, with its new orchestral efforts, its exaggerated dynamic marks and pretty subsidiary subjects. A major occurence in British stage music was the return from Vienna, in 1787, of the Storace family – the composer Stephen and his sister, Nancy (Mozart's first Susanna in *The Marriage of Figaro*). Stephen Storace, together with William Shield, were to become the leading composers of British opera, the heirs of Thomas Arne, who had died in 1778, a year after William Boyce, a native British composer whose symphonies still sounded like Handel rather than Stamitz.

Haydn's influence, after his two British sojourns in 1791–2 and 1794–5, was in instrumental music almost as pervasive and long-lived as had been Handel's in the sacred style. Because most of Mozart's music was still unpublished at his death in 1791, it took many years before his music achieved any lasting popularity in England. By the time works like the late symphonies were fashionable in London (in the 1820s), Beethoven's music was just beginning to conquer (some) British hearts. Yet Beethoven's Septet had been well received when it was first played in London as early as 1801 – significantly the same year as the first London performance of Mozart's Requiem.

A substantial part of the British musical scene was coloured by the enormous number of foreign musicians, especially performers, who had settled in the country and dominated the whole of London's concert life as well as the Italian opera house – the violinist and impresario Johann Peter Salomon (who brought Haydn to England and was buried in Westminster Abbey because of it); the violinist and leader Wilhelm Cramer and his talented son, Johann Baptist, the pianist and composer; Muzio Clementi, the piano virtuoso and composer; Giovan Battista Viotti, violinist and composer, who fled to London during the French Revolution; and many singers such as Gertrud Mara and, in the 1790s, Brigida Banti-Giorgi. Later, Jenny Lind created a furore in London (1847) and ended her life in the country. But there were distinguished British singers, too, such as Michael Kelly (Mozart's first Bartolo in *The Marriage of Figaro*) and the famous soprano Elizabeth Billington. The oratorio tradition in Britain ensured a continuing number of excellent singers for the genre.

The opera in London was divided into two groups: the native British variety, sung in English, and the Italian opera, staffed by native Italians, including for a period in the 1790s and early 1800s Lorenzo Da Ponte, Mozart's librettist, who was briefly involved (to his distress) in British music publishing. Taste in the London opera largely favoured the more popular operas by fashionable Italians, but there were usually resident Italian composers, or at least those who visited, including Francesco Bianchi, Martin y Soler, Rossini, Bellini and, in 1847, Verdi himself. One operatic event of international consequence was the London invitation to Carl Maria von Weber to compose an English opera: the work was *Oberon* (1816), but the composer died two months after its successful première.

Composers continued to flock to the country, where they were richly rewarded. Indeed, Britain had the same kind of mystical attraction for musicians as New York does today. Louis Spohr (1784–1859) came and conquered, Felix Mendelssohn-Bartholdy (1809–47) became a darling of British audiences, visiting the country ten times, beginning in 1829, as pianist, composer and conductor. His oratorios revived an industry which was becoming completely historical (largely surviving on Handel and Haydn's *The Creation*), and Queen Victoria had 'dear Mr Mendelssohn' come and play at Buckingham Palace.

In England, all during this richly varied period, it was the general public which supported composers and performers. The amount of money to be made in England was enormous. Singers were the best paid, of course, as they are today; but performers, if the British liked them, were also huge successes, such as Niccolò Paganini, the violin virtuoso, in 1831. Yet for some curious reason, the English had a reputation for being not only unmusical but Philistines as well, especially the upper classes. Certainly, there is no hint of such 'unmusicality' in the correspondence of Haydn or Weber or Mendelssohn. A visiting Italian in 1847 – one of Verdi's entourage – has this to say on the subject:

THE MORNING CONCERT.

Swell (doesn't care for Music himself). " MY DEAR, IS THIS—AH—(*yawns*)—TE-DIUM OVAR ?" ! !

'The morning Concert', a cartoon for Punch *by Charles Keene.*

We in Italy imagine that the English don't love music; this is a mistake. It is said that the English know nothing but how to pay for the pleasure of hearing great artists, but that they don't understand anything; this is a mistake that the French have spread about and that the Italians have adopted because it's a French ideas. I say that no man pays for things he doesn't like and which don't give him pleasure. The English have never hissed a masterpiece. They have never received with indifference a Barber of Seville, as Rome has, or a William Tell, as Paris has, and they have never hissed an Otello, as Naples did on its first appearance.

(Frank Walker, *The Man Verdi*, 1962)

British orchestras were always considered excellent, though in 1794, during Haydn's second visit, one native London musician (Sir George Smart) noted that 'many foreigners were employed by [Haydn's impresario] Salomon at these concerts at very low salaries'. A tremendous boost to orchestral tradition in the country as a whole was the foundation, in 1813, of the Royal Philharmonic Society, an organisation that tried to persuade Beethoven to come to London and in his absence cultivated his music, which was then considered difficult:

A Haydn trembles at his own boldness; his hands recoil even at the sounds he himself has made; but still he goes on: more fearless, steps in a Mozart; and, at length, a Beethoven plunges into a congregation of sounds, that might raise from the very grave the spirits of his early predeccessors. The audience keeps pace, but it is a lagging one, with these innovations; first wondering what they mean, and lastly wondering at their former insensibility. Such is the progress of human ears; and of human improvement too, in many other matters . . . Many of us remember when Beethoven was Greek and Hebrew to our ears, – we have lived to see; that scarcely another could command the attention of the audience. Nay, there are some of us who can recollect when Haydn, and even Boccherini, was as Beethoven; when the shorter step from Haydn to Mozart was a serious effort; and when the prudent kept silence, and pretended to believe, in hopes, that the day of admiration would come at last.

(*Macculloch's Letters to Sir Walter Scott, on the Highlands and Western Isles of Scotland*, 1824, Vol. ii)

By the middle of the nineteenth century, Beethoven had become the most widely respected symphonic composer in Britain. The opera was, as before, divided into two classes, the local English (where taste was veering more and more to the vulgar) and the foreign opera, which was at first almost exclusively Italian, but gradually became infiltrated by French opera as well. All during this period British music publishing flourished, but soon a distinct change in taste began to be registered. Both the aristocratic and middle-class Victorian drawing room heard a vast quantity of music. Every well-bred young lady usually sang and also studied the piano, which became the focal point in home music-making. This new piano industry obviously required a vast amount of new music. Songs, arrangements of operas for voice and piano, and purely piano music began to be produced in staggering quantities. All this concentration on the piano went hand-in-hand with the development of the actual instrument. As early as 1795, Haydn took back to Vienna a British grand pianoforte 'with the additional keys' (that is, a treble extension) and with the technical novelty of a shifting pedal, then virtually unknown in Austria. (Beethoven sent Viennese piano-makers to study and copy his former teacher's exceptional instrument.) At the end of the eighteenth century, partly because France was in the throes of the Terror, England became the world's leading manufacturers of pianos, both of quantity and quality (their mahogany cases with rosewood inlay were much admired, too). In the course of the nineteenth century, she lost that pre-eminence, but the amount of reliable, sturdy pianos made in England continued to be impressive.

The quality of music being produced for the Victorian amateurs was less impressive. In fact it deteriorated rapidly as the century progressed: *kitsch* became fashionable. Of course, publishers continued to issue good music as well as bad; but the trash, vocal and instrumental, soon vastly outnumbered the classics.

Dominated as it was by foreigners, British music was nearly stifled – nearly, but never entirely. Even in this famously 'bad' period, respectable English composers did exist – Sir William Sterndale Bennett was one. Apart from producing some very interesting vocal and instrumental music, he also founded the English Bach Society in 1849. From then on, J.S. Bach would increasingly come to be loved and revered in Britain – though all during the nineteenth century nothing rivalled the deep-seated popularity of *Messiah*. Victorian organists, long starved of true masterpieces, welcomed the Bach revival with especial fervour. The organ, enriched by this Bachian cornucopia, again began to occupy a position of central importance in British musical life. There had always been the British Cathedral tradition in vocal music; now they had suitable music for the organ, and in enormous quantities.

Finally, there was a peculiarly English form of music that flourished in this period, the Glee, vocal ensemble music performed in clubs, in homes and also in public concerts. The 'Glee Club' was formed in London in 1787, and a whole group of composers – their names now largely forgotten – came to specialise in the Glee. The Glee especially appealed to the English for its exaltation of the amateur: there had been a grand tradition of such singing from the madrigals of Elizabethan times. In the church it flourished with the anthem and the hymn, to such an extent that even foreign composers such as Haydn (a staunch Catholic) enjoyed trying their hand with this distinctively English kind of religious music.

Handelian echoes

The Handel celebrations of 1784 were so successful that they were repeated, with ever increasing forces, in 1785–7, 1790 and in 1791, the year in which Haydn arrived in England. The 1791 festivities were held in Westminster Abbey 'by command and under the patronage of their Majesties'. There were by now over one thousand performers, including the best of available singers and orchestral players; the instruments included the famous 'large double basses', 'double bass Kettle drums' (tuned an octave lower than normal timpani), double bassoons and massed wind instruments – all of which no doubt made a 'sight . . . really very fine, and the performance magnificent; but the chorus and kettle-drums for four hours were so thunderfull, that they gave me a head-ache, to which I am not at all subject,' Sir Horace Walpole wrote describing the 1786 celebrations.

In 1791, the ladies came in full *toilette*, and their head-dress caused much annoyance. The King and Queen, with six royal princesses, came in full court dress. The orchestra was built up *en amphithéâtre* with Joah Bates sitting at the organ and leading the whole. To the right and left were the two musical prodigies, J.N. Hummel (later a celebrated composer) and G.P. Bridgetower (for whom Beethoven would later compose the so-called 'Kreutzer' Sonata), helping Bates with the registration of the huge organ. The massed rows of trumpets were decorated with banners rich in gold and silver threads.

When they did *Messiah* on 1 June, Haydn had a box near the royal family and was witness to the King, the Queen and the whole congregation rising to the 'Halleluja' Chorus. Haydn was thunderstruck; perhaps it was on that evening that the first idea of a 'modern' oratorio was implanted on his mind – an idea that would one day give the world *The Creation* and *The Seasons*.

Handel continued to dominate the musical scene in Britain all during the nineteenth century. At the 'Grand Musical Festival' of York Cathedral in 1823, for example, there were thirty-five composers, of which Handel was represented by twenty-five works (including *Messiah* complete) as compared to four each by Haydn and Beethoven, five by Mozart and seven by Rossini. In the musical festivals held in the provinces all during this period, Handel continued to dominate. One reason for this extraordinary predominance is extra-musical, and was summed up by Burney in his Preface to the 'Account' mentioned earlier:

Indeed Handel's Church-Music has been kept alive, and has supported life in thousands, by its performance for charitable purposes: as at St. Paul's for the Sons of the Clergy; at the Triennial Meetings of the Three Choirs of Worcester, Hereford, and Gloucester; at the two Universities of Oxford and Cambridge; at the Benefit Concerts for decayed Musicians and their Families; at the Foundling-Hospital; at St. Margaret's Church for the Westminster Infirmary; and for Hospitals and Infirmaries in general, throughout the kingdom, which have long been indebted to the art of Music, and to Handel's Works in particular, for their support.
('Account of the Musical Performances in Westminster-Abbey and the Pantheon, May 26th, 27th, 29th; and June the 3rd, and the 5th, 1784 in Commemoration of Handel')

The Handel festivals of the 1780s and 1790s set another precedent: vast forces. It was a very long cry from Handel's Foundling Hospital *Messiahs*, with fifteen violins and a choir of six boys and eighteen other singers (including the soloists), to the forces of 1000 at the London *Messiah* of 1791. The York *Messiah* performance, of which an engraving has survived, consisted of

> semi-chorus of 26
> main choir: 60 sop., 48 alt., 60 ten., 72 basses
> orchestra: 'above 450 performers'.

The monster festivals of the eighteenth century suggested to a British composer and organist, Dr Samuel Arnold, the idea of issuing the first collected edition of Handel's music. The project was a marked success, and the tall folio scores, which appeared between 1787 and 1797, were the first attempt at a critical complete edition of any composer. (Beethoven was given the set shortly before he died; he thought Handel the greatest composer who had ever lived.)

Another Handel festival, that of 1834 in Westminster Abbey with 644 participants, suggested to a distinguished British musician that he should embark on a new Handelian publishing project. Novello had been the organist of the 1834 series (his daughter, Clara, aged sixteen, sang soprano solo in *Messiah*), and he soon entered the world of music publishing, founding the famous firm that bears his name. In the 1840s, Novello began to issue octave piano-vocal scores of religious music, beginning with *Messiah* which, as Christopher Hogwood has written, was 'the cheapest musical publication ever offered to the public' (six shillings), and made Handel's most popular oratorios available very inexpensively to the many choral societies throughout the country.

In short, by the middle of the nineteenth century, Handel had become a British institution. A man closely associated with the festival of 1784, Burney, was also on *his* way to become a national institution: not as a composer (Burney's talents along those lines were distinctly modest) but as a writer on music. In the 1770s he had created a solid reputation through his travel books about the state of music on the continent, and in 1776 he had issued the first volume of his *General History of Music*, dedicated and personally presented to Queen Charlotte. The second volume appeared in 1782, the third and fourth in 1789, two years before Burney could welcome Haydn to England both personally and with a huge poem entitled 'Verses on the Arrival in England of the Great Musician Haydn'. By that time Burney was himself a national British figure, loved and respected by everyone from George III to members of the London orchestras. Burney also contributed largely to the important work, edited by Abraham Rees, entitled *The Cyclopaedia; or, Universal Dictionary of Arts, Sciences, and Literature* (London, 1802–20). In his way, Burney had fulfilled a double function: that of launching the Handel revival and of paving the way in his writings for appreciation of Haydn in England.

The rise of Haydn

It was in about 1765 that the English began importing European editions of Haydn's music. These were soon so successful, it would seem, that a few years later (certainly by 7 January 1772, when Bremner, in the Strand, offered several sets of works by Haydn for sale) British publishers found it worth their while to engrave and sell music by this relatively unknown Austrian composer. For many years Haydn continued to sell moderately well, along with works by the Mannheim school (Richter, the two Stamitzes, Beck) and by Haydn's Austrian contemporaries, such as Hofmann and Ditters (later Dittersdorf, when he had been ennobled). Then, in 1781, a Haydn symphony (it was No. 53, later known as 'L'impériale') was performed at the subscription concerts given by J.C. Bach and C.F. Abel; it turned into the hit of the year, and was played in piano arrangement by every cultivated young lady throughout the kingdom. In 1782 a serious attempt was made to lure

Haydn to England and he not only considered going but wrote three new symphonies (Nos. 76–78) to take with him. But Haydn's Prince Esterházy was against the idea – who could otherwise enliven those long evenings in Esterháza Castle?

The fact was that Haydn was immensely beholden to Prince Nicolaus Esterházy – not only because he was now the third highest-paid employee of the vast (perhaps 10,000-man) establishment which made up the Esterházy 'kingdom within a kingdom', but for a specific reason. Haydn's little house in Eisenstadt, in which the composer had invested all his capital, had burned down twice, most recently in 1776, and had been entirely rebuilt at Prince Nicolaus's expense. How could Haydn leave a Prince who behaved like that? The English heard curious rumours about Haydn's domestic life; they even had a plan:

> There is something very distressing to a liberal mind in the history of Haydn. This wonderful man, who is the Shakespeare of music, and the triumph of the age in which we live, is doomed to reside in the court of a miserable German Prince, who is at once incapable of rewarding him, and unworthy of the honour. Haydn, the simplest as well as the greatest of men, is resigned to his condition, and in devoting his life to the rites and ceremonies of the Roman Catholic Church, which he carries even to superstition, is content to live immured in a place little better than a dungeon, subject to the domineering spirit of a petty Lord, and the clamorous temper of a scolding wife. Would it not be an achievement equal to a pilgrimage, for some aspiring youths to rescue him from his fortune and transplant him to Great Britain, the country for which his music seems to be made?
>
> (*Gazetteer & New Daily Advertiser*, 17 January 1785)

Alas, no aspiring youths could be found to rescue Haydn from Schloss Esterháza, but five years later, in September 1790, Prince Nicolaus died, and, as it happened, his successor, Prince Anton, had no particular use for Haydn (though retaining him nominally as Capellmeister). Meanwhile, Johann Peter Salomon, the young German who had settled in London as a successful violinist and impresario, was in Cologne that same month, to hire singers and instrumental soloists for the 1791 London season. Salomon read in a local newspaper of Prince Nicolaus Esterházy's demise; he dropped everything and hastened to Vienna. Having arrived, he enquired where he might find Haydn (who was living in rented quarters on the Wasserkunstbastei), had himself announced and marched in with the historic words, 'I am Salomon from London and come to fetch you; tomorrow we shall reach an accord'. Haydn always told people that he had been very amused by this whole scene, and particularly by Salomon's play on the word 'accord' (both musical and financial). Salomon also came to engage Mozart to follow Haydn to London.

Haydn went twice to England, in 1791–2 and 1794–5, and the English heaped stupendous success, love, gratitude and financial rewards on him (and which they would, without question, have heaped on Mozart, had he gone to London as intended in 1792). Strangers came up to Haydn on the street in London, looked him up and down and said, 'You are a great man'. After Haydn's last benefit concert in May 1795, when the composer made the equivalent of 4000 gulden (equal to four years' annual pension granted by Prince Nicolaus Esterházy in 1790), the *Morning Chronicle* wrote:

A Gentleman, eminent for his musical knowledge, taste and sound criticism, declared this to be his opinion. That, for fifty years to come Musical Composers would be little better than imitators of Haydn; and would do little more than pour water on his leaves.

This was after the première of symphony No. 104, 'which', the *Morning Chronicle* judged, 'for fullness, richness, and majesty, in all its parts, is thought by some of the best judges to surpass all his other compositions'.

Haydn obviously intended to settle in England for good. After the first season of 1791–2 he had arranged to return to Austria, settle his affairs and come back to England in 1793 (taking with him his new pupil, Ludwig van Beethoven). In the event, the Napoleonic Wars began and Haydn decided to remain in Austria, so that the second journey to London in 1794–5 turned out to be only a temporary sojourn. But when he had rejoined a very annoyed Prince Anton Esterházy at the coronation of Emperor Francis II in Frankfurt in 1792 – annoyed because Prince Anton had wanted Haydn to come and arrange the musical part of the Esterházy contribution to the coronation ceremonies, and had been obliged to engage others to do so instead – Haydn fully expected to conclude 'the finale of his days, with the "Roast Beef of Old England"' (*Public Advertiser*, 12 April 1792).

Haydn had many friends and pupils among British musicians in the 1790s. Some began to imitate his music:

We are glad to observe that some sparks of the fire of *Haydn* begin to communicate themselves to our English Composers. An overture, written by Mr. *Alday*, was performed here, in which we were continually reminded of that great master. It is true the imitations were so strong as, occasionally, to make us suspect they were transcripts of *Haydn* himself: but we suspect men of genius frequently, if not always, begin with imitating. Originality is an acquirement of slow growth.

(*The Morning Chronicle*, 9 April 1796)

Alas, no lasting 'Haydn school' developed in Britain, as it did in Germany and Austria, because of a lack of talent. But among the rewards of Haydn's presence in London was his symphonic writing for a modern virtuoso orchestra. There was a vast difference between Handel's baroque orchestration, with its harpsichord or organ continuo holding everything together, and Haydn's modern orchestral scores, which by 1795 were taking into account the new string technique of yet another foreigner, Viotti, who had come to England from Paris and brought with him the beginning of the modern string orchestra technique. (Basically, this meant that the violin was strengthened to give it more force and tone, and the bow was made less curved so as to produce a greater sound.) Foreigners were by now an essential and omnipresent part of British musical life, and we must examine, in a little more detail, who they were and what they accomplished.

Foreigners, great and small

Professional musicians are a very arrogant race: they despise amateurs. In one of Haydn's London notebooks is this description of a fellow musician: 'Mr

Antis, Bishop and a minor composer' (this was the Moravian-American composer John Antes). There were many 'minor composers' in England then and for the next half-century, most of them foreigners. Lured to England by the promise of a comfortable existence, many enjoyed successful careers and some were of international stature. But there were also many major composers and performers who came to England and stayed, some all their lives (like Clementi), others for brief visits (like Verdi).

One of the most distinguished foreign musicians to settle in Britain in the period under review was Muzio Clementi, the Roman composer and piano virtuoso. Born in Rome in January 1752, he had achieved sufficient local fame by the age of about sixteen to attract the attention of a travelling Englishman, Sir Peter Beckford, who persuaded Clementi's parents to entrust him with their son's further education in Beckford's seat in Dorsetshire. After a systematic and thorough education,

His success was equal to his zeal and assiduity: at eighteen he not only surpassed all his contemporaries in execution, taste, and expression, but had already composed (though it was not published till three years after) his celebrated Op. 2, – a work which, by the common assent of all musicians, is entitled to the credit of being the basis on which the whole fabric of modern piano-forte sonatas has been founded; and which – though it is now [1831], from the immense progress which manual dexterity has made in the last sixty years, within the powers of even second-rate performers – was, at the period of its production, the despair of such pianists as J.C. Bach and Schroeter, who were content to admire it, but declined the attempt to play what the latter professor declared could only be executed by its own composer, or that by the great performer of all wonders, and conqueror of all difficulties, the Devil.

(*Harmonicon*, London, 1831)

Undoubtedly the solo sonatas of Opus 2 (which also included flute or violin sonatas) astounded the musical world when they appeared in 1779.

This brief biography of Clementi cannot enter into the details of his life, but it must be said that posterity's judgement of this great musical revolutionary has been adversely coloured by Mozart's opinion when he engaged, at Vienna in 1781, in a kind of musical duel with the Roman. 'He is a mere *mechanicus*', wrote Mozart, who admired his execution in thirds but thought 'he hasn't a farthing's worth of taste or feeling'. Probably Clementi's playing developed; certainly his compositions did. Apart from his fabulous piano technique, of which the most spectacular outward trappings were rapid passages in octaves and thirds, he also possessed a 'most beautiful *legato*'. As a teacher, Clementi spread this new technique to many small fingers over many years, and among his star pupils were John Field (the composer of celebrated Nocturnes) and Theresa Jansen, for whom Haydn composed his last great piano sonatas (Nos. 60–62, 1794) and piano trios (Nos. 43–45, ?1796).

Apart from composing, performing and teaching piano, Clementi entered the businesses of piano manufacturing and music publishing towards the end of the eighteenth century. Among his many services in those two fields one is of special interest. In 1807 Clementi came to Vienna, where he was introduced to Beethoven and arranged to publish his music in England. Beethoven thought very highly of Clementi:

. . . He had the greatest admiration for [Clementi's sonatas] and placed them in the front rank of works dedicated to beautiful piano-playing; he also loved them for their beautiful, pleasing and fresh melodies. For Mozart's piano music he had little liking.

(Anton Schindler, *Ludwig van Beethoven*, 1927)

At Clementi's instigation Beethoven rewrote the Violin Concerto Op. 61 as a Piano Concerto, adding a fascinating cadenza in the first movement for piano and timpani. At the same time Clementi persuaded 'that haughty beauty' to give Clementi's firm the British rights for the Razumovsky Quartets (Op. 59) and various other works including the 'Emperor' Concerto Op. 73, of which the English edition is actually the first.

As a composer, Clementi's reputation has in recent years been thoroughly revised by the appearance of his late symphonies. They had been performed in London and Paris (as well as elsewhere) between 1813 and 1834 but were never published. It is thought he completed six, and in 1978 Pietro Spada was able to reconstruct and publish four from the autographs (mostly in the Library of Congress, Washington). The rediscovery of these magnificent 'English' symphonies by Clementi have not only restored to the repertoire among the greatest works of the genre and period after Beethoven, but they show their composer to have been a bold experimenter and a symphonist of the first rank – a far better monument to his talents than the (otherwise indispensable) *Gradus ad Parnassum*, the famous piano school, and his 'Practical Harmony'. Clementi retired to Evesham, Worcester, where he died on 9 March 1832, 'his intellectual and musical faculties unimpaired'.

Giovan Battista Viotti was born in Fontanetto (province of Turin) on 12 May 1755, the son of a blacksmith. The child prodigy studied with Gaetano Pugnani, then a celebrated violinist and composer, in Turin, and became a member of the court orchestra there. In 1780 Pugnani asked the young Viotti to accompany him on a European tour. In 1781 Viotti's Op. 1 – six string quartets – was published in Paris. His spectacular career had begun. It led him, on these early journeys, also to Germany and Russia, where he was much fêted by Catherine the Great. Finally, in 1782, he settled in Paris, where he became a fashionable composer, performer and opera director. But the Revolution found him in disfavour with the authorities, and with the help of that generous impresario, Salomon, Viotti left for London in July 1792. Salomon introduced his colleague in the famous Hanover Square subscription concerts on 7 February 1793, when Viotti played his new Concerto No. 21 in E. A week later, on 14 February, he performed his most famous and best loved Violin Concerto, No. 22 in A minor, dedicated to his friend left behind in Paris, Luigi Cherubini. It is a profoundly beautiful work, with a very full orchestration (including clarinets, trumpets and kettledrums) and was to have enormous influence on the concerto form; Brahms thought it a masterpiece, and Joachim, the great violinist of the nineteenth century, ranked it above the concertos of Mendelssohn and Brahms.

On 26 April 1793, Viotti gave his first London benefit concert, in which there were two Haydn symphonies, while Viotti played a violin concerto and a duet with Salomon. After an unexpected trip to Italy because of his mother's death in 1793, Viotti was back with the Salomon concerts of 1794, sharing the limelight with Haydn, both on their second visits. When the latter's 'Military' Symphony was being cheered, the *Morning Chronicle* of 9 April 1794 wrote:

Some of the connoisseurs profess to like the playing of Viotti better than his Music. – Judgments differ; we will not pretend to affirm they are mistaken; we can only say, though his Compositions partake of the Old French School, there is yet a richness, unity and grandeur in them, that in our opinion place them far beyond the jigs, quirks and quackery, in which modern music is so apt to indulge. Not that we are the enemies of modern music: it has many essential improvements, but it has no few radical vices. Another new Symphony, by Haydn, was performed for the second time; and the middle movement was again received with absolute shouts of applause. Encore! encore! encore! resounded from every seat: the Ladies themselves could not forbear . . .

By the end of 1794, Viotti was acting manager of the King's Theatre and the next year leader of the Opera Concert, for which Haydn composed his Symphonies Nos. 102–104. The British public loved Viotti: his career seemed assured. Then, in 1798, he was denounced as a Revolutionary agent and obliged to leave the country within twenty-four hours. Shattered at being forced into exile again, he fled to Hamburg, but he left behind devoted friends, especially William Chinnery and his family, to whose children he taught music. By 1801 he was able to return to England, welcomed by his friends and the music world in general. Nevertheless he hoped to settle in Paris, but by 1810 he had still not been able to secure a position in the Napoleonic capital and returned once more to England, where he was one of the founders of the Philharmonic Society in 1813. At last he did secure a position in Paris under the Restoration – Viotti had been, after all, a refugee in 1792 – as director of the opera, starting in November 1819. But times had changed and Viotti's direction was not to modern taste; in 1822 he retired, with a modest pension and spent his declining years with his friends the Chinnerys in England. The late Boris Schwarz wrote:

What was the secret of Viotti's success? Virtuosity alone does not explain it. When he appeared in Paris in the 1780s, the public was ready for a new sound. Formerly, the ideal violin tone was sweet and slightly nasal, like the Amati and Stainer instruments that the previous generation of performers favored. Now Viotti arrived with a powerful Stradivari violin and produced a sound richer and more brilliant than anything heard before. His bow, too, may have contributed to the carrying power of his tone. Viotti must have used the new model developed at that time by François Tourte: the stick was thicker and heavier, the bow hair broader, and the balance had shifted toward the frog, which favored stronger accentuation and attack. At times, Viotti could sound 'brusk and hurtful', as one contemporary critic observed; but it was precisely that assertive style that enthralled a public tired of graceful gallantry. He replaced the dainty with the dramatic. Finally, Viotti is known to have used a more pronounced vibrato (the critics called it 'tremulando'), which gave his tone a more sensuous, expressive quality.

(*Great Masters of the Violin*, New York, 1983)

When in 1795 Viotti's string technique was allied to Haydn's last three symphonies, the modern orchestral sound was born – in London.

As an old gentleman, Viotti attended a Philharmonic Concert in 1820 at which the audience witnessed the London début of an extraordinary violinist and composer named Louis Spohr, who later wrote, 'I was delighted to learn that old Viotti . . . had praised my playing. He had always been my model, and in my youth I had hoped to study with him.'

In 1819, the Philharmonic Society invited Louis Spohr, a native of Braunschweig born on 5 April 1784, to come to London and give concerts. The invitation was extended by Beethoven's pupil Ferdinand Ries, one of the founders of the Society in 1813. In his autobiography we have an amusing account of Spohr's visit, on which he was accompanied by his wife Dorette, a harpist. We learn that the Philharmonic Society had been formed for the purpose of

giving a series of eight concerts during the session of Parliament. The demand for subscriptions, despite the high cost of tickets, was so great that several hundred subscribers could not be accommodated and had to take their places on a waiting list. The Society's resources were, accordingly, such that it could engage, not only the best singers and instrumentalists of London as soloists, but also distinguished artists from abroad.

Thus it was that I was engaged for the season of 1820. Against a substantial fee, covering travel over and back and a four-months' subsistence in London, I had a fourfold obligation: to conduct some of the concerts, to appear as soloist in several, to play in the violin section in all of them, and finally, to offer one of my orchestra compositions to the society as its permanent property. In addition to my fee, I was guaranteed a benefit concert in the hall of the society, with its orchestra participating. Although my wife was not included in these arrangements I could not bring myself to leave her for four months. Our family council therefore decided that she would accompany me and that she would appear as harpist in London, at least in my own concert. . . .

The time was now at hand for me to conduct my first Philharmonic concert, and I occasioned hardly less excitement than with my first appearance as soloist. It was still the custom in London that, in the playing of overtures and symphonies, the pianist sat at the piano with the score before him. He did not conduct, but rather read along and joined in when it suited him, which made a very bad effect. The actual conductor was the first violinist, who gave the tempo and, when things went wrong, beat time with his bow. An orchestra as large as the Philharmonic, with the musicians standing so far apart, could not achieve real precision under such a system. Despite the excellence of the individual musicians, the ensemble was much worse than that to which one was accustomed in Germany. I had decided, accordingly, that when it came my turn to conduct, I would attempt to improve matters.

Fortunately, when the time came, Ries was at the piano and gladly agreed to turn the score over to me and remove himself from the proceedings. I took my place, with the score before me, at a desk especially set up in front of the orchestra, drew my baton from my pocket and gave the signal to begin. Shocked at such an innovation, some of the directors wished to protest. However, when I asked them at least to give it a try, they consented. I had conducted the symphonies and overtures on the programme many times in Germany and was abundantly familiar with them. Then I could not only set the tempi with authority, but also signal the entrances to the woodwinds and brass, giving them a degree of security they had never previously enjoyed. I also took the liberty of interrupting when things were not satisfactory, and politely but firmly making my wishes known, with Ries acting as interpreter. By this means the orchestra was prompted to extraordinary attentiveness. The visible outline of the beat contributed to security, and they all played with a fire and precision never achieved by them before.

The success of the concert itself was even greater than I had hoped. The listeners were, to be sure, disturbed at first by the novelty, and there was a good deal of whispered comment. But when the music began, and the orchestra attacked the familiar symphony with such unwonted force and precision, prolonged applause after the first movement confirmed the favorable verdict. The victory of the baton was complete and never again was a pianist to be seen during the playing of overtures and symphonies.

Spohr had experienced great difficulty by his insistence upon playing only his own compositions at this début, but Ries 'assured them that in Germany my violin concertos were considered to be in the same class as' the great classics; hence the directors relented and Spohr's compositions were cordially received. He now began to compose new works for the Philharmonic Society. Spohr wrote exceptional words of praise for the performance – a point that ought to be stressed when the quality of London orchestras of the period is doubted. Here, after all, is the opinion of a professional:

My first work was a symphony (the second, in D minor, Opus 49), which I introduced at a Philharmonic concert on April 10, 1820. It found general favour at the rehearsal and real enthusiasm at the concert. This success was due in part to the excellent strings of this orchestra, to whom I had given a special opportunity to display their virtuosity in pure and precise ensemble playing. As a matter of fact, with respect to the strings, I never again heard this symphony played so well.

Gioacchino Rossini and his wife, the famous singer Isabella Colbran, were engaged by the King's Theatre in London for the 1824 season. She (born in 1785) was perhaps past her prime, Rossini (born in 1792) at the height of his career, having just produced the famous *Semiramide* in Venice which made his international fame. The couple arrived in December 1823 after one of those terrible crossings which reduced Rossini to a state of near-hysteria, and it was not until 29 December that he felt up to a journey to Brighton for a presentation to George IV. What happened then is described in the *Morning Post* of 1 January 1824:

His Majesty, with that discrimination and fine taste which so eminently characterise all his actions, in introducing Rossini into the music-room and to the principal professional Gentlemen there, commanded his inimitable band to play the Overture to the Opera of La Gazza Ladra, and also the beautiful concerted piece 'Buona Sera', from his popular Opera, Il Barbiere di Siviglia. Both these pieces were performed in such a stile of superior excellence as to obtain the most unqualified approbation of the composer, who expressed to his Majesty his astonishment that such powerful effects could have been produced by wind instruments alone . . .

Rossini was seated at the piano-forte and accompanied himself in two songs, one of which, an Aria Buffa, he gave with true comic spirit and humour; the other, Desdemona's beautiful Romance, from his own Othello, he sang most divinely, with exquisite pathos and expression of voice and countenance: his voice is a good clear tenor. His Majesty honoured him several times with marks of his royal approbation.

As with Haydn in 1791, George IV (then Prince of Wales) had set the tone in recognising a distinguished foreign composer; and Rossini was within weeks the darling of the capital. Of course, he had been engaged to write an opera for the King's Theatre, and on 24 January he made his London début with *Zelmira*, with Colbran in the title rôle. The critics thought her style pure and 'the delivery of her voice is in the manner of the best schools' but found her voice deteriorated. Moreover '*Zelmira* has not pleased, it must be admitted; why, we cannot tell: perhaps the reason is, that the music is too good.' Rossini had organised the orchestra in a different fashion; but, noted the same critic,

... Mackintosh, the best bassoon-player in England, is thrown out, to make way for a stranger, whose tones on the night of the opening, excited – not that pleasure and admiration which this instrument has hitherto never failed to produce in the orchestra of the King's Theatre, but downright laughter.

(*Harmonicon*, January 1824)

It was not exactly an auspicious beginning, and what then occurred must have made Rossini doubt British sanity. 'Rossini's *Barbiere di Siviglia* has been brought out here, but has not proved very successful ... this revival has proved a failure'. If Rossini had planned to produce a new opera for the King's Theatre, it was rapidly abandoned and for the six months that the composer stayed in England, he and *la* Colbran pursued a different object: money. They charged the huge sum of £50 per joint appearance and received it many times, but on occasion he received much more. He wrote, or rather rewrote, one new piece, 'Il pianto delle muse in morte di Lord Byron', an octet for voices arranged in large part from *Maometto II* (Naples 1820), which was performed at one of two benefit concerts Rossini gave at Almack's. The concerts, in which Rossini himself sung the part of *Apollo* in that 'Lament of the Muses for the death of Lord Byron', were financial successes but the *Harmonicon* thought 'we never heard a duller concert'. Rossini was still the main-stay of the King's Theatre with *Tancredi* (Pasta in the title-rôle) and *La donna del lago*. As for the new opera, *Harmonicon* tells us of its fate:

The new opera, so often announced, *Ugo, Re d'Italia* is in *status quo*. It is not likely to be finished by Signor Rossini here, for there is, as usual, a complete misunderstanding between all the high contracting powers in the theatre ...

Rossini, it might be said, was laughing all the way to his bank in Paris: he took home 175,000 francs, according to Francis Toye.

If Rossini's sojourn in the foggy island was like the subtitle of Francis Toye's book, 'A Study in Tragi-Comedy', the history of the next great composer to visit England is a sad end to his budding career. Carl Maria von Weber, born in 1786 at Eutin near Lübeck, came from a family which had given the world many musicians, such as the singers Aloysia (whom Mozart wished to marry) as well her sisters Josepha (Mozart's first Queen of the Night) and Constanze (Mozart's wife). Carl Maria went to study with Joseph Haydn's brother, Johann Michael, at Salzburg in 1798 and 1801. Weber's career was solid and successful – he composed symphonies, church music, concertos, chamber music but above all operas, of which the most successful were *Der Freischütz* (Berlin, 1821) and *Euryanthe* (Vienna, 1823). His activities covered the whole of German-speaking Europe, including Breslau (now Poland), Stuttgart, Mannheim, Darmstadt, Prague, Dresden, and Vienna.

It was from Dresden that Weber ventured forth to London, where he was the guest of Sir George Smart, who contracted to arrange all the contracts for

Weber (they had met during Smart's tour of Germany in 1825). Sir George also told Weber to bring some new compositions with him, 'which will assume a novel feature when directed by yourself'. With great kindness, he instructed Weber what he should do when he arrived: Weber arrived in Sir George's house on 5 March 1826, and he at once set to work completing the opera he was contracted to write for Covent Garden – *Oberon* – the greatest opera in the English language between Purcell's *Dido and Aeneas* and Britten's *Peter Grimes*. On 12 April 1826, the 'Romantic and Fairy Opera' was given its world première at Covent Garden. Weber himself conducted the orchestra and was received by the public with a rare warmth. On 26 May Weber gave his benefit concert in the Argyll Rooms and made a handsome profit of £96 11s. Meanwhile his English, which he studied especially for the composition of *Oberon*, had improved to the extent that he could compose a new English song and find a mistake in the manuscript copy of the words when he began to set it.

But then, Smart wrote, 'We were preparing a performance [of *Der Freischütz*] under Weber's direction at Covent Garden Theatre and I conducted a rehearsal of it for Weber, on the 2nd of June, on account of his illness'. It seemed that no one, least of all Weber, realised how ill he was. Three days later, on 5 June, he was found dead from tuberculosis in Smart's guest-room. A memorandum was found showing the amount of payments he had received in London:

From the Proprietors of the Theatre Royal, Covent Garden.

	£	s.	d.	£	s.	d.
For the copyright of *Oberon* in London	500	0	0			
For conducting this opera twelve nights	255	0	0			
For conducting selections from *Der Freischutz* five nights during the performance of oratorios	125	0	0			
				880	0	0
Performance at the Marquis of Hertford's concert				26	5	0
Ditto at Mrs. Coutts's concert				26	5	0
Profit of the benefit concert at the Argyll Rooms				96	11	0
For conducting the Philharmonic concert				15	15	0
From W. Ward, Esq., for composing a song				26	5	0
				1071	1	0

Eleven years later Victoria, pretty and much loved, assumed the throne and another great musician almost died on a tour to England centering round the Coronation festivities – Johann Strauss Senior.

The Coronation year of 1838 drew entertainers to England in vast quantities, and among them was the first of the great Strauss dynasty, Johann Senior, who would bring the waltz to all Europe. Born in Vienna in 1804, Johann Strauss had joined forces with the first Viennese 'waltz king', Joseph Lanner. By September 1825 Strauss had formed his own orchestra and with it he toured the whole of mainland Europe, playing his own waltzes and

A sketch by William Thackeray of Queen Victoria and Prince Albert, in a letter to J.R. Planché requesting seats for the Royal Command Performance of his coronation masque The Fortunate Isles *(1840).*

polkas and works by others, and conquering in the 1830s Berlin, Prague, Amsterdam, Brussels and then, in no less than three tours during 1837 and 1838, Paris.

Strauss and his orchestra arrived in England and took up residence in the 'Hotel de Commerce' in London. Their first concert was in the venerable Hanover Square Rooms, and as had happened with Haydn at his first concert in the same rooms in 1791, the British public needed to be persuaded of the new artist and the rooms were half empty. The concert was nevertheless a marked artistic success, and the next day the *Morning Post* reported to its readers:

So perfect a band was never before heard on this side of the Channel! The perfection of such an ensemble our orchestras never yet reached. The accuracy, the sharpness, the exquisite precision with which every passage is performed, can be the result only of the most careful and persevering practice . . .. We must notice the superior element of Strauss himself on the violin: he performs with peculiar energy, and imparts much of his own spirit to the band, the combined effect of which more resembles the unity of one single, powerful instrument than any orchestra that has yet been heard in this country. At all events we have no doubts that he will find himself appreciated here as he has been in all the principal cities of the Continent.

After such a review, the second concert, in Willis's Rooms, King Street, was sold out, and very soon Strauss was printing on his invitations 'Under the patronage of His Serene Highness Prince Esterházy', the Austrian Ambassador to St James. Paul Prince Esterházy, who had embraced the old Haydn, had engaged the Strauss orchestra at his installation ceremonies in Eisenstadt. Esterházy gave Strauss good financial advice: he was to read through every contract not twice but three times. English law was incorruptible. Strauss was not only prudent – though he was soon robbed of £97 – but clever, and within a few days the papers were asking 'whether Arnold & Dent send their chronometers hither (instead of Greenwich) to ascertain if they keep true Strauss time'.

On 10 May, Strauss and his orchestra played at a court ball and received £250, on 15 June he played for Prince Esterházy's ball at Richmond, which ended at 6.0 a.m., and where the astonished British aristocracy saw Austria's representative at the coronation, Prince Schwarzenberg, Strauss and Prince Esterházy traversing the ballroom arm in arm. It was a signal honour for any musician in those days.

Coronation Day, 28 June 1838, saw Strauss and his orchestra established in front of the Reform Club, where the procession was to pass. In the course of the festivities Strauss played nine times at court and earned a huge sum of money. He dedicated his Op. 103, a waltz, to Queen Victoria, which had been first played on 26 June at a court ball in front of the sovereign. There followed an exhausting tour through the provinces, across the Channel to Boulogne, Abbeville, Le Havre and Rouen, back to England and ending in Scotland with colds for most of the orchestra. Strauss fled back to the Continent but broke down in a concert at Calais. He was brought very ill to Paris and sent home in a coach. By the time he reached Strasbourg he was unconscious and lay in a coma for four days. He arrived so ill in Vienna that his family thought he was dying. But the Strauss family was of a robust nature, and to the joy of posterity, he survived; his two sons Johann Junior and Joseph lived to bring to the dynasty even greater glories.

Nine years later, one of London's most illustrious visitors arrived – Giuseppe Verdi, to produce his new opera *I Masnadieri*, with Jenny Lind. Verdi's young assistant, Emmanuele Muzio, has provided us with entertaining accounts of life in London as seen through the eyes of an amused, sympathetic Italian musician. He preceded Verdi to make the arrangements.

What a chaos is London! What confusion! . . . People shouting, poor people weeping, steamers flying, men on horseback, in carriages, on foot, and all howling like the damned . . . Milan is nothing. Paris is *something* in comparison with London; but London is a city unique in all the world. . . .

It's a mistake to say that all Englishmen speak French; there is nobody, one can say, in the shops and stores, who speaks French. The Englishman hates the Frenchman and his language. The high society of the Lords speak Italian well, having almost all been for years in Italy for amusement and diversion, and when one goes into society at least one can make oneself understood; otherwise it would be sheer desperation. You will have guessed, without my telling you, that we are working from morning to night. We get up at five in the morning and we work until six in the evening (supper time);

then we go for a while to the theatre and return at eleven and go to bed, so as to be up early next morning. The opera progresses, and two acts are already at the copyist's and by next Monday, perhaps, everything will be finished; then there's the scoring to be done. I am of the opinion – mark my words! – that, after *Ernani*, it's the most popular opera that Verdi has written, and the one that will have the widest circulation . . . .

Muzio then heard Jenny Lind but thought she sang in an old-fashioned way, with an excess of ornaments and arbitrary trills. 'We Italians are not accustomed to things of this sort and if *la* Lind came to Italy she would abandon her mania for embellishments and sing simply.'

They had a box at their disposal for the opera and Muzio was fascinated by the richness of the dresses and jewels worn by the audience during *Norma*. But

It's cold in London; it does nothing but rain, with wind all the time, and the Maestro [Verdi] doubts whether there is any sun, for he has never seen it shining owing to the mist, which is continual. It's weather that gets on one's nerves in an incredible manner. Blessed Italy, where we have at least got the sun!

The abominable weather made Verdi 'more lunatic and melancholy than usual' and slowed the completion of *I Masnadieri*; but Jenny Lind proved to be ugly and thoroughly professional. Verdi refused most social invitations 'because he can't eat those foods full of drugs and pepper . . . and wine so strong it's like rhum'. Despite all the disadvantages – 'Those Covent Garden singers, the old ones that is, are all hostile to Verdi's music . . .' – *I Masnadieri* was a resounding success:

The opera created a furore. From the prelude to the last finale there was nothing but applause, *evvivas*, recalls and encores. The Maestro himself conducted, seated on a chair higher than all the others, baton in hand. As soon as he appeared in the orchestra-pit there was a continuous applause, which lasted a quarter of an hour. They hadn't finished applauding when there arrived the queen and Prince Albert . . . . At half past four the doors were opened and the people burst into the theatre with fury such as had never been seen before . . . . The takings amounted to £6,000.

Verdi and Muzio left at the end of July for Paris, and Muzio went on to Milan, to witness the popular unrest and opposition to the Austrian occupation. 'The scene', wrote Frank Walker in *The Man Verdi*, 'was set for the revolution' of 1848.

The foreigner who had the most influence on British music society after Handel (and to a lesser extent Haydn) was Felix Mendelssohn-Bartholdy, of a cultivated Berlin Jewish family. He made his first visit to London in 1829 and presented himself as a rich young man who happened to be a musician: the trick worked and Felix was accepted at once by society as well as by his colleagues at the Royal Philharmonic Society concerts. On a memorable trip to Scotland, he conceived the idea of putting into music some of the feeling of the misty north; three years and three versions later, London heard the *Hebrides* Overture and was enchanted. 'Works such as this are like "angel's visits"', wrote the influential *Harmonicon*, 'and should be made the most of'. He played the piano: 'people went mad'; and tried the organ at St Paul's, where he improvised in triple counterpoint (his friend Thomas Attwood was

The first performance of Mendelssohn's Elijah *at Birmingham Town Hall on 26 August 1846.*

the organist there and, as a pupil of Mozart's, appreciated Felix's skill). In short, Mendelssohn became a success on several levels, the English liked his cultivated manners and his flawless command of the language.

For his third visit in 1833, Felix brought with him his new *Italian* Symphony, and played the solo part in Mozart's D minor Concerto. The *Harmonicon* thought the symphony ' . . . a composition that will endure for ages'. The celebrated Paganini was there and wanted to play Beethoven violin sonatas with Felix. Later in the same year Mendelssohn returned again from abroad and witnessed the official emancipation of the Jews: 'that pleases me tremendously'.

In 1837, Felix was in London for the British première of *St Paul* at Exeter Hall, which was repeated shortly afterwards at the Birmingham Festival. By the summer of 1842 he was making his seventh visit to Britain: this time it was the *Scottish* Symphony – like the *Hebrides* Overture conceived in 1829 in situ – which was first given by the Philharmonic Society. He now went to Buckingham Palace to play with Queen Victoria and Albert. Mendelssohn thought Victoria sang 'quite delightfully . . ., cleanly, in strict time'. He invited her to the next Philharmonic concert and she accepted: 'you can imagine what a tizzy the Philharmonic directors are in . . .'. The *Scottish* Symphony was dedicated to her, by permission.

Mendelssohn had made a friend in the British composer Bennett, and it was Bennett who extended the next invitation in November 1843, which was Mendelssohn's eighth visit to the 'dear old smoky city'. This time he displayed another side of his talents – as a champion of J.S. Bach, whose *St Matthew Passion* he had resurrected in 1829. He placed at the end of the first part the Overture for Orchestra in D, a British première (what did the trumpeters make out of their incredibly difficult part?). The critics considered the Bach 'a curiosity, more obscure and less effective' than Handel's overtures, and when Mendelssohn tried to perform Schubert's newly discovered 'great' Symphony in C, the orchestra laughed it aside and it was not heard in London until 1871. Another Schubert work, the Overture to *Fierabras*, was considered 'literally beneath criticism'. Mendelssohn, furious, withdrew his own *Ruy Blas* Overture. But the grand success of the season was the new incidental music to *A Midsummer Night's Dream*, which had to be given on two successive Philharmonic evenings. Among Mendelssohn's many friends and admirers was now Charles Dickens.

It is to England, and more specifically to the Birmingham Festival, that we owe Mendelssohn's chef d'oeuvre and in many critics' opinion the greatest oratorio of the century – *Elijah*. Its ardent religious flavour was in perfect harmony with the times, especially in England, where its success was such that Prince Albert felt constrained to write to its composer, comparing him with the prophet Elijah. The year after saw the final journey to England with six performances of *Elijah*, one attended by the Queen and the Prince Consort. But Mendelssohn was exhausted, and half a year later was dead. His new oratorio soon proved to rival Haydn's *The Creation* and Handel's *Messiah* in popularity with choral societies in the Anglo-Saxon world. *Elijah* also had many enemies: but its slightly sanctimonious tone was what Victorian England wanted, and it became a legend within a few years. Mendelssohn had rejuvenated the moribund oratorio form.

Some of the great foreigners who graced London's musical society have been discussed and although brief visits by Hector Berlioz (1847–8) and Frédéric Chopin (1848) have been omitted there were a host of lesser figures as well. A particularly bleak picture of life in London when Rossini visited it is drawn by Francis Toye:

London was then the milch-cow of every foreign musician, regarded, not without reason, as a source of income rather than a musical centre. English music had in truth sank to about the lowest depths of its too often depressed history . . . . [The public's] ignorance seems to have been positively sublime. [The English] were the prey of every quack and charlatan . . . .

(Rossini, 1934)

Probably Britain's bad reputation during this period is exaggerated. Mendelssohn considered musical life in Austria at the same period a great disappointment: 'The people around me [in Vienna] were so trashy and worthless that I took a spiritual turn and behaved like a theologian among them.' It was the general European debasement of taste, musical and otherwise, which England shared, and though European music had its giants, the general level was distinctly poorer than in 1780.

British opera and vocal music

A generation ago, even educated musicians might have been forgiven for
ignoring British opera during this period. The works and their composers had
been all but completely obliterated. A noble attempt to rehabilitate this dark
corner of British musical history was undertaken by the late Dr Roger Fiske,
whose work on the subject, *English Theatre Music in the Eighteenth Century*
(1973), has become a classic. Whether the actual music will ever again
become part of the repertoire is doubtful; but that is no excuse for ignoring
it. One of the difficulties in studying these operas is that virtually nothing has
survived except vocal scores. The recent revival of Shield's *Rosina* (1782) was
only possible because the orchestral parts have survived in the British
Library; the same applies to Storace's *No Song No Supper* (1790), where we
can study the effects of the composer's sojourn in Vienna and friendship with
Mozart, especially noticeable in the suave orchestration and use of the
woodwind. Fiske considers Storace's *The Pirates* (1792), set in Naples (which
the composer knew well), to be his masterpiece, 'remarkable for its action
ensembles and long finales in several sections'. 'Storace's early death' – he
died in 1796 at the age of thirty-four – 'was . . . one of several disasters that
beset English opera in the eighteenth century', concludes Fiske.

English opera soon attracted a huge public and made their composers rich
and successful. Shield, who was to become a friend of Haydn, was paid 1000
guineas for *The Woodman* in 1791. Haydn went to see it and wrote:

> The common people in the galleries of all the theatres are very impertinent; they set
> the fashion with all their unrestrained impetuosity, and whether something is repeated
> or not is determined by their yells.

This was quite a different audience from that which attended the Italian
opera, which was firmly in the hands of Italian *maestri* (as Storace found out
when he tried to gain an entrée after returning from Vienna). In English
opera, there was spoken dialogue between the song numbers, in Italian opera
there was recitative. It is a moot question how much Italian the average
London opera-goer understood in those days, but it is astonishing how long
and with what continuing success Italian operas persevered in Britain. During
the Napoleonic Wars it was not considered patriotic to perform French
operas, but after 1815, the occasional work originally written in French was
performed at the King's Theatre, usually translated into Italian (such as
Spontini's *La Vestale*, given in London in 1826 and 1832). In 1832, the
King's Theatre was actually host to three companies, one singing in Italian,
one in French and one in German (Weber's *Der Freischütz* and Beethoven's
Fidelio). There were also operas in English playing at Drury Lane and
Covent Garden for much of this period. London audiences also had the best
of foreign singers – the heroes and heroines of Milan, Vienna and Paris also
came to London – and all the latest operas as well. But it was always Italian
opera that predominated, first Rossini, then Bellini (less appreciated),
Donizetti, Verdi and scores of lesser composers.

One of the few native opera composers of this period was Henry Bishop
(1786–1855), who had a thoroughly professional knowledge of form, the voice

and orchestration. Bishop was forced to make a living in the theatre as best he could, in particular with pasticci and insertion numbers: his famous 'Home, sweet home', a song of pre-Victorian sentimentality, was such an insertion (in *Clari, or the Maid of Milan* of 1823). Bishop launched his career a year after Haydn's death, in 1810, with *The Maniac, or the Swiss Banditti*, which had a considerable success. However, by 1823, when Bishop produced *Cortez, or the Conquest of Mexico* at Covent Garden, the critic of the *Harmonicon*, after praising the music ('a superior kind') and noting that Bishop's work ' . . . announced in every part the scientific composer', had to admit that 'it is not music of a popular kind; not a single piece is encored; not one air is carried out of the theatre to haunt the imagination for the next fortnight'. Of Bishop's following work, a 'Fairy Opera', entitled *Alladin, or the wonderful lamp*, the *Harmonicon* wrote:

Aladdin did not prove successful; after it had been performed a few nights it was entirely withdrawn . . . .. It displays great labour, and but little invention: every part of it exhibits the experienced musician, while it betrays the vexatious inactivity of the composer's imagination . . . .

Partly, of course, it was the sensational qualities of Weber's *Oberon* which killed *Aladdin*. It was a discouraging attempt on the part of a British composer to compose native opera. In the event it was operetta, not opera, in which British talent would surpass.

Another attempt, perhaps more successful, to resuscitate native opera was made by the Irishman, Michael Balfe (1808–70), whose career began,

A scene from Michael Balfe's opera The Maid of Artois *(1836).*

curiously, with Italian, not British, opera. But unlike Bishop, Balfe's English operas were extremely successful and soon became eminently exportable. *The Siege of Rochelle* (1835) was followed by *The Maid of Artois* (1836) and then by his masterpiece, *The Bohemian Girl* (1843), which was even given at Vienna three years later. Having demonstrated his ability to compose Italian and English opera, Balfe now turned to French *opéras comiques* and won the hearts of Parisian audiences in the 1840s. Considering the enormous success of his English operas, it is curious that not even he was able to form a lasting school. The fault was certainly not his.

The piano: from Georgian salon to Victorian parlour

One of the most important developments of British piano manufacturing had been the invention of the square piano in the 1760s – an instrument ideally suited to the small room in a typical London house. Such a small piano was, of course, far less expensive than a grand piano, which was used primarily in public concerts and, in private town houses, limited to spacious salons. The small piano created a whole new public for the instrument, and by the end of the eighteenth century composers were writing music especially suitable for modest and private music-making: substantial amounts of dance music, for use in private balls, were now printed, along with sonatas, songs and extracts of operas and oratorios. Chamber music, too, could be played with the pianist at his (or more increasingly her) square instrument.

Mechanically, British pianos in the 1790s were superior to their main European rivals, and this superiority was encouraged by the chaotic political situation in France, removing that country temporarily from competition. The British speciality, which Haydn took back to Vienna with his new Longman and Broderip piano, was the *sopra una corda*, or shifting, pedal. This device shifted the keyboard away from three strings to two or one; the use of a single key was curiously ethereal and gave the music a silvery quality. The cases for British grand pianos were usually mahogony with delicate rosewood inlay and the whole was placed on a sturdy trestle. As time went on, attempts were made to reinforce the wooden frame and wrest-plank (where the pegs for the strings were attached) which tended to warp due to the tremendous pressure on the top register, extended from f″ to c‴ in the late 1780s ('with the extended keys'). The bass was then extended downwards from F to C. Thus the piano became not a five-octave F-oriented instrument, as it had been, but a C-oriented instrument, of six octaves: one such instrument, for Spain, was built by Broadwood, the leading London piano makers, in 1796 (Deerfield Museum, Massachusetts). The use of metal for the frame soon made both square and grand piano much more stable. With the development of the grand, empty virtuoso playing was coming into the fore. At the same time, people in the country could own an instrument without having to employ a professional to repair it constantly (a wooden-framed piano needs frequent attention).

The rise of the piano, its widespread distribution and its technical improvement, went hand in hand with the increasing power and wealth of the

middle class. By the middle of the nineteenth century, the piano had become
the bourgeois instrument par excellence all over Europe. It had become an
almost essential feature of the Victorian parlour, especially when space was
further saved by creating the upright piano (replacing, as it were, the square
instrument). The gradual prominence of the piano is closely linked with
another development: that of music publishing.

It is significant that the first publication of Haydn's twelve London or
'Salomon' Symphonies in Britain was in an arrangement for piano trio by the
impresario Salomon himself. Many music-lovers who had not heard the
original performances in London came to know these masterpieces in their
own homes: the string parts were dispensable and one could play the music
using only the piano. Soon, amateur pianists caused their music to be bound
in volumes. A typical, late eighteenth-century volume of piano music in
Britain might contain: some Haydn symphonies arranged for piano; a
Clementi sonata; a Dussek concerto with two versions, one for the 'extended
keys' and one for the old, restricted range; a collection of dances 'for the year
1796'; the Overture to Piccinni's *La buona figliola* arranged for piano; and Mr
Kotzwara's 'Battle of Prague' (the piano imitating guns, salutes and
marching). One of Britain's – or rather Ireland's – most endearing figures was
John Field (1782–1837), a pupil of Clementi whom Haydn admired in 1795,
and who was soon used by Clementi to display the new pianos of his firm
Clementi and Co. Field soon began composing and became one of the first to
exploit the tonal possibilities of the new piano. He realised that the piano
could be used in ways undreamt of in earlier music and on the fragile,
delicate instruments of the late eighteenth century. Field investigated the
running left hand accompaniment that we remember in Chopin (for example,
the *Revolutionary Etude*), on whose music Field had considerable influence.
But Field's speciality soon became the smaller forms, in which the delicate
shades of the new piano's upper register, and the sonorous possibilities of the
bass, could be turned into delightful miniatures – washes of colour. Field's
principal claim to fame is his invention of a miniature form called the
'Nocturne', of which his first was published in St Petersburg in 1812, and
whose delicate sonorities and interesting harmonies captivated musical Europe
and especially Chopin. Field's problem was that he was not a master of the
larger forms – a difficulty he shared with Chopin, too. Hence Field's
concertos for piano are less memorable than his piano pieces in shorter forms.
Field performed his technical wizardries with a 'deadpan expression on his
face which [noted Liszt] did not excite curiosity'. His dissipated style of life
contributed to a decline in his technical powers and, hence, his popularity. In
a sense, he wasted his very considerable gifts, but that is no excuse for the
neglect of his compositions today.

As the nineteenth century progressed, the number of music publishers in
the country multiplied. First, London had a virtual monopoly, but then
subsidiary centres in Dublin and Edinburgh began to register financial
success and a steadily growing public. The public's taste began to change as
published music penetrated into miners' cottages in Wales and seamstresses'
flats in Liverpool. London publishers continued to print the latest sonatas by
Beethoven and Hummel and mazarkas by Chopin, but the best sellers were

not those European heroes but 'Home sweet home' by Bishop and the latest English theatre tune. There arose an acute need to supply *kitsch*, and by 1850 an abundant supply of sentimental drawing-room ballads, songs, dance music of all kinds and solo piano music – good, bad and indifferent – was flooding the market. 'George Eliot gives an amusing description of this kind of music-making in the home in *Middlemarch*:

Celia was playing an 'air with variations', a small kind of tinkling which symbolised the aesthetic part of the young ladies' education.

(ch. 5)

The typical bound volume of piano music of 1850 was a far cry from the (on the whole) good music found in our specimen volume of 1796. Taste had become debased and the greatest compositions were becoming the exclusive property of a very limited minority. That minority was, however, well organised and staunch, so that there were always first-rate orchestral concerts, oratorio and the best operatic singing in the world. Popular opera in English began to move further and further away from its Italian, French and German counterparts. Shield's *Rosina* was certainly up to the best European standards in 1782, but the average fare at London's Olympia Theatre in 1850 – *The Yellow Dwarf*, for instance – was in a class by its British self.

The Bach revival and the English cathedral tradition

In some respects, British insularity was at its most homely and endearing in its church music – it is often referred to as the 'English cathedral tradition'. One composer, Thomas Attwood (1765–1838), who had been Mozart's pupil, had many gifts, both as a composer and as a musical bureaucrat: but his compositional talents were limited, whether by design or by circumstance, to Services and anthems for the church (some very superior) and to some attractive settings of songs and organ music. He also wrote music in larger forms, including a whole series of operas. It is a pity that somehow Attwood – potentially the most talented musician of his generation – never found the medium in which to express himself at his very considerable best.

The Wesley family, of which the English divine John, the founder of Methodism, was the most celebrated, came from Somerset and gave the English their only equivalent of a musical dynasty along the lines of the Bach family. John's brother, Charles, ordained in 1735, went to Georgia as secretary to Colonel Ogelthorpe, the Governor, and when he returned to England became the poet of the Evangelical Revival, writing some 6500 hymns. Samuel Wesley, the son of Charles, was a most precocious composer and he was instrumental in the Bach revival. His brother, Charles, also an excellent organist, was the father of Samuel Sebastian Wesley (1810–76), whose many anthems were justly admired for their complexity and brilliance. Among the most celebrated are his Service in E of 1845 and the anthems 'Blessed be the God and Father', 'The Wilderness' (for the inauguration of the Hereford Organ, of which he was the master, in 1832) and 'O Lord, Thou art my God'. These works are all part of the distinguished English cathedral tradition, which persisted in solitary excellence all through this otherwise undistinguished period of British music.

British organs were still rooted in the technical system of the eighteenth century, in that until 1850 or thereabouts there was no proper pedal and hence Bach's great organ music was literally unplayable on them. Moreover, only one organ – that of Surrey Chapel – was reported to have been tuned in equal temperament and thus able to be used for Bach's *Well-Tempered Clavier* which Samuel Wesley is said to have played there. In fact pianos in Britain were tuned in so-called mean temperament until Broadwood began to use 'well tempered' tuning in 1846. Percy Scholes in *The Great Dr Burney* (London, 1958) rightly asks the question: 'How could Wesley play the forty-eight preludes and fugues of the *Well-Tempered Clavier* on the organs and pianos of the day, since these were not "well-tempered"?'

Nevertheless interest in the music of J.S. Bach rose steadily during the first half of the nineteenth century, not only in Britain but in the rest of Europe. The Motet 'Jesu, meine Freude' had been heard at the Hanover Square Rooms in 1809, and exactly forty years later the British composer William Sterndale Bennett (later knighted) founded the British Bach Society, a year before the Germans began to publish the Collected Works (Gesamtausgabe). It was to bring to British organists the greatest boon of their lives, but it would take years before the instruments were rebuilt (or newly built) that could accommodate Bach's pedal parts and equal temperament. It was largely the passionate desire of British organists for Bach that forced the builders to adopt the German system of pedals and thus enable British cathedrals – and later smaller churches as well – to hear the greatest organ music of all time.

The Drawing Room at the Athenaeum (1828–30). Decimus Burton.

7 The Athenaeum

ALEXANDRA WEDGWOOD

One of the most characteristic developments of metropolitan life in the first quarter of the nineteenth century was the construction of large and grand purpose-built club houses, mostly within the parish of St James, Piccadilly, and concentrated in Pall Mall. Clubs had, of course, existed from the late seventeenth century and originated in assemblies 'of good fellows meeting under certain conditions' (in Dr Johnson's definition), usually in a coffee house or tavern. Politics and gambling were the chief stimuli which drew like-minded men together, and for some like Johnson himself and Goldsmith, it was literature and Grub Street gossip. During the second half of the eighteenth century it became the custom to provide a special building for the club, financed solely by the members, and from which (unlike the coffee house or tavern) unelected persons could be barred. Such buildings usually had the appearance and plans of town-houses. Surviving examples include Brooks's, built by Henry Holland, White's, probably by James Wyatt, but altered later, and Boodle's by John Crunden, all in St James's Street and all built between 1775 and 1788.

By the beginning of the nineteenth century, however, a change took place in the style of club buildings, which was the result of a radical alteration in the composition of club membership:

Intellectuals, graduates from universities, officers in the armed forces, all began to commission club buildings, and the image of responsible respectability that they wished to promote was some way from the raffish frivolity of the membership of the first clubs.

(Ian Grant, 'Club', in the *Dictionary of Art*, ed. J. Shoaf Turner, forthcoming 1994)

Henceforth club houses were designed to give the general suggestion of public buildings.

It seems to have been easy to start a new club. John Wilson Croker (1780–1857), the politician and essayist who is generally regarded as the founder of the Athenaeum, said on 23 November 1823: 'All that is necessary to create a Club in these times is a Circular Letter of Invitation'. He had a particular membership in mind and had been planning his club throughout

The Athenaeum, exterior from Waterloo Place (1828–30). Decimus Burton.
The building is shown before the attic storey was added in 1899.

that year. In March he wrote to Sir Humphry Davy, who was then President of the Royal Society:

I will take the opportunity of repeating the proposition I have before made to you about a Club for Literary and Scientific men, and followers of the Fine Arts. The fashionable and Military Clubs not only absorb a great portion of society, but have spoiled all the Coffee Houses and Taverns, so that the artist, or mere literary man, neither of whom are members of the established Clubs, are in a much worse situation, both comparatively and positively, than they were. I am therefore satisfied that a Club for their accommodation is desirable and would be very successful.

As everything must have a beginning, I would propose in the first instance to write to each member of the Council of the Royal Society, and each Royal Academician, to propose to them to be of the Club – perhaps also a dozen letters to persons of acknowledged literary eminence might be ventured, such as Sir Walter Scott, Mr. Moore, Mr. Campbell, Mr. Rogers, Mr. Rose etc.

This measure would produce enough to form a Committee which might then proceed to fill up the Club; which, in the first instance, ought, I think, to be limited to the number of 300 and to be composed of persons who are members of the Royal Society, or the Antiquarian Society, the Colleges of Physicians and Surgeons, the Royal Academy, or who shall have published any work, or shall have exhibited a certain number of pictures.

I do not propose that all such persons should be *ipso facto* elected; but only that they should be eligible, and that from amongst them, by selection, or ballot or otherwise, the Club should be formed. I attach great importance to a good situation . . .

These early negotiations proceeded smoothly, but Croker was determined to insist on strict conditions for membership, which have bden substantially followed ever since:

In order to keep our Club what it is intended to be, a Club of literary men and artists, we must lay down clearly and positively, as our first rule, that no one shall be eligible into it, except Gentlemen who have either published some literary or professional work, or a paper in the Philosophical Transactions – Members of the Royal Academy – Trustees (not officials) of the British Museum – Hereditary and Life Governors of the British Institution: the latter will open our doors to the Patrons of the Arts; I do not see any other classes which could be admitted, unless Bishops and Judges who are *par état* literary men although they may not have published any literary work.

A prospectus inviting membership from 'Authors known by their scientific or literary publications; Artists of eminence in any class of the fine arts; and Noblemen and Gentlemen, distinguished as liberal patrons of science, literature, or the arts' was sent out on 12 December 1823 and the first meeting of the distinguished Committee took place on 16 February 1824. In May the name of the Club was officially decided upon as 'The Athenaeum' and in the same month the number of members reached 300, which had originally been set as the limit. The success of the club was assured, and there was already a long waiting list of candidates. In December 1824 it was proposed to extend the limit of members to 1000, and there, more or less, it has remained, creeping up slowly to a nominal 1200.

Croker, right from the start, attached great importance to the situation of his club and an early decision by the committee was that it 'should be situated in a very public thoroughfare'. The obvious choice was the area of St James's with its proximity to the Palace, the Court, Government and Parliament. A temporary house was taken at No. 12, Waterloo Place, but a purpose-built club was always intended and in April 1824, Decimus Burton (1800–81) was appointed as the architect. He was then still a young man, but had made a precocious start, helped by his father, James, who was 'the most enterprising and successful London builder of his time' (Colvin), and his father's friend, John Nash. He soon obtained important commissions in the Royal Parks, such as the Ionic screen at Hyde Park corner and the archway, now on Constitution Hill, but originally designed as the Royal Entrance to Buckingham Palace, and he was known as an original neo-classical architect.

The Committee of the Athenaeum was negotiating for land in Trafalgar Square when in December 1825 it learned of the decision to demolish Carlton House and develop the area; so it applied for a site there. Waterloo Place, with Carlton House Terraces beyond, therefore, became the grand southern end to Nash's great scheme for Regent's Street, which had been planned in 1811 and finally completed in 1826. Opposite the Athenaeum, the United Services Club had been granted a site. Their architect was Nash whose overall plan for the area was approved in January 1827. It was always assumed by the Commissioners for the Office of Woods and Forests, who were the agents for the Crown, that these two buildings should have some degree of uniformity and in February 1827 they instructed the two architects, Nash and Burton, to consult, laying down the stipulations that there should be a continuous first floor balcony and no upper portico to the entrance. Burton attempted to consult Nash in order to produce complementary elevations but Nash behaved with his usual lack of attention to details, whether details of architectural design or details of the truth. He said that his plans were settled and unalterable and the United Services Club was built rapidly during 1827.

The Athenaeum had been delayed in the effort to achieve an agreement with Nash but started in the spring of 1828. By this date it became obvious that the design for the United Services Club included a Corinthian portico above the entrance porch to the north, or Pall Mall, elevation, which had been expressly forbidden by the Commissioners. The building committee of the Athenaeum was much aggrieved and felt that the presence of the portico tended 'to throw an air of inferiority over the Athenaeum, which they think may be in some degree corrected by giving a bolder proportion and more ornamental character to the Cornice and Frieze'. This, then, is the origin of the most distinctive feature of the exterior of the Athenaeum, a frieze on three sides of the building carved with a facsimile of the Panathenaic procession from the frieze on the Parthenon. The Athenaeum was thus released from its agreement with the Commissioners and made several alterations to the original design. The frieze was carved in Bath stone by John Henning and his sons in 1828 for £1300. Its present painted condition, in blue and cream colours, is not original. The decision to make a feature of the frieze and the choice of its subject was no doubt due to the presence on the building committee of W.R. Hamilton, the antiquary, diplomatist and sometime secretary to Lord Elgin.

Apart from the frieze with a cornice and balustrade above, the exterior of the Athenaeum is plain and covered with stucco; the two other main features are the porch with paired Roman Doric columns in the centre of the seven-bay elevation to Waterloo Place and the continuous balcony around the building at first floor level which is supported on finely detailed brackets. The attic storey, which spoils the proportions, was added in 1899 by T.E. Collcutt. Over the porch a gilt statue of Pallas Athene by the sculptor E.H. Baily was placed in 1830.

The plan is one of great dignity. The three-bay entrance porch leads to an entrance hall divided into three parts by columns. The middle has the widest section and is covered by a shallow tunnel-vault. The hall leads directly to the impressive staircase with handsome cast-iron balusters which rises in one flight, splits into two at right angles, and then turns again at right angles to reach the first floor landing, the centre of which rests on the tunnel-vault below. There is a glazed octagonal dome above the staircase. Thus the lighting in the entrance hall is dark and dramatic with the bright staircase beyond. The decoration throughout is slight, but always dignified and with erudite references to classical subjects and Athenian buildings. In the hall there are casts of classical statues in niches over the fireplaces and facing downstairs above the intermediate landing, is a cast of the Apollo Belvedere framed by columns. There are very few paintings in the Club.

The main room on the ground floor was the dining room, called, as was traditional in clubs, the coffee room. It runs the full width of the building,

The Entrance Hall.

The Coffee Room.

five bays, overlooking Carlton House Gardens. On the opposite side of the entrance hall is the two bay square morning room, and, beyond it, another small room, originally the writing room. Upstairs is the drawing room, the grandest room in the building. It runs the entire length of the building, overlooking Waterloo Place. The room has the traditional tri-partite division, here discreetly marked by pairs of columns. There is an identical chimneypiece to each section, one at either end of the room and one in the centre, with large plate mirrors above the fireplace. Behind the drawing room, to either side of the stairwell, are rooms devoted to the excellent library which has been an important feature of the Athenaeum since its foundation. The other two rooms essential for club life were a smoking room and a billiard room, and these were provided, the former at the top of the building, the latter in the basement. The furnishings are mostly of solid mahogany. At the end of the nineteenth century, some redecoration was done by two eminent painter-members, Sir Lawrence Alma-Tadema and Sir Edward Poynter.

The great appeal of gentlemen's clubs in the nineteenth century is well described by Thomas Walker in his periodical, *The Original*, the first number of which appeared in May 1835.

The only club I belong to is the Athenaeum, which consists of twelve hundred members, amongst whom are a large proportion of the most eminent persons in the land in every line, – civil, military, and ecclesiastical – peers, spiritual and temporal (ninety-five noblemen and twelve bishops), commoners, men of the learned

The Library.

professions, those connected with science, the arts, and commerce, in all its principal branches, as well as the distinguished who do not belong to any particular class. Many of these are to be met with every day, living with the same freedom as in their own houses for twenty-five guineas entrance and six guineas a year. Every member has the command of an excellent library, with maps; the daily papers, English and Foreign; the principal periodicals; writing materials, and attendance. The building is a sort of palace, and is kept with the same exactness and comfort as a private dwelling. Every member is master, without any of the trouble of a master: he can come when he pleases, and stay away when he pleases, without anything going wrong; he has the command of regular servants, without having to pay or manage them; he can have whatever meal or refreshment he wants, at all hours, and served up as in his own house. He orders just what he pleases, having no interest to think of but his own. In short, it is impossible to suppose a greater degree of liberty in living.

Clubs, as far as my observation goes, are favourable to economy of time. There is a fixed place to go to, every thing is served with comparative expedition and it is not customary in general to remain long at table. They are favourable to temperance. It seems that when people can freely please themselves, and when they have an opportunity of living simply, excess is seldom committed. From the account I have of the expenses at the Athenaeum in the year 1832, it appears that 17,323 dinners cost, on an average, 2s 9¾d each, and that the average quantity of wine for each person was a small fraction more than half-a-pint.

The effect of being able to visit a 'palace', where one can behave as in one's own home is vividly recorded by a young scientist from a provincial gentry background, Charles Darwin, who wrote on 9 August 1838, to his friend Charles Lyell, the geologist, who was a member:

I go and dine at the Athenaeum like a gentleman, or rather like a lord, for I am sure that the first evening I sat in that great drawing-room on a sofa by myself, I felt just like a duke. I am full of admiration for the Athenaeum, one meets so many people there that one likes to see . . . Your helping me into the Athenaeum has not been thrown away, and I enjoy it the more because I fully expected to detest it.

This was the building too where Dickens and Thackeray made up their quarrel, where Macaulay spoke his mind and where Trollope decided to change the course of his novel *Barchester Towers* and put an abrupt end to the life of Mrs Proudie, when he overheard two bishops criticising her in the library. Such a place could not fail to raise expectations and facilitate the exchange of ideas. And though it is not easy to calculate, the Athenaeum must have had a significant effect on the cultural life of Britain during the middle years of the nineteenth century.

Detail from a Bedfordshire enclosure map, showing surveyors at work (1798).

8 Enclosure and the English Hedgerow

TOM WILLIAMSON

The author of the Middle English poem *The Owl and the Nightingale* described

> a thick neglected hedge
> mixed with reed and green sedge.

As these lines indicate, the idea that before the eighteenth century hedges had been rare in England is a myth. In the south-eastern parts of the country, and in the west, most of the arable land had long taken the form of hedged or walled fields occupied and exploited by individual farmers.

Nevertheless, in the eighteenth century there were still many areas in which hedges and walls were comparatively scarce. The Midlands, and much of the north east of England, were traditionally 'champion' regions, in which open-field agriculture on the familiar textbook pattern was practised. Here, farms and cottages were usually clustered together in villages, with the arable holdings lying in small unhedged strips, intermixed in two or three vast fields and subject to communal organisation and rights of access. Yet it would be wrong to imagine that even these areas were completely devoid of trees or hedges. Hedges existed around the crofts in the immediate vicinity of the villages, and sometimes around the periphery of the great fields, or around meadows and areas of common grazing. Moreover, enclosure had been nibbling away at the open fields for centuries. This had partly taken place piecemeal, as proprietors consolidated strips through purchase or exchange and took them out of communal cultivation: and partly it had occurred through various forms of legal agreement, whereby all the remaining commons and open fields in a township were removed at one go. Nevertheless, many parishes in these areas remained largely unenclosed in the second half of the eighteenth century. One writer, commenting in 1744 on the appearance of Northamptonshire, stated that 'most of it is champion and lies so open to the eye in many places that 20 or 30 churches present themselves at one time to view'.

Even in those regions in which open fields had never existed, or had entirely disappeared at an early date, many areas of unenclosed commonland survived into the period of Parliamentary Enclosure, especially in the upland areas of the north and west of England. Commons were not the common property of a community. Since the early middle ages they had been owned by someone – usually the lord of the manor within which they lay. They were called 'commons' because certain defined groups of individuals had rights to their use. Such rights were usually attached to specific properties, frequently those which fronted directly onto the common. The existence of common rights, and especially the most important of these, the right to grazing, meant that commons remained open: while their perimeter might be demarcated by a stout hedge or other barrier, sections within them could not be permanently fenced off.

What was new in the eighteeenth and nineteenth centuries was not so much the hedge itself, but the speed with which new hedgerows were appearing in the landscape. Before the late eighteenth century, enclosure had been a gradual or episodic process, and one which had had comparatively little impact on areas of commonland. Parliamentary Enclosure dealt with the vast residue of unenclosed land – perhaps 25 per cent of the total land area of England – with remarkable rapidity. Although enclosure by Parliamentary Act continued from the early eighteenth century until the end of the nineteenth, the overwhelming majority of Acts were, in fact, passed within two fairly short periods. The first phase of enclosure, in the 1760s and 1770s, was mainly concerned with the open fields on the heavy clay soils of the Midlands. These enclosures seem to have been associated with an expansion of the area of land under pasture.

The second phase, which spanned the two decades after 1795, principally affected areas of lighter soils in the eastern parts of England and, in particular, areas of common grazing and waste. It was stimulated by the steep rise in agricultural prices brought about by the French Revolutionary and Napoleonic Wars. It was often associated with the ploughing up of land like the moors to the east of Helpston in Northamptonshire which up to this time had, in John Clare's words, 'never felt the rage of blundering plough'. The main subject of Constable's picture *A Mill on a Common*, painted in 1816, is not the post-mill owned by the artist's father, but a dramatic change taking place in the appearance of the Suffolk countryside. The common is being ploughed for the first time in recorded history, a year after the passing of the Enclosure Act.

The pre-enclosure landscape of open fields and commons is poorly represented in visual art. Although with the growing influence of the Picturesque towards the end of the eighteenth century, unenclosed upland scenery began to be painted, artistic appreciation of lowland heaths and commons developed only gradually. These more level and uniform landscapes lacked the sublime characteristics which might, in the mind of the educated public, have compensated for their primitive and unimproved state. Artists concentrated on the picturesque features which were characteristically associated with commons, such as tumbledown cottages or old windmills: few paintings dealt with the broad expanses of these landscapes, although there are notable exceptions – such as John Crome's panorama of Mousehold Heath in Norfolk.

Mezzotint by David Lucas (1830) based on John Constable's oil sketch A Mill on a Common. *This shows East Bergholt Common in Suffolk under the plough in 1816, a year after enclosure.*

John Crome, Mousehold Heath, a Norfolk view *(c.1818–20).*

But if paintings of commons are rare, those of open fields are almost non-existent. These lacked the complexity and variety necessary for a truly picturesque landscape, while earlier in the eighteenth century their almost featureless expanses would have been difficult to organise within contemporary principles of pictorial composition. Their formlessness made them seem profoundly unsettling and unsightly: ' . . . roughened by sluggish frost and strident wind the wild fields extended, and unbroken tracts strained and tortured the sight', as the Reverend James Tyley remarked of the unenclosed landscape in 'Inclosure of Open Fields in Northamptonshire'.

In those rare cases – all dating from the earlier eighteenth century – when open fields do appear in paintings and other illustrations, they do so as incidentals. Thus the view of Averham Park from the East, painted around 1720 by an unknown artist, shows the house dominating a park within which can be seen the familiar 'ridge and furrow' earthworks of former open-field plough-ridges, fossilised under grass: in the foreground the still-ploughed ridges of a working open field can be seen. This painting has a wider significance, however, for it encapsulates the nature of the changes occurring in the English countryside throughout the post-medieval period, and especially in the later-eighteenth and early-nineteenth centuries. A landscape directly exploited by small farmers, who organised their farming on local, traditional, customary lines, was gradually giving way to one dominated by large estates and tenant farms. The reasons for this change are complex, but there is a general agreement among historians that the decline of the small freeholder was both a precondition for, and a further consequence of, enclosure.

Its proponents claimed that enclosure was necessary for greater efficiency, for the adoption of new agricultural methods and for the development of agricultural specialisation. Thomas Batchelor, in the poem *The Progress of Agriculture* (1804), expressed a number of widely held beliefs when he contrasted the pre- and post-enclosure landscape of an area in Bedfordshire:

> Yet have I seen, nor long elapsed the day,
> When yon rich vale in rude disorder lay;
> Each scanty farm dispread over many a mile,
> The fences few, ill-cultur'd half the soil;
> Seen rushy slips contiguous roods divide
> Mid worthless commons boundless stretching wide.

(53–8)

Unknown artist, Averham Park (Nottinghamshire) from the East *(c.1720)*.

According to the author, improvements were impossible in such an environment; the skills of the farmer were employed in vain where 'all share a common fate'. Within the open fields, the organisation of agriculture was based, not on scientific principles, but on 'custom's law'. The poem is particularly interesting for the way in which agricultural backwardness and ugliness are seen as synonymous. A local common, prior to enclosure, is described by the author as a

> Dull scene! where nature, with herself at strife
> Teemed but with useless vegetable life.

> (66–7)

But all has now changed:

> To distant fields no more the peasants roam
> Their cottage-lands and farms surround their home
> And hawthorn fences, stretch'd from side to side
> Contiguous pastures, meadows, fields divide.

> (273–6)

Such was the rhetoric of enclosure and improvement, but the reality was often rather different. Some of the new agricultural techniques of the eighteenth century could be adopted in the open fields, and frequently were. Moreover, the idea that most commons could be profitably cultivated was not entirely true. Many were poor-quality, marginal land, unsuitable for arable agriculture even when 'improved' by using all the techniques available to the eighteenth-century farmer. This was a point not lost on George Crabbe:

> Lo! where the heath, with withering break grown o'er
> Lends the light turf that warms the neighbouring poor,
> From thence a length of burning sand appears,
> Where the thin harvest waves its withered ears.

> (*The Village, Book 1,* 1783)

The removal of open fields and commons was, no doubt, motivated by a desire for improvement, but there were other important incentives. The fact that a Parliamentary Enclosure Act terminated all existing lease agreements must have been an important consideration for landowners when the profits of their tenant farmers rose dramatically during the Napoleonic Wars. In addition, there is little doubt that enclosure, and especially the enclosure of commons, was also motivated by a desire to improve labour discipline, by making the poor more dependent on wages. This was certainly its effect. Enclosure removed a valuable safeguard against hunger and destitution, for it virtually eliminated the customary practice of small cottagers keeping their own livestock. This was a greater loss than it might seem to some modern historians. Arthur Young calculated that a single milking cow was worth around six shillings a week – a sum equivalent to the wages of a full-time labourer – to say nothing of the other benefits lost when commons were enclosed, such as the right to collect wood and cut turves for fuel. The enclosure of open fields was also a serious blow, as it deprived small farmers and cottagers of their rights to graze the fallows, and to glean after the harvest. Those who received a small allotment had to pay for it to be

The landscape of Parliamentary Enclosure: a view over north Buckinghamshire, from Combe Hill near Wendover.

surrounded by a hedge, wall, or fence – normally within 12 months of the passing of the Enclosure Act – as well as for the legal costs of the enclosure. The overall expense of enclosure, as compared with the value of the land received, was proportionately greater for smaller allotments.

It is, therefore, hardly surprising that in eighteenth- and nineteenth-century England the hedgerow was an evocative political symbol. To many people today the hedge represents the traditional English countryside, something which we should strive to preserve against the depredations of modern agriculture. Yet to many in the eighteenth and nineteenth century it had a rather different significance – as a symbol of theft and despotism, of a new and revolutionary social order which was overturning custom and tradition. Just as Batchelor in *The Progress of Agriculture* found the unenclosed common aesthetically, as well as economically, distasteful, so the opponents of enclosure considered the newly enclosed landscapes, and the hedgerows themselves, to be ugly as well as wrong. Cobbett wrote of 'a large common, *now enclosed*, cut up, disfigured, and the labourers driven from its skirts'. Clare's aesthetic response to the landscape created by the enclosure of his native village of Helpston in Northamptonshire was similar, but his poems also convey something of the changes which enclosure brought about in the way in which landscape was experienced. Enclosure involved a profound reorganisation of social space, a curtailment of customary rights and patterns of movement. In *The Mores*, Clare describes the freedom of movement before enclosure, and then the new landscape, in which

> Fence now meets fence in owners little bounds
> Of field and meadow large as garden grounds
> In little parcels little minds to please
> With men and flocks imprisoned ill at ease.

(47–50)

Hedges both changed the appearance of the countryside, and limited most people's experience of it. Yet even for Clare the hedgerows – or at least, the fewer, more ancient hedges of the pre-enclosure landscape – remained objects of beauty: the 'old lane hedges' which

> like the pasture brook
> Run crooking as they will by wood and dell.

Like Clare, Ebenezer Elliott might write in *The Splendid Village* (1833) of the '. . . commons, sown with curses loud and deep', but could yet describe the experience of

> Stealing through lanes, sun-bright with dewy broom
> by fragrant hedgerows sheeted o'er with bloom.

The hedge could be such an ambiguous symbol in the poetry of this 'anti-pastoral' tradition precisely because not all hedges were the result of Parliamentary Enclosure. The straight new quickset hedges planted across the former commons represented the forces of agricultural capitalism destroying the independence of an ancient peasant society: the ancient hedges whose origins had long been forgotten, in contrast, could be associated with the timeless peace and beauty of this threatened lifestyle. It is noteworthy that there are few eighteenth- or early nineteenth-century pictures of the kinds of hedged landscapes created by recent enclosure. The flimsy, ruler-straight hawthorn hedges, wide straight roads, and geometric fields which are the hallmark of the Enclosure Acts appear in the background of many hunting prints, but they are otherwise as rare in visual art as the open fields they replaced. The tall hedges and sunken lanes of Constable's Suffolk were created centuries, if not millennia, before the first Enclosure Act.

The hedges created by Parliamentary Enclosure also eventually came to be viewed as timeless elements of a picturesque landscape: their historical significance was soon forgotten. Indeed, even at times and in places where enclosure was actually taking place, their significance could be ignored in order to foster an ahistorical myth of an unchanging countryside. William Cowper wrote *The Task* in 1783, while living at Olney in Buckinghamshire. There is little indication in the oft-quoted line, 'God made the Country and Man made the Town', that at this precise moment the landscape of Olney itself, like that of the surrounding villages, was being revolutionised by Parliamentary Enclosure.

Enclosure in the eighteenth and nineteenth centuries changed the landscape of England directly, by adding a network of hedges and walls to formerly open areas. But perhaps more important were its indirect, longer-term effects. Enclosure created possibilities for further landscape change, at a time when the landed gentry were increasingly concerned to organise elements of the rural landscape for aesthetics and display. This kind of thing was difficult to achieve in unenclosed areas. In particular, it was impossible to plant trees on land subject to rights of common grazing, as livestock would simply eat, grub up or knock down young trees, or else commoners would help themselves to the wood. It was for these reasons that most commons had lost their tree cover centuries before. Enclosure, combined with the gradual concentration of land ownership in relatively few hands, created a private landscape, of continuous blocks of property under the absolute control of individuals.

The most obvious consequence was a vast increase in the number of parks. Until the eighteenth century, the majority of parks had been concentrated in the old-enclosed areas of England, and especially in the south-east, in the vicinity of London. With the spread of enclosure in the eighteenth and nineteenth centuries they proliferated in all areas, but especially in the former open-field regions: the number of parks in England more than doubled in the period between 1760 and 1840. Equally important for the development of the landscape was the massive wave of tree-planting which swept across Britain during this time. Plantations were created for game cover, for timber, and to enhance the beauty of estates: most, indeed, were planted for a mixture of reasons. Many were planted on former heaths and moors; they represented an alternative use for marginal land, and they symbolised the triumph of private property over older concepts of landownership. Some great estates were

Nineteenth-century plantations on the Holkham estate, near Castle Acre, Norfolk.

particularly noted for their tree-planting activities. On the Brocklesby estate in Lincolnshire, the Earls of Yarborough planted seventeen and a half million trees between 1787 and 1889: by the end of the nineteenth century the estate contained 8000 acres of ornamental and commercial woodland. But such plantations, many of which consisted of foreign conifers, were not universally welcomed. Wordsworth in particular bemoaned the expansion of forestry in the Lake District:

To those who plant for profit, and are thrusting every tree out of the way to make room for their favourite, the Larch, I would utter . . .a regret, that they should have selected these lovely vales for their vegetable manufactory, when there is so much barren and irreclaimable land in the neighbouring moors, and in other parts of these islands.

Moreover, to some people the planting of softwoods had ideological implications. Repton associated indigenous hardwoods like oak and beech with long-established families and traditional values. They took a long time to mature, and planting them implied a confidence in the long-term stability of society and property. The fast-growing conifers, in contrast, symbolised the more commercial concerns and short-term commitment of the parvenu, entering the ranks of landed society from the world of commerce and industry.

Towards the end of the eighteenth century, the hegemony of the landed élite over the countryside allowed a more radical involvement in landscape change, involving an appropriation of elements of the 'traditional' landscape. The minutiae of the rural environment began to be seen as fitting objects for aesthetic manipulation. The idea of the *ferme ornée* – an ornamental and, to some extent, symbolic landscape created around what was basically a working farm – had originated in the first half of the eighteenth century. In the later-eighteenth and early-nineteenth century, however, this concept was simplified and extended into more general attempts to combine beauty and utility. In a series of articles in the *Annals of Agriculture*, Thomas Ruggles explained the principles of 'picturesque farming', advocating such things as the extension of hedgerows to blur the edges of geometric fields, the careful planting of individual trees, and even the selective replanting of hedgerows with a range of indigenous trees and shrubs.

This kind of beautification of the countryside often went on in the immediate vicinity of country houses, and it was especially popular with those whose educated sense of landscape was not equalled by their resources. Today, the hedgerows of glebelands still often display the relics of picturesque planting. For the owner of an estate, large or small, the hedgerow had become something more than just a boundary to property or a stock-proof barrier. It had become an element in a picturesque landscape of élite display.

The Theocritus Cup, a silver-gilt vase with stand, designed by John Flaxman. Made by Paul Storr of Storr and Co. for Rundell, Bridge and Rundell (1811–13).

9 The 'Applied Arts': Design, Craft and Trade

PAT KIRKHAM

Introduction

This chapter deals with the design, production and business organisation of the more fashionable urban crafts, such as furniture, ceramics, metal-work and glass, which are often collectively known as the 'applied arts'. They are also known as the 'decorative arts' and – at the time – as the 'lesser arts' or 'minor arts' because they were considered inferior to the fine arts to which true 'artists', as opposed to designer/craftworkers, brought their genius and talents. In this snobbish hierarchy of artistry there were certain crafts which were (and often still are) considered inferior to the 'applied arts', namely the making of baskets, carts, ploughs and other objects which it was not thought necessary to 'design' self-consciously.

The history of designed and manufactured objects, perhaps more than any other 'art' objects, is inextricably linked to the social and economic conditions of the period in which they were produced. The years 1784–1851 in Britain can be seen as transitional between the Augustan 'age of elegance' (so-called), when taste and consumption were dominated by the aristocracy, and the period of High Victorian design based on middle-class prosperity and mass consumption. These years witnessed the extension and consolidation of the process of industrialisation; by 1851 Britain was undoubtedly the 'workshop of the world'. In their eagerness to study the growth of machine production and the major industries such as coal, cotton, iron and steel, however, historians have all too often ignored the fact that in the nineteenth century a great deal of manufactured goods was still produced by hand. Even where machinery was introduced, it was not always applied to every stage of production; indeed, by 1850 textile production was the only major British manufacturing industry which had been extensively mechanised. Yet it needs to be remembered that the largely unmechanised trades, such as pottery and furniture, were increasingly subjected to capitalist organisation. Pressure to increase output and profits led to workshops increasing in both size and scope as well as to the appointment of managers and overseers to control the workforce and scrutinise production, which was increasingly based on a division of labour. Most crafts and trades witnessed an increasing degree of specialisation in this period. Mechanisation, when it came, simply speeded up production processes which were already sub-divided or added power to a hand machine, the working of which still required considerable skill on the part of those using them.

Another division of labour must also be borne in mind when discussing designed objects – that between design, entrepreneurial activities and the craft process. Design attracted a great deal of attention in the years 1785–1851. Its importance grew with the increasing necessity to sell goods, at home and abroad, and it became recognised as a separate profession, just like architecture or painting. The separation between craft, design and business developed apace in this period which also saw the emergence of the entrepreneur/businessman who neither designed nor worked at the bench. This basic division still prevails in manufacture today.

Markets continued to increase with the general expansion of population and the growth of overseas trade (mainly as a result of colonial expansion). They also widened: the cheaper range of quality Staffordshire pottery from firms such as Wedgwood reached an ever widening consumer group, while such was the demand for furniture by the lower middle- and working-classes that a very distinct sector of the furniture trade grew up in East London from the 1830s and 1840s specifically to cater for it and also, of course, to promote it. Differentiation by sex and age was another feature of the market at this time, with objects, such as hairbrushes, being divided into distinct types so that they would appeal exclusively to women or to men. Similarly, the market in goods aimed at children grew enormously, with chairs, pottery and other items specially produced in child-size proportions as manufacturers added variety to the ever increasing range of products made.

Marketing techniques varied from trade to trade but the overall trend was to greater sophistication. The growth of shops and shopping in the eighteenth and nineteenth centuries is well documented. Windows increased in size so that more goods could be displayed and more customers tempted. Sale tickets were increasingly used although the grander shops also hired assistants (usually agreeable-looking females) to answer the queries of prospective customers. What is not sufficiently appreciated is the sheer splendour of some of the larger London showrooms which were deemed among the sights of the capital. Ackerman's *The Repository of the Arts*, an important indicator as well as influencer of taste published in monthly parts 1809–28, featured some of these, including those of Wedgwood and Byerley, the pottery firm, and Morgan and Saunders, furniture makers patronised by that epitome of the newly socially elevated client, Admiral Lord Nelson.

Rundell and Bridge, gold and silversmiths of Ludgate Hill, opened new showrooms in 1806 and in the following year exhibited the silver plate designed and made for the Prince of Wales for use on state occasions. For three days every week, it was reported, the rich, famous and fashionable of the capital made their way across London to see these extravagant pieces.

At the same time as markets were ever widening, the patronage of the wealthy and influential remained an important factor in the fashionable sectors of the trades. In a country where royalty has not been particularly

*Silver-gilt dessert stand, one of
a set of four. Made by Paul
Storr and Co. for Rundell,
Bridge and Rundell
(1812–13).*

noted for its patronage of the arts, the period 1784–1851 covers two royal
patrons who, each in his own way, influenced the taste of the day, particularly
in the decorative arts. They were, of course, George IV (as Prince of Wales,
Regent and King) and Prince Albert.

Revivalism was the keynote in design as various styles, including Gothic,
Classical, Renaissance, Tudor and Elizabethan, were adopted by architects
and designers, while exotic touches were added through free adaptations of
Oriental and Egyptian styles. This revivalism was rooted in a Romantic view
of the world and resulted in an eclecticism which gave equal validity to each
style. Thus it was possible for, say, John Nash to design in the Gothic,
Classical and Oriental styles at one and the same time (and sometimes in one
and the same building) without any sense of impropriety or contradiction.
This changed in the 1830s: with some historians dating the change precisely
to 1836, the year in which A.W.N. Pugin (1812–52) published his famous
Contrasts wherein the contemporary world was unfavourably compared with
the medieval one. From this time onwards design issues and the 'battle of the
styles' took on a moral flavour. Pugin argued that the art and design of a
society reflected its wider aims, ideals and social reality. For him Gothic came
to stand for all that was good; Classicism for all that was bad. The medieval
world was good, the modern world was sadly lacking in true Christian virtue
as well as any decently designed objects (see colour plate 10, The Royal
Throne, House of Lords).

The son of A.C. Pugin, an aristocratic French émigré who made his living
as an architectural draughtsman of some note, Augustus Welby Northmore

Pugin worked on the refurnishing of Windsor Castle in 1827 when he was only fifteen years old. He designed a complete range of Gothic furniture in a style developed by his father, from simple oak pieces for the Buffet Room to more elaborate ones in rosewood and gilt for the State Dining Room. Greatly admired today, this type of work was denounced by Pugin himself in 1841 when he criticised much of the design work which purported to be in the Gothic manner:

> everything is crocketed with angular projections, innumerable mitres, sharp ornaments, and turreted extremities . . . I have perpetrated many of these enormities in the furniture I designed some years ago for Windsor Castle . . . all my knowledge of Pointed Architecture was [then] confined to a tolerably good notion of details in the abstract; but these I employed with so little judgement or propriety, that, although the parts were correct and exceedingly well executed, collectively they appeared a complete burlesque of pointed design.
>
> (*The True Principles of Pointed or Christian Architecture*, 1841)

By the time he organised, virtually single handed, the Medieval Court at the Great Exhibition his Gothic style of furniture was altogether heavier and in a more authentically Gothic style than that designed for Windsor.

The Windsor Castle commission also reveals George IV as a discerning patron. By any criteria, he was the most important British royal collector of the decorative arts. A compulsive builder and decorator, he had a relaxed approach to his many precious possessions which he saw essentially as ingredients in interior design schemes. He was ready to alter or 'improve'

The Medieval Court at the Great Exhibition (1851).

pieces of furniture as and when it was necessary to achieve a particular overall effect in an interior. Furthermore, he also appreciated the part which paintings (of which he was a considerable connoisseur) played in interior design schemes. A great Francophile, he followed the example of the French collectors of the eighteenth century who hung Dutch and Flemish pictures in rooms filled with French furniture. When barely out of his teens, he bought French pieces in the Louis XVI style and his transformation of Carlton House from the 1790s, using French designers and craftsmen, led contemporaries to claim that it outshone the splendour of the Winter Palace in St Petersburg.

When he finally succeeded to the throne in 1820, George IV had become bored with Carlton House and Brighton Pavilion was almost finished. He had been discussing plans for a new palace based on Buckingham House but, with his father's death, his attentions turned to Windsor Castle and he took up residence in 1823. He initiated considerable rebuilding in the Gothic style by the architect Wyattville, in keeping with the old building; but not all the furnishings were in the same style, although they were all made or supplied by the firm of Morel and Seddon of London.

A great deal was in the French taste and designed by François-Honoré-Georges Jacob-Desmalter, son of Georges Jacob (a favourite furniture maker of Napoleon and Josephine), who came out of retirement to execute this important work for an English royal palace. His work is in a severe *style Empire* and remains at Windsor Castle today. Some earlier French furniture was brought from Carlton House and additional pieces were made to match when there was not sufficient. The State Drawing Rooms are furnished in an English Empire style, which itself was influenced by French design trends. Some French pieces are shown in the original schemes for these rooms but they were eventually removed because the King felt they did not look correct there. As it was, some of the higher royal officials found these rooms too gaudy and dazzling. Others loved them and, after all, they were, as Wyattville constantly reminded people, 'His Majesty's taste'. If the drawing rooms were dazzling, then the ballroom (now the State Reception Room) was even more so. It is one of a remarkable series of interiors designed in the 1820s and 1830s in the Louis XVI revival style by the Wyatt family which included Belvoir Castle, Rutland (colour pl. 9), and Crockford's Club, Apsley House and York House, all in London. The adoption of what was then the very latest style at Windsor Castle shows that even in the last decade of his life, George IV remained open to new ideas which he energetically put into practice.

Case studies: pottery, silver and silver plate, furniture and interior design

Pottery

Developments in pottery centred around new materials rather than machinery and a considerable emphasis was placed on design. By 1784 the firm of Josiah

Wedgwood was already well established as the leading pottery manufacturer, with an emphasis on product innovation, rationalised workplace organisation including marketing, and a recognition of the importance of design as a selling point (colour pl. 7). After the death of the founder in 1795, Wedgwood continued as a family enterprise on much the same basis as before, except that in the early nineteenth century steam power was applied to the potter's wheel which could then revolve slowly or faster at will. Despite much that has been written about Wedgwood and technological innovation during the 'Industrial Revolution', the basic machinery remained the traditional potter's wheel.

The fame of the firm of Wedgwood should not blind us to the activities of other potters. The Staffordshire industry grew enormously in the first half of the nineteenth century, as cream ware, blue printed and bone china found markets all over the world. In the early 1790s Josiah Spode perfected bone china (as it was later called), producing a durable translucent pottery which was to prove one of the most popular materials of the nineteenth century. In 1813 Charles James Mason patented his distinctively patterned and coloured hard ironstone earthenware china, in a wide range of items. The energies of certain potters such as Roses of Coalport, Minton and Copeland, went into reproducing pre-Revolutionary French Sèvres porcelain which was enormously popular and very costly in Britain in the 1820s. Indeed, so good an imitation was that made at the Madeley factory of Thomas Randall from 1825, that the one was often mistaken for the other.

A particularly hard porcelain, originally developed by both Copelands and Mintons in the 1840s for making scaled-down sculptural figures, was Parian porcelain. It resembled marble and therefore was ideal for translating large sculptures into small-scale pieces to grace the bourgeois drawing room. The work of several leading sculptors was reproduced in Parian by a variety of firms, including Summerley Art Manufactures, and shown at the Great Exhibition of 1851.

Minton's main contribution in terms of new materials was to produce a new version of an old heavy earthenware with coloured glazes known as majolica. Shown at the Great Exhibition, it soon proved extremely popular, particularly for jardinières holding plants, which today grace almost as many middle-class 'best rooms', as they did in the nineteenth century. Mintons were to dominate the English pottery trade from 1840, as had Wedgwood in the previous sixty years or so. Another important revival was that of the medieval craft of making inlaid tiles, usually known as encaustic tiles. This development, spearheaded by Herbert Minton (son of Thomas Minton who founded the firm in 1793) re-established the virtually moribund British tile industry which by 1870 was booming.

An entrepreneur in the mould of Wedgwood, Minton experimented with materials and production throughout the 1830s. He ensured commercial success for his venture by buying shares in two patents: one for the production of inlaid tiles and the other for pressing clay dust into tiles. Design was not ignored; he studied examples from the past, particularly the medieval period, and in 1842 published a catalogue of *Old English Tile Designs*. Minton's efforts and products were applauded by A.W.N. Pugin

Octagonal Chelsea vase, by Mintons
(c.1840–5). Height 45 cm.

Earthenware wine cooler with decorations
on a hunting theme, by Mintons (c.1851).
Height 65 cm.

who advocated the use of encaustic floor tiles in Gothic Revival churches.
Not all Minton tiles went into ecclesiastical buildings; in the 1840s they
were used in a decorative pavement for Queen Victoria at Osborne House,
Isle of Wight, and in the New Palace of Westminster. Other firms also
produced inlaid tiles in the early Victorian period, particularly Chamberlains
of Worcester and Copeland and Garrett of Stoke on Trent. The latter also
produced some of the earliest transfer printed tiles, the pattern books for
which still exist.

Silver and silver plate

Silver and silver plate continued to be fashioned by skilled crafts-workers but
by 1790 Sheffield plate sold at one-third of the price of silver plate. Produced
by fusing a copper ingot between two silver plates and rolling out the whole
into a thin composite sheet, Sheffield plate had been used for domestic ware
since 1758 when Joseph Hancock had devised a lapped edge to cover the
layer of copper which showed through the silver sandwiching it. Mainly
manufactured in Sheffield (although the well-known Soho Plate Company

founded by Matthew Boulton and continued by his son was located in
Birmingham), production continued until the middle of the nineteenth
century by which date most firms partly, if not completely, used the new
method of electroplating. This latter process, which involved the deposit of
metal by means of the continuous action of a battery, was the direct result of
a series of scientific developments dating from Volta's invention of the electric
battery in 1799–1800. It was not until 1840, however, that George and Henry
Elkington successfully developed electroplating on a commercial basis, but
such was its speed and cheapness that it soon became the most popular
method of plating. It needs to be distinguished from electrotyping, by which
pieces of historic interest were copied or facsimiles made of natural objects
such as leaves or flowers, the novelty of which had great popular appeal.

Some firms used the same designs for both plate and solid silver. Sheffield
plate manufacturers produced a few of their most successful designs in silver
and many electroplated pieces were also reproduced in the solid metal.
Elkingtons employed French designers, much of whose work featured the
highly modelled figures and naturalistic sculpture relief so popular in the
mid-nineteenth century. Other manufacturers used French designs which
were bought abroad or copied from those illustrated in the periodical *Art
Union* or circulated to manufacturers by the Government School of Design.
The employment of specialist designers was by no means specific to the

*Sheffield plate candlestick with
silver mounts, by James Dixon
and Sons (c.1835–7).*

The Trafalgar Vase (1805–6), designed by John Flaxman, made by Digby Scott and Benjamin Smith. One of a series for presentation to admirals and captains at the Battle of Trafalgar. Height 43 cm.

The Macready Testimonial, a silver centrepiece presented to the actor William Charles Macready (represented by the seated figure). Designed by Charles Grant for Benjamin Smith (1841–2).

electroplate trade. Throughout the period leading goldsmithing and silversmithing firms employed their own permanent designers as well as putting out special commissions for items such as commemorative ware to outside artists or designers. These were mainly painters and sculptors, and include John Flaxman, Francis Chantrey, Daniel Maclise, George Hayter and Edward Cotterill. Flaxman is perhaps better remembered for his designs for Wedgwood ceramics but he also designed in the neo-classical manner for Rundell and Bridges, the largest London silver firm of the early nineteenth century which employed over 1000 workers.

Furniture and interior design

In 1784 London was the largest single furniture-making centre in Britain. It remained so in 1851 but in the intervening years, and particularly after 1800, the provincial trade developed enormously. The large firms in each of the major cities competed in size and scope with those of the metropolis and many local families who would have previously brought their furniture from London turned to local firms such as Pratts (Bradford), Kendall or Constantine (Leeds) and Gillows (Lancaster – with an Oxford Street branch from the turn of the century).

The largest firms in London and the provinces, which ranged in size from about 50–300 workers, brought together all the main furniture-making crafts. They employed cabinet-makers, upholsterers, chair-makers and carvers under one roof in order to rationalise production, and foremen and managers to supervise production. They also bought in a range of other items such as carpets, oil cloths, curtains and bedding so as to offer their customers a complete range of furnishings. This process evolved gradually from the mid-eighteenth century but by 1800 several firms could boast that a client could furnish a house from top to bottom in a few hours. Some firms also offered advice on interior decoration: indeed, the term 'interior decorator' came to be used early in the nineteenth century to distinguish those furniture-makers who set themselves up as connoisseurs in all matters pertaining to the decoration and furnishing of houses. Until the new term came into being the word 'upholsterer' was used to describe the person who undertook this new activity, whilst still being used to describe a particular type of craftworker.

The rapid growth of a market composed of clients who were neither self-confident in matters of taste nor wealthy enough to seek the advice of an architect concerning the decoration of their home increased the numbers who relied on the furniture-maker. The 'upholsterer' decorator was the product of the commercial, financial and industrial revolutions which had created a large and wealthy bourgeoisie in Britain. As such, it was a unique feature and the envy of its European counterparts; this all-embracing service was unknown elsewhere in the world, including Paris. A not unsympathetic account of the nouveaux riches, unconfident of their taste yet anxious to have their houses in keeping with their recently elevated status, was given by a foreign journalist who in 1800 discussed their dependence on the 'upholsterer' to save them from embarrassing mistakes when furnishing their homes. This mentor in matters of taste could tell at a single glance from the house and the clients which furnishings would be appropriate:

As if worked by strings, he tells one immediately what colours go together, how much each article costs, what one must choose in order to guard against the shape and style becoming old-fashioned after some years, what changes must be made in a house, what sort of carpets to go in the dining room and what sort in the dressing room, what materials last longest; how much time he needs to furnish the whole house and so on and so on.

(*London and Paris*, vol. IV, 1800)

Such an absolute arbiter of taste appeared in literature as Mr Soho, the 'first architectural upholsterer of the age' (wittily described by Maria Edgeworth in *The Absentee*, 1812), who decreed that 'the whole face of things must be changed'.

Not all changes were carried out tastefully or conscientiously, however, and John Ruskin bitterly regretted giving the furniture-making firm of Snell of Albemarle Street £2000 and carte blanche to decorate and furnish a house in the 1850s. Effie Ruskin declared that Snell had done it as cheaply and vulgarly as possible and pocketed half of the money. Despite this experience, the Ruskins continued to use the services of the 'upholsterer'/interior decorator as did many others. So great was the demand for the services

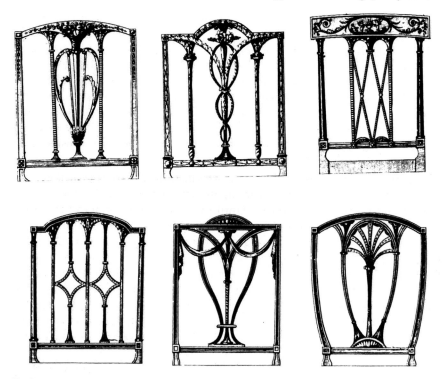

Designs for painted chairs (top) *and parlour chairs* (bottom), *from* The Cabinet-Maker and Upholsterer's Drawing Book *by Thomas Sheraton (1791–3).*

offered that by the mid-nineteenth century leading firms such as Jackson and Graham established separate departments to deal with interior decoration.

The three most popularly known names in English furniture design are Chippendale, Hepplewhite and Sheraton, all of whom enjoy an international reputation as authors of pattern books. Thomas Chippendale, known as the 'Shakespeare of English furniture makers', was craft trained, ran his own firm of about fifty employees and also worked as a designer. He died in 1779 and therefore lies outside the scope of this volume, but the other two members of the triumvirate demand our attention, not least because George Hepplewhite is one of the most elusive figures in furniture history. His reputation is in inverse proportion to the few facts known about him. His fame rests on the attribution to him of the unsigned designs which constitute *The Cabinet Maker and Upholsterer's Guide* (1788), published two years after his death by 'A. Hepplewhite & Co., Cabinet-maker'. This was almost certainly his widow, Alice Hepplewhite, who presumably carried on the business after her husband's death as was customary in the trade. The grounds for attribution are therefore not entirely convincing. Even accepting that he did design the pieces in the *Guide*, there is no evidence that he was ever a leading figure in the trade or worked on any important commissions.

The designs were by no means avant-garde in the sense of introducing a new style; indeed Sheraton commented on their somewhat out-of-date quality. Furthermore, the very low fee recorded when he took on an apprentice suggests that he was by no means in the forefront of the trade.

Whilst the very fact of Hepplewhite being a designer, let alone a leading one, needs to be challenged, the reputation of Thomas Sheraton (1751–1806) appears to be well deserved. He worked for many years as a journeyman cabinet-maker, but from about 1793 supported himself 'by his exertions as an author', concentrating mainly, but not exclusively, on furniture and design. He moved to London from Stockton upon Tees about 1790 and, according to his trade card, taught 'Perspective, Architecture and Ornaments', designed for furniture-makers and sold all sorts of books and drawings. Today he is best remembered as the author of three pattern books: *The Cabinet-Maker and Upholsterer's Drawing Book* (1791–3), *The Cabinet Dictionary* (1803), and *The Cabinet-Maker, Upholsterer, and General Artist's Encyclopaedia* (1803–6).

Little is known of other furniture designers in the early nineteenth century although John Richard Taylor, who published two small volumes of furniture and drapery designs, is known to have worked for the firm of Oakley in the 1830s and must be one of the first outside designers to be employed in the trade. Morel and Seddon of Great Marlborough Street, London, employed designers but that was specially for the Windsor Castle commission in 1827. The firm not only employed four designers but also design assistants. It proved expensive to hire such people but the Parliamentary committee, which examined the bills for Windsor and reported to the House of Commons in 1831, struck out charges for drawing and designing on the grounds that 'a manufacturer should be his own designer'. This assertion echoed the customary practice that furniture-makers did not normally charge for design. It was assumed that the design for a piece of furniture would originate in the establishment in which it was manufactured and the lack of clear distinctions between craft and design in furniture-making meant that the cost of design was included in the overall cost of an item. When an architect designed furniture, however, he was always paid a separate fee because he was recognised as a professional designer and there was no question of his making it.

The decision of the Parliamentary committee led to a reluctance on the part of furniture-makers to employ designers, because they could not rely on being able to charge for their work. It was the crusade led by Henry Cole (1808–82) and others to improve standards of design by promoting art manufactures (see below) which was mainly responsible for encouraging certain leading manufacturers to reconsider the employment of professional designers. The problem then became one of finding suitable designers.

Henry Whitaker, architect and furniture-designer, commented in 1845 on a changing attitude towards design and reported 'brighter days' ahead since the public was beginning to realise that 'many years of hard study in the art of design, and exclusive attention to it, can alone make a designer'. The attempts to emulate foreign design by erecting a system of design education similar to that of France and Prussia had less immediate effect on the furniture trade than the direct employment of foreign designers. Jackson and Graham employed the French designer, Eugène Prignot, in the late 1840s, and in 1850 Alfred Lormier, or Lorimer as he was sometimes referred to, was also appointed. These two 'artists of no common order' headed the firm's design team in the 1850s. The policy was successful commercially; the large amount of business conducted by the firm was attributed to the high standard of its designs. The example set by Jackson and Graham and the desire to make a good impression at the 1851 Exhibition encouraged more firms to employ designers, if only for important exhibition pieces.

Design reform and the Great Exhibition

Some of the radical Members of Parliament elected after the 1832 *Reform Act* articulated the fears of manufacturers that all was not well with British design. Certain products such as textiles suffered from foreign, particularly French, competition, in the field of well-designed goods. The belief was that if design could be reformed then sales and profits would improve. A Parliamentary Select Committee on Arts and Manufactures in 1835 heard a great deal of evidence from manufacturers, designers and artisans. France (with 80 Schools of Design) and Germany (33 in Bavaria alone) were held up as examples of enlightened policies towards commercial design. As a consequence the Committee's *Report* of 1836 recommended the establishment of Government Schools of Design, as well as improved protection for design patents and more exhibitions and art galleries which, it was hoped, would elevate the level of public taste.

Unfortunately, the main emphasis within the design schools was on an arbitrary conjunction of 'art' and 'industry' whereby fine artists with no experience of manufacturing processes or materials were drafted into the commercial sector to design a variety of products. This, of course, refers back to the opening remarks of this chapter concerning the élitist and hierarchical view of art and design prevailing at the time. There was no emphasis on re-training designers already working within the various trades or an insistence that designing a product should involve an understanding of the nature of the materials used and the possibilities and limitations defined by the production process. Not surprisingly, a later *Report* of 1846 acknowledged the complete failure of the schools to meet the needs of manufacturers.

The two leading figures pressing for design reform in the 1840s were Prince Albert and Cole, a civil servant at the Public Record Office who not only reformed the system of preserving public records, but also introduced the Penny Post system and was responsible for the publication of the first English Christmas card. Together these two men breathed new life into the Society of Arts, founded in 1754 to encourage 'Arts, Manufacture and Commerce', but which had long since ignored design or matters related to commerce. Under Prince Albert's Presidency (1843), however, the Society changed direction and began to organise small exhibitions of British manufactured goods, offering prizes for tea services and beer mugs designed for everyday use in 1845.

Cole took up the challenge and collaborated with Mintons over a tea service, recalling later in his autobiography how he worked at the British Museum studying Greek pottery and spent three days at the Minton factory

Tea service by Henry Cole (1847).

'superintending the throwing, turning, modelling and moulding of a tea service'. The Society of Arts stipulated that the manufacturer's name be given with every entry but Minton was reluctant to attach his lest Cole's design was a failure and his firm's reputation suffered. Cole therefore entered the tea set under the pseudonym of Felix Summerley.

Both it and a beer jug, also made by Mintons, won medals. The tea set in particular proved a great success and remained in production at the time of Cole's death. In about 1874 he wrote:

> . . . the manufacture of the Summerley Tea Cup and Saucer and Milk Jug has kept several workmen at Mintons China Works . . . incessantly at work since 1846, and it may be estimated that many hundreds and thousands of the articles have been made and sold for the benefit of industry.
>
> (*Cole, Fifty Years of Public Work*, 1884, Vol. I)

Cole's success convinced him that he could forge an alliance between 'art' and 'industry' to 'promote public taste', add beauty to 'mechanical production' and manufacture well-designed saleable objects. He therefore, in 1847, established 'Summerley's Art Manufactures', a scheme whereby a host of well-known artists and manufacturers were drafted into designing for industry. Richard Redgrave, H.J. Townsend, Sir Richard Westmacott and John Bell were some of the artists, while manufacturing firms included Coalbrookdale Iron Company, Holland & Co. (furniture), Wedgwood and Minton (pottery), Jennens and Bettridge (papier-mâché) and Rodgers, Joseph and Sons (cutlery).

It is no coincidence, however, that Cole, with no 'artistic' training, did as well as the painters and sculptors he drafted into his scheme when it came to designing everyday objects for batch or mass production (whether made by hand or machine). This was because these fine artists had little interest in manufacturing processes and did not have the time or inclination to visit the factories and liaise with the manufacturers. Some of the objects were criticised because a design in one material was too readily translated into another with very different qualities. Redgrave's design 'Well Spring' for a clear-glass decanter made by J.F. Christy of Lambeth, for instance, was adapted by Minton as a porcelain vase and Cole's own milk jug was reproduced in silver. There was often an over-literal emphasis on 'appropriate' decoration, such as hops for beer jugs, and also there was a lack of understanding of craft skills and production processes. A silver tea service which adopted different forms for each item meant that six times the normal number of dies were needed, while Holland & Co. found it impossible to manufacture a sideboard designed by the sculptor, John Bell.

If nothing else, the work of the Society of Arts and Summerley's Art Manufactures publicised the need to improve design standards and encouraged manufacturers to confront the issue. Soon, however, the activities of Cole and Prince Albert were taken up with a far bigger scheme – the Great Exhibition. The years of detailed planning resulted in what Cole and his followers regarded as a stocktaking of the state of design in the manufacturing sector. For Prince Albert, and for many others, the exhibition had a far wider import: it represented an optimistic view of the benefits of Industrial Capitalism and the inevitability of progress.

The Great Exhibition

Without the enormous amount of energy and enthusiasm shown by both Prince Albert (who persuaded a not over enthusiastic Government to support it) and Cole (who is on record as proposing a national exhibition as early as January 1848), *The Great Exhibition of the Works of Industry of All Nations* would not have been the success it was. After the Paris Industrial Exhibition of 1849, both men considered it imperative that Britain stage a major exhibition. In Cole's words, 'a great people invited all civilised nations to a festival, to bring into comparison the works of human skill'. Privately funded, it cost the tax payers nothing and most critics were silenced by the £186,000 profit it made. It proved immensely popular and was seen by over 6 million people; the average attendance was over 42,000 per day but on 7 October over 100,000 people viewed the exhibition. Season tickets were available (three guineas for men and two guineas for women) and, after the first three weeks, entrance prices dropped to one shilling per day on Monday to Thursday, two shillings and sixpence on Fridays and five shillings on Saturdays. The varied entrance fees meant that different social classes did not need to mix if they did not want to, while the one shilling minimum charge meant that, in the main, the poorer classes were represented by skilled artisans. The Exhibition was not open on Sundays and smoking, alcohol and dogs were banned.

The Exhibition proved wrong the fears of Colonel Sibthorp and others about the introduction into Britain of 'foreign stuff of every description'. At the same time, it was the Colonel who put up the greatest protectionist fight

The Great Exhibition (1851). Hardware exhibits, with Jennens and Bettridge papier-mâché displays on the right.

to save the magnificent elm trees of Hyde Park which were threatened by the whole scheme. Although several were chopped down, Joseph Paxton (1801–65), the architect of the 'Crystal Palace', was instructed by the Building Committee to roof in some of them. He encased the three largest ones within a magnificent arched transept which made the building seem more like a cathedral of light than a mere exhibition space. The interior was as magical as the exterior; a veritable Aladdin's cave of delights. The objects exhibited in 1851 were not typical of the everyday products of the firms showing them: they were either examples of what manufacturers deemed their best design and craftsmanship or pieces illustrating novelty or virtuosity.

Although the exhibition claimed to display the work of 'All Nations', over half of the exhibitors (7381) came from Britain and the Empire, the remainder (6000) from the rest of the world. The total number of exhibits was over 100,000 with the goods valued at over £2 million (excluding the Koh-i-noor diamond). Two types of medals, rather than money, were awarded as prizes to what were considered the best products. 'Council Medals' were given for novelty of invention in materials or techniques, or originality combined with 'great beauty of design', while 'Prize Medals' were given for excellence in workmanship and production. Much novelty and ingenuity was displayed at the Exhibition as, for instance, in the steam ship furniture which converted into a life raft, corsets that 'opened instantaneously in case of emergency', a 'patent ventilating hat', an alarm bedstead, and a cricket catapult 'for propelling the ball in the absence of a first-rate bowler'.

Many materials were imitations of others, such as slabs of glass produced to imitate marble and specimens of wood painted in imitation of various marbles. Others were used for unusual purposes such as metal, papier-mâché and gutta percha (a latex substance) for furniture. At the same time, furniture made in wood was exhibited with carvings executed by a series of patent devices, from burning with a hot template to carving machines which routed out the basic forms which were then hand finished. Certain critics felt, however, that it was novelty for novelty's sake; an affirmation of technical ingenuity and craft skills for their own sake. Owen Jones (designer and friend of Cole) claimed it was 'Novelty without beauty, beauty without intelligence, all work without faith'. Arising out of the Great Exhibition came the foundation of the first public museum of the applied arts in this country. Some of the profits from the Exhibition went towards buying 87 acres of land at South Kensington to house a complex of museums and educational institutions, including what today are called the Science Museum and the Royal College of Art. Cole, now Sir Henry (he was honoured for his work), purchased £5000 worth of items from the exhibition itself, including Elkington electrotypes and ceramics from Mintons and Sèvres, which he exhibited in his own Museum of Manufacturers at Marlborough House. The collection included both contemporary and historical examples of what Cole and other design reformers, such as Pugin and Jones, considered aesthetically pleasing, well-designed objects and was meant to improve the taste of designers and manufacturers as well as the general public. The latter attended the museum, soon to be renamed The Museum of Ornamental Art, in considerable numbers, particularly its exhibitions of 'good' and 'bad' design (Cole set up a 'Chamber of Horrors' of what he considered badly designed objects). It later moved to South Kensington where it eventually became known as the Victoria and Albert Museum, which today remains the most important national repository of the 'decorative' or 'applied' arts.

Model of T.B. Jordan's woodcarving machine (1845).

Group of electrotypes shown at the Great Exhibition (1851) made by Elkington.

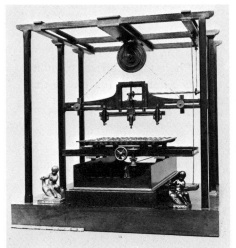

Part III
Appendix: Further Reading and Artists' Biographies

CHRISTOPHER GILLIE

Contents

Introduction

This *Appendix* is a selective guide to further reading. The main sections correspond to the chapters in the book and, after The Cultural and Social Setting section, are arranged alphabetically. Place of publication, unless otherwise stated, is London.

Individual authors, artists, architects and musicians are also introduced with thumbnail biographies.

A more comprehensive further reading list and artists' biographies can be found in the hardback edition of this volume, published as *The Cambridge Guide to the Arts in Britain: Romantics to Early Victorians*.

1   The Cultural and Social Setting

Histories: political, social and economic

Ashworth, W., *English Economic History, 1800–1870* (1960)

Aspinall, A. and Smith, A.E. (eds), *English Historical Documents (1785–1832)* (1959)

Briggs, A., *The Age of Improvement* (1961)
  (ed.), *Chartist Studies* (1959)

Brown, L.M. and Christie, I.R., *Bibliography of British History 1789–1851* (1977)

Bryant, Sir A., *The Years of Endurance* (1942)
  The Years of Victory (1944)
  The Age of Elegance (1950)

Butler, Marilyn (ed.), *Burke, Paine, Godwin and the Revolution Controversy* (1984)

Chapman, S.D. and Chambers, J.D., *The Beginnings of Industrial Britain* (1970)

Court, W.H.B., *A Concise Economic History of Britain from 1750* (Cambridge, 1954)

Deane, P., *The First Industrial Revolution* (Cambridge, 1965)

Flinn, M.W., *The Origins of the Industrial Revolution* (1966)

Gash, N., *Politics in the Age of Peel* (1977)

Gayer, A.D., *et al.*, *The Growth and Fluctuation of the British Economy 1790–1950* (1950)

Halévy, E., *A History of the English People 1815–1915* (1951)

Leslie, Shane, *George IV* (1926)

Low, D.A., *Thieves' Kitchen: the Regency Underworld* (1968)

Thompson, E.P., *The Making of the English Working Class* (1963; Penguin Books, 1968)

Trevelyan, G.M., *Illustrated English Social History Vol. IV* (1942; Penguin Books, 1964)

White, R.J., *From Waterloo to Peterloo* (1968)

Social and cultural background

Bagwell, P.S., *The Transport Revolution in Britain from 1770* (New York, 1974)

Bovill, E.W., *English Country Life 1780–1830* (1962)

Briggs, A., *Victorian People* (1954) *Victorian Cities* (1963)

Bradley, E. and Simon, B. (eds), *The Victorian Public School* (Dublin, 1975)

Chapman, R., *The Victorian Debate: English Literature and Society, 1832–1901* (1968)

Denvir, B., *The Early Nineteenth Century: Art, Design and Society, 1789–1852* (1984)

Dyos, H.J. and Wolff, M.Y. (eds), *The Victorian City: Images and Realities* (1972)

Emsley, C., *British Society and the French Wars 1798–1815* (1979)

Fay, C.R., *Palace of Industry, 1851* (Cambridge, 1951)

Horn, P., *Labouring Life in the Victorian Countryside* (Dublin, 1977)

Jones, E.L., *Agriculture and the Industrial Revolution* (1972)

Kitson Clark, J., *The Making of Victorian England* (1962)

Laqueur, T.W., *Religion and Respectability: Sunday Schools and Working Class Culture 1780–1850* (1976)

Laver, J., *The Age of Illusion: Manners and Morals (1750–1848)* (1972)

Low, D.A., *That Sunny Dome. A Portrait of Regency Britain* (1972)

Mayhew, H., *London Labour and the London Poor* (1862; repr. 4 vols. 1968; Selections ed. S. Rubinstein 1947) *The Unknown Mayhew* eds E.P. Thompson and Eileen Yeo (1971; Penguin Books, 1973)

Mingay, G.E. (ed.), *The Victorian Countryside* (1981)

Petrie, Sir Charles, *The Victorians* (1960)

Phelps-Brown, E.H., *The Growth of British Industrial Relations* (1959)

Pike, E.R., *Human Documents of the Victorian Golden Age* (1967)

Silver, H., *English Education and the Radicals 1780–1850* (1976)

Smith, K., *The Malthusian Controversy* (1951)

Ward, W.R., *Religion and Society in England 1790–1850* (1972)

Willey, B., *The Eighteenth Century Background* (1940; Penguin Books, 1962)

Williams, Raymond, *Culture and Society 1780–1950* (1958; Penguin Books, 1961) *The Long Revolution* (1961; Penguin Books, 1965) *The Country and the City* (1973)

Young, G.M., *Victorian England* (Oxford, 1936)

2   The Applied Arts

Bell, Q., *The Schools of Design* (1963)

Bemrose, G., *Nineteenth-Century English Pottery and Porcelain* (1952)

Cole, Sir H., *Fifty Years of Public Work* (2 vols, 1884)

Cornforth, J., *English Interiors 1790–1848: The Quest for Comfort* (1978)

Denvir, B., *The Early Nineteenth Century: Art, Design and Society, 1789–1852* (1984)

Edwards, H.C.R. and Jourdain, M. (eds), *Georgian Cabinet Makers 1700–1800* (1965)

Edwards, H.C.R. and Ramsey, L.G.C. (eds), *The Connoisseur's Complete Period Guides* (1968)

Forty, A., *Objects of Desire* (1986)

Joy, E.T., *English Furniture 1800–1851* (1977)

Lucie-Smith, E., *Furniture: A Concise History* (1979) *The Story of Craft: The Craftsmans Role in Society* (1981)

Musgrave, C., *Regency Furniture 1800–30* (1977)

Naylor, G., *The Arts and Crafts Movements; a Study of its Source, Ideals and Influence on Design Theory* (1971)

Pevsner, N., *High Victorian Design: a Study of the Exhibition of 1851* (1951)

Stanton, P.A., *Pugin* (1971)

Wakefield, H., *Nineteenth Century British Glass* (1961)

3   Architecture

General studies

Addison, W., *English Spas* (1951)

Clark, K., *The Gothic Revival* (2nd edn 1950)

Cornforth, J., *English Interiors 1790–1848: The Quest for Comfort* (1978)

Dale, A., *History and Architecture of Brighton* (Brighton, 1950)

Davis, T., *The Architecture of John Nash* (1960)

Hitchcock, H.R., *Early Victorian Architecture* (2 vols, 1954)

Hussey, C., *English Country Houses: Late Georgian 1800–1840* (1958)

Jourdain, M., *English Interior Decoration, 1500–1830* (1950)
   English Furniture: The Georgian Period, 1750–1830 (1953)

Reilly, P., *An Introduction to Regency Architecture* (1948)

Summerson, Sir J., 'Architecture in Britain 1530–1830' (Pelican History of Art, 1977)
   Georgian London (1945; Penguin Books, 1962)

Watkin, D., *The Buildings of Britain: Regency, A Guide and Gazetteer* (1982)

The Great Exhibition

Briggs, A., *Victorian People* (1954)

Fay, C.R., *Palace of Industry, 1851* (1951)

ffrench, Y., *The Great Exhibition* (1951)

Gibbs-Smith, C.H., *The Great Exhibition* (1950)

Luckhurst, K.W., *The Great Exhibition of 1851* (1951)

Architects

Barry, Sir Charles (1795–1860)
Architect; son of a stationer. Won first prize for new Houses of Parliament (built 1840–60) in 1835. He preferred the Italianate neo-classical style (e.g. Travellers' and Reform Clubs, Pall Mall) but the competition required Gothic or Elizabethan. In 1841: Royal Academician; 1852: Knighthood.

Barry, A., *Life and Works of Sir Charles Barry* (1867; 2nd edn, 1870)

Whiffen, M., *The Architecture of Sir Charles Barry in Manchester and Neighbourhood* (Manchester, 1950)

Brunel, Isambard Kingdom (1806–59)
Engineer; son of the engineer Sir Marc Isambard Brunel, of French origin. 1825–28: resident engineer of Thames Tunnel project designed by his father, completed 1846. 1831: designed suspension bridge over Avon, completed 1864. 1833: engineer for Great Western Railway – Box Tunnel. 1844: designed Royal Albert Bridge over Tamar (completed 1859). He also designed steamships, e.g., Great Western (first voyage 1838) – the first ship to make regular crossings of the Atlantic. He helped to promote the Great Exhibition in 1851.

Hay, P., *Brunel: His Achievement in the Transport Revolution* (1973)

Knell, K.A., *Brunel – 'Engineer extraordinary'* (Cambridge, 1973)

Pudney, J., *Brunel and his Work* (1974)

Pugsley, A., *The Works of Isambard Kingdom Brunel* (1976)

Rott, L.T.C., *Isambard Kingdom Brunel* (1970)

Nash, John (1752–1835)
Leading architect in neo-classical Regency style, famous for the harmony of his street architecture and use of Stucco, e.g., the terraces around Regent's Park, and Regent Street, since replaced. 1797–1802: partnership with Humphry Repton, landscape-garden designer, working on alterations to country houses. His country house architecture attracted the patronage of the Prince Regent (future George IV) for whom he redesigned the Brighton Pavilion. His work on Buckingham Palace was suspended on the death of George IV in 1830.

Davis, T., *The Architecture of John Nash* (1960)
   John Nash, the Prince Regent's Architect (1966; 2nd edn, Newton Abbot, 1973)

Summerson, J.M., *John Nash, Architect to King George IV* (1935; 2nd edn, 1949)

Paxton, Joseph (1801–65)
Architect and gardener; son of small farmer in Bedfordshire. Became professional gardener. 1826: superintendent of Duke of Devonshire's Chatsworth estate; expert in designing garden buildings, especially the great conservatory (1836) later used as basis for his Crystal Palace, designed at short notice in 1850. 1851: knighted. 1854: MP for Coventry.

Pugin, Augustus Welby Northmore
(1812–52)
Architect: son of an architect who had made
extensive study of English medieval
architecture. Pugin strongly advocated
Gothic as honest architecture in preference
to emulation of neo-classical Italiante styles.
Became Catholic in 1835; influenced
architecture of the Anglican High Church
(Tractarian) movement of the 1840s. His
ideas were on the whole more important
than his actual buildings. Among his
written works: *Contrasts; or a Parallel
between Architecture of the 15th and 19th
centuries* (1836); *True Principles of Christian
Architecture* (1841).

Gwynn, D.R., *Lord Shrewsbury, Pugin and
the Catholic Revival* (Intro. S.J.
Gosling) (1946)
Trappes-Lomax, M., *Pugin, a Medieval
Victorian* (1932)
Stanton, P., *Pugin* (Intro. N. Pevsner)
(1971)

Ruskin, John (1819–1900)
Critic of art and architecture. Born London,
son of vintner who, with his wife, educated
him into strong architectural interests. 1843:
Vol. I of *Modern Painters* included an
eloquent defence of Turner. 1849: *The
Seven lamps of Architecture*; 1851–3: *The
Stones of Venice*, both works maintaining
that architecture is the expression of a
nation's spiritual values. Completed *Modern
Painters* in 1860. Thereafter devoted
himself mainly to studies of the health of
society – e.g., *Unto this Last* (1862); *Sesame
and Lilies* (1868).

Bell, Q., *Ruskin* (1963; repr. 1978)
Conner, P., *Savage Ruskin* (1979)
Garrigan, K.O., *Ruskin on Architecture*
(Madison, Wis., 1973)
Pevsner, N., in *Some Architectural Writers
of the Nineteenth Century* (1972)
Rosenberg, J.D. (ed.), *The Genius of John
Ruskin* (1964)
Whitehouse, J.H., *Vindication of Ruskin*
(1950)

Soane, Sir John (1753–1837)
Architect. Of humble origin; changed his
name from 'Swan'. Acquired Royal
Academy medals (1772 and 1776). 1777–80:
studied in Italy. Combined Greek with
Italianate classical styles. Designed Bank of
England, Westminster Law Courts,
Dulwich Art Gallery. Most of his important
buildings now destroyed or altered, e.g.,
Bank. His house at 13 Lincoln's Inn, and
Pitzhanger Manor, Ealing, remain as fine
examples.

Summerson, J.N., *Sir John Soane R.A.*
(1952)

Telford, Thomas (1757–1834)
Engineer; son of Dumfriesshire shepherd.
1780: employed in Edinburgh building
houses in the 'New Town'. 1793: began to
acquire reputation for canal construction.
Constructed roads in Scottish Highlands
and Wales and famous for his bridges, e.g.,
over Tay at Dunkeld, Menai Bridge (begun
1820), Conway Bridge (1822). Also built
Dean Bridge in Edinburgh and Broomielaw
Bridge in Glasgow.

Bracegirdle, B. and Miles, P.H., *Thomas
Telford (Great Engineers and their
Works)* (Newton Abbot, 1973)
Gibb, Sir A., *The Story of Telford; the Rise
of Civil Engineering* (1935)
Knell, K.A., *Thomas Telford, Civil Engineer
in the Stage Coach Era* (Cambridge,
1974)
Rolt, L.T.C., *Thomas Telford* (1958)

Wilkins, William (1778–1839)
Architect in 'Grecian style', reacting against
more ornate roman classicism of Adam.
1806: Downing College, Cambridge; 1807:
Haileybury School. 1823: New Court of
Corpus Christi College, Cambridge –
Gothic in a classically regular framework.
1828–9: St George's Hospital, Hyde Park
Corner, London; 1832: National Gallery.

Crook, J.M., *Haileybury and the Greek
Revival* (Hertford, N. Carolina, 1964)
Reilly, P., *An Introduction to Regency
Architecture* (1948)
Richardson, A.E., *Monumental Classic
Architecture in Great Britain and
Ireland* (1914)
Summerson, J., *Georgian London* (1948)

Wyatt, James (1746–1813)
Architect; son of Staffordshire builder.
Studied in Italy. He was a classicist in spirit
but also practised Gothic, e.g., Pantheon in
Oxford Street, London, in restrained
classicism and Fonthill Abbey, Wiltshire, a
Gothic mansion for William Beckford.
Attracted hostility of Pugin and others for
his restoration work in Westminster Abbey
and Durham, Salisbury and Lichfield
Cathedrals.

Dale, A., *James Wyatt* (1956)
Turnor, R., *James Wyatt 1746–1813* (1950)

4   The Athenaeum

Cowell, F.R., *The Athenaeum, Club and
Social Life in London 1824–1974* (1975)

Timbs, J., *Club Life of London*, 2 vols
(1866)
Ward, H., *History of the Athenaeum,
1824–1925* (1975)

5 The City of Edinburgh

Catford, E.F., *Edinburgh, the Story of a
City* (1975)
McKean, C. and Walker, D., *An Illustrated
Architectural Guide* (1982)
Minto, C.S. and Armstrong, N.E.S.,
*Edinburgh Past and Present; A Pictorial
Record of the Ancient City of Edinburgh*
(1975)
Scott-Moncrieff, G., *Edinburgh* (1947)
Youngson, A.J., *The Making of Classical
Edinburgh 1750–1840* (1966)

6 Enclosure and the English Hedgerow

Bovill, E.W., *English Country Life
1780–1830* (1962)
Fox, H.S.A. and Butlin, R.A., *Change in the
English Countryside: Essays on Rural
England* (1979)
Jones, E.L., *Agriculture and the Industrial
Revolution* (1972)
Mingay, G.E. (ed.), *The Victorian
Countryside* (1981)
Yelling, J.A., *Common Field and Enclosure
in England 1450–1850* (1977)

7 The Fine Arts

General studies

Boase, T.S.R., *Oxford History of English
Art 1800–1870* (1959)
Clark, Sir K.M., *The Gothic Revival. An
Essay in the History of Taste*
Cundall, H.M., *A History of British Water
Colour Painting* (1929)
Edwards, R. and Ramsey, L.G.G., *The
Connoisseur Period Guides, IV: The
Late Georgian Period 1760–1810
V: The Regency Period 1810–1830*
(1956–58)
Einstein, L., *Divided Loyalties* (1933)
Pevsner, N., *The Englishness of English Art*
(1956)
Pilcher, D., *The Regency Style* (1947)
Redgrave, R. and S., *A Century of British
Painters* (1981)
Steegman, J., *The Rule of Taste from George
I to George IV* (1936)
Todd, Ruthven (ed.), *A Century of British
Painters* (1947)

Whitley, W.T., *Art in England 1800–1820*
(Cambridge, 1928)
Art in England 1821–1837 (Cambridge,
1930)
Young, G.M., *Early Victorian England*
(1934)

Sculpture

Gunnis, R., *Dictionary of British Sculptors
1660–1851*
Penny, N., *Church Monuments in Romantic
England* (1977)
Physick, J., *Designs for English Sculpture
(1680–1860)* (1969)
Read, B., *Victorian Sculpture* (1982)
Whinney, M., *Sculpture in Britain
1530–1830* (1964)
English Sculpture 1720–1830 (1971)

Special themes

Barbier, C.P., *William Gilpin: his Drawings,
Teaching and Theory of the Picturesque*
(1963)
Barrell, J., *The Political Theory of Painting
from Reynolds to Hazlitt: 'The Body of
the Public'* (Yale, 1986)
Bayard, J., *Works of Splendor and
Imagination. The Exhibition Watercolor
1770–1870* (Yale Center for British Art
1981)
Bermingham, A., *Landscape and Ideology*
(1986)
Brion, M., *Art of the Romantic Era* (trans.
D. Carroll, 1966)
Clark, K.M., *Landscape into Art* (1949;
Penguin Books, 1956)
Clarke, M., *The Tempting Prospect: a Social
History of English Watercolours* (1981)
Clifford, D., *Watercolours of the Norwich
School* (1965)
Fawcett, T., *The Rise of English Provincial
Art* (1974)
Graves, A., *The British Institution
1806–1867* (1908)
Hardie, M., *Watercolour Painting in Britain*,
3 vols. (1966–68)
Hawes, L., *Presence of Nature: British
Landscape 1780–1830* (1982)
Hemingway, A., *The Norwich School of
Painters 1830–33* (1979)
Hughes, C.E., *Early English Water Colour*
(1913; ed. J. Mayne, 1950)
Hussey, C., *The Picturesque* (1927)
Hutchison, S., *The History of the Royal
Academy 1768–1968* (1968)
Klingender, F.D., *Art and the Industrial
Revolution* (1947; revised Sir A. Elton,
1968)
Lister, R., *British Romantic Art* (1973)

Mayne, J. (ed.), *A History of English Water Colour* (1950)

Moore, A.W., *The Norwich School of Artists* (1985)

Ormond, R., *Early Victorian Portraits* (1973)

Parvis, L., *Landscape in Britain c.1750–1850* (1973)

Pointon, M., *Milton and English Art* (1970)

Quennell, P., *Romantic England: Writing and Painting 1717–1851* (1970)

Rajnai, M., *Painters of the Norwich School* (1978)

Roget, J.L., *History of the Old Water Colour Society* (1891)

Rosenthal, M., *British Landscape Painting* (1982)

Sitwell, S., *Conversation Pieces* (1936); *Narrative Paintings* (1937)

Stainton, L., *British Landscape Watercolours 1600–1860* (1985)

Tinker, C.B., *Painter and Poet: Studies in the Literary Relations of English Painting* (Cambridge, Mass., 1938)

Williams, I.A., *Early English Water-colours* (1952)

Wilton, A., *British Watercolours 1750–1850* (1979)

Artists

Bewick, Thomas (1753–1828)
Wood-engraver. Born near Newcastle upon Tyne, son of a coalmine renter. Apprenticed to an engraver in Newcastle. 1784: *Select Fables*, of unprecedented excellence for its wood engravings. Greatest achievement: *British Birds* (1797–1804).

Memoir of Thomas Bewick by Himself (1862)

Blake, William (1757–1827) (See also under **9 Literature:** *Authors*.)
Painter and engraver. Apprenticed at 14 to James Basire: engravings of medieval sculpture. Subsequently engraved illustrations for Flaxman's *Iliad*. 1787: began engraving his own poetry; developed his personal mythology with influence of Fuseli in succession to Flaxman. Invented new tempera and printing techniques for his 'Prophetic Books'. Most famous engravings for Dante, the Book of Job, *Milton* and *Jerusalem*. Life by A. Gilchrist (1880).

Bentley, G.E., *Blake Books* (1977)

Bindman, D., *Blake as an Artist* (1977)

Binyon, L., *Engraved Designs of William Blake* (1926)

Butlin, M., *The Paintings and Drawings of William Blake* (1981)

Clark, K., *Blake and Visionary Art* (Glasgow, 1973)

Figgis, D., *The Paintings of William Blake* (1925)

Grierson, H.J.C. (ed.), *Blake's Illustrations to Gray's Poems* (1922)

Keynes, G., *Illustrations to Young's Night Thoughts Done in Water Colour by William Blake* (1925)

Lister, R., *Infernal Methods: a Study of Blake's Art Techniques* (1975)

Pinto, V.de S. (ed.), *The Divine Vision: Studies in the Poetry and Art of William Blake* (1957)

Raine, K., *The Human Face of God: William Blake and the Book of Job* (1982)

Bonington, Richard Parkes (1801–28)
Painter of landscapes, street scenes and genre pictures mainly in water colour. Born in Nottingham, spent much of his short life in Paris; friend of Delacroix; considered a precursor of French Barbizon school. Some of his paintings at Wallace Collection, London. Died of tuberculosis.

Dubuisson, A. (trans. C.E. Hughes) *Richard Parkes Bonington: his Life and Work* (1924)

Pointon, M., *The Bonington Circle* (1985) *Bonington, Francia and Wyld* (1985)

Shirley, A., *Bonington* (1940)

Callcott, Augustus Wall (1779–1844)
Landscape painter. Born in London, son of a builder; student at Royal Academy under Hoppner. Achieved early success in portraiture, but after 1804 exhibited only landcapes; from 1830 mostly in foreign settings. Knighted in 1827.

Brown, D.B., *Augustus Wall Callcott, Catalogue* (1981)

Chantrey, Francis Legatt (1781–1841)
Sculptor. Born near Sheffield, son of carpenter and small farmer. Apprenticed to a Sheffield wood-carver. 1802: London; worked at portrait-painting, bust-sculpture, clay-modelling. 1808: exhibited at the Royal Academy ('Head of Satan'). Much encouraged by the sculptor Nollekens. Acquired a high reputation for the grace and dignity of his portraiture of public figures. Knighted in 1835. Founded the 'Chantrey Bequest' for the encouragement of fine art.

Holland, J., *Memorial of Sir Francis Chantrey, Sculptor* (1851)

Jones, G., *Sir Francis Chantrey, R.A. Recollections of his Life, Practice and Opinions* (1854)

Raymond, A.J., *Life and Work of Sir Francis Chantrey* (1904)

Constable, John (1776–1837)
Born in Suffolk, son of proprietor of wind
and water mills; educated at Dedham
Grammar School. 1799: student at Royal
Academy. His mature work, influenced by
Gainsborough, the Dutch School and
Thomas Girtin, developed after 1811. 1819:
ARA; made Royal Academician in 1829.
His sympathy with the natural environment
was very strong, but he abandoned the
concept of the 'ideal landscape', working
much more by direct study of the
environment. This for a time inhibited
public appreciation, but his exhibiiton in
Paris (1824) aroused strong interest there.
Major collection of paintings and studios at
Victoria & Albert Museum. Life by C.R.
Leslie (1843) revised and enlarged by A.
Shirley (1937), edited by J.Mayne (1951).

Althusen, *John Constable* (1976)
Beckett, R.B., *John Constable and the
    Fishers* (1952)
    (ed.), *John Constable's Correspondence* (6
    vols) (1962–68)
    John Constable's Discourses (1970)
Cormack, M., *Constable* (1986)
Fleming-Williams, I., and Paris, L., *The
    Discovery of Constable* (1984)
Gadney, R., *Constable and his World* (1976)
Hawes, L., *Constable's Stonehenge* (1975)
Key, S.J., *Constable* (1948)
Parris, L., *The Tate Gallery Constable
    Collection* (1981)
Parris, L. and Shields, C. *Constable: The
    Art of Nature* (Exhibition Catalogue)
    (1971)
Parris, L. Shields, C. and
    Fleming-Williams, I. (eds), *John
    Constable: Further Documents and
    Correspondence* (1976)
Paulson, R., *Literary Landscape: Turner and
    Constable* (1982)
Reynolds, G., *Constable: the Natural
    Painter* (1966)
    *Catalogue of the Constable Collection in the
    Victoria and Albert Museum* (2nd edn,
    1973)
    *The Later Paintings and Drawings of John
    Constable* (comprehensive bibliography,
    1984)
Rosenthal, M. (ed.), *Constable: Selected
    Correspondence* (forthcoming)
    Constable: the Painter and his Landscape
    (1983)
    Constable (1987)
Tate Gallery: *Constable: Paintings,
    Watercolours and Drawings Exhibition
    Catalogue* (1976)
Taylor, B. *Constable: Paintings, Drawings,
    Watercolours* (2nd edn, 1975)

Cotman, John Sell (1782–1842)
Painter, etcher, engraver: son of Norwich
draper. 1800: London, assisted by Dr
Monro, patron of Girtin and Turner.
Exhibited at Royal Academy. 1803–5: visits
to Yorkshire; architectural studies. 1806:
return to Norwich. 1811: succeeded Crome
as President of Norwich Society of Painters.
Settled as drawing teacher at Yarmouth.
1817–19: visited Normandy for architectural
studies. 1834: with Turner's influence,
became Professor of Drawing at King's
College, London. His reputation among
contemporaries was small, but he is now
distinguished for his abstract qualities of
composition and contrast in tone.

Mallalieu, H., *The Norwich School: Crome,
    Cotman and their Followers* (1974)
Moore, A.W., *John Sell Cotman 1782–1842*,
    catalogue (1968)
Rajnai, M., *John Sell Cotman 1782–1842*,
    catalogue (1978)
Rajnai, M. and Allthorpe-Guyion, M., *John
    Sell Cotman 1782–1842 Early Drawings
    in the Norwich Castle Museum* (1979)
    *John Sell Cotman: Drawings of Normandy
    in the Norwich Castle Museum* (1975)

Cox, David (1783–1859)
Landscape painter. Born Birmingham, son
of a smith practising traditional crafts. Early
training in scene painting, and he received
instruction from John Varley. Became art
teacher and author: *Treatise on Landscape
Painting and Effect in Water Colour*
(1814–15). His production was large; a
distinguished example, 'The Night Train',
is in the Birmingham City Art Gallery.

Cox, G.T., *David Cox* (1947)
Roe, F.G., *Cox, the Master: the Life and
    Art of David Cox 1783–1859* (1946)
Scrase, D., *Samuel Prout and David Cox*,
    catalogue 1983–4
Solly, N.N., *Memoir of the Life of David
    Cox* (1873)
Wildman, S. (ed.), *David Cox 1783–1842*,
    catalogue (1983)

Crome, John (1768–1821)
Landscape painter, first of the Norwich
School. Son of a Norwich weaver. Became
house-painter, sign-painter, eventually
drawing master. 1805: President of the
newly established Norwich Society of
Painters. 1806: exhibited at Royal Academy.
Most of his work is East Anglian landscape;
see 'The Poringland Oak' and 'Mousehold
Heath' in the National Gallery.

Baker, J., *Crome. With an Introduction by
    C.J. Holmes* (1921)

Binyon, L., *John Crome and John Sell
    Cotman* (1897)
Clifford, D. and T., *Crome* (1968)
Howcroft, F., *John Crome 1768–1821*,
    catalogue (1968)
Mallalieu, H., *The Norwich School: Crome,
    Cotman and their Followers* (1974)
Mottram, R.H., *John Crome of Norwich*
    (1931)
Theobald, H.S., *Crome's Etchings* (1906)

De Wint, Peter (1784–1849)
Landscape painter. Born at Stone,
Staffordshire, son of a physician of Dutch
extraction. Studied art in London and
exhibited frequently from 1812 at the
Society of Painters in Water Colour and
with the Royal Academy. Excelled in water
colour, but also painted in oil. Life by W.
Armstrong.

Fitzwilliam Musem, *Drawings and
    Watercolours by Peter de Wint* (1979)
Smith, H., *Peter De Wint 1784–1849* (1982)

Dyce, William (1806–64)
Painter. Born in Aberdeen, son of a
physician. Attended Marischal College; MA
at 16. Studied art at the Royal Scottish
Academy, and then in London and Rome.
Painted portraits, and especially religious
and legendary subjects, e.g., for the
robing-room and the House of Lords in
Parliament. RA in 1848.

Pointon, M., *William Dyce 1806–1864*
    (1979)

Etty, William (1787–1849)
Painter, especially of historical and
legendary scenes. Born in York, son of a
baker. 1807: private pupil of Sir Thomas
Lawrence. Became famous for his nudes,
and much influenced by Rubens and the
Venetian Renaissance. Made Royal
Academician in 1828. Examples: 'The
Combat' (Scottish National Gallery), 'The
Judgement of Paris' (Port Sunlight),
'Ulysses and the Sirens' (Manchester).

Farr, D.L., *William Etty* (1958)
Gaunt, W. and Roe, F.G., *Etty and the
    Nude: the Art and Life of William Etty
    R.A.* (1945)

Flaxman, John (1755–1826)
Sculptor and illustrator. Born in York, son
of moulder and dealer in sculptors. A
foremost exponent of neo-classicism, e.g., in
his designs for Wedgwood ceramic ware. In
his illustrations used contour drawing as in
antique vases. Works by Flaxman: *Lectures
on Sculpture* (1865); *Designs in Illustration to
the Iliad of Homer* (1793); *Designs in*

Illustration to the Odyssey of Homer (1793);
*Illustrations of the Divine Poem of Dante
Alighieri* (1802); Compositions from the
Tragedies of Aeschylus (1881).

Constable, W.G., *John Flaxman* (1927)
Irwin, D., *John Flaxman 1755–1826:
    Sculptor, Illustrator, Designer* (1979)

Fuseli, Henry (1741–1825)
Illustrator and writer on art. Originated in
Zurich, son of portrait painter and art
biographer, John Füssli; left Switzerland in
1765 and eventually settled in England.
Assisted Cowper in translation of Homer
and became a close associate of Blake.
Famous for the poetic energy of his
illustrations to Dante, Virgil, Shakespeare,
the *Niebelungenlied*.

Antal, F., *Fuseli Studies* (1956)
Keay, C., *Henry Fuseli* (1974)
Mason, E.C., *The Mind of Henry Fuseli;
    Selections from his Writings with
    Introductory Study* (1951)
Powell, N., *The Drawings of H. Fuseli*
    (1951)
Tomory, P., *The Life and Art of Henry
    Fuseli* (1973)
Weinglass, D.H. (ed.), *The Collected English
    Letters of Henry Fuseli* (New York,
    1982)

Girtin, Thomas (1775–1802)
Painter and etcher. Born Southwark, son of
cordage maker. Remarkable for his rich use
of water colour as a medium instead of
merely tinting; Turner's verdict: 'Had Tom
Girtin lived I should have starved'.

Binyon, L., *English Watercolours, from the
    Work of Turner, Girtin, Cotman,
    Constable and Bonington* (1939)
    Thomas Girtin; his Life and Works (1900)
Girtin, T. and Loshak, D., *The Art of
    Thomas Girtin* (1954)
Mayne, J., *Thomas Girtin* (Leigh-on-Sea,
    1949)

Haydon, Benjamin Robert (1786–1846)
Historical painter and writer. Born in
Plymouth, son of printer and publisher.
Made a big reputation with pictures such as
'Entry into Jerusalem', 'Lazarus', 'The
Judgement of Solomon', and engaged
extensively in controversy, e.g., about the
Elgin Marbles acquired in 1806. Despite
much public success, conflicts and money
difficulties led to his suicide.

Beardsworth, E., *The Life and Death of
    B.R. Haydon, Historical Painter* (1967)
Pope, W.B. (ed.), *Invisible Friends; the
    Correspondence of Elizabeth Barrett*

Browning and B.R. Haydon
(Cambridge, Mass., 1972)
B.R. Haydon: Diary (Cambridge, Mass., 1963)

Hoppner, John (1758–1810)
Portrait painter; born in London of German parents. 1789: appointed portrait painter to Prince of Wales. Became rival to Thomas Lawrence and fashionable as a court painter; especially gifted in portrayal of women and children.

McKay, W. and Roberts, W., *John Hoppner R.A.* (1909–14)

Landseer, Edwin (1802–73) Animal painter. Born in London, son of engraver and writer on art. Made an early reputation; singled out by Géricault (for 'Rat Catchers') on his visit to England in 1820. Designed the bronze lions round the Nelson Monument in 1867.

Lennie, C. *Landseer: the Victorian Paragon* (1976)
Marison, J.A., *Sir Edwin Landseer R.A.* (1902)
Ormond, R., *Sir Edwin Landseer* (1981)
Stephens, F.G., *Memoirs of Sir Edwin Landseer* (1880)

Lawrence, Sir Thomas (1769–1830)
Narrative and portrait painter. Born in Bristol, son of inn-keeper. Brought a new Romantic mode to portrait painting and acquired a reputation in Europe unprecedented for an English painter. Involved with theatre world, e.g., portrait of Kemble as Coriolanus.

Armstrong, W., *Sir Thomas Lawrence* (1913)
Garlick, K., *Sir Thomas Lawrence* (1954)
Goldrinc, D., *Regency Portrait Painter: the Life of Sir Thomas Lawrence* (1951)
Gower, Lord R.C., *Sir Thomas Lawrence* (1900)
Layard, G.S., *Sir Thomas Lawrence's Letter-Bag* (1906)
Williams, D.E., *Life and Correspondence of Sir Thomas Lawrence* (1851)

Linnell, John (1792–1882)
Painter and engraver. Born London, son of a carver and gilder. 1805: student at the Royal Academy school of art, showing precocious gifts. Later engraved outlines of Michelangelo's frescos, and plates based on pictures in the royal collection. Chiefly known for paintings of landscapes with small figures; 'St John Preaching'; 'Journey to Emmaeus'. A close friend and patron of William Blake.

Story, A.T., *Life of John Linnell* (2 vols) (1892)
Craian, K., *John Linnell*, Catalogue (1982)

Martin, John (1789–1854)
Painter. Born Haydon Bridge, near Hexham, Northumberland; 1806: moved to London where he supported himself partly by painting on glass. This influenced his use of colour in the large apocalyptic narrative paintings which made him famous, e.g., 'Joshua' (1815) and 'Belshazzar's Feast' (1821). He was also an engraver, e.g., illustrations to Milton and the Bible.

Balston, T., *John Martin (1789–1854); his Life and Works* (1947)
Feaver, W., *The Art of John Martin* (1975)
Penchard, M., *John Martin, Painter; his Life and Works* (1923)

Morland, George (1763–1804)
Painter of animals and rustic scenes. Born in London, the son and grandson of artists. Precociously talented, he exhibited at the Royal Academy at the age of ten. 1786: married Anne, the sister of James Ward. Painted several series of didactic paintings, but then fled to Leicestershire to escape creditors and took to rustic and animal painting for which he is best known.

Barrell, J., *The Dark Side of the Landscape: the Poor in English Painting* (Cambridge, 1980)
Dawe, G., *The Life of George Morland* with introduction and notes by J.J. Foster (1904)
Gilbey, W. and Cuming, E.D., *George Morland: his Life and Works* (1907)
Image, S., *Some Reflections on the Art of Rowlandson and George Morland*, Lecture-Print Collectors' Club (1929)

Mulready, William (1786–1863)
Painter of scenes from ordinary life (genre painting). Born in Ireland, son of leather-breeches maker. Educated in Wesleyan and Roman Catholic schools in London. Became a pupil teacher in the studio of John Varley. Early paintings on legendary themes. 1807–09: illustrated children's books. 1816: Royal Academician. Strongly humorous 'game' pictures till 1839, when he became more sentimental. Designed first penny-postage stamp issued by Rowland Hill.

Heleniak, K.M., *William Mulready* (1980)
Pointon, M., *William Mulready 1786–1863* (1986)

Palmer, Samuel (1805–81)
Landscape painter and etcher, born in
London. In his youth he was one of a group
(including Edward Calvert and George
Richmond) known as 'The Ancients',
strongly influenced by William Blake. His
best years were 1826–32 at Shoreham,
Kent, producing mystical paintings and
wash drawings. In later life his work
became conventional.

Cecil, D., *Visionary and Dreamer; Two
    Poetic Painters, Samuel Palmer and
    Edward Burne-Jones* (1969)
Grigson, G., *Samuel Palmer; the Visionary
    Years* (1947)
Lister, R., *Beulah to Byzantium; a Study of
    Parallels in the Works of W.B. Yeats,
    William Blake, Samuel Palmer and
    Edward Calvert* (Dublin, 1965)
    Samuel Palmer; a Biography (1974)
Palmer, A.H., *The Life and Letters of
    Samuel Palmer, Painter and Etcher*
    (1892) (New edition with introductory
    essay by R. Lister and preface by K.
    Raine, 1972)
Peacock, C., *Samuel Palmer; Shoreham and
    After* (1968)
Sellars, J., *Samuel Palmer* (1974)

Raeburn, Henry (1756–1823)
Portrait painter. Born in Edinburgh, son of
manufacturer; apprenticed to goldsmith and
then studied in Italy. Began career in
Edinburgh in 1787, achieving great success
as a portraitist of Scottish society, using
vivid colours and varied light. His
reputation extended to London from 1810.

Andrew, A.R., *Life of Sir Henry Raeburn*
    (1886)
Armstrong, Sir W., *Sir Henry Raeburn.
    With introduction by R.A.M. Stevenson
    and descriptive catalogue* (1901)
Greig, J., *Sir Henry Raeburn: His Life and
    Works. With Catalogue* (1911)

Turner, Joseph Mallord William
(1775–1851)
Painter. Born in London, son of a barber.
He received little education but began art
training at thirteen. His career started in
commercial practice for architects and
engravers. He duly became a topographer, a
marine and country-house painter, a prolific
artist of watercolours, and of mythological,
genre and historical subjects: and also a
poet and enthusiastic angler. Was elected
ARA and RA at youngest possible age, and
Professor of Perspective in 1809. His
enormous output included 541 oil paintings,
1578 finished water-colours, and over
19,000 sketches and studies. An
indefatigable traveller. The bulk of his
pictures were of places visited. From 1799
his work grew more poetic, and he became
famous for his rendering of light in land
and seascapes. In this he was much
influenced by the French painter Claude. At
the age of 40 was described as 'the first
genius of the day'. His visits to Italy in
1819 and 1828 made his use of colour even
more remarkable in his later work. Was
strenuously championed by Ruskin.

Armstrong, Sir W., *Turner* (1902)
Butlin, M. and Joll, E., *The Paintings of
    J.M.W. Turner* (revised edn.
    comprehensive bibliography, 1984)
Clare, C., *J.M.W. Turner, his Life and
    Work* (1951)
Finberg, H.F., *The Life of J.M.W. Turner*
    (2nd edn, 1961)
Foss, K., *The Double Life of J.M.W. Turner*
    (1938)
Gage, J., *Colour in Turner: Poetry and
    Truth* (1969)
    Turner: A Wonderful Range of Mind
    (1987; comprehensive bib.)
Hermann, L.J., *J.M.W. Turner
    (1775–1851)* (1963)
Hill, D., *In Turner's Footsteps* (1984)
Hind, C.L., *Turner's Golden Visions* (1925)
Lindsay, J., *Turner: his Life and Work, a
    Critical Biography* (1973)
Mauclaire, C., *Turner* (trans. from French
    by E.B. Shaw) (1939)
Powell, C., *Turner in the South* (1987)
Ruskin, J., *Modern Painters* (1843–60;
    abridged and edited by A.J. Finberg,
    1927)
Shanes, E., *Turner's Picturesque Views in
    England and Wales* (1979)
    Turner's Rivers, Harbours and Coasts
    (1981)
    The Genius of the Royal Academy (1981)
Swinburne, C.A., *Life and Work of J.M.W.
    Turner* (1902)
Thornbury, W., *The Life of J.M.W. Turner
    RA* (1877; new edn, 1970)
Wilkinson, G., *The Sketches of Turner R.A.
    1802–30: Genres of the Romantic* (1974)
Wilton, A., *J.M.W. Turner* (1987)

Varley, John (1778–1842)
Painter in water colours and draughtsman.
Born in London, son of a teacher with
strong scientific interests. He painted
buildings and found his most congenial
landscapes in north Wales. Taught drawing
to leading artists and was a member of the
circle centred on William Blake.

Bury, A., *John Varley of the 'Old Society'*
    (1946)

Butlin, M. (ed.), *The Blake-Varley
Sketchbook of 1819* (2 vols) (1969)
Kauffmann, C.M., *John Varley
(1778–1842)* (1984)

Ward, James (1769–1851)
Animal painter and engraver. Born in
London. Apprenticed to engraver. Acquired
an interest in painting from George
Morland. Achieved a reputation for animal
paintings, e.g. of an Alderney cow for an
agricultural society and 'Bull-Bait' (1797).
He also painted landscapes and portraits.

Fussell, G.E., *James Ward* (1974)
Grundy, C.R., *James Ward R.A.* (1909)
Nygren, E.J., *James Ward's Gordale Scar*
(1982)

West, Benjamin (1738–1820)
Painter. Born in Pennsylvania, acquired a
reputation for his portraits in New York;
after a period in Italy he settled in London
where he became historical painter to
George III in 1772. 1792: became President
of the Royal Academy on the death of
Joshua Reynolds. His reputation arose
largely from the new fashion for historical
paintings which he executed meticulously.

Galt, J., *Life and Studies of Benjamin West*
(1816)
Dillinger, J., *Benjamin West: The Context of
his Life and Work* (San Antonio, Texas,
1977)
von Erffa, M. and Staley, A., *The Paintings
of Benjamin West* (1986) (Full
bibliography)

Wilkie, Sir David (1785–1841)
Anecdotal painter. Born in Fifeshire, son of
Presbyterian minister. Moved to London in
1805, and achieved great success with his
painting 'The Village Politicians'. Much
influenced by the seventeenth-century
Dutch genre painters, especially Teniers.
After visiting Italy in 1826 he attempted
more imposing compositions, but lost the
intimacy of detail. Knighted in 1836.

Errington, L., *Tribute to David Wilkie*,
Catalogue (1985)
Gower, Lord R.C., *Sir David Wilkie* (1902)
Mollett, J.W., *Sir David Wilkie* (1881)
Pinnington, E., *Sir David Wilkie and the
Scots School of Painters* (1900)

8 Graphic Satire and Illustration

General studies

George, M.D., *Hogarth to Cruikshank:
Social Change in Graphic Satire* (1967)

Harvey, John, *Victorian Novelists and their
Illustrators* (1970)
Klingender, F.D., *Hogarth and English
Caricature* (1944)
Low, D., *British Cartoonists and Comic
Artists* (1932)

Artists

Browne, Hablot Knight ('Phiz')
(1815–82)
Illustrator. Born in London of poor parents;
early apprenticed to Finden, an eminent
steel engraver. 1836: illustrated Dickens's
The Pickwick Papers. He later illustrated
*Martin Chuzzlewit, David Copperfield,
Dombey and Son, Bleak House*, and became
famous for his rendering of character. He
also illustrated novels by Charles Lever and
Harrison Ainsworth.

Forster, J., *Life of Charles Dickens* (1874)
Johannsen, A., *Phiz: Illustrations from the
Novels of Charles Dickens* (1956)
Kitton, F.G., *'Phiz': a Memoir* (1882);
Charles Dickens and his Illustrators
(1899)
Leavis, Q.D., 'The Dickens Illustrations:
their function', Chapter VII in Leavis,
F.R. and Q.D., *Dickens the Novelist*
(1970)
Spielmann, M.H., *The History of Punch*
(1895)
Steig, M., *Dickens and Phiz* (1978)
Thomson, D., *Hablot Knight Browne,
'Phiz': Life and Letters* (1884)

Cruikshank, George (1792–1878)
Caricaturist and illustrator. Born in
London, son of a painter. By 1811 already a
popular caricaturist, rivalling Gillray. 1820:
illustrated *Life in London* and later novels
by Ainsworth (*Old St Paul's*) and Dickens
(notably, *Oliver Twist*). In later life devoted
himself to pictorial propaganda for
temperance movements. Influential in the
tradition of Victorian book illustration, e.g.,
'Phiz' (Hablot Knight Browne).

Jerrold, B., *The Life of George Cruikshank*
(1882)
McLean, R., *George Cruikshank, his Life
and Work as a Book Illustrator* (1948)
Patten, R. (ed.), *George Cruikshank: A
Revolution* (1973), a special double
number, in volume form, of the
Princeton University Library Chronicle
Thackeray, W.M. (ed. W.E. Church), *An
Essay on the Genius of George
Cruikshank* (1884)

Gillray, James (1757–1815)
Caricaturist. Born Chelsea, son of Chelsea
Pensioner. Influenced by Hogarth in his

satirical studies of politicians and events remarkable for their wit and vigour. He directed his satire at both political parties though the French Revolution made him more conservative.

Grego, J., *The Works of James Gillray, the Caricaturist; with the History of his Life and Times* (1873)

Hill, D., *Mr Gillray the Caricaturist, a Biography* (1956)
Fashionable Contrasts (1966)
(ed.), *The Satirical Etchings of James Gillray* (New York, 1976)

Rowlandson, Thomas (1756–1827)
Caricaturist. Born in Old Jewry, London, son of a city man of business. Developed an early talent for painting, but ruined himself by gambling; friendship with Gillray led him into caricature to recover his income. Achieved success especially with the 'Dr Syntax' series: 'The Schoolmaster's Tour' (1809–11) reissued as the 'Tour of Dr Syntax in Search of the Picturesque' (1812), followed by 'Dr Syntax in Search of Consolation' (1820) and 'Third Tour of Dr Syntax in Search of a Wife' (1821)

Falk, B., *Thomas Rowlandson: his Life and Art* (1949)

Hayes, J., *Rowlandson: Watercolours and Drawings* (1972)

Paulson, R., *Rowlandson: a New Interpretation* (Encounters: Essays on Literature and the Visual Arts, 1972)

9   Literature

General studies

Abrams, M.H., *The Mirror and the Lamp: Romantic Theory and the Critical Tradition* (New York, 1953);
Natural Supernaturalism: Tradition and Revolution in Romantic Literature (1971)

Altick, R.D., *The English Common Reader 1800–1900* (Chicago, 1957)

Ashton, R., *The German Idea* (Cambridge, 1980)

Bate, W.J., *From Classic to Romantic* (Cambridge, Mass., 1946)

Bembaum, E., *Guide through the Romantic Movement* (1948)

Bowra, Sir C.M., *The Romantic Imagination* (1950)

Buckley, J.H., *The Victorian Temper: A Study in Literary Culture* (1968)

Butler, M., *Romantics: Rebels and Reactionaries* (1981)

Collins, A.S., *The Profession of Letters 1780–1832* (1928)

Cruse, A., *The Englishman and his Books in the Early Nineteenth Century* (1930)

Dowden, E., *The French Revolution and English Literature* (1897)

Ford, B. (ed.), *The New Pelican Guide to English Literature* (vols 5 and 6) (1982)

Harrison, F., *Studies in Early Victorian Literature* (1895)

Hazlitt, W., *The Spirit of the Age* (1825; Worlds Classics 1904)

Hilles, F.W. and Bloom, H., *From Sensibility to Romanticism* (New York, 1965)

Horne, R.H., *A New Spirit of the Age* (1844; Worlds Classics, 1907)

House, H., *All in Due Time* (Oxford, 1963)

Lovejoy, A.O., 'On the Discrimination of Romanticism' in *Essays on the History of Ideas* (1948)

McFarland, T., *Romanticism and the Forms of Ruin* (Princeton, 1981)
Romantic Cruxes (1987)

Neff, E., *A Revolution in European Poetry, 1660–1900* (New York, 1940)

Piper, H.W., *The Active Universe* (1962)

Pipkin, J., *English and German Romanticism: Crosscurrents and Controversies* (Heidelberg, 1985)

Praz, M., *The Romantic Agony* (1933; rev. edn 1951)

Renwick, W.L. and Jack, I., *Oxford History of English Literature vols IX, X* (1963)

Sales, R., *English Literature in History 1780–1830* (1983)

Selincourt, E. de, *Wordsworthian and Other Studies* (Oxford, 1947)

Sewell, E., *The Orphic Voice* (1960)

Stokoe, F.W., *German Influence in the English Romantic Period* (Cambridge, 1926)

Sutherland, D., *On Romanticism* (New York, 1971)

Wellek, R., 'The Concept of Romanticism' in *Concepts in Criticism* (1963)

Williams, R., *Culture and Society, 1780–1950* (1958)

The Novel

Allen, W., *The English Novel* (1954; Penguin Books, 1958)

Allott, Miriam, *Novelist on the Novel* (1959)

Birkhead, E., *The Tale of Terror, A Study of the Gothic Romance* (1921)

Block, A., *The English Novel 1740–1850: A Catalogue* (1939; rev. edn, 1961)

Cecil, Lord D., *Early Victorian Novelists* (1934; new edn, 1964)

Colby, V., *Yesterday's Woman: Domestic*

Realism in the English Novel (Princeton, 1974)

Harrison, F., *Studies in Early Victorian Literature* (1895)

Howells, C.A., *Love, Mystery and Misery: Feeling in Gothic Fiction* (1978)

Kelly, G., *The English Jacobin Novel, 1780–1805* (1976)

Kettle, A., *An Introduction to the English Novel* (1951)

Leavis, F.R., *The Great Tradition* (1948; Penguin Books, 1967)

Leavis, Q.D., *Fiction and the Reading Public* (1932)

'The Englishness of the English Novel' in *Collected Essays* (1983)

MacCarthy, B.G., *The Later Women Novelists: 1744–1818* (Oxford, 1947)

Punter, D., *The Literature of Terror* (1980)

Summers, M., *The Gothic Quest* (1938)

Tillotson, K., *Novels of the Eighteen Forties* (Oxford, 1954)

Tompkins, J.M.S., *The Popular Novel in England, 1770–1800* (1932)

Poetry

Abrams, M.H. (ed.), *English Romantic Poets: Modern Essays in Criticism* (1960; rev. edn, 1975)

Barth, J.R., *The Symbolic Imagination* (Princeton, NJ, 1977)

Bateson, F.W., *English Poetry and the English Language* (Oxford, 1934; 3rd edn, 1973)

Bloom, H., *The Anxiety of Influence: A Theory of Poetry* (1973)

The Visionary Company (New York, 1961)

Bradley, A.C., *English Poetry and German Philosophy in the Age of Wordsworth* (Manchester, 1909)

Bush, D., *Mythology and the Romantic tradition in English Poetry* (Cambridge, Mass., 1937)

Science and English Poetry (New York, 1950)

Davie, D., *Purity of Diction in English Verse* (1952)

Foakes, R.A., *The Romantic Assertion* (1958)

Grierson, Sir H.J.C., *The Background of English Literature: Classical and Romantic* (1934)

Grigson, G., *The Harp of Aeolus* (1948)

Hough, G., *The Romantic Poets* (1953)

Knight, G. Wilson, *The Starlit Dome* (Oxford, 1971)

Leavis, F.R., *Revaluation* (1936; Penguin Books, 1964)

Read, Sir H., *The True Voice of Feeling: Studies in English Romantic Poetry* (1953)

Ruskin, J., *Pre-Raphaelitism* (1851)

Saurat, D., *Literature and Occult Tradition* (1930)

Simpson, D., *Irony and Authority in Romantic Poetry* (1979)

Warren, A.H., *English Poetic Theory 1825–65* (Princeton, 1950)

Watson, J.D., *English Poetry of the Romantic Period 1789–1830* (1985)

Woodring, C., *Politics in English Romantic Poetry* (Cambridge, Mass., 1970)

Authors

Austen, Jane (1775–1817)
Daughter of Hampshire clergyman with two daughters, six sons. Lived in Hampshire with an interval in Bath. She never married but had rich relationships, though almost none with contemporary writers. Her novels appealed to the Prince Regent and were admired by Walter Scott. Writers she especially admired included Dr Johnson, the novelist Samuel Richardson, and the poets William Cowper and George Crabbe. Novels: *Sense and Sensibility*, published 1811; *Pride and Prejudice*, 1813; *Mansfield Park*, 1814; *Emma*, 1815; *Northanger Abbey*, the first written, was published posthumously with *Persuasion*, 1818. *Letters*, ed. R.W. Chapman (Oxford, 1932; enlarged edn London, 1954)

Austen-Leigh, J.E., *A Memoir of Jane Austen* (1871; Oxford, ed. R.W. Chapman, 1926)

Bradbrook, F.W., *Jane Austen and Her Predecessors* (1966)

Brown, J.P., *Jane Austen's Novels: Social Change and Literary Form* (Harvard, 1979)

Butler, M., *Jane Austen and the War of Ideas* (Oxford, 1975)

Cecil, D., *A Portrait of Jane Austen* (1978)

Chapman, R.W., *Jane Austen – Facts and Problems* (Oxford, 1948)

Craik, W.A., *Jane Austen in her Time* (1969)

Devlin, D.D., *Jane Austen and Education* (1975)

Duckworth, A.M., *The Improvement of the Estate: a study of Jane Austen's Novels* (Baltimore, 1971)

Gillie, C., *A Preface to Jane Austen* (1985)

Hardy, B., *A Reading of Jane Austen* (1975)

Jenkins, E., *Jane Austen, a Biography* (1956)

Kirkham, M., *Jane Austen: Feminism and Fiction* (1983)

Laski, M., *Jane Austen and her World* (1969)

Leavis, Q.D., *A Critical Theory of Jane Austen's Writings* (Cambridge, 1963)

Lodge, D., in *The Language of Fiction* (1966)

Monaghan, D. (ed.), *Jane Austen in a Social Context* (1982)

Mudrick, M., *Jane Austen: Irony as Defense and Discovery* (Princeton, 1952)

O'Neil, J. (ed.), *Critics on Jane Austen* (1970)

Page, N., *The Language of Jane Austen* (1972)

Phillips, K.C., *Jane Austen's English* (1970)

Pinion, F.B., *A Jane Austen Companion* (1973)

Roberts, W., *Jane Austen and the French Revolution* (1979)

Southam, B.C. (ed.), *Jane Austen: the Critical Heritage* (1969)

Tanner, P.A., *Jane Austen* (1986)

Watt, I., (ed.), *Jane Austen: a Collection of Essays* (1963)

Bentham, Jeremy (1748–1832)
Lawyer and philosopher, especially concerned with legal and penal reform; founder of school of thought later known as Utilitarianism. Started the *Westminster Review* (1832) and was one of the initiators of London University. Life by C.W. Everett (1966). *The Correspondence*, ed. Sprigge, T.L.S. and Christie, I.R. (in progress). *Works* ed. Burns, J.H. (in progress).

Baumgardt, D., *Bentham and the Ethics of Today* (1953)

Leavis, F.R., *Mill on Bentham and Coleridge* (1967)

Long, D.C., *Bentham and Liberty: Jeremy Bentham's Ideas of Liberty in Relation to his Utilitarianism* (Toronto, 1977)

Mack, M., *Jeremy Bentham: An Odyssey of Ideas* (1962)

Mill, J.S., Essays on Bentham (1838) and Coleridge (1840), ed. F.R. Leavis

Blake, William (1757–1827)
(See also under 7 **The Fine Arts**). Poet, painter engraver. Son of a London haberdasher, he lived all his life in London except 1800–03 in Felpham, Sussex. For a time, an ardent supporter of the French Revolution and moved in the radical circle of William Godwin and Tom Paine. He rceived support from a few friends, but his visionary art of poetry blended with engraving was too original for the public, especially because he invented his own mythology. Works: *Poetical Sketches* (1783); *Songs of Innocence* (1789); *Songs of Experience* (1794). His 'prophetic books'

began with *Tiriel* (1788–89) and thereafter include *The French Revolution* (1791); *The Four Zoas* (1797), *Milton* and *Jerusalem* (1804). Lives by A. Gilchrist (1863: rev. ed ed. R. Todd, 1945); Mona Wilson (1927: rev. edn 1948); Kathleen Raine (1870).

Beer, J.B., *Blake's Humanism* (1968)
Blake's Visionary Universe (1969)
William Blake 1757–1827 (1982)

Bentley, G.E. (ed.), *William Blake: The Critical Heritage* (1975)

Blackstone, R., *English Blake* (Cambridge, 1949)

Bottrall, M., *The Divine Image: A Study of Blake's Interpretation of Christianity* (Rome, 1950)

Bronowski, J., *A Man Without a Mask* (1943; rev. as *William Blake and the Age of Revolution*) (New York, 1965; rev. edn, 1972)

Damon, S.F., *A Blake Dictionary: The Ideas and Symbols of William Blake* (Providence R.I., 1965)

Damrosch, L., *Symbol and Truth in Blake's Myth* (Princeton, 1980)

Dorfman, D., *William Blake in the Nineteenth Century* (New Haven, Conn., 1969)

Erdman, D.V., *Blake: Prophet against Empire* (Princeton, 1970)
A Concordance to the Writings of William Blake (Berkeley, 1968)

Frosch, T., *The Awakening of Albion* (New York, 1974)

Frye, N., *Fearful Symmetry: A Study of William Blake* (1947)

Gardner, S., *Infinity on the Anvil* (1954)

Gaunt, W., *Arrows of Desire* (1956)

Gillham, D.G., *Blake's Contrary States; the Songs of Innocence and of Experience as Dramatic Poems* (Cambridge, 1966)

Glen, H., *Vision and Disenchantment: Blake's Songs and Wordsworth's Lyrical Ballads* (Cambridge, 1983)

Keynes, G., *Blake Studies* (1949; rev. and enlarged, 1971)

Margoliouth, H.M., *William Blake* (1951)

Paley, M.D., *William Blake* (1978)

Paley, M.D. and Phillips, M., *William Blake: Essays in Honour of Sir Geoffrey Keynes* (1973)

Raine, K., *Blake and Tradition* (1969)

Saurat, D., *Blake and Modern Thought* (1929)

Schorer, M., *William Blake: The Politics of Vision* (New York, 1946)

Swinburne, A.C., *William Blake* (1868; ed. H.J. Luke, Lincoln, Neb., 1970)

Wicksteed, J., *Blake's Innocence and Experience* (1928)

Bowles, William Lisle (1762–1850)
Poet, critic, clergyman. Born King's Sutton, Northamptonshire, son of a clergyman; educated at Winchester and Trinity College, Oxford. 1789: *Fourteen Sonnets*, his best known poetry, strongly appealing to Wordsworth and Coleridge. 1806: published an edition of Pope's poetry with a preface establishing principles of 'natural' imagery in opposition to Pope's artificiality. This provoked controversy, angering Byron but defended by Hazlitt. Life by G. Gilfillan, prefacing vol. II of Bowles's *Poetical Works* (Edinburgh 1855).

Greever, G., *A Wiltshire Parson and his Friends: The Correspondence of W.L. Bowles* (1926)
Van Rennes, J.J., *Bowles, Byron and the Pope Controversy* (Amsterdam, 1927)

Brontë, Charlotte (1816–55) Third of five daughters of Patrick Brontë, rector of Haworth, Yorkshire. In adolescence, with her sisters Emily and Anne and their brother Patrick, she cultivated her imagination by writing romances. After brief formal education she became a governess; in 1842 went with her sister Emily to Brussels (Pension Héger) to learn French and returned there to teach in 1843. 1844: with her sisters Emily and Anne published poems under pseudonyms Currer, Ellis and Acton Bell. Novels; *Jane Eyre* (1847); *Shirley* (1849); *Villette* (1853). *The Professor*, an earlier version of *Villette*, was published posthumously.

Brontë, Emily Jane (1818–48)
Her one novel, *Wuthering Heights* (1847) was on publication overshadowed by Charlotte's *Jane Eyre*, but has since been considered pre-eminent among the Brontës' works as has her poetry. She had a close bond with her brother Patrick Branwell who died in the same year. Life by Elizabeth Gaskell (1857; rev. edn 1908)

Allott, M. (ed.), *Charlotte Brontë: The Critical Heritage* (1974)
Craik, W.A., *The Brontë Novels* (1968)
Duthie, E., *The Foreign Vision of Charlotte Brontë* (1975)
Eagleton, T., *Myths of Power* (1975)
Gérin, W., *Charlotte Brontë* (Oxford, 1967)
  Emily Brontë (Oxford, 1971)
Hanson, L. and E.M., *The Four Brontës* (Oxford, 1967)
Martin, R.B., *The Accents of Persuasion: Charlotte Brontë's Novels* (1966)
Petit, J.P., *Emily Brontë* (1973)
Ratchford, F., *The Brontës' Web of Childhood* (New York, 1967)

Sangar, C.P., *The Structure of Wuthering Heights* (1968)

Browning, Robert (1812–89)
Poet; son of Bank of England clerk; privately educated. Earlier poems: *Pauline* (1833); *Paracelsus* (1835); *Strafford* (tragedy, performed Covent Garen 1837); *Sordello* (1840); *Bells and Pomegranates* including *Pippa Passes* (1841–46). 1846: married the poet Elizabeth Barrett. Most of his major works (*Men and Women, Dramatis Personae, The Ring and the Book*) published after 1850. *Letters* ed. T.L. Hood (1933); Life by W. Irvine and P. Honan (1975); J. Maynard (Cambridge, Mass., 1977).

Armstrong, I. (ed.), *Robert Browning, Writers and their Background* (1974)
Jack, I., *Browning's Major Poetry* (1973)
Langbaum, R., *The Poetry of Experience* (New York, 1957)
Raymond, W.O., *The Infinite Moment and Other Essays on Robert Browning* (Toronto, 1950)
Shaw, W.D., *The Dialectical Temper: The Rhetorical Art of Robert Browning* (New York, 1968)
Smalley, D. and Litzinger, B., *Browning: The Critical Heritage* (1970)

Burns, Robert (1759–96)
Poet. Born in Alloway, Ayrshire, son of a tenant farmer. Famous for his poetry in Lowland Scottish: *Poems. Chiefly in the Scottish Dialect* (1786); *Tam O'Shanter* (1790). Worked as a farmer until he became an excise officer in 1791. Life by F.B. Snyder (New York, 1932); M. Lindsay (1954; rev. edn 1968). *Letters*, ed. J. de L. Ferguson (2 vols Oxford, 1929). *Burns: Poetry and Prose*, ed. R. Dewar (Oxford, 1929) *The Poems and Songs of Robert Burns* (3 vols., 1968).

Crawford, T., *Burns: A study of the Poems and Songs* (Edinburgh, 1960)
Daiches, D., *Robert Burns* (1952) (rev. edn, 1966)
Lindsay, M., *The Burns Encyclopaedia* (1959; rev. and enlarged 1970)
Low, D.A., *Critical Essays on Robert Burns* (1971)
  Robert Burns: The Critical Heritage (1974)

Byron, George Gordon, Lord (1788–1824)
Born with deformed foot, but became famous for the glamour of his personality, notorious for private scandals, and popular for his romantic verse tales and plays, e.g. *Childe Harold I and II, The Giaour, The*

Bride of Abydos, The Corsair, Cain (all from 1812 to 1821). But he admired Alexander Pope and some of his best work is more acerbic: *Childe Harold III and IV* (1816–18), *The Vision of Judgement* (1821) and *Don Juan* (1818–24). His radical politics led to his support in the war for the independence of Greece where he died. Life by L.A. Marchand (1958); *Letters and Journals*, ed. L.A. Marchand (1973–8)

Blackstone, B., *Byron: A Survey* (1975)
Joseph, M.K., *Byron the Poet* (1964)
Jump, J.D. (ed.), *Byron: A Symposium* (1975)
Leavis, F.R., 'Byron's Satire' in *Revaluation* (1936; Penguin Books, 1964)
Lovell, E.J. (ed.), *His Very Self and Voice: Collected Conversations* (1954)
Marchand, L.A., *Byron's Poetry* (1965)
Origo, I., *Byron, the Last Attachment* (1949)
Quennell, P., *Byron: the Years of Fame* (1935)
    Byron in Italy (1951)
Read, H., *Byron* (1951)
Robson, W.W., *Byron as Poet* (British Academy Lecture, 1957)
Rutherford, A., *Byron: The Critical Heritage* (1970)
West, P., *Byron and the Spoiler's Art* (1960)

Carlyle, Thomas (1795–1881)
Philosopher and historian. Son of Scottish peasant; he renounced Presbyterian faith but remained deeply concerned with religious values under the influence of Goethe. Wrote in eccentric poetical prose. *Sartor Resartus* ('Tailor Repatched', 1834) is a disguised spiritual autobiography. Principal later works; *French Revolution (1837); On Heroes and Hero Worship* (1841); *Past and Present* (1843); *Oliver Cromwell's Letters and Speeches* (1845); *Latter Day Pamphlets* (1850); *Frederick II of Prussia* (1858–65); *Shooting Niagara – And After?* (1867). Life by J.A. Froude (4 vols London 1882–84); J. Symons (1952); I. Campbell (1974); F. Kaplan (1983).

Clubbe, J. (ed.), *Carlyle and his Contemporaries* (Durham, N. Carolina, 1976)
Fielding, K.J. and Tarr, R.L. (eds), *Carlyle Past and Present* (1976)
Shine, H., *Carlyle's Early Reading, to 1834* (1953)
Siegel, J.P., *Carlyle: The Critical Heritage* (1972)

Clare, John (1793–1864)
Poet. Born Helpston, Northamptonshire, of labouring stock. Lived as farm worker, gardener, militiaman, vagrant, until his mental breakdown in 1837; thereafter lived in asylums with intervals of relative lucidity. Befriended by publisher, John Taylor, who issued his *Poems descriptive of rural life and scenery* in 1820; highly praised. Later works: *The Village Minstrel and other Poems* (1821); *Shepherd's Calendar* (1827); *The Rural Muse* (1835). Wrote more poems in asylums. Life by J.W. and A. Tibble (1932; rev. edn, 1972). *Letters* ed. M. Storey (1985).

Barrell, J., *The Idea of Landscape and the Sense of Place 1730–1840: An Approach to the Poetry of John Clare* (Cambridge, 1970)
Robinson, E. and Summerfield, G. (eds), *The Later Poems of John Clare* (Manchester, 1964)
Storey, M. (ed.), *Clare; the Critical Heritage* (1973)
    The Poetry of John Clare: a Critical Introduction (1974)
Tibble, J.W. (ed.), *The Poems of John Clare* (2 vols. 1935)
Tibble, J.W. and Tibble, A. (eds), *The Prose of John Clare* (1951)
    The Letters of John Clare (1951)

Coleridge, Samuel Taylor (1772–1834)
Poet, critic, philosopher; born Ottery St Mary, Devon, son of clergyman; educated at Christ's Hospital and (1791–94) Jesus College, Cambridge. Wrote his best poetry between 1795 and 1805 during his close friendship with William and Dorothy Wordsworth; collaborated with Wordsworth in *Lyrical Ballads* (1798). Thereafter lectured, engaged in political journalism (*The Friend*, 1809–10), and developed a radical and philosophical style of literary and political criticism partly under the influence of contemporary German thought (Kant and Schelling): *Biographia Literaria* (1817); *Aids to Reflection* (1825); *Church and State* (1829). Lives by J.D. Campbell (1894); W.J. Bate (New York, 1968). *Letters* ed. E.L. Griggs (1956–71).

Appleyard, J., *Coleridge's Philosophy of Nature* (Cambridge, Mass., 1965)
Barfield, O., *What Coleridge Thought* (1971)
Beer, J.B., *Coleridge the Visionary* (1959)
    (ed.) *Coleridge's Variety: Bicentenary Studies* (1974)
Brett, R.L. (ed.), *Writers and their Background; S.T. Coleridge* (1971)
Coburn, K., *The Self-Conscious Imagination* (on the Notebooks) (1974)
    The Notebooks of S.T. Coleridge (1957–74)

Colmer, J., *Coleridge, Critic of Society* (1959)

Dekker, G., *Coleridge and the Literature of Sensibility* (1978)

Everest, K., *Coleridge's Secret Ministry* (1979)

Fruman, N., *Coleridge the Damaged Archangel* (1972)

Hamilton, P., *Coleridge's Poetics* (1983)

Harding, A.J., *Coleridge and the Idea of Love* (Cambridge, 1974)

House, H., *Coleridge* (the Clark Lectures, 1951–52) (1953)

Jackson, J.R. de J. (ed.), *Coleridge: the Critical Heritage* (1970)

Leavis, F.R. (ed.), *Mill on Bentham and Coleridge* (1950)

Lowes, J.L., *The Road to Xanadu* (1927; rev. edn 1951)

Margliouth, H.M., *Wordsworth and Coleridge 1795–1834* (1953)

McFarland, T., *Coleridge and the Pantheist Tradition* (1969)

Prickett, S., *Coleridge and Wordsworth: the Poetry of Growth* (Cambridge, 1970)

Read, H., *Coleridge as Critic* (1949)

Shaffer, E., *'Kubla Khan' and the Fall of Jerusalem* (Cambridge, 1975)

Walsh, W., *Coleridge: the Work and the Relevance* (1967)

Whalley, G., *Coleridge and Sara Hutchinson and the 'Asra' Poems* (1955)

Wheeler, K.M., *Sources, Processes and Methods in Coleridge's 'Biographia Literaria'* (Cambridge, 1980)

Willey, B., *S.T. Coleridge* (1972)

Crabbe, George (1754–1832)
Poet. Born Aldeburgh, Suffolk, son of a customs warehouse keeper. 1768: apprenticed to surgeon. 1775–79: practised as surgeon-apothecary; developed a strong interest in botany. 1775: *Inebriety, a Poem*. 1779: abandoned medicine for literature under patronage of Edmund Burke. 1781: took Holy Orders. Later works: *The Village* (1783); *The Newspaper* (1785); *Poems* including *The Parish Register* (1807); *Tales* (1812). 1814: Rector of Trowbridge. Life by his son, G. Crabbe (1834; ed. E.M. Forster, 1932; ed. E. Blunden 1947).

Haddakin, L., *The Poetry of George Crabbe* (1955)

New, P., *George Crabbe's Poetry* (1976)

Pollard, A., *Crabbe: The Critical Heritage* (1972)

De Quincey, Thomas (1785–1859)
Essayist and critic. Born Manchester, son of a merchant; educated at Bath and Manchester grammar schools and Worcester College, Oxford. Best known for his autobiography, *Memoirs of an English Opium-Eater* (1822; enlarged edn 1856). He also wrote fine essays on a wide range of subjects, e.g. 'The English Mail Coach', 'Knocking at the Gate in Macbeth', 'The Logic of Political Economy', and studies of contemporary writers known collectively as 'Recollections of the Lake Poets'. Lives by E. Sackville-West and H.A. Eaton; *The Opium Eater* by G. Lindop (1981).

De Luca, V.A., Thomas De Quincey: The Prose of Vision (Toronto, 1980)

Jordan, J.E., *Thomas De Quincey, Literary Critic: His Method and Achievement* (Berkeley, 1952)

(ed.), *Reminiscences of the English Lake Poets* (1961)

Dickens, Charles John Huffam (1812–70)
Novelist. Born Portsea, Hampshire, son of clerk in Navy Pay Office; little education. 1824: father's imprisonment for debt forced him to work in blacking warehouse. 1835: parliamentary reporter for *Morning Chronicle*. 1836–7: *Sketches by Boz, Illustrative of Every-Day Life and Every-Day People*. Popularity established by *The Pickwick Papers* (1837), published, like all his novels, serially. 1837–9: *Oliver Twist;* 1838–39: *The Old Curiosity Shop; Nicholas Nickleby*; 1840–41: *Barnaby Rudge*. Major novels followed from *Martin Chuzzlewit* (1843–44). 1848: *Dombey and Son*; 1849–50: *David Copperfield*; 1852–53: *Bleak House*; 1854: *Hard Times*; 1857–58: *Little Dorrit*; *1859: A Tale of Two Cities*; 1860–61: *Great Expectations*; 1864–65: *Our Mutual Friend*. *Edwin Drood* left unfinished. Edited two weeklies: *Household Words* (started 1850) and *All the Year Round* (started 1859). Life by John Forster (1872–74); G.K. Chesterton (1906); U. Pope-Henessey (1945); J. Lindsay (1950); Edgar Johnson (1953; rev. 1965).

Butt, J. and Tillotson, K., *Dickens at Work* (1957)

Collins, P, *Dickens and Crime* (1962)

Dickens and Education (1963)

(ed.), *Dickens: Critical Heritage* (1971)

Fielding, K.J., *Charles Dickens: A Critical Introduction* (1958; rev. edn, 1966)

Ford, G.H. and Lane, L., *The Dickens Critics* (1963)

Garis, R., *The Dickens Theatre* (1965)

Gissing, G., *Charles Dickens: A Critical Study* (1898)

Gross, J. and Pearson, G. (eds), *Dickens and the Twentieth Century* (1962)

House, Humphrey, *The Dickens World* (1941)

Leavis, F.R. and Leavis, Q.D., *Dickens the Novelist* (1970)

Lucas, J., *The Melancholy Man* (1970; rev. edn 1980)

Orwell, G., 'Charles Dickens' in *Critical Essays* (1946)

Pope, N., *Dickens and Charity* (1978)

Slater, M. (ed.), *Dickens* (1970)

Wall, S. (ed.), *Dickens: A Critical Anthology* (1970)

Hazlitt, William (1778–1830)
Essayist and critic. Born Maidstone, Kent, son of Unitarian Minister: educated by tutors and at day-school. Developed radical politics, contributing miscellaneous essays and essays on art and literature to the Hunts' *The Examiner, The Edinburgh Review* and other journals. Early friendship with Coleridge, Wordsworth: *My First Acquaintance with Poets* (1823). Made a study of the culture of the period in *The Spirit of the Age* (1825). Life by P.P. Howe (1922; rev. 1947) and Herschel Baker (1962). *Letters*, ed. H.M. Sikes (New York, 1978).

Albrecht, W.P., *Hazlitt and the Creative Imagination* (Lawrence, Kansas, 1965)

Brinton, C., *The Political Ideas of the English Romanticists* (1926)

Keats, John (1795–1821)
Poet. Born London, son of manager of livery stable. Parents died 1804 and 1810; guardianship of Richard Abbey. Educated Enfield. 1811: apprenticed to surgeon. 1815: gave up surgery. 1817: *Poems*. Joined radical circle of John and Leigh Hunt. 1818: *Endymion*; hostile reception by Tory reviews. 1819: most creative year – narrative poems including *Hyperion* and Odes. Passionately in love with Fanny Brawne. 1821: died in Rome of tuberculosis. Life by S. Colvin (1917); R. Gittings (1970); Ayleen Ward (1963). Keats is famous for his letters – ed. H.E. Rollins (1958); Selection ed. R. Gittings (1970).

Aske, M., *Keats and Hellenism* (Cambridge, 1985)

Bate, W. J., *The Stylistic Development of Keats* (1945)

Blackstone, B., *The Consecrated Urn* (1959)

Ford, G.H., *Keats and the Victorians: A study of his Influence and Rise to Fame* (1946)

Ford, N.F., *The Prefigurative Imagination of John Keats* (1951)

Jack, I., *Keats and the Mirror of Art* (1967)

MacGillivray, J.R., *Keats: A Bibliography and Reference Guide* (1949)

Matthew, G.M. (ed.), *Keats: the Critical Heritage* (1971)

Muir, K. (ed.), *John Keats: A Reassessment* (Liverpool, 1958)

Murry, J.M., *Keats and Shakespeare* (1926) *Studies in Keats* (1930; rev. 1955)

Ricks, C., *Keats and Embarrassment* (1974)

Walsh, W., *Introduction to Keats* (1981)

Kingsley, Charles (1819–75)
Novelist, poet, clergyman; born Devon, son of clergyman; educated King's College, London and Magdalene, Cambridge. Strong supporter of Chartism and Christian socialism. Best known works; *Alton Locke* (1850); *Westward Ho!* (1855); *The Water Babies* (1863); *Hereward the Wake* (1866). Life by R.B. Martin (1960); S. Chitty (1974).

Egues, G., *Apologia for Charles Kingsley* (1969)

Hartley, A.J., *The Novels of Charles Kingsley* (Folkestone, 1977)

Kendall, G., *Kingsley and his Ideas* (1974)

Smith, S., *The Other Nation* (1980)

Lamb, Charles (1775–1834)
Essayist. Born London, son of assistant to Bencher of Inner Temple. Educated Christ's Hospital – beginning of friendship with Coleridge. Clerk at South-Sea House, 1791; East India House, 1792. Aimed to popularise classics: *Tales from Shakespeare* (1807); *The Adventures of Ulysses* (1808). Contributed to periodicals; famous for miscellaneous *Essays of Elia* (1823; 2nd series, 1833). Life by E.V. Lucas (1905; rev. 1921). *Letters* ed. E.W. Marrs (3 vols, New York, 1976–78).

Courtney, W., *Young Charles Lamb 1775–1802* (1982)

Lucas, E.V. (ed.), *Lamb's Letters* (3 vols, 1933)

Park, R., *Lamb as Critic* (1980)

Randel, F.V., *The World of Elia: Charles Lamb's Essayistic Romanticism* (1975)

Macaulay, Thomas Babington (1800–59)
Historian, essayist, poet, politician. Son of secretary to firm, Babington and Macaulay, founders of Sierra Leone and leading opponent of slave trade. Educated privately and Trinity College, Cambridge. 1825: became contributor to *Edinburgh Review*. 1830: Member of Parliament. 1833: Member of Supreme Council for India. 1839: War miniser under Melbourne. 1842: *Lays of Ancient Rome*; 1843: *Essays*; 1848–55: *History of England*. 1857: made Baron. Life by G.O. Trevelyan (1876; new edn, 1978); A. Bryant (1932); J. Clive (1973). Complete Works (1905–7).

Burrow, J.W. in *A Liberal Descent*
  (Cambridge, 1981)
Firth, Sir C., *A Commentary on Macaulay's
  History of England* (1938)
Pinney, T. (ed.), *Letters* (Cambridge,
  1974–81)
Young, G.M., *Selected Prose and Poetry*
  (1967)

Mill, John Stuart (1806–73)
Born London, son of James Mill, the
leading disciple of Jeremy Bentham.
Invented 'utilitarianism' as term for
Benthamite philosophy; became
disillusioned with its limitations; see his
essays on Bentham (1838) and Coleridge
(1840). 1848: *Political Economy*. Later
works: *On Liberty* (1859); *Thoughts on
Parliamentary Reform* (1859); *Representative
Government* (1860); *Utilitarianism* (1861);
On the Subjection of Women (1869);
Autobiography (1873). Life by M.St J.
Packe (1954).

Abrams, M.H., *The Mirror and the Lamp*
  (New York, 1973)
Alexander, E., *Matthew Arnold and John
  Stuart Mill* (1967)
Amschutz, R.P., *The Philosophy of J.S. Mill*
  (1953)
Duncan, G., *Marx and Mill* (Cambridge,
  1973)
Himmelfarb, G., *On Liberty and Liberalism:
  the Case of John Stuart Mill* (New
  York, 1974)
Leavis, F.R., *Mill on Bentham and Coleridge*
  (1950)
Ryan, A., *John Stuart Mill* (1975)
Stephen, J.F. (ed. R.J. White), *Liberty,
  Equality, Fraternity* (Cambridge, 1968)
Stephen, Sir Leslie, *The English Utilitarians*
  (1900)
Willey, B., in *Nineteenth Century Studies*
  (1949)

Peacock, Thomas Love (1785–1866)
Novelist and poet. Born Dorset, son of
merchant. 1805: *Palmyra, and Other Poems*.
1815: *Headlong Hall*; 1817: *Melincourt*;
1818: *Nightmare Abbey*. 1819: entered East
India Company. 1822: *Maid Marian*; 1829:
The Misfortunes of Elphin; 1831: *Crotchet
Castle*; 1860: *Gryll Grange*. Novels
composed of satirical dialogue with little
attention to plot. His essay *The Four Ages
of Poetry* (1820) provoked Shelley's famous
Defence of Poetry (1821). Life; Carl Van
Doren (1911); H.F.B. Brett-Smith (vol. 1 of
Halliford edition of *The Works*, 1934).

Butler, M., *Peacock Displayed: A Satanist
  in his Context* (1979)

Dawson, C., *His Fine Wit: a Study of
  Thomas Love Peacock* (1970)
Freeman, A.M., *Thomas Love Peacock: A
  Critical Study* (1911)
Madden, J.L., *Thomas Love Peacock* (1967)
Mills, H., *Peacock: His Circle and his Age*
  (Cambridge, 1969)

Radcliffe, Mrs Ann (1764–1823)
A famous 'Gothic' novelist. Born London,
daughter of William Ward, merchant;
married 1787. *The Castles of Athlin and
Dunbayne* (1789); *A Sicilian Romance*
(1790); *The Romance of the Forest* (1790);
The Mysteries of Udolpho (*1794 – subject of
satire in Jane Austen's Northanger Abbey*);
The Italian (1797).

McIntyre, C.F., *Ann Radcliffe in Relation to
  her Time* (1921)

Scott, Sir Walter (1771–1832)
Novelist and poet. Born Edinburgh, son of
lawyer; educated Edinburgh High School
and University, 1778–83. 1792: called to the
Bar. Began literary career as poet. 1802:
Minstrelsy of the Scottish Border (partly
anthology); 1805: *The Lay of the Last
Minstrel*; 1808: *Marmion*; 1810: *The Lady of
the Lake*. Began career as historical novelist
in 1814 with *Waverley*. 1815: *Guy
Mannering*; 1816: *The Antiquary; Old
Mortality*; 1817: *Rob Roy*; 1818: *The Heart
of Midlothian*. Novels with English
background: *Ivanhoe* (1819); *Kenilworth*
(1821). Scott wrote many other novels,
many of them in desperate haste and great
concern to pay off his debts. Life by
son-in-law J.G. Lockhart (1837–38); H.J.C.
Grierson (1938); John Buchan (1932).

Cockshut, A.O.J., *The Achievement of
  Walter Scott* (1969)
Fiske, C.F., *Epic Suggestion in the Imagery
  of the Waverley Novels* (1940)
Gordon, R.C., *Under Which King? A Study
  of the Scottish Waverley Novels*
  (Edinburgh, 1969)
Grierson, H.J.C., *Sir Walter Scott Today*
  (1932)
Grierson, H.J.C. *et al.*, Sir Walter Scott
  Lectures (Edinburgh, 1950)
Jeffares, A.N. (ed.), *Scott's Mind and Art*
  (Edinburgh, 1969)
Lewis, C.S., in *They Asked for a Paper*
  (1962)
Mayhead, R., *Walter Scott* (Cambridge,
  1973)
McMaster, G., *Scott and Society*
  (Cambridge, 1981)
Muir, E., *Scott and Scotland: the
  Predicament of the Scottish Writer* (1936)

Parsons, C.O., *Witchcraft and Demonology in Scott's Fiction* (1964)

Pritchett, V.S., 'Scott' in *The Living Novel* (1946)

Shelley, Percy Bysshe (1792–1822)
Poet. Born Sussex, son of rich landowner; educated at Eton (1804–10) and University College, Oxford, from which he was sent down for his pamphlet *The Necessity of Atheism*. Joined the circle of the revolutionary philosopher William Godwin. Friendship with Byron. Notable Works: 1813: *Queen Mab*; 1816: *Alastor, or The Spirit of Solitude*; 1817: *The Revolt of Islam*; 1818: *Julian and Maddalo*; 1819: *The Cenci*; *Prometheus Unbound*; *The Mask of Anarchy*; 1820: *The Witch of Atlas*, *The Cloud*, *To a Skylark*; 1821: *Adonais* (elegy for Keats); *Hellas*; *Defence of Poetry* (prose). Working on *The Triumph of Life* at the time of his death by drowning off Spezia. Life by N.I. White (1947); K.N. Cameron, *The Young Shelley: Genesis of a Radical*, (1950); Edmund Blunden (1946).

Baker, C.H., *Shelley's Major Poetry: The Fabric of a Vision* (1948)

Barnard, E., *Shelley's Religion* (1937)

Blunden, E., *et al.*, *On Shelley* (1938)

Butter, P., *Shelley's Idols of the Cave* (Edinburgh, 1954)

Cameron, K.N. and Reiman, D.H. (eds), *Shelley and his Circle 1773–1822* (6 vols, Cambridge, Mass., 1961–73)
Shelley: The Golden Years (Cambridge, Mass., 1974)

Fogle, R.H., *The Imagery of Keats and Shelley* (1949)

Foot, P., *Red Shelley* (1980)

Grabo, C., *The Magic Plant: The Growth of Shelley's Thought* (1936)
A Newton Among Poets (1930)

Hughes, A.M.D., *The Nascent Mind of Shelley*

Jones, F.L., *The Letters of Percy Bysshe Shelley* (1964)

Norman, S., *Flight of the Skylark: The Development of Shelley's Reputation* (1954)

Robinson, C.E., *Shelley and Byron: The Snake and Eagle Wreathed in Fight* (1976)

Rogers, N., *Shelley at Work: a Critical Enquiry* (1956; rev. 1967)

Solve, M.T., *Shelley: His Theory and Poetry* (Cambridge, 1927)

Stovall, F., *Desire and Restraint in Shelley* (Cambridge, 1932)

Wasserman, E.R., *Shelley, A Critical Reading* (1971)

Webb, T., *Shelley: A Voice Not Understood* (Manchester, 1977)
The Violet in the Crucible: Shelley and Translation

Welburn, A., *Power and Self-consciousness in the Poetry of Shelley* (1986)

Southey, Robert (1774–1843)
Poet, biographer, journalist. Born in Bristol, son of linen draper; educated Westminster and Balliol, Oxford. Supported the French Revolution. 1794: began collaboration with Coleridge on Utopian 'Pantisocracy' project. 1795; married Edith Fricker, Coleridge's sister-in-law. 1801: completed epic *Thalaba the Destroyer*. Began friendship with Wordsworth. 1805: *Madoc; Metrical Tales*; 1810: *The Curse of Kehama*. 1813: Poet Laureate. 1814: *Roderick the last of the Goths*. Opinions now conservative; contributor to the Tory *Quarterly Review*. 1821: conflict with Byron; Southey's *Vision of Judgement* answered by Byron's famous satire with same title. Biographies include the famous *Life of Nelson* (1813) and the *Life of Wesley (1820)*. Life by J. Simmons (1945); K. Curry (1975). *Poems* ed. M.H. Fitzgerald (1909). *Life of Nelson* ed. E.R. H. Harvey (1953); *Life of Wesley* ed. M.H. Fitzgerald (1925); *Letters from England* ed. J. Simmons (1951).

Carnall, G., *Robert Southey and his Age* (1960)

Madden, L., *Robert Southey: The Critical Heritage* (1972)

Tennyson, Alfred (1809–92)
Poet. Born Somersby, Lincolnshire, son of rector; educated Louth Grammar School and Trinity College, Cambridge, where he began deep friendship with Arthur Hallam. 1830: *Poems, Chiefly Lyrical*. 1833: maturer volume, including 'The Two Voices', 'Oenone', 'The Lotos-Eaters'. Influenced pessimistically by Lyell's *Principles of Geology*. The death of Hallam caused him to begin *In Memoriam*. 1842: new volume of poems established his reputation. 1850: Poet Laureate; *In Memoriam* published. Among later works, *Idylls of the King* were most popular. Made peer in 1884. Life by his son Hallam (1897) and grandson Charles (1949); R.B. Martin: *Tennyson: the Unquiet Heart* (1980).

Auden, W.H., *Tennyson: a Selection and Introduction* (1946)

Bradley, A.C., *A Commentary on Tennyson's 'In Memoriam'* (1901; rev. 1930)

Buckley, J.H., *Tennyson: the Growth of a Poet* (Cambridge, Mass., 1960)

Jump, J.D. (ed.), *Tennyson: The Critical Heritage* (1968)

Kilham, J. (ed.), *Critical Essays on the Poetry of Tennyson* (1960)

Leavis, F.R., in *New Bearings in English Poetry*

Nicolson, H., *Tennyson* (1923)

Ricks, C., *Tennyson* (1972)

Tennyson, H. (ed.), *Studies in Tennyson* (1981)

Turner, P., *Tennyson* (1976)

Thackeray, William Makepeace (1811–63)
Novelist. Born Calcutta, son of civil servant; educated Charterhouse and Trinity College, Cambridge. Became journalist, contributing to *Frazer's Magazine* and *Punch* (*Book of Snobs*, 1846). 1848: his masterpiece, *Vanity Fair*. 1850: *Pendennis*; 1852: *The Newcomes*; 1852–53: *Henry Esmond*; 1854: *The Newcomes*; 1859: *The Virginians*; *Denis Duval* unfinished at his death. Life by G.N. Ray (2 vols 1955, 1958).

Carey, J., *Thackeray: Prodigal Genius* (1977)

Greig, J.Y.T., *Thackeray: a Reconsideration* (1950)

Hardy, B., *The Exposure of Luxury: Radical Themes in Thackeray* (1972)

McMaster, J., *Thackeray: the Major Novels* (Manchester, 1971)

Peters, C., *Thackeray's Universe* (1987)

Saintsbury, G., *A Consideration of Thackeray* (1931)

Sutherland, J., *Thackeray at Work* (1974)

Tillotson, G., *Thackeray the Novelist* (1954)

Tillotson, G. and Hawes, I. (eds), *Thackeray: the Critical Heritage* (1968)

Wordsworth, William (1770–1850)
Poet. Born Cockermouth, Cumberland, son of law-agent. 1778–91: educated Hawkshead Grammar School and St John's College, Cambridge. Early sense of deep affinity with nature. Admirer of French Revolution until 1793. 1793: *Descriptive Sketches*. 1795: beginning of friendship with Coleridge. 1798: (with Coleridge) *Lyrical Ballads*. 1799: settled in Cumberland with sister Dorothy. 1805: completed early (unpublished) version of *Prelude*. 1807: *Poems in Two Volumes*. 1814: *Excursion*. 1843: made Poet Laureate. 1850: pub. of revised *Prelude*. Life by Mary Moorman (2 vols, 1957–65); G.M. Harper (1916; rev. 1929).

Bateson, F.W., *Wordsworth: A Re-intrpretation* (1954)

Beer, J.B., *Wordsworth and the Human Heart* (1978)
Wordsworth in Time (1979)

Bradley, A.C., 'Wordsworth' in *Oxford Lectures on Poetry* (1909)

Darbishire, H., *The Poet Wordsworth* (1950)

Davies, H.S., *Wordsworth and the worth of Words* (Cambridge, 1986)

Garrod, H.W., *Wordsworth's Lectures and Essays* (1923; rev. 1929)

Hartman, G.H., *Wordsworth's Poetry, 1787–1814* (1964)
The Unremarkable Wordsworth (1987)

Jacobus, M., *Tradition and Experiment in Wordsworth's 'Lyrical Ballads' (1798)* (1976)

Jones, J., *The Egotistical Sublime* (1954)

King, A., *Wordsworth and the Artist's Vision: An Essay in Interpretation* (1966)

Margoliouth, H.G., *Wordsworth and Coleridge, 1795–1834* (1953)

McConnell, F.D. (ed.), *The Confessional Imagination* (1974)

Moorman, M. (ed.), *Journals of Dorothy Wordsworth* (1971)

Read, Sir H., *Wordsworth* (1970)

Rehder, R., *Wordsworth and the Beginnings of Modern Poetry* (1981)

Smith, J.C., *A Study of Wordsworth* (1944)

Ward, J.P., *Wordsworth's Language of Men* (1984)

Wordsworth, J., *The Music of Humanity* (1969)
William Wordsworth: the Borders of Vision (Oxford, 1982)

10 Music

General studies

Contemporary Periodicals: *The Harmonicon* (1823–33)
The European Magazine (London) 1785, et seq.

Baines, A. (ed.), *Musical Intruments through the Ages* (Penguin Books, 1952)

Blume, F. (trans. M.D. Herter Norton), *Classic and Romantic Music: A Comprehensive Survey* (1972)

Fiske, R., *English Theatre Music in the Eighteenth Century* (1973, rev. edn 1986)
Scotland in Music; a European Enthusiam (1983)

Kassler, J.C., *The Science of Music in Britain 1714–1830: a Catalogue of Writings, Lectures and Inventions* (1979)

Montagu, J., *The World of Romantic and Modern Musical Instruments* (1981)

Milligan, T.B., *The Concerto and London's Musical Culture in the Late Eighteenth Century* (1983)

Petty, F., *Italian Opera in London 1760–1800* (AnnArbor, Mich., 1980)

Robbins Landon, H.C., *Haydn in England* (1976)

Haydn: a Documentary Study (1981)

Handel and his World (1984)

Sadie, S. (ed.), *The New Grove Dictionary of Music and Musicians* (1980)

Shonimsky, N. (rev.), *Baker's Biographical Dictionary of Musicians* (1978)

Wallace, R.K., *Jane Austen and Mozart: Classical Equilibrium in Fiction and Music* (Bloomington, Ind., 1983)

Musicians and composers

Balfe, Michael William (1808–70)
Composer. Born Dublin, son of dancing master; music education from his father and the musician C.E. Horn. 1823: joined Drury Lane orchestra. Became operatic singer and composer, working extensively in France and Italy. Best known work; *The Bohemian Girl* (1843). Composed some famous songs, e.g., 'I dreamt that I dwelt in marble halls'. Life by W.A. Barrett (1882).

Bennett, Sir William Sterndale (1816–75)
Composer. Born Sheffield, son of an organist. Received his musical education from his grandfather at Cambridge; 1824 entered King's College choir; 1826 entered the Royal Academy of Music. 1836–42: made frequent visits to Germany where he had success as a composer, under the influence of Mendelssohn. 1856; Professor of Music at Cambridge; 1866: Principal, Royal Academy of Music. Life by J.R. Sterndale Bennett (1907).

Burney, Charles (1726–1814)
Music historian. Born Shrewsbury, educated at the free school; studied music under the composer Dr Arne. Had some success as a composer, and became Doctor of Music at Oxford. Chiefly famous for his history of music: *A General History of Music from the Earliest Ages to the Present Day – 1789*; see edition with critical historical notes by F. Mercer, 1935.

Lonsdale, R., *Dr Charles Burney; a Literary Biography* (1965)

Scholes, R.A., *The Great Dr Burney* (2 vols, 1948)

Field, John (1728–1837)
Composer and pianist. Born Dublin, son of a violinist; musically educated by his grandfather, an organist. Became a pupil of Clementi in London, and accompanied him on his European tours. 1820: finally settled in Moscow. As composer, he was famous for his nocturnes. Lives by P. Piggott (1973); A. Nikolaev, trans. H.M. Cardello (New York, 1973).

Branson, D., *John Field and Chopin* (1972)

Wesley, Samuel (1766–1837)
Organist and composer, son of Charles Wesley, hymn writer, and nephew of John Wesley, the evangelist. Famous for his organ-playing; introduced J.S. Bach's organ music to England.

E. Wesley (ed.), *Letters from Samuel Wesley to Mr Jacob relating to the introduction of the works of J.S. Bach.* Life by J.T. Lightwood (1937)

Wesley, Samuel Sebastian (1810–76)
Composer and organist; son of Samuel Wesley. 1832: appointed organist to Hereford Cathedral, the first of a succession of similar appointments. 1834: conducted the Festival of the Three Choirs. Well known for anthem compositions e.g. 'The Wilderness', 'Blessed be the God and Father', 'Ascribe unto the lord', 'O Lord, Thou art my God'.

S.S. Wesley, *A few words on Cathedral music and the musical system of the Church* (New York, 1849; reprinted 1965)

Sources of Illustrations

The publishers gratefully acknowledge the help of the many individuals and organisations who cannot be named in collecting the illustrations for this volume. In particular, they would like to thank Callie Crees for the picture research. Every effort has been made to obtain permission to use copyright materials; the publishers apologise for any errors and omissions and would welcome these being brought to their attention.

2, 122 Reproduced by courtesy of the Trustees, The National Gallery, London
44t, 172, 175, 177 By permission of the Trustees of the British Museum
44b Yale Center for British Art, Paul Mellon Collection
47, 48, 49b By courtesy of Edinburgh City Libraries
49t Royal Commission on Ancient Monuments, Scotland
50 Photograph by courtesy of The National Trust for Scotland; Crown copyright, reproduced with the permission of the Controller of Her Majesty's Stationery Office
52 The National Trust for Scotland
56 Leeds City Art Galleries
64, 151r Reproduced by permission of the Syndics of the Fitzwilliam Museum, Cambridge
74 By kind permission of Mrs Douglas Cleverdon; photograph by permission of the Syndics of Cambridge University Library
86 Cliché des Musées Nationaux, Paris
115 By permission of the Syndics of Cambridge University Library
118 By courtesy of P.M. Gallimore; photo National Portrait Gallery

121, 147b, 276, 279r, 281l, 286, 288, 289r By courtesy of the Board of Trustees of the Victoria & Albert Museum
126, 134, 165, 265b The Tate Gallery, London
130 National Museums & Galleries on Merseyside, Lady Lever Art Gallery, Port Sunlight
137t By courtesy of Athenaeum of Ohio
137b, 160 National Gallery of Ireland
138, 147t National Gallery of Scotland
139 Witt Library, Courtauld Institute of Art/Victoria & Albert Museum
140–141 National Museums & Galleries on Merseyside, Walker Art Gallery, Liverpool
144, 174 Reproduced by permission of the Huntington Library, San Marino, California; photograph by permission of the Syndics of Cambridge University Library
145 By kind permission of the Earl of Mansfield
146 Royal Academy of Arts, London
151l Viscount Coke and the Trustees of the Holkham Estate
153, 154, 186, 200, 201t, 205, 213, 214, 222, 256 Royal Commission on the Historical Monuments of England
156 The Conway Library, Courtauld Institute of Art
158 The Metropolitan Museum of Art; Bequest of Edward S. Harkness, 1940 (50.135.5)
161, 275 Reproduced by Gracious permission of Her Majesty the Queen
164 Manchester City Art Galleries
166 Norfolk Museums Service (Norwich Castle Museum)
167 Ashmolean Museum, Oxford
171 By courtesy of His Grace the Duke of Northumberland, Alnwick Castle, Northumberland

Index